Three days after Christmas 2007, thousands of fans were at the Mandalay Bay Event Center in Las Vegas, Nevada, to see the Ultimate Fighting Championship's top star, "The Iceman" Chuck Liddell, square off with the fearsome "Axe Murderer" Wanderlei Silva. The crowd was loud and boisterous as the competitors stripped down and got on a scale. That's right. These fans weren't there for the fight; they were there for the weigh-ins. It was a clear signal of just how far the sport had come.

Just ten years earlier, the UFC was lucky to draw a few thousand fans to backwater locations like Alabama and Mississippi. To make matters worse, it was banned from pay-per-view television nationwide. Even after the mega-rich Fertitta brothers bought the company in 2001, the UFC had come close to going under. A fortuitous cable television show called *The Ultimate Fighter* had given the promotion a new lease on life.

Now the fledgling sport of MMA was being hailed as the next big thing. Almost every news medium that mattered covered the story of the sport's rise like a phoenix from extinction with various degrees of accuracy. The most important point was clear. MMA was hot and UFC 79 was proof positive. Not only did the UFC sell out the arena and draw a gate of almost $5 million, they sold more than a thousand additional tickets to see the fight on closed-circuit television.

"I can't tell you the last time I was this excited for a fight," UFC President Dana White said. It was a fight he had traveled around the globe to set up in 2003, entering Liddell in the Pride Middleweight Grand Prix, only to be bitterly disappointed when "The

Iceman" fell to Quinton "Rampage" Jackson before getting a shot at Silva. Wanderlei had demolished Jackson in the finals, rankling White because it showed hard-core fans that the Japanese promotion, and not the UFC, had the toughest fighters in the world. White had been obsessed with putting the fight together ever since, even promoting it on UFC broadcasts before it had been signed.

Pride had been reluctant to allow Silva to appear in the UFC's famous Octagon. White settled that issue by buying the Japanese group. Now he could finally book his personal dream match. It didn't matter to fans or White that both fighters were coming off losses. This was more than just Liddell versus Silva. This was UFC versus Pride personified. "Silva was definitely the face of that organization [Pride] and one of the most exciting fighters in the world," he said. "He and Chuck have the exact same fighting style. Both are aggressive knockout artists, both come forward, and both try to finish fights with knockouts. I've been trying to put this fight together for six years. Finally, here we are. I can't tell you how much this fight means to me. Seriously, I'm shaking right now."

White may have been shaking, but Liddell wasn't fazed in the least. At the weigh-in, Liddell had made Silva wait for the customary stare-down while he slowly put his clothes back on. The sponsors' logos so garishly displayed on that clothing, after all, helped pay his bills and would want to be in the money shot, sure to be broadcast nationwide on ESPN. The fiery Brazilian Silva didn't appreciate the delay (or Liddell's press conference promise to knock him out). He pulled his shirt off, and as the two stared into each other's eyes, he faked a head butt. Liddell didn't flinch, calmly taking a step back and flipping Silva the bird. "The Axe Murderer" lost control and went after Liddell. It looked like a professional wrestling pantomime, but it was completely real. In a moment, it demonstrated the UFC's appeal to the young male market. MMA combined the flash and bombast of professional wrestling with the gravitas and excitement of a real sporting event. In the WWE, that kind of tomfoolery would have been in the script. In the UFC, it just added intensity to what was already a much anticipated fight.

"He got stupid at the weigh-in and any time someone does that, it just fires Chuck up even more," Liddell's trainer John Hackleman said. "As soon as he did that, we went in the back and I was ten times more confident than I had been. You do that to Chuck, you're going to fire him up a lot more."

The fight was everything the hype had promised. It was years in the making, and fans got exactly what they expected: two powerful strikers exchanging punch after punch. After a slow start, the two began throwing bombs. For once, it was Liddell with the straighter punches, using his reach to land blows when the Brazilian's looping punches were coming up short. "Two warriors who love to bang and knock people out went toe-to-toe and showed tons of heart," White said. "It was one of the best fights I've ever seen."

Although Silva landed plenty of counter shots when Liddell uncharacteristically came forward, Liddell punished him with precision punching. Silva was in trouble in every round, back to the cage and swinging wildly just to get some room to breathe. Liddell was known for his knockout power, but Silva took punches flush on the chin and survived where others might have fallen.

"He did a great job to keep fighting. He didn't want to give up," Liddell said. "There were a couple of times he could have covered up in the corner and the ref probably would have stopped it. But he came out slugging. It was a fun fight."

Liddell's unanimous-decision win capped off an amazing year for the UFC. The company had turned the corner. Once banned from pay-per-view, this show would bring in more than 600,000 households paying $39.95 for the pleasure of watching Liddell get back on track. The sport was a regular feature on local and cable news, and made the cover of *Sports Illustrated,* the ultimate sign of mainstream sports acceptance. It had come a long way since a skinny young Brazilian, too frail to actually participate, watched a Japanese judo master teach his brothers the basics of ground fighting.

THE BIRTH OF BRAZILIAN JIU-JITSU

Rio de Janeiro is known as "A Cidade Maravilhosa," the marvelous city. It's a tropical paradise, with some of the world's most beautiful beaches. Millions of tourists visit every year, drinking chope from a Botequim and having a good time in their Speedos or string bikinis. But Rio is also one of the world's most dangerous cities. Today the violence often leads to murder, but in the 1980s scores were settled with fists. And the most dangerous gang in Rio was the Gracies, a family with an obsession for proving its toughness that extended through the generations.

The toughest of them all was Rickson Gracie, a muscular street fighter with a hair-trigger temper and an unquenchable thirst for violence. For years the Gracies had been defending the honor of the family in rings, dojos, nightclubs, and in the streets. In 1988, Rickson was continuing the family tradition and gave beach goers a shock when he and a passel of his students, family, and friends descended on noted tough guy Hugo Duarte at Praia do Pepe beach.

"When our group arrived at the beach, Rickson was there with a group of more than 50 guys," future Gracie conqueror Eugenio Tadeu said.[1]

Duarte offered to shake hands with Rickson, who would have none of it. Rickson Gracie was there to prove a point and slapped Duarte in the face with an open palm — the ultimate insult, and for years an act that necessitated a duel to the death.

"Before Rickson moved to the United States, he heard Hugo Duarte wanted to fight him, that Denilson Maia wanted to fight him, and Rickson went to the beach one day and fought that fight where he slapped Hugo," Royler Gracie said. "Rickson said, 'Let's go,' and Hugo said, 'Dude, I'm not ready.' So Rickson slapped him across the face and said, 'Now you have to,' so they had it out. On the beach, Renzo [Gracie] and Eugenio also had an altercation, but the crowd split it up."[2]

Duarte would get off lightly. Surrounded by jeering jiu-jitsu students kicking sand and taunting, Duarte was videotaped being pummeled by Rickson.

"I tried to help Hugo, making a circle and not allowing jiu-jitsu people to attack him, throwing sand in his eyes like they were doing," Tadeu said. "It was not fair. They were planning to get us in this trap for a long time."

The tape would be edited to make it appear Rickson dominated the fight: Duarte's knees to Rickson's body were removed, and the times he had the advantage on the ground. Then the tape was used to sell the Gracie brand of "self-defense." Welcome to the world of the Gracie family and Gracie jiu-jitsu, where unprovoked thuggery is commendable and promoting the family name paramount.

But this story more properly begins in Tokyo during the late 1800s, where a 5'2", 90-pound jujutsu expert named Jigoro Kano realized he needed to train smarter instead of harder.

THE GENTLE WAY

Jigoro Kano was a little guy, picked on by bullies and desperate to defend himself. The solution to that problem in 19th-century Japan was jujutsu, an ancient Japanese fighting system that had roots in feudal Japan and the time of the samurai. Originally the "gentle art" focused on everything — punches, kicks, throws, arm locks, strangles — and was truly martial in nature. It was one of more than a dozen martial arts a samurai would study during his life, but the only one that focused on weaponless combat.

The samurai were a dying breed. Commodore Matthew Perry had opened the islands up to the world, and Japanese society was experiencing severe culture shock. What was once a focus, the budo spirit of the samurai, suddenly seemed antiquated and dangerous. Jujutsu was dying.

In Kano's time, each ryu, or school, had a different focus and there was no unified approach. There were hundreds of jujutsu offshoots, each with their own traditions and techniques. Kano was a meticulous man, highly organized and thoughtful. He had studied at several ryu and was frustrated by the state of jujutsu. Kano decided to study each of the major jujutsu schools and take the best from each, creating judo, "the gentle way."

"In my youth I studied jujutsu under many eminent masters. Their vast knowledge, the fruit of years of diligent research and rich experience, was of great value to me. At that time, each man presented his art as a collection of techniques. None perceived the guiding principle behind jujutsu. When I encountered differences in the teaching of techniques, I often found myself at a loss to know which was correct. This led me to look for an underlying principle in jujutsu, one that applied when one hit an opponent as well as when one threw him," Kano said. "After a thorough study of the subject, I discerned an all-pervasive principle: to make the most efficient use of mental and physical energy. With this principle in mind, I again reviewed all the methods of attack and defense I had learned, retaining only those that were in accordance with the principle. Those not in accord with it I rejected, and in their place I substituted techniques in which the principle was correctly applied. The resulting body of technique, which I named judo to distinguish it from its predecessor, is what is taught at the Kodokan."[3]

Jujutsu was a martial art, judo a way of life. Kano wasn't happy with the types of students who were studying jujutsu, men who were too often street fighters and common thugs. His judo included a strict code of ethics.

"Kodokan instructors and students were expected from the beginning to be outstanding examples of good character and honest conduct," judo historian Dr. Keo Cavalcanti said. "Any hand-to-hand combat outside of the dojo, public demonstrations for profit, or any behavior that might bring shame to the school could lead to suspension or expulsion from the Kodokan."[4]

Kano's creation was brilliant. The ideas seem so simple now, but at the time they were revolutionary. Judo would include a belt system to distinguish beginning and advanced students. Students would advance from basic to complex skills studying lessons from Kano's teaching background. And most important was the creation of randori, or free play. This is what separated judo from most other martial arts of the time. While they promised to teach deadly techniques, there was no way to practice the "death touch" or the eye gouge without seriously diminishing your student population.

Kano understood that training students at full speed but allowing them to practice less deadly techniques — throws, elbow locks, and chokes — would create a much more effective fighter. Randori didn't allow striking or many submission holds. These were reserved for more theoretical training. But every day, the students at the Kodokan fought each other as hard as they could in techniques that would not cause lasting harm. It made them the toughest men in Japan, and they were out to prove it.

As you would expect, a rivalry grew between Kano and the old school jujutsu men. And while people respected Kano's theories and his idealism, there was a real question about whether his style would work, whether Judoka would be able to defeat jujutsu men in real combat. A tournament was organized by the chief of the Metropolitan Police in Tokyo, pitting 15 men handpicked from both schools of combat. In a very real sense, the fate of Kano's judo depended on the results of this tourney. Winning would prove once and for all that judo was not only creating strong and model citizens, but also competent fighters.

The Kodokan won 13 bouts and had two draws (against two unusually large and physically powerful opponents). Judo was here to stay.

Maeda

It was Kano's dream to spread judo around the world. He traveled overseas more than a dozen times to spread the art of judo and worked hard to have judo recognized as an Olympic sport. Kano saw judo as a way of life that could benefit people throughout the world: through the pursuit of physical perfection, the Judoka would make himself valuable to society. Many of his students traveled all over the world to settle in distant lands and spread the philosophy and combat system developed by Kano. One of these students was Mitsuya Maeda.

Maeda traveled to the United States to spread the word about judo. His companions were Soishiro Satake and Tsunejiro Tomita, a respected teacher and veteran of the 1886 Tokyo Police tournament. They arranged a demonstration at the West Point Military Academy in New York, where a wrestler who wanted to see their techniques in action confronted the two. Maeda accepted his challenge and was immediately taken down. Here, there was some confusion about the rules of the contest. The westerners thought the fight was over when their guy pinned Maeda clean. Maeda continued to fight from his back and submitted the bigger man with an arm bar. He also demonstrated his judo against a boxer, winning the match.

Maeda and Tomita attended a reception that evening and demonstrated kata there. Out of the crowd came a challenge from a giant football player. The Americans turned to Tomita, the senior man, to represent judo in a second challenge. Tomita was past his prime, but could not honorably refuse the challenge. He was pinned and helpless against the bigger man. This was a setback, but judo was getting plenty of press, including a complimentary article in the *New York Times* and demonstrations at Columbia University and the New York Athletic Club.

Tomita and Maeda parted ways when Maeda began to associate with professional wrestlers and prizefighters. Maeda was not satisfied with the impression they had made in New York. He wanted to stay and show Americans the power of judo the best way he knew how. He wasn't a philosopher like Tomita or Kano. He would show judo on the mat in a series of challenge matches. He got a Japanese businessman to front him $1,000 and took on all comers.

Fighting became a passion for Maeda, and he would travel all over the Americas and even to Europe with a troupe of Japanese pro wrestlers, demonstrating the art of judo, even challenging the heavyweight boxing champion of the time, Jack Johnson. Maeda had over 2,000 fights and only a handful of documented losses, despite being 5'4" and 145 pounds. When he did lose, he was typically pinned by a larger wrestler. It is said he never lost a match while wearing the gi. Of course, it is hard to say which of the fights were legitimate contests and which were part of his wrestling act.

For example, in Mexico City, Maeda established himself at the Principal Theatre. His act was typical of the carnival wrestler. Maeda challenged any man in the house to face off with him. If he couldn't throw you, you earned 100 pesos. If you managed to throw him, you got 500 pesos. Nobody ever collected, and Maeda quickly developed a reputation as a tough hombre. The Mexican fans were excited when Nobu Taka arrived to challenge Maeda for the world jujutsu title. Taka surprised everyone when he won the fight, held at the Colon Theatre on November 16, 1909. At an impromptu rematch just four days later, a rematch likely with very different betting lines, Maeda reclaimed his reputation with an easy win. Taka, of course, was really Maeda's friend Soishiro Satake. This was how the group operated, seeing the world, making a buck, and spreading judo to the local populace, if not always in a manner Kano would have approved.

In Cuba, Maeda and his boys were known as the Four Kings, and they defeated a succession of Cuban tough men. In Spain they called Maeda "Conde Koma" (The Count of Combat), a name he would assume in place of his own on his subsequent travels.

After traveling all over the Western world, Maeda settled in Brazil, where he met a politician named Gastao Gracie and agreed to teach his sons how to fight.

THE GRACIES

"At the time it was considered a crime against the nation for a Japanese national to teach jiu-jitsu to a non-Japanese. But Count Koma decided to teach my dad. I think because my father was so skinny, Count Koma didn't think much about teaching him; he could never have guessed it would develop into such a large thing," Carlson Gracie said. "My father was the only one of the brothers to learn jiu-jitsu, and he taught all of his brothers. The brothers then passed the knowledge on to their sons."[5]

Of course, this is patently ridiculous. Maeda was not only permitted to teach the martial arts to non-Japanese nationals; it was the purpose of his trip to the Americas. It's all part of the Gracie myth, an attempt by the family to sell their brand of judo to the masses. It sounds better to be in possession of a secret system, known only to the Gracies, than to be particularly gifted proponents of judo ne-waza (ground fighting). The Gracies are adamant that they are practitioners of "jiu-jitsu," not judo, that Maeda taught them ancient techniques, not Kano's judo. This seems unlikely, as Maeda was a Judoka and the system he taught the Gracies looks strikingly similar to judo. There is some confusion about the use of the term jujutsu instead of judo. They were interchangeable in Maeda's time, with Kano's judo seen as just a school of jujutsu. No matter what Maeda called it, there is little doubt that what he taught Carlos Gracie was judo, though perhaps it was tempered by his real world fighting experience.

Renzo Gracie writes in his book *Mastering JuJitsu*: "Maeda taught Carlos the excellent training methods of kodokan judo, with its emphasis on live randori [free sparring] and ne-waza [ground fighting] skills [Maeda was a kodokan student at the beginning of the ne-waza revolution in judo]. He also taught classical submission holds that were not part of the judo curriculum. In addition, because Maeda had been exposed to numerous fighting styles during his travels, he did not limit his teachings to judo. In fact, in one old photograph, Maeda is shown training without the traditional Japanese gi jacket, and it reveals him using a standard control and submission technique of Western catch wrestling: a half nelson and hammer lock. Maeda was a regular competitor in catch wrestling events while in England, and there is no doubt that he absorbed what he took to be useful from these arts and incorporated them into his training and teaching."

Carlos trained with Maeda for four years, but ever the wanderer, Maeda moved on to a new part of Brazil. But Carlos did not move on from judo; he was hooked on the art and taught his brothers Osvaldo, Gastão, and Jorge. His youngest brother, Hélio, was considered too sickly to be an active participant, but he sat in on the classes, studying every move.

"After learning jiu-jitsu from Koma, my father decided he would make that his life. And he started to motivate his brothers in order to create an unbeatable team, 'The Gracie Brothers,'" Carlos's daughter Reila Gracie said. It was the start of Gracie jiu-jitsu and the birth of the Gracie propaganda machine.

"My father moved to Rio in 1925, where he opened the first known jiu-jitsu school in the country. At that time, Carlos and his brothers were challenged to prove the superiority of jiu-jitsu. My father always tried to have a good relationship with the press. This way, he always got their victories on the front pages of the newspapers. This was very important for the beginning of the Gracie family's popularity in Brazil."[6]

Maeda had set the table for Carlos, but now it was up to the Gracies to continue to learn and progress. Based on descriptions of what Maeda taught Carlos, it is likely he wasn't even a judo black belt when he struck out on his own. This means he would have learned ground fighting and some throwing techniques, but none of the striking that advanced Judoka would use to throw their opponents off balance so they could get in close for a takedown. This would have a tremendous impact on how Gracie jiu-jitsu developed in Brazil. The Gracies continued to figure it out on their own, and by the late 1920s, the Gracies were confident enough in their art to accept challenges from all comers. They were developing a reputation as men not to be trifled with, as Carlos and George won many challenges for the honor of the family. Carlos took out ads in the newspaper, challenging Brazil's tough guys: Want a broken rib? Look for Carlos Gracie.

It was only by accident that Gracie jiu-jitsu continued to advance as more than a judo spin-off. One afternoon, Dr. Mario, the director of the Bank of Brazil, arrived for his lesson and Carlos was nowhere to be found. His younger brother Hélio took over the instruction and changed the course of martial arts history forever.

THE INNOVATOR

In old pictures, Hélio Gracie looks a bit like movie star Douglas Fairbanks. With his dashing good looks and reputation as the best Vale Tudo fighter in Brazil, it's hard to imagine Hélio as a sickly young man, so frail he couldn't even participate in his brothers' jiu-jitsu classes. His brothers George and Carlos were excellent athletes and good-sized men. Hélio was just 140 pounds and would have to find a different path. In many ways he was like Kano, a smaller man who needed to find the most effective techniques in order to compete with larger and better athletes. He was also a revolutionary, discarding techniques that didn't work and improvising what he needed from the judo framework he inherited.

"I adapted the jiu-jitsu to my characteristics. I was weak and awkward, light. I could not manage to do what my brother [Carlos] did, because his jiu-jitsu depended on strength and ability. I had neither of those. Then I made that which is known today. I perfected the flawed technique of my brother on behalf of weaker people, using the principles of physics, like force and leverage," Hélio said. "You, for example, cannot lift a car with the strength of your arms, but with a jack you can lift a car. That's what I did. I discovered techniques of leverage that optimize force. These modifications made a form of jiu-jitsu that is superior to the jiu-jitsu that existed before that, and today the jiu-jitsu that the entire world knows is my jiu-jitsu."[7]

Hélio's focus was on the groundwork of jiu-jitsu. He knew he would likely end up on his back and concentrated on winning the fight from there. He spent much of his time perfecting the guard position, controlling his opponent with his legs and hips. Everything in jiu-jitsu was based on the real fighting situations the Gracies encountered in challenge matches and in the ring. In most grappling sports like wrestling, and even judo, being on your back is a losing proposition. The pin is the primary way to win on the ground. In real life, being pinned is not enough to make someone tap out. So the Gracies disregarded it. Getting on the back of your opponent wasn't a key technique in judo or wrestling. But the Gracies found it was the single most effective position for finishing a fight. So the family focused on it. It was beautiful in its simplicity.

Gracie's true genius was strategic. Submission locks and chokes existed for years in jujutsu and judo prior to Gracie jiu-jitsu. What separated Hélio's jiu-jitsu was the focus on successfully applying these holds in a real-life fight. The key to Gracie jiu-jitsu isn't a collection of chokes or holds; it's the development of a theory of positional dominance.

In *Mastering JuJitsu*, Renzo Gracie writes: "Once a fight goes to the ground, the two combatants can fall into a variety of positions relative to each other, and these positions range from very good to very bad. Between them are positions that are more or less neutral, with neither fighter having a decisive advantage. The Gracies developed a set of skills that enable a fighter to move from position to position, escaping from bad ones and entering into and maintaining good ones. They learned that both position and control of position are the keys to victory when matches are fought on the ground. Some positions enable one fighter to unleash a torrent of unanswerable blows on an opponent, whereas others make it exceedingly difficult for your opponent to control and strike you. In addition, the Gracies noted a strong correlation between positional dominance and the use of submission holds. Dominating positions tend to make the successful use of submission holds much easier. The opponent can be put under so much pressure that he is far more likely to make a mistake and unwittingly expose himself to a simple submission hold. In addition, they found that once a dominant position was attained, it was much more difficult for an opponent to successfully apply a submission on you."[8]

THE GRACIE CHALLENGE

As with all new things, people were skeptical, not content to just accept the Gracies' word that their jiu-jitsu was the world's best self-defense system. Hélio and his brothers would have to prove it in the ring.

Hélio said, "The Gracie Challenge was a way of improving our system and letting people see how good the techniques were. It was not a personal thing or an ego trip. If you really look at it from the right perspective, the challenge was very much for ourselves because it put us in constant difficulty, and we had to develop new techniques and strategies to deal with other systems. It was never a personal thing. When I fought, I did it for a cause and for a reason. The reason was to prove the efficiency of the method of jiu-jitsu that I was developing. I never did it for money. Today, fighters do it simply for money, and that's their only objective. It's understandable that when the reason a person is doing something changes, the whole picture changes, too."[9]

Like his son Royce, Hélio had his first professional fight with a boxer. He was just 19. It took Royce more than two minutes to dispatch Art Jimmerson in his jiu-jitsu versus boxer matchup at UFC 1. Hélio beat Antonio Portugal in just 30 seconds. His next fight would be much harder. He and catch wrestler Fred Herbert fought for more than two hours before the fight was broken up by police. Gracie also went to a draw with World Wrestling Champion Wladek Zbyszko. But Gracie's most famous opponent practiced a sister art: World Judo Champion Masahiko Kimura.

KIMURA

At UFC 1, the announcers were quick to lay out the Gracie myth for viewers: "When Royce Gracie steps into the Octagon, he brings 65 years of tradition with him. That's how long the Gracie family has been undefeated in no-holds-barred competition."

This was how the propaganda began. Royce came from a line of undefeated champions. But, of course, questions arose almost immediately. The Gracies were taking a lot of money out of the pockets of traditional martial artists by claiming that their systems were unsuitable in real fighting situations. But such a bald faced lie could never stand up to scrutiny. The Gracies were valiant warriors, but far from undefeated. In fact, Hélio's most famous fight was a loss to one of the greatest Judoka of all time. And so the story shifted.

> **GRACIES:** We are undefeated.
> **SKEPTICS:** What about Masahiko Kimura?
> **GRACIES:** Well, Hélio lasted a long time before losing. Plus, Kimura was heavier. So it was like a win. . . .

SKEPTICS: Well, what about Waldemar Santana?
GRACIES: You know about that?
SKEPTICS: Yes.
GRACIES: Well, Hélio was really old.

Gracie's first loss was to the greatest grappler of the 20th century. Masahiko Kimura was so good no one in Japan could touch him on the mats. After winning the All Japan Judo Championships for the third year in a row in 1939, he was awarded the Championship Flag, the only person ever so honored.

"Kimura is the greatest fighter Japan ever produced. I think he was national champion about a dozen times," Olympic Judo silver medalist Doug Rogers said. "In ten years, he was never off his feet. They say, 'No one before Kimura, no one after.'"[10] Kimura would remain undefeated in judo competition for 13 years before the expense of treating his wife's tuberculosis would lead him into the world of professional wrestling. The wrestling took him to Hawaii and from there to Brazil. In Brazil he was wrestling three matches a week, making good money, and teaching judo techniques everywhere he went. It's this last bit that likely made Hélio Gracie challenge the wrestler to a fight for supremacy. The rules were different from those Kimura was used to, as throws and pins weren't counted. It was a grappling battle that could be won only by submission or choke. Before he faced off with Kimura, Gracie would first battle his understudy, Kato. By traditional judo rules, Kato dominated the bout but was eventually choked unconscious after more than 30 minutes of fighting. Now Gracie would get his fight with Kimura, but not everyone was happy about this. There were serious doubts about taking on the Japanese judo machine.

Hélio said, "I wasn't the only one who thought that nobody in the world could defeat Kimura. My brother Carlos was worried that I would never give up under any condition. He thought I would get seriously injured. So he gave me permission to fight with Kimura on the condition that I would 'give up' without fail. I didn't regret it at all either before or after the fight. I was so focused on jiu-jitsu at that time, fear was surpassed by desire to know what on earth such a strong man like Kimura would do in the fight — he might open the door to an unknown world for me."[11]

The Gracies' story about the Kimura fight continues to shift. Hélio claims that Kimura agreed that if Hélio lasted more than three minutes, it would be considered a moral win for him. Of course, there is nothing about this agreement in Kimura's biography, and the Gracies also claim Kimura was a giant, more than 220 pounds. Kimura was 5'6" and approximately 185 pounds. Stuff like this is why Brazil's top judo instructor, George Mehdi, doesn't care for Hélio: "Fighting and lying I don't like. Judo should make a better person, not someone who fights in the street."[12] Mehdi trained with Kimura in Japan the year after his fight with Gracie and says he wasn't any more than 180 pounds. Pictures of the two men, and the film clips that have survived, show Kimura and Gracie to be roughly equal in size. They weren't equal in skill. Kimura tossed Gracie like a rag doll. Kimura recalled the wild spectacle in his autobiography, *My Judo*.

Kimura wrote: "Twenty thousand people came to see the bout, including the president of Brazil. Hélio was 180 centimeters and 80 kilograms (six feet and 176 pounds). When I entered the stadium, I found a coffin. I asked what it was. I was told, 'This is for Kimura. Hélio brought this in.' It was so funny that I almost burst into laughter. As I approached the ring, raw eggs were thrown at me. The gong rang. Hélio grabbed me by both lapels and attacked me with o-soto-gari and kouchi-gari. But they did not move me at all. Now it's my turn. I blew him away up in the air by o-uchi-gari, harai-goshi, uchimata, ippon-seoi. At about the ten-minute mark, I threw him by o-soto-gari. I intended to cause a concussion. But since the mat was so soft, it did not have much impact on him. While continuing to throw him, I was thinking of a finishing method. I threw him by o-soto-gari again. As soon as Hélio fell, I pinned him by kuzure-kami-shiho-gatame.

"I held still for two or three minutes and then tried to smother him by belly. Hélio shook his head trying to breathe. He could not take it any longer and tried to push up my body extending his left arm. That moment, I grabbed his left wrist with my right hand and twisted up his arm. I applied Udegarami. I thought he would surrender immediately. But Hélio would not tap the mat. I had no choice but to keep twisting the arm. The stadium became quiet. The bone of his arm was coming close to the breaking point. Finally, the sound of bone breaking echoed throughout the stadium. Hélio still did not surrender. His left arm was powerless. Under this rule, I had no choice but to twist the arm again. There was plenty of time left. I twisted the left arm again. Another bone was broken. Hélio still did not tap.

When I tried to twist the arm once more, a white towel was thrown in. I won by TKO. My hand was raised high. Japanese Brazilians rushed into the ring and tossed me up in the air. On the other hand, Hélio let his left arm hang and looked very sad withstanding the pain."

Hélio, over 40 years old, retired from active competition and concentrated on running the Gracie Academy. But he was called out of retirement when one of his own instructors, Waldemar Santana, started wrestling professionally for money. Hélio thought that kind of tomfoolery could bring his school into disrepute and forbade Santana from wrestling. Santana went ahead with his bout, which was actually a Vale Tudo match, and lost his job with the Gracie Academy. He also made some disparaging comments about Gracie in the newspaper. Gracie asked him to retract his comments and he refused. The fight was on. Again, the Gracie PR machine made Santana out to be a monster of a man. He was actually a well-proportioned 195 pounds, hardly a giant. His fight with Hélio in 1955 lasted more than three hours before Santana knocked Gracie unconscious with a kick to the head. Santana had involuntarily retired Hélio, and it was time for a new Gracie to defend the family's honor.

THE FREE SPIRIT

When Santana knocked out his uncle Hélio, Carlson Gracie was the first one in the ring. He and Santana had been very close friends, but now things had changed. Hélio had taken him in when he moved to Rio at 15; he lived and breathed jiu-jitsu at the famous Gracie Academy. When the family suffered such an important loss, Carlson felt an obligation to restore its honor. He was the only man who could. After all, the best fighter in the gym was Carlos Gracie's son Robson, and he was only 124 pounds. Only Carlson could possibly stand and face Santana.

"I was a friend of his and told him, 'Look, Waldemar, we are friends, but now I can't let it pass. You beat Hélio, and now you're going to have to fight me. I have nothing against you, but in the ring, I'm going to beat the shit out of you!' And I did," Carlson said. "I fought him six times. I won four times, and two were a draw. He was tough shit. If it were today, he would be one of the best fighters."[13]

Because Carlson was underage, his father, Carlos, had to forge paperwork saying he was 21. Winning was imperative. Students and money were flowing out of the Gracie Academy and to Santana's new school. Without their reputation as the best fighters in the world, the future of Gracie jiu-jitsu was at stake.

"If it were not for me, after I beat Waldemar Santana, the Gracies would be selling bananas in a public market," Carlson said.[14] The fight took place August 3, 1956, in front of 40,000 fans at the Maracananzinho Stadium. Carlson and his friend showed each other no mercy.

Carlson said, "It was a really violent fight — 39 minutes of pure hitting from side to side. Waldemar had great endurance. It was one of the greatest MMA fights ever. He lost because he wasn't able to continue. He was bleeding from everywhere, so his corner threw in the towel, afraid he might die." It is reported that Santana's manager, Carlos Barretto, said, "I prefer a living friend to a brave and dead one." Watching the fight clips on YouTube is a revelation. The two are so evenly matched, and the back and forth action could be inserted in a modern MMA fight and no one would blink an eye. These were truly two of the all-time greats going toe-to-toe for four ten-minute rounds. Gracie knew the moment the fight was over: "I felt when he caved in. I was really punching and he fled. He used to flee a lot, didn't he? I was relentless. I could fight all day and I would never feel tired."[15]

He would be the standard bearer for the family through the 1970s and led the family with a new focus: sport jiu-jitsu. Vale Tudo fights became a flash-in-the-pan success on television in the 1970s, but the Gracies did not participate. They had nothing to prove.

"Jiu-jitsu practitioners don't need to fight anymore to prove that Brazilian jiu-jitsu is an effective self-defense and fighting method," Carlos Gracie Jr. said. "Everybody knows it is. I remember my father sitting and telling me that once jiu-jitsu was accepted, there was no reason to keep doing challenges and Vale Tudo matches anymore. They did it for respect and recognition, not money."[16]

The Gracies read the winds correctly: Brazilian politicians banned the fights and Vale Tudo was dead for years. The new game in town was sport jiu-jitsu, and Carlson was its master.

"Hélio always faced jiu-jitsu as ideology, the fight where the weak must beat or at least not lose to the strong," said master Joao Alberto Barreto. "Therefore, he demanded students follow a complete program, where the person had to defend, take down — or be taken down, and in this case sweep — pass guard, mount and submit. Carlson was different. To him, jiu-jitsu was a game. The important thing was winning."[17]

Life was good in Brazil, and the Gracies were content to play the sport jiu-jitsu game, surf, and hang glide. Everything was fine until Rorion Gracie wanted to live the American dream, and Gracie jiu-jitsu had to be established in a new country. It was time to resurrect the Gracie Challenge.

2
THE WAR OF THE WORLDS

They say if you can make it there, you can make it anywhere. Frank Sinatra was talking about New York, but Rorion Gracie was thinking of America. "I always knew that if you make it in America, the whole world is going to know about it," he once said.[18] Rorion believed that Gracie jiu-jitsu was the strongest martial art. His family had proven that time and time again on the streets of Brazil. But how could the Gracies make these Americans understand what they were missing?

"Man, I'm going to tell you that it was a question of proving it. People will . . . want to test you and see if you're really good," Rorion's brother Royce Gracie said. "If you're going to come to a place and tell everybody you are the best in the world, people are going to look at you and say, 'Prove it.' Anywhere, not just in America, anywhere in the world. All the more with Americans because they love what's theirs."[19]

Rorion had reached a stumbling point. He had all of this great information; he just didn't know how to share it. The martial arts community had followed the money, teaching ineffective and flashy kung fu and karate styles that looked great in Bruce Lee movies but were less effective in real life. Gracie trained the students he could find in his own garage, offering one free class and a second if you brought a friend.

He made ends meet cleaning houses until the wife of a movie producer told him he ought to be in pictures. With small roles on such television shows as *Starsky and Hutch* and *Hotel,* Gracie got his foot in the door and started attracting students from the movie business. But acting was not his passion. He desperately wanted to bring the Gracie mythos to America. His uncle had once posted a notice in the newspaper: "If you want a broken arm or rib, contact Carlos Gracie." Rorion would try a variation of the same strategy, challenging and defeating local karate teachers and kickboxers and giving classes to local law enforcement agents. A producer saw him battle kickboxer Ralph Alegria and hired him to choreograph the final fight scene in the movie *Lethal Weapon*. From there he taught Chuck Norris jiu-jitsu for an upcoming fight scene and started teaching more and more connected students.

Rorion was thriving in California but still hadn't accomplished his goal of making Gracie jiu-jitsu a worldwide phenomenon. He upped the ante on the Gracie Challenge, accepting matches with all comers in a winner-take-all contest for $100,000. There were no takers, but he did attract the attention of *Playboy*. An article simply titled "Bad" introduced a world of readers who really did subscribe for the articles to Gracie and his fighting system, proclaiming "The toughest man in the United States holds no official titles and has had only one fight in years."

It's safe to say that without *Playboy* we wouldn't have MMA as we know it today. Adman Art Davie read the piece and was intrigued. He was looking for a new sports hero for an ad campaign for Tecate beer. "My company did the advertising for a client in the beer importing business. They asked me to develop alternative sponsorship ideas that didn't involve boxing but yet could attract 18-to-34-year-old males," Davie said. "When I was in the Marine Corps, we used to sit around and talk about which martial arts would win if they would actually get into a ring and fight. Could a boxer beat a karate master? Could a judo fighter take on a kung fu expert? So when Tecate asked me for sponsorship ideas, that concept immediately popped into my head. My research produced a list of everyone promoting martial arts in America. That is how Gracie jiu-jitsu came to my attention, when I read the *Playboy* article that came out in September of 1989."[20]

The ad campaign didn't work out, but Davie saw huge potential in Gracie jiu-jitsu and helped Rorion promote his *Gracies in Action* tapes. These videos featured Gracies through the years in challenge matches with foolish martial arts masters in over their heads. The fights were narrated by Rorion in his trademark broken English, and when people saw them, their minds were blown. Davie saw dollar signs. He liked to think big and proposed a grand idea to Rorion. What about expanding the Gracie Challenge into a big tournament, a battle of styles in which the various martial arts would compete for supremacy? Along with movie director John Milius (*Conan, Red Dawn*), they came up with the idea for what would eventually become the UFC.

David said, "Milius, Gracie, and I were sitting around talking one night, and we began to have a conversation, like guys used to have in Vietnam, about if Sugar Ray Robinson were alive and fought Bruce Lee, who would win. People always have those 'what if?' conversations in the martial arts. Out of it came a desire to do this event. I went back to my agency and had my art department put together a comp called 'The War of the Worlds.' I said, 'Let's do a tournament.' I sat down with Milius and Gracie. Milius said he'd help develop the fighting circles. Rorion said he'd show what technically would work. I said I would do the marketing and raise the money."[21]

Getting the show on television turned out to be the tricky part, just like it would be for the Zuffa-run UFC a decade later. Televising a quasi-legal street fight with unknown fighters squaring off in a cage was a tough sell. By the time Davie was pitching the project to Semaphore Entertainment Group (SEG), the concept was barely breathing, having been rejected by all the other pay-per-view entities in what was a relatively new market.

SEG programmer Campbell McClaren said, "I was last on his list of phone calls. He called Showtime and they went, 'Get the fuck out of here.' He called HBO and they said, 'What? Shut up.' He probably didn't even get anyone on the phone. But we were doing some pretty out there programming at the time." SEG was investigating what could work in this new medium. What would people pay a premium for? They had limited success with concerts and comedians and needed a new idea.

SEG executive David Isaacs said, "When you looked at pay-per-view, all they had was wrestling, porn, and Mike Tyson. We kept trying to create new categories. I did a children's pay-per-view with the people that do *Thomas the Tank Engine*. We were trying to find things that people would pay extra for. That was really the mantra. We were actively looking for stuff like this. Campbell was leading the charge on the programming side and I was leading the charge on the 'We can't keep doing these concerts, they're paying crap' side. We saw the Gracie tape and had to figure out how we could do it. Was it really safe? Was it really sport? We saw this tape of

Rorion's brother on the beach. 'This man has insulted the Gracie family.' And the guy is a big bodybuilder, and one of these scrawny Gracie brothers beat the crap out of him. We got this tape and suddenly the office was filled with people. It was so compelling, and our gut instinct was, 'Holy crap! This is really interesting stuff.' How do we do it?"

The War of the Worlds was exactly what SEG had been searching for. McClaren had been looking at lucha libre wrestling (the high flying Mexican style of professional wrestling, complete with masked heroes and villains) and demolition derbies. But he put those ideas aside: this was the next big thing. McClaren said, "We were always looking for things that were very different and very wild. When the Ultimate Fight came in, I was looking for something wild. What I didn't expect to get were people with the integrity of the Gracies. In life, particularly in the entertainment business, integrity is not really in great supply. I met these guys and they were for real. They were no-bullshit, straight up for real. By then I was hooked, and I had to convince everyone that we had to do this."

McClaren was enthusiastic about the project and carried it personally to Bob Meyrowitz, his boss. Meyrowitz had made his name in the radio industry with the syndicated King Biscuit Flower Hour but had a flair for the dramatic, promoting a Jimmy Connors and Martina Navratilova tennis match like the Billy Jean King–Bobby Riggs "Battle of the Sexes" debacle. Meyrowitz likes to take credit for creating the UFC, but in reality, at the beginning, he was not entirely sold on the idea.

McClaren said, "What's the expression? Success has many fathers and failure is an orphan? And that's really how it is with the UFC. I was talking to Bob and he was saying that he conceptualized it. Which made me laugh, because we were there and Bob didn't even go to the first Ultimate Fight. The truth of the matter is that in a lot of ways, Rorion conceptualized it. In reality it was a Gracie Challenge. It was Art's energy, and Rorion's life's work and his family's, and David Isaacs bringing order to chaos. Bob Meyrowitz takes all the credit for it, even though the truth of the matter is he let me do it. You've got to give someone credit when they let their employees do their jobs. And that's just the producers. What about the fighters? Manny Yarbough did as much as anyone to launch the UFC. The ninja that Pat Smith beat up at UFC 2? His bloody face did as much to launch the UFC as anything."

With SEG firmly on board, a rough sketch of an idea had to be prepared for television. "They wanted to do a multi-month tournament and War of the Worlds wasn't going anywhere," Isaacs said. "We added the sexiness to it and made it a one-night tournament. I don't think if they put on War of the Worlds you would have ever heard of this again."

They settled on a one-night tournament to crown a martial arts champion. Now they needed a place to fight. A ring was out because Rorion told them it wouldn't effectively contain the fighters and keep them safe. Milius had studied ancient Greek Pankration and suggested a pit like the one surrounded by Greek structures and columns he had used in his Conan movies. Davie wanted a pit too, but one surrounded by a moat or Plexiglas. They eventually settled on the Octagon, a $34,000 structure that was dramatic and different, but also provided a good view for the television audience. When SEG vice president of marketing Michael Abrahamson came up with the name "Ultimate Fighting Championship," the show was ready to go. With a plan in place, Davie and Rorion had a new task: to find eight warriors willing to compete in an all-out fight for the championship.

THE FIGHTERS

Rorion wanted his brother, Royce, to represent the Gracie family. The more obvious choice would have been Rickson, the family champion, who was muscular and an aggressive street fighter. He was close to his prime and would have smashed his opponents in a most convincing manner. But Rorion didn't think this was the right way to display the full potential of Gracie jiu-jitsu. It would have fixed the focus on the athlete, not the system. More importantly, Rickson had opened a competing school to train Americans in the art of jiu-jitsu.

"Rickson had more experience than Royce, but he'd decided to make his own move," Rorion said. "I felt that Royce would be a very convincing example of what jiu-jitsu can do for people."[22]

While SEG and Davie had the goal of promoting an entertaining show, Rorion still had his own aim. He was, first and foremost, promoting Gracie jiu-jitsu.

"Since my arrival in America a quarter century ago, my primary goal has been to alert people to the importance of ground fighting," Rorion said. "I wanted everyone to learn the art that did so much for me. . . . I saw in the

UFC an opportunity to expose to the world the truths and fallacies inherent in contemporary martial arts theory."[23]

Royce was the smallest man in the tournament, and that wasn't by accident. When this scrawny Brazilian made larger men cry uncle, the efficiency of jiu-jitsu would be apparent.

"I think Rorion has never been anything but really forthright with us about his interests," Isaacs said. "Rorion had this whole business agenda selling videos and doing seminars, and to do that he really needed Gracie jiu-jitsu to be the big dog."

Rorion Gracie picking opponents for his own brother on a show he promoted as, essentially, an infomercial for his family's martial arts system was an obvious conflict of interest. But Gracie didn't use his position to secure an advantage for his brother. He didn't think he needed to. He and Art Davie looked for the best fighters they could find.

"I told Rorion, 'The only one who picks the fighters is going to be me. If that's acceptable and if we keep this thing open so all styles can have an equal, fair shake, then I'll do it on that basis. I won't do it any other way.' Everyone has been very good about that," Davie said. "We structured it that way so I could have that kind of decision-making power. Otherwise I didn't want to be involved in it. I wanted to find the best fighter in the world. If it's a Gracie, fine. If not, the UFC goes on. The UFC isn't dependent upon Royce Gracie winning."[24]

The fighters selected for UFC 1 were a motley crew. Gracie had wanted a world-class kickboxer, but when Denis Alexio and Ernesto Hoost turned them down, they were stuck with past-his-prime '80s star Kevin Rosier, who was sporting a monster gut to go along with his considerable gumption. Zane Frazier and local star Pat Smith were also kickboxers of lesser acclaim. Frazier was the one fighter that Rorion had personally requested. He had impressed the Gracies when he beat up Frank Dux, the fighter who inspired Jean Claude Van Damme's *Bloodsport,* at a local karate tournament.

Gerard Gordeau was a Savate expert and karate man from Holland and a vicious street fighter. He would later maim an opponent in Japan with a continued assault on the eyes. He was a bouncer and a bodyguard for pornography producers in Europe and was absolutely not messing around. He would face a 400-pound sumo wrestler named Teila Tuli in the first round. Tuli didn't speak the whole week leading up to the fights. When fighters were arguing about the pre-fight restrictions (no eye gouging and no groin strikes) and the lack of hand wraps, Tuli stood up and simply said, "I came here to fight. I'll fight anyone who wants to fight. See you tomorrow."

For SEG, the most important fighter besides Royce was boxer Art Jimmerson. The Gracies had dreamed of fighting a top boxer for years. Hélio had challenged Joe Louis and Ezzard Charles, while Rorion and Rickson had both offered Mike Tyson a match. The problem then, as it is now, is that the economics simply don't work to entice a top boxer into the Octagon. They had contacted James "Bonecrusher" Smith, but when the top prize for winning three fights in one night is just $50,000, it's hard to get boxers interested. Luckily for the UFC, Jimmerson was looking to buy a house and needed some quick cash. For a $20,000 appearance fee, a former top-ten fighter would compete inside the Octagon. The Gracies are accused of designing the brackets of the Ultimate Fighting Championship tournaments to make it easier for Royce. Only in this one case was it true, and it was so a Gracie could finally face a top boxer.

The final entrant in the eight-man tournament was possibly the most important fighter in UFC history, a pro wrestler from Lodi, California, who was confident that no one scheduled to appear that night could beat him.

KEN SHAMROCK

Kenny Kilpatrick grew up fighting. He was on the street before he turned 13 and was in and out of juvenile detention facilities, group homes, and foster homes. His path led to jail or the morgue until Bob Shamrock came into his life.

Shamrock had given his life to troubled young men and had raised hundreds of adolescents by stressing discipline and encouraging athletics. Disputes were settled out back with gloves on to prevent tensions from building. Ken was soon the champion of Bob's backyard and a star athlete in football and wrestling. A broken neck prevented him from pursuing his professional football dreams, but it never stopped him from fighting. He was fighting in underground tournaments and toughman contests by the time he was 19 years old. When fighting got him into trouble, his adopted father Bob suggested fake fighting. Ken trained with Buzz Sawyer and was wrestling for peanuts in North Carolina as Vince Torelli. Wrestling on the smaller shows barely paid the bills, so Ken continued to earn some extra cash on the toughman circuit, earning the nickname "One Punch" in honor of his big right hand.

Pro wrestler Dean Malenko thought Shamrock's natural aggressiveness and amateur skills would be perfect for a new style of wrestling that had caught fire in Japan. Shoot-style wrestling in the Universal Wrestling Federation (UWF) was as close as it came to the real thing. Kicks were full force, and much of the match happened on the mat with the wrestlers exchanging suplexes and submission holds. Malenko introduced Shamrock to Sammy Soronaka, who put Ken through a grueling tryout, a test of guts and fortitude that Shamrock would put his own students through when he opened his training center, the famous Lion's Den.

He went through another tryout when he made it to Japan. Ken considered himself a tough guy, but when he hit the mat with future Pancrase (the first professional wrestling company to promote legitimate contests in almost 100 years) founders Minoru Suzuki and Masakatsu Funaki, Shamrock realized he had a lot to learn. He could take them down with his strength and wrestling, but he was getting arm-barred, leg-locked and choked out by both of the smaller Japanese. He was getting trounced and loving it. He stayed in Japan and learned these locks himself, becoming a top student of Funaki and his teacher, the legendary professional wrestler Karl Gotch. When Funaki and Suzuki started their own promotion that would feature real pro wrestling, legitimate competition under traditional pro wrestling rules, Ken was in.

He stood out in Pancrase, just as he had in toughman contests and underground fights. He was a solid 215 pounds and as skilled as anyone in Japan on the mat. At Pancrase's inaugural show, he choked out his old teacher Funaki in the main event.

Shamrock said, "It was our first shoot, and I was really uncomfortable because I was fighting my trainer Funaki. And you know you are going to go in and you are shooting with a guy, and it's like you know this guy and it is tough to bring yourself to take that extra step. If you get a submission are you going to break it? Are you going to make him tap? Or are you going to let it go because he won't tap? We went in and we did it and it worked out fine and nobody got hurt."[25]

When his student Scott Bessac saw an advertisement for the UFC in

Black Belt magazine, Ken was intrigued. "I fought in Japan [for Pancrase] four days prior to the event. I flew out and arrived in Denver three days prior to the event. It's a mile high with a 16-hour time difference from Japan, and I'm thinking they're going to come to me and say, 'This is how it works.' But they never did, so I'm walking out going, 'This is the real deal.'"[26] Shamrock wasn't the only one who wasn't sure what to expect. When they locked the cage door on November 12, 1993, at the McNichol Arena in Denver, no one knew what was going to happen.

3
FIGHT NIGHT

The first Ultimate Fighting Championship started not with a bang, but with a belch. "Superfoot" Bill Wallace could rest his foot on your head, but he wasn't much of a broadcaster. He screwed up the show's name too, calling it "The Ultimate Fighting Challenge." Wallace wasn't the only one in over his head.

SEG programmer Campbell McClaren said, "Not a fucking clue. We were in the truck, which is the mobile control center for the TV show. You use these giant semis with TV studios inside. The director is in there and if you're the producer you sit in there and watch everything. There are 11 cameras and you're watching everything. We're in that truck for the first fight between Teila Tuli and Gerard Gordeau and it lasted, like, four seconds or something. And we're thinking, 'We've got 11 fights, we've got a three-hour block, but this might be a four-minute show.' We had no idea even how long the fights were going to last."

Gordeau had sidestepped a charging Tuli and planted a round kick into his mouth. Tuli's tooth flew right past broadcaster Kathy Long, a kickboxing world champion. Two more of Tuli's teeth were embedded in Gordeau's foot. The whole thing was over in less than 30 seconds.

Ken Shamrock said, "In the locker room, you hear the popping of the pads and the guys getting all angry before they go out and fight. It's the first time anybody's even thought of putting something like this on, and it really hadn't sunk in to anybody what it really was. He kicks him in the mouth and the teeth go flying in the front row. And I kid you not, when all this happened, you could

33

hear a pin drop in that place. And at that moment, everybody realized what the UFC was really about. The original no-holds-barred MMA. That was the fight that set the tone."[27]

After a slobber knocker between Kevin Rosier and Zane Frazier that left Rosier with a busted jaw and sent Frazier to the hospital, it was time for Royce Gracie to make his Octagon debut. His opponent, Art Jimmerson, was shaken by the violence. It was like nothing he'd ever seen. Boxing was a brutal business, but it was an organized chaos. Anything could happen in the Octagon, and Jimmerson had a fight coming up with "The Hitman" Thomas Hearns. He wasn't sure he really wanted to be there.

McClaren said, "Art Jimmerson was buying a house and was short on the down payment. So his needs and our needs came together. He was a nationally ranked boxer. He was a real guy, a professional. But he was more interested in getting out of there with his arms still attached to his body. I talked him into doing it . . . but I realized it's not a good thing to talk a fighter into doing a fight. There's too much at stake; it's not a game. If you didn't come physically prepared you might lose or things might not go the way you wanted. But if you didn't come mentally prepared you were in serious jeopardy. Ken Shamrock told me, and Ken had fought everywhere in the world, when he went into the Octagon for the first time and that door closed and that metal bolt slammed, it freaked him out. And he was one tough guy. I thought, if that freaked him out, what's it going to do to a first-time guy?"

Jimmerson had been confident that his quick jab and movement would give him an advantage over the other fighters on the show. Martial artists could punch and kick hard, but they tended to move straight forward all the time. Jimmerson would move around and pick them apart. Art was feeling pretty good about his chances until he saw Ken Shamrock working out and talked to future UFC referee "Big" John McCarthy. McCarthy was there with his training partner Royce Gracie, and Jimmerson was needling him about how Royce had never seen a punch like his. McCarthy tried to explain to Jimmerson that he was in trouble and even demonstrated a little jiu-jitsu before the match.

"The one thing I remember today as clearly as that day back on November 12, 1993, was Art Jimmerson having a panicked look on his face when he said, 'Oh my God, he is going to break my arms and legs, isn't he?'

I told him all he had to do if he felt pain or discomfort was tap out."[28]

Even when Jimmerson came out, looking completely ridiculous with a single boxing glove on his left hand, the audience was conditioned to expect him to win. He was a professional boxer. Surely he would dismantle this skinny kid in the white pajamas.

McClaren said, "When Royce went in with that boxer at UFC 1, I was 1,000 percent convinced that boxer was going to kill him. I don't mean knock him out; I mean actually kill him. He's going to swing, throw a punch from his hips, hit Royce on his head, and knock his head off his skinny little body. But when I went down before the fight and Art Jimmerson asked me, 'Do I tap with my left hand or my right hand?' I started to realize maybe the fight wasn't going to go the way I originally thought."

Royce beat Jimmerson with ease, taking him down and getting the mount position. Jimmerson was so intimidated by his workout with McCarthy that he tapped out before Royce could even attempt a submission hold. The crowd didn't understand the grappling on the ground and was furious. It only got worse when Ken Shamrock defeated local favorite Patrick Smith by heel hook in the final first-round fight.

"I remember walking to the back after beating Patrick Smith and people were booing me," Shamrock said. "They were actually booing me. I broke the guy's ankle! But they didn't have an education about that stuff."[29]

After Gerard Gordeau easily dispatched an exhausted Kevin Rosier, Shamrock and Gracie matched up in what would become a legendary semifinal match. Royce Gracie would be in the cage with the one other fighter in the whole tournament who was familiar with the ground. Shamrock was convinced he had already beaten the toughest guy in the competition. He had fought the best ground fighters Japan had to offer. Royce hadn't impressed him much in his fight with Art Jimmerson.

"When I went in there, I didn't know who Royce Gracie was," Shamrock said. "When he came out and I saw him with a gi, I said, 'Karate guy. I'll take him no problem.' I saw all these boxers and said, 'Everybody's stand-up. I'll smoke these guys.'"[30]

Royce charged Shamrock with a double leg takedown attempt and got stuffed. He pulled Ken into his guard position, which was fine with him. The Gracies were just as dangerous from the bottom as they were on top.

In the early UFCs, Royce often utilized heel kicks from his back to his opponent's kidneys. These kicks weren't going to make anyone quit but would cause serious internal problems following the fight. They were eventually banned, but were still legal here, and Royce used them but to Ken's advantage. He caught Gracie's leg and tried the same kind of leg lock he had beaten Smith with earlier in the evening. Royce was ready for it and used Ken's own momentum to propel himself back on top. In the scramble that followed, he was able to snake his arm under Shamrock's throat and force him to tap the mat.

The announcers were as new to the sport as the fans in the arena. No one was sure what had happened, including the referee, who didn't stop the fight after the tap out. Royce whispered in Ken's ear, "You know you tapped." Ken was a man of honor. "I tapped the mat and the referee didn't see it. He was going to let it go, but I tapped the mat. I'm not going to lie. Otherwise the referee was going to let it go. He let go of his hold already. It wouldn't be fair for me to say 'Keep going.' He'd already let go of the hold."

Backstage it looked like a war zone, with only the cautious Jimmerson unscathed by the evening's battles. One fight remained to crown the first Ultimate Fighting Champion. Royce Gracie would face Gerard Gordeau, and Gordeau didn't look to be in any condition to fight.

McClaren said, "Gerard Gordeau kept his left hand in a bucket of ice after his first fight because he'd broken a couple of knuckles. And after his second fight he had his other hand in a bucket of ice because he'd broken those knuckles. So he goes in to fight Royce with two broken hands. He can't even tap! But he iced them down and he was going to fight Royce even with the broken knuckles. I couldn't figure him out, and he was scary and nasty. But when I saw that I thought, 'What does this take?' You could go and sit in a Zen monastery and not achieve this."

Gordeau was furious with the UFC and the Gracies. He believed that he was initially supposed to be Royce's first-round opponent and was switched with the timid Jimmerson when Rorion heard about Gordeau's fearsome reputation from the Japanese press in attendance. He was sure the fight doctors had told Royce about his injuries, taking away what slim hopes he had. When Gracie got him down to the mat, Gordeau attempted a Tyson. "He got a piece of my ear," Gracie said. "He didn't take a piece off, but he bit my ear and I had to pull it out of his teeth. He was trying to bite it, but it just got scratched and bled a little bit." The foul play would have cost Gordeau part of his purse but wouldn't have disqualified him. The UFC had very few rules, and even the ones it did have were more like suggestions.

Royce was able to free his ear and the UFC avoided the spectacle of a biting scandal. Royce instead secured the rear naked choke for the win. He was $50,000 richer and the first Ultimate Fighting Champion.

AFTERMATH

The UFC was an immediate success. No one was sure why. They had no TV programming, no TV advertising, and still did 86,000 pay-per-view buys. Compare that to the hundreds of copycat shows that have tried to follow the UFC's lead as a pay-per-view powerhouse. Even the Pride Fighting Championships, featuring former UFC stars and powered by FoxSportsNet, still only drew just over 30,000 buys in 2007. It's an unwritten rule that you can't sell on pay-per-view without television, but somehow the show sold.

Wrestling Observer Newsletter editor Dave Meltzer said, "It had never happened before; it hasn't happened since. It will probably never happen again. They had an intriguing question that everyone was curious about. It violated every rule we know about promoting a pay-per-view. It was kind of a once-in-a-lifetime lightning-in-a-bottle thing. People were intrigued by the concept of style versus style. People have debated that forever. What if a wrestler fought a boxer or fought a jiu-jitsu guy. That was the original lure, and then I think a couple of the personalities, Royce and Shamrock, were intriguing to people. Word of mouth, 'Oh my God, you have to see this.' People talked about it."

The fighters were unknown, and it would have been easy for people to dismiss the athletes as simple bar fighters. One man helped keep that from happening. He exuded credibility and was well known to a generation of sports fans as a legitimate tough guy. SEG's decision to bring in football legend Jim Brown as its color commentator really paid off, as he was an integral part of their successful initial broadcast.

"Jim was a great addition because Jim is a real tough guy. He's just a no-bullshit tough guy. Jim was maybe 60 and you could tell by the way he walked in the room and the way he acted that he figured he could still take these guys," Isaacs said. "He was Jim fuckin' Brown. When he spoke on the air I think it had that authenticity. This is a tough guy telling us that this is a tough sport. And Jim told it like it was. You couldn't buy Jim Brown. You couldn't get him to say it unless he really thought it."

Brown was like the Michael Jordan of his generation, and his celebrity paid off. When they ran into potential problems in Denver, Brown played golf with the mayor and the problems went away.

McClaren said, "I'm not really into sports; the only sport I know is Ultimate Fighting. I thought Jim Brown was O.J. Simpson. I went to Jim's house in Beverly Hills, going to meet O.J. Simpson in my mind. And Jim does all this work with gangs and he had called a truce of the Bloods and the Crips. In his house. And he had all these church ladies, these African American ladies who raised these kids, in the house keeping the peace. And this is Jim's idea of a joke. I got to know him really well. He invites me, but he has no intention of going. So it's Bloods and Crips and I am a 37-year-old Scottish TV executive. Chubby, graying, wearing a TV producer's outfit, surrounded by Bloods and Crips for three hours as I wait for him to come home. One guy came up to me, and these are, like, 17-year-old kids. And young men who have never been given any respect are so prickly about getting respect. And they are half-cocked and angry. And this kid comes up to me and looks me right in the eye and goes, 'I'm not just in the Bloods. I'm in the Diabolical Bloods.' And I go, 'That is cool,' and the only thing I could think to do was give him my business card. He looked at it, and it was just such a moment. And then when he finally comes home and says he's Jim Brown, I'm thinking, no you're not. Where's the running-through-the-airport guy?"

THERE ARE NO RULES

In the absence of a traditional marketing platform (or an accompanying budget), the UFC had to do whatever it could to get attention. The tagline was "Two Men Enter, One Man Leaves." When they put the first advertisements together, there were no images to sell. The Octagon hadn't been built, the fighters hadn't been chosen, and there was no history to draw on. What was left but to focus on blood and violence?

"The fact is that when we started this, it didn't exist. We started it . . . they didn't know what it was. . . . We had to do something to bring people in to see this sport," SEG owner Bob Meyrowitz said. "The first year or two we marketed really aggressively, we thought with a sense of humor, but we did say a lot of very aggressive stuff."[31]

The focus on blood and gore would eventually come back to haunt SEG. It's hard to argue with critics when your own promotional materials exhibit and exaggerate the worst human impulses.

McClaren said, "When we talked about how wild it was, the press loved that story, and the press became our advertiser. In retrospect was it the wrong decision? No, because if we hadn't done it there would be no Ultimate Fight. It's one thing to look back and say, 'That success was built on scandal' or 'that success was built on outrageousness.' But if you don't get to the point where it's a success, there's nothing else to talk about. We were doing the line 'Banned in 49 States' after we had done it in seven states."

The show changed martial arts overnight. Royce Gracie demonstrated to karate practitioners and other exotic martial arts practitioners that their arts may be flashy, but they just don't work. Needless to say, the martial arts establishment was not happy about this. Gracie was costing them money, and they struck back the only way they knew how: by writing mean letters in *Black Belt* magazine. Their own announcer, Bill Wallace, was among the first to blast the event in print. He, like his friends in the industry, had a lot at stake. No one was keen to see their art depicted as a fraud in front of the entire world.

UFC matchmaker Art Davie said, "I think when some people see that a particular stylist of their style goes in and doesn't do well, they ask me why I don't get somebody who's doing a national seminar in that style. Invariably we've asked that person, some known name, and he doesn't do it. The last thing he wants to do is to go in the Octagon and lose; it would hurt his business. I get the toughest young guys out there in a particular style. In some cases, when they get in the Octagon and it's a real fight like this is, virtually a street fight, the guys forget a lot of what they've learned. And a lot of what they've learned doesn't apply. It really doesn't apply when you go in an all-out fight like that. Everyone looks good punching bricks."

Although the UFC would later draw the ire of politicians and cable executives for its lack of rules, after UFC 1 the main criticism was that there were too many rules. The karate men demanded groin shots, and Davie convinced Rorion Gracie they were necessary to appease the strikers who actually trained to deliver a quick shot to the testicles. Rounds were also out, as no fight had gone more than five minutes. Everyone agreed that jiu-jitsu trainer Joao Alberto Barreto had done a horrible job as the referee. Davie's solution was to remove the referee completely and have an observer outside the Octagon attempt to maintain order. Sanity prevailed and Rorion recommended police officer John McCarthy be the new official inside the cage. McCarthy had no experience, but he was a tough cop and an experienced jiu-jitsu player. And at over 250 pounds, he could control even the biggest fighters. "Big John" became a mainstay and almost as recognizable as the fighters themselves, starting hundreds of fights with his trademark "You ready? You ready? Let's get it on!"

The new rules didn't change much. Royce Gracie was declared the Ultimate Fighting Champion a second time, beating a returning Patrick Smith in the finals. Gracie looked even more dominant in the second tournament, possibly because there was no Ken Shamrock to challenge him. Shamrock had broken his arm training with his student Vernon White and missed the show. Fans were clamoring to see him in a rematch with Gracie, and SEG was quickly realizing that style versus style was already a dated concept. They needed stars and hoped Ken Shamrock could be their Jack Dempsey.

SHAMROCK VS. GRACIE: THE REMATCH

"We had the Gracies, but we needed a foil. And that was Ken Shamrock. A lot of the stories that were there were real and weren't some marketing guys idea. Ken Shamrock was a street kid from a very rough and tumble background," McClaren said. "And the Gracies, even though it's a fighting family, are all about family. You had Ken who was kind of a street orphan versus this whole clan, and it was pretty compelling stuff. He was the gunslinger, the cold professional, and the Gracies were kind of pure."

Shamrock was obsessed with getting revenge for his loss at UFC 1. Although he managed to keep his composure when he was interviewed on live television after his loss, backstage he was furious and threw a tantrum. He felt Royce had cheated, that the gi gave him an unfair advantage.

"He wrapped the gi around my neck, and I tried to pull his arm off, but there was no arm to pull off," Shamrock said. "I thought, 'Wait a minute, you can't do that.' It's cheating. It's not his arm. He's got this rope around my neck. How is that fair?"[32] Even after the fight, his students couldn't believe he had lost. He was Ken Shamrock. He never lost.

"I was very surprised when he lost. It was like jiu-jitsu was the new kung fu. When kung fu first came around back in the '70s, it was mysterious. People didn't understand it," Vernon White said. "Ken was stronger, he was more athletic, he was more aggressive, but he didn't understand jiu-jitsu. Now it's no mystery."

Ken had brought a Judoka into his camp, and his brother Robbie Kilpatrick got gis for his students to wear. "He was determined to fight Royce again, whether it was in the Octagon, in a dojo, or in a parking lot," Bob Shamrock said.[33] Ken Shamrock was focused like a laser on Gracie and was just hoping for another opportunity — one he wasn't sure was coming.

"After UFC 1, I honestly thought because of the performance I had against Royce Gracie, that I didn't know if I'd be back . . . I didn't realize how much I'd connected with the fans," Ken Shamrock said. "The fans and the people were picking up on it and dying to see more."[34]

They wouldn't get Shamrock-Gracie right away, at least not at UFC 3 on September 9, 1994. The event was marketed based on seeing the two square off, but the draw for the tournament was done randomly, with numbered ping-pong balls. The two men were on opposite sides of the bracket. If they were going to meet, it would be in the finals. Instead, neither made it that far. The tournament was packed with flamboyant and exciting fighters. Art Davie, who had to beg for fighters to compete at UFC 1, had hundreds of applications for UFC 3. That meant the show would feature people with the right look and skills to provide entertaining television.

The man with the best look, a character right out of a pro wrestling show, was known only as Kimo. He was a muscle-bound street fighter who emerged from the smoky entranceway carrying a gigantic wooden cross on his back. It was quite a sight, and Kimo put up quite a fight against Gracie. For the first time in the UFC, Gracie was in trouble and looked flustered. He was having a hard time getting the bigger man down and was paying the price in the currency of the ring: hard punches to the head. Gracie turned things around by grabbing a handful of hair to control his opponent. Not against the rules, but a "bitch move," Lion's Den fighter Guy Mezger said. Gracie finished Kimo off with an arm bar but had to be dragged backstage.

Ken Shamrock was there watching, waiting for his chance to get at Gracie. He had beaten one of America's top judo players, one of the flying Lennigers, and took his time. He won a dull fight with punches on the ground. He was equally cautious against alternate Felix Lee Mitchell in the semifinal round. Nothing was going to keep him away from Gracie.

Nothing except Kimo. When it was time for Royce's semifinal match with Canadian "Wildman" Harold Howard, Royce couldn't continue. Royce Gracie said, "Before we made the ring entrance I stopped and said, 'Wait a second, let me just lay here on the ground to rest a bit.' I laid down, took a breath, and got up. What I don't remember is that when I laid on the ground, Fabio Sanos and Relson Gracie came up to me and said, 'Do you want anything, Royce?' And I told them, 'I want some watermelon juice.' And they told me, 'There's no watermelon juice here, bro! Let's go! Get up!' But I don't remember this conversation. So I fainted before the fight and I didn't even know it."[35]

His corner threw in the towel, and Kimo and his manager, Joe Son, hit the ring to celebrate. The final fight would be Ken Shamrock against Harold Howard, who advanced when Gracie couldn't continue. But Ken wasn't interested in coming out. "Ken had a funny way of looking at things," Bob Shamrock said. "He came to the event to fight Royce; he didn't care about anyone else."[36]

It was just one of what would become a pattern of disappointing Shamrock performances. "I always expected more from Ken, in a way. Not that he didn't achieve a lot, but I always felt that right when he could really take it over the top, he couldn't do it," David Isaacs said. "Ken's a pioneer and there's no doubt he's done great things for the sport. Early I felt like he was close to achieving what Chuck Liddell did for the Zuffa UFC, but not quite. When they needed a big win and a star, Chuck was able to deliver. Ken got injured, and it was all real stuff, and it just didn't happen perfectly. We built a lot of stuff around him, and I wish that he had really knocked it out. Then Ken would have been on the cover of *Sports Illustrated*."

Instead of Shamrock-Gracie, UFC 3 had a final fight featuring Harold Howard, who advanced after a Gracie injury, taking on Steve Jennum, an alternate. Jennum was proclaimed the Ultimate Fighting Champion, but everyone knew the real champions were backstage, not in the cage. The Shamrock-Gracie rematch would have to wait until UFC 5. But UFC 4 on December 16, 1994, introduced the world to SEG's next big star: Dan Severn.

4
HYBRID WRESTLING: PANCRASE

Many people think that modern MMA made its debut with "Superfoot" Bill Wallace's belch heard 'round the world. But those people are wrong. Modern MMA actually got its start on September 21, 1993, at Tokyo NK Hall. Inside the beautiful convention center next to the Tokyo Bay Hilton, Japanese wrestling fans were treated to a bold new experiment: fights without predetermined outcomes. The mad scientist was a young wrestler named Masakatsu Funaki.

Funaki was a rising star in the world of professional wrestling. In Japan, the mat wars had taken a dramatic step away from their American counterpart. While Americans embraced the cartoonish antics of Hulk Hogan and "Rowdy" Roddy Piper, the Japanese fans were craving something very different.

Japan had a long established martial arts culture. After all judo, jiu-jitsu, and karate can all trace their roots to the small island chain. Professional wrestlers and their fans wanted to place their discipline ahead of the other fighting arts, establishing it as the toughest of all. This desire for legitimacy led to the creation of the Universal Wrestling Federation in 1984. This style of wrestling, though still predetermined, featured real kicks and punches and submission holds straight out of jiu-jitsu and judo. Instead of a match ending with a power bomb or pile driver, it was more likely to end with the juji-gatame (the dreaded arm bar). The matches were predetermined, but the training was very real.

"A lot of those [matches] were worked shoots, but in the training we shot [wrestled for real]," former Ultimate Fighting Champion and King of Pancrase Ken Shamrock said. "That's where

I learned most of my submissions. . . . I got hooked a couple of times. I got hooked, I learned it. I got hooked again, I learned that one. As I got better and better, there weren't too many people who could hook me."

Eventually young up-and-comers Masakatsu Funaki and Minoru Suzuki, tired of biding their time behind established pro wrestling stars like Yoshiaki Fujiwara, stepped out of the shadows and into the spotlight, creating Pancrase. Funaki and others were convinced the audience was ready for the next step. Real submission wrestling, wrestling without scripted results. Along with former Olympic wrestling alternate Suzuki, Funaki took wrestling back to the days of Frank Gotch and Farmer Burns — to a time before shows were more morality play than athletic contest.

No one was sure exactly what to expect, least of all the fighters.

"Someone came to me and told me about a guy who was taking people to Japan to fight, and at first I said, 'Nah' because I didn't want to be on the airplane. But after they told me how much money I could make, then I decided I wanted to go," Pancrase veteran Vernon "Tiger" White said. "I got six months to train. I had no idea what the ground was all about. Even though I had worked with Ken [Shamrock], when I got over there it was totally different. It was people trying to rip your arms off, rip your legs off. I don't want to say it was horrible because it was a learning experience. I got to fight a couple of guys on my level, and I had to fight guys who got angry and tried to end my career. I took a beating like a pro. I took it and I came back. Some people, they lose and say, 'This sucks. I don't want to lose and look like a fool.' But you never get anyplace quitting."

White lost his first fight by arm bar in less than two minutes, but he was amazed by the experience. That first show wowed the 7,000 fans in attendance, too. They had never seen real combat, not like this, but it didn't go exactly as promoters hoped. It turns out that real fights don't last long, especially when only one of the combatants is schooled in submission, certainly not as long as the 15- or 20-minute matches shoot-style fans were used to. The six fights that night lasted a total of 13 minutes and five seconds. Something had to change, and it turns out the solution was simple. Funaki, Suzuki, Shamrock, and other experienced fighters would take their time with their opponents, extending the fights long enough to give the crowd their money's worth before finishing their opponent.

THE RULES

Since Pancrase had its roots in pro wrestling, it's natural the rules would be the same. Like pro wrestling, you were allowed to punch the body with a closed fist but could only strike the head with an open hand. Elbow strikes were also illegal, as were knees and stomps to the head on the ground. For knockouts, a ten-count similar to boxing was used. If the fighter couldn't answer the count, a TKO was declared and the fight was over. If the fighter could get back on his feet, the fight resumed and one point was deducted.

Submission holds were legal, but you had to break the lock if your opponent made it to the rope. Unlike traditional pro wrestling, however, Pancrase did not allow unlimited rope escapes. Fighters were penalized a point for using this way out. Competitors had a total of five rope escapes at their disposal, but after a fighter lost five points, the contest was over. If a fight made it to the end of the 15-minute regulation period, the winner was the fighter who had lost the fewest points. If the fighters both lost the same amount of points, or if neither lost points, the fight was declared a draw.

Pancrase also featured a unique gentleman's agreement.

Pancrase star Jason DeLucia said, "The gentleman's agreement was that it was legal to hit shotei [palm strikes] to the head on the ground and fist to the body, but that we would preserve the submission art and promote Pancrase as something different and more dignified than UFC. Especially since it would have been easy for the experienced wrestlers to pound out the stand-up guys."

The gentleman's agreement led to very interesting and dynamic mat work and also helped extend the length of fights that might have ended very quickly if striking on the ground was allowed. Even some submission holds, like the heel hook, were eventually banned from competition because of their tendency to cause injury. The mandatory Pancrase boots made it easier to apply leg locks, and a heel hook can cause serious damage before the victim even registers pain.

"In our first fight, I made Bas [Rutten] grab a rope escape with a heel hold," DeLucia remembers. "So three months later I get Bas again. Funaki says to me, 'You know how to win?' I say, 'Yes, heel hold.' So I train heel hold like crazy for a whole month, pulling heel holds out of thin air. I arrive in Japan to find out then that the heel hold has been made illegal."

Eventually Pancrase would bow to the economic pressure in Japan to present the same kind of mixed martial arts matches fans saw in Pride and UFC. But during its height, Pancrase rules were truly unique, and every fight card was covered in all of the papers, magazines and on television.

"Pancrase was the stuff back in the day. It was the height of pro wrestling then, and we were pro wrestlers that did it for real," former King of Pancrase Guy Mezger said. "We were the shoot wrestlers in a sport everyone knew wasn't real, and we really captured the imagination of the Japanese audience. It was a lot of fun back in those days, and there was a lot of notoriety to be had then."

MAKING STARS

Pancrase, like other professional wrestling companies, had a regular roster of fighters at its disposal. Fighters with potential, like the Dutchman Bas Rutten, weren't quickly beaten and disposed of. After losses to Funaki and Shamrock, Bas was sent home with a book to study wrestling. Funaki wasn't looking out for himself as a fighter. Funaki the promoter needed strong opponents to draw crowds to arenas all over Japan. He'd learned his formidable submission skills from wrestling legend Karl Gotch, and he was so desperate for solid competition that he actually trained most of his original Pancrase adversaries.

"I learned the most from Funaki when I went to Pancrase and we started doing real shoots," Ken Shamrock explained. "I started learning a lot more technical stuff. I lived and breathed training."

Pancrase quickly established three top-tier fighters: Funaki, Suzuki, and Shamrock. Shamrock was crowned the first champion, the King of Pancrase, after winning a tournament in 1994. But three fighters didn't give the promoters much flexibility in creating new and exciting matchups. Naturally, the pro wrestler in Funaki took over, and he took it upon himself to create a new star in Lion's Den newcomer Jason DeLucia.

DeLucia's quest to refine the traditional martial arts had led him to a place he never expected to go: the ground. After losing a dojo challenge to Royce Gracie in 1992, DeLucia realized that kung fu alone wouldn't be enough to compete in this new sport. Studying the ground game emboldened him, and he was ready to challenge Gracie again, winning an alternate match at UFC 1 and his first fight at UFC 2 before falling to Gracie in the rematch at UFC 2. It was at those early UFCs that Jason was discovered by

Pancrase's North American talent scout, Ken Shamrock, and within months he was in Japan joining Shamrock's legendary Lion's Den. Pancrase saw Jason's potential and tested him right away. His first fight was in a main event. His opponent was Pancrase's founder, Masakatsu Funaki.

"You know they say, 'Don't be affected by hype and don't listen to the crowd,' but it's hard not to when you see someone who commands energy from a crowd as Funaki does," DeLucia said. "In my case, that energy inflamed my will, whereas I think he was a bit too comfortable."

The Pancrase newcomer shocked fans at Amagasaki Gym, making Funaki tap out to a knee bar in just over a minute. Pancrase had a new superstar.

"From what I understand," DeLucia said, "he was supposed to carry me three rope escapes into the match and miscalculated his distance upon the first rope escape [necessitating the tap] — it happens. The promoters were very unhappy, needless to say."

It was commonplace for established fighters in Pancrase to make opponents look good. "Jason DeLucia is correct about many of the fights in Pancrase not being on the level," former Pancrase competitor and future Pride executive Matt Hume said. Hume was involved in several of the bouts that ringsiders thought were questionable, including a fight that saw Ken Shamrock use a professional wrestling move called a northern lights suplex. He put his head under Hume's arm and grabbed him in a clinch before flipping him over his head. It is a move nearly impossible to pull off cleanly without cooperation.

The Pancrase promotion was competing with several pro wrestling organizations, companies like Akira Maeda's RINGS and Nobuhika Takada's UWF-I, companies that presented a similar product. It was important for Pancrase to create stars that could draw fans to the arena, and sometimes that meant the fighting arts gave way to the fight business.

"When fight companies are small, there are works [fixed fights] — it is necessary. For example, in those days a fighter like Matt Hume would not be able to fight Bas Rutten unless it was worked or they didn't care about Bas losing," DeLucia said. "Because if they fought, Matt could go to the ground game, mount, and pound Rutten out in a UFC-style fight. It's just a fact that Matt was schooled as a wrestler and Bas as a Thai boxer. It's a matter of securing business objectives."

Rutten, the charismatic Dutch kickboxer with a sculpted physique and great stage presence, was a pet project of Pancrase's promoters. They already had homegrown Japanese stars, and several Americans had also made their mark. They now needed their own European star to combat RINGS' duo of Dick Vrij and Volk Han and began grooming the Dutchman.

"People can say what they will, but I doubt many besides Ken will have as intimate knowledge of the goings-on as I did," DeLucia said. "Basically, the way many organizations wind up operating is this: you can build the drama and gambling concessions better if you're sure of the outcomes."

Rutten would eventually become an outstanding fighter, but Pancrase wasn't ready to wait for that to happen naturally. Instead, they tried to make a big splash by buying Rutten a win.

"They have been asking Ken all along to put Bas over, but he won't; he doesn't feel he deserves it, based on character more than anything," DeLucia remembers. "Ken agrees to carry Bas for some time to build him, but they want him to put Bas over. Because Ken and I both have wins over Funaki, they don't want both to have wins over Rutten. They're trying to build fighters from many countries, and that would push him too far down. Until Ken puts him over, they can't risk it with me so they begin working me . . . Great mental pressure before and during the fights was how these fights were worked, and with good reason. . . . Business reasons."

Rutten denies ever being involved in a worked fight, and it's likely that much went on without his knowledge. Others close to the situation don't deny that some early Pancrase bouts were worked, but don't believe Rutten needed any help to beat DeLucia.

"Bas beat the crap out of Jason," DeLucia's former teammate Mezger says. "I love Jason to death, but he took a beating from Bas from start to finish. There was no throwing in those fights. I watched those fights and Bas pretty much took it to him. Were there fixed fights? I'll be honest — I think there probably were before my time. No one ever approached me and I never heard of any fixed fights. And I could see them asking me, because I was one of the more dominating fighters. The closest they ever came with me was asking me to take it easy on some of the younger guys, so I wouldn't beat them up bad or hurt them or knock them out because I kept most of the fight on the feet and I jacked up some of those guys pretty good."

THE OTHER SHAMROCK

Mezger and DeLucia weren't the only Pancrase stars to come out of Ken Shamrock's Lion's Den. Americans who wanted to make a name in what was then Japan's most prestigious fight league had to come through Shamrock. And Ken had an eye for marketable talent. His adopted brother, Frank Shamrock, like Rutten, was brought into Pancrase with a big build. Like Rutten, his looks and charisma branded him a future star. And the simplest way to make a star was to give him a big win over an established name.

"I know that it went on. I don't know if I was just too young, or didn't need to know, but no one ever shared anything with me. I had a feeling . . . there were always secret meetings and whatnot, but I never knew anything about it," Frank Shamrock said. "No one ever asked me to end it a certain way. I do know that it went on, but I was never approached or had any experience with it. I believe some of the fights that I fought with the upper-echelon guys, they may have let me win or had some sort of ending in mind. But I always fought my heart out and fought as hard as I could and gave as much as I could."

Of course, the Shamrock brand had already been established when Frank Juarez Shamrock burst onto the Pancrase scene and became an instant contender. The Lion's Den was a successful stable of fighters, perfect foils for the homegrown Japanese stars. Brother Ken was one of the sport's most successful and charismatic fighters, having connected to fans both in Japan and at home in the United States. Despite not being related by blood, Frank had that same raw charisma, the same natural athleticism. His first fight was a win over one of Pancrase's other big foreign superstars, Bas Rutten, and he also handled himself quite well in a hard-fought loss to Funaki.

"I didn't really know what I was getting in to. I turned pro after six months of training and they threw me to the wolves. It was kind of cool because no one really knew anything. . . . We'd look at guys' outfits and look at what country they were from and sort of guess what they do," Shamrock said. "It was a fantastic time. Cut your teeth in fighting. No one knew anything. We were all just making it up, screwing around and I didn't take it seriously for the first couple of years, I just sort of hung out. . . . I didn't really understand what it took and what it entailed [to be a great fighter]. Now that I'm older I realize I probably wasted some valuable time there, but I had the time of my life."

A troubled kid who had grown up in a series of foster homes and crisis centers, Shamrock was enjoying his new surroundings. He had recently dropped out of college and was pushed into the fight game by his adopted father. Frank didn't like it at first, didn't approve of violence. Soon, however, it became apparent that he had a real affinity for fighting and his combination of looks, charisma, and skill made him a star in a culture that reveres the martial arts.

"It was really unique, and I had never experienced anything like celebrity. All of it was new to me. And I experimented with everything, tried to do everything," Shamrock said. The lifestyle and Tokyo nightlife might have been great for a young man enjoying his newfound fame, but it may not have been the best thing for Shamrock's burgeoning career.

"I smoked for the first year of my fighting career," Shamrock said. "In Japan, Lucky Strike was our biggest sponsor, so you got free cigarettes. It never dawned on me. The Japanese all smoked. It never dawned on me that I needed a bigger commitment to be a great fighter."

THE EYE-OPENER

Whether or not his early matches in Pancrase were worked is unclear, but Shamrock is sure they weren't full-out fights. That much became evident on the evening of May 13, 1995. Shamrock was just settling in as a Pancrase fighter, with five matches under his belt — fights with the best Pancrase had to offer. His opponents' names still carry the ring of legend: Funaki, Rutten, Suzuki. This was supposed to be a night off, an easy fight. After all, if you weren't a regular on the circuit, well, you just didn't mean much in the insular world of Pancrase.

"I had taken a month off from training. They told me I was fighting a Brazilian guy, and at that time if you weren't Japanese you weren't really a threat in the Pancrase game," Shamrock said. "It was an elaborate game. . . . The day before I was smoking and having wine and relaxing with my girlfriend."

It would be one of the fights that made Frank re-evaluate himself, not just as a fighter, but also as a man. Instead of a quick win, Frank had a brutal introduction to the intensity of MMA courtesy of Carlson Gracie black belt Allan Goes. It was Goes' first professional MMA fight, but he was no timid rookie. He had more than 200 jiu-jitsu matches and plenty of experience on the mean streets of Brazil.

Immediately, it was clear that it would be no average Pancrase bout. Instead of intricate and flowing mat work, the audience at Tokyo Bay NK Hall saw an aggressive and sparse form of jiu-jitsu on display. This wasn't the "smooth art" of Royce Gracie. This was the jiu-jitsu of Rickson: strong and pitiless. Normally Pancrase bouts were fought with the gentleman's agreement firmly in place. Frank found out the hard way that Goes was no gentleman.

"We had a knock-down, drag-out battle. Alan came from Brazil and was a Brazilian street fighter," Shamrock said. "I don't think anyone told him about the [gentleman's] agreement. It was a big eye-opener when he mounted me and started punching me in the head. . . . It was a whole other level, but I enjoyed it and it was big for me in the realm of fighting because it led to stiffer studies for me."

Goes dominated the fight, raining down blows from the mount and almost finishing Shamrock with a choke. But Frank's Lion's Den training helped him grab a leg lock, and it looked like the fight was over when Goes let out a startling scream.

"I truly felt at that time that I was at a place where my submission wrestling techniques would take care of any issue," Shamrock said. "And when striking became involved it certainly changed the amount of energy put into it [ground fighting] and the strategy involved in it. I also started to realize the difference between a sporting event and a fight. I broke Alan's leg and he didn't stop. That there is a fighter. If you break my leg, I'm giving up. . . ."

Shamrock escaped with a draw but left the arena that night with the realization that things would have to change for him to achieve his true potential.

"The camp I was with at the time, the Lion's Den, didn't advance their knowledge of fighting like you should if you're going to be a professional at anything," Shamrock said. "That was before the days of cardiovascular training. I never really knew anything about it. I was just a regular guy. My biggest sports were volleyball and hacky-sack. I didn't have a clue what it took to be a professional athlete and a competitor. And Ken, my original teacher, didn't know either. . . . We just fought hard and trained hard and did the best that we could."

Frank continued to fight in Pancrase for the next 18 months, stepping into the ring an incredible 13 times. But when his brother and mentor Ken Shamrock had a falling-out with the organization in 1996, it was time for Frank to pursue a new challenge: true mixed martial arts in the UFC.

DUTCH DYNAMO

While the Shamrocks were able to dominate on the ground, Bas Rutten was able to make his presence felt with a minimum of grappling training. Rutten almost never made it to Japan. After a disappointing kickboxing performance in his native Holland, he was about to retire from fighting altogether. Only his wife's premonition of future stardom convinced him to try out.

"She looked at me, and she had this strange look on her face. I said, 'What are you thinking?' She said, 'You're going to be a famous fighter in Japan.' I said, 'Nope, because I'm not going to fight anymore.' Four months later I get a telephone call for a tryout, which was in Amsterdam. I had to go that night. I put somebody in the hospital that tried to knock me out. And that's when Funaki and Suzuki were pointing their fingers at me and they said, 'We want him.' It came out of the blue."

Pancrase turned Rutten into a star. He was a breath of fresh air in a promotion built primarily on grapplers. His dynamic striking and undeniable charisma added a new dimension to the cards, and his ability to speak Japanese helped endear him to the crowds.

"The audience went wild for me. I couldn't believe it. In Holland, if you're a foreign guy and you beat a Dutch guy, hopefully you're going to make it out alive," Rutten said in a *T-Nation* interview. "But these people, they're putting babies in my hand, taking pictures. I couldn't believe it. The next day I was walking in the street and people were bowing to me. I was in the papers. I just couldn't believe it."

After early losses to both Shamrocks and Masakatsu Funaki, Rutten went on a 19-fight win streak, unheard of in Pancrase's history. But to maintain his winning record, he needed to learn how to fight on the ground.

"It was the loss against Ken. I really had it. I'm a very sore loser, and I knew what the problem was," Rutten said. "It was because I didn't train any ground. That decided it for me. Forget about striking, nobody's going to strike with me anyway. Even [famous kickboxer] Maurice Smith took me down in a fight. So I start concentrating on grappling twice a day, seven days a week. I really took it to the next level. I always told Ken, 'Thank you for that, buddy, because that actually made me very good.' I never lost again."

Rutten is adamant that none of his Pancrase bouts were anything but legitimate. Even so, the promotion used other methods to protect him and the Japanese stars they needed to remain strong.

"They'd switch opponents on us all the time," Mezger said. "When I fought Bas Rutten, they told me I was fighting this Australian guy, a nice guy but my mom could beat him. So I really didn't train that hard, and then I found out they had put me in a 30-minute match with Bas and I said, 'Holy crap.' They wouldn't tell you who you were fighting until a week ahead of time or they would change it at the last minute. Pride did that a lot, too. They wouldn't give you an opponent until the last week or two, so you wouldn't know how to freakin' train. But the Japanese fighter would know exactly who he was fighting or the guy they wanted to have a push would know who they were fighting. They'd pull a lot of crap like that."

Rutten won the King of Pancrase title in September of 1995 but had to take several months off after an injury. At the time, Pancrase expected stars to work an insane monthly schedule, and the company could ill afford to be without a champion for long. Frank Shamrock beat Minoru Suzuki for a provisional championship and, upon his return, Rutten established himself as the company's top fighter by beating the provisional champ.

Rutten had accomplished everything he could — everything except beating Pancrase founder Funaki. Their fight, on September 7, 1996, will forever be known as the most brutal in Pancrase history. Rutten destroyed Funaki standing and had come so far on the ground that the master of the submission lock couldn't hook him. For 15 long minutes, Rutten pounded Funaki with knees, palm strikes, and kicks, but the Pancrase founder refused to stay down.

"He gave me the slit throat to the neck sign. I looked at my manager, 'Now, I'm gonna kill him.' I totally fucked him up," Bas said in *Full Contact Fighter Magazine*. "Broke his nose. Broke the bone under his eye. Heavy fight, man. I knocked him down five times. There was blood everywhere."

The Funaki-Rutten fight was the high point for Pancrase as a promotion. Funaki was thrilled with the result, despite the fact that he lost.

"I don't think he lost to Bas on purpose, but I don't think he was trying to win. I think he was trying to have a great fight. He was trying to make a moment and he succeeded," Dave Meltzer said. "When it was over he was thrilled because he created the fight he wanted to create. He wasn't mad. Usually, when you're trying to win, you get mad at a loss. He wasn't mad when he lost that fight. He thought that was great."

This pro wrestling mindset controlled much of the company's decision making. When Ken Shamrock was set to fight Dan Severn at UFC 6, Pancrase had him lose his title to founding father Minoru Suzuki. Shamrock had held on to his Pancrase title while facing Royce Gracie at UFC 5. Shamrock losing to Royce was an acceptable risk. Shamrock losing to Dan Severn was unacceptable. Severn was a fellow professional wrestler and wasn't even considered a top performer for UWF-I, Pancrase's competitor. Not only that, but he was the NWA champion, the representative of fake pro wrestling. Losing to Severn was not in the cards, at least not as an official representative of Pancrase. This unique Japanese mentality often baffled the Americans fighting in Japan.

THE DECLINE

Many of the earliest foreign stars were leaving to fight in the UFC, and the promotion couldn't afford some of the talent they had signed. After a bitter disagreement with Pancrase over his UFC appearances, Ken Shamrock and many of his Lion's Den fighters left the promotion for good. Bas Rutten was soon to follow. The King of Pancrase title was left vacant when Rutten left to spend more time at home with his family.

"My wife was pregnant, and she had a pregnancy poisoning," Rutten said. "It's very serious. She and the baby both could have died. At that time she was in the hospital and couldn't leave her room. I had to go to Japan to defend my title and I told them, 'Listen, I'm going to stay home.' They said, 'If you're going to stay home, we'll strip the title from you.' I said, 'Okay, then you take my title.'"

A tournament was held to crown a new king. DeLucia earned his first title shot with tournament wins over Osami Shibuya and rising star Yuki Kondo. He would get his chance at Pancrase's ultimate prize on December 15, 1996. The opponent? Masakatsu Funaki. DeLucia was at his best that night, out-grappling the Japanese submission wizard, and he looked to be on his way to becoming the fourth King of Pancrase. And then his leg snapped.

"I broke my leg only a few minutes into that fight and continued to fight for about four minutes," DeLucia said. "And he knew he broke it when he blocked my round kick with an elbow. Then every chance he got, he went after that leg with low kicks. To be honest, I was glad he did it that way. These are defining moments for fighters."

Funaki was King of Pancrase for the first time, and Pancrase drew 12,000 to the Budokan Hall in Tokyo. The company thought it had a new star in Yuki Kondo, but he didn't have the charisma of Suzuki or the talent of Funaki. When he won the King of Pancrase title over Funaki in 1997, whispers from Japan were that Funaki threw the fight to his young protégé. Pancrase wasn't quite sure about their new champion. When the tough Guy Mezger became the top contender for Kondo's title, they had Kondo fight a return match with Funaki first.

"Funaki kind of hopscotched over me to fight Kondo," Mezger said. "Because I was going to fight Kondo for the title and they thought only Funaki could beat me. Everybody thought I was going to lose."

Pancrase was so confident in Funaki's invincibility that they booked him in appearances around Japan even before the fight was contested. Instead, Mezger showed how far he'd come as a fighter. The only way for Funaki to beat Mezger was on the ground. But first he'd have to get him there. No one in Pancrase could take Mezger down, and he was happy to methodically beat them standing. After years as a top contender, Mezger finally sat on the king's throne.

"It was my favorite win because Funaki was the only guy who had beaten me twice. Anyone else who's beaten me, I've either beaten them back or never had the opportunity to fight them again," Mezger said. "The King of Pancrase was supposed to speak to an elementary school the next day. They were so confident Funaki was going to beat me that they had the King of Pancrase scheduled to talk at this Japanese school. So the next day I had to give a talk at the school, and my Japanese is not very good."

Mezger would defend his title twice before joining his fellow foreign stars in the UFC. He would have been happy to stay on and fight in Pancrase as well, but the company didn't want to take the risk of having its champion lose to a fighter on another company's card. Mezger vacated the title.

"They didn't want me to go in there as the King of Pancrase. They felt if their guy were to lose, it would make their company seem not as good as the UFC," Mezger said. "It's just business, I guess. I didn't really care. I enjoyed my time with Pancrase, but I didn't mind leaving and giving up the title. They had been good to me, and some of my best years, the best times I remember were in Pancrase. But I wanted to fight and move on to some other things, so I didn't mind giving it up. It kind of hurt my feelings, but I understood where they were coming from, so it didn't bother me that much."

Mezger was scheduled to fight Vitor Belfort at UFC 19. When Belfort dropped out with an injury, Mezger would enter the Octagon with Tito Ortiz for the second time, igniting one of the hottest feuds the sport of MMA had ever seen. With the loss of Mezger, Pancrase's glory days were clearly behind them. Although the promotion continues to run shows to this day, they would never again be Japan's biggest mixed martial arts promotion. A new power was on the rise in the land of the rising sun. Pride Fighting Championships would run their first show in the Tokyo Dome in 1997.

If you wanted to be somebody in MMA during the mid-1990s, Ken Shamrock was like Willy Wonka. He held the magic ticket. As the official U.S. contact for the Pancrase promotion, he could get you fights in Japan. As the UFC's top star, he had the pull to get you on pay-per-view. Soon Shamrock went from struggling to find training partners to having flocks of restless young men from all over the country showing up on his doorstep.

"The UFC had brought submission wrestling to the forefront of the martial arts world. People knew I lived in Lodi, California, so they started looking me up and asking me what it took to join my gym," Shamrock said.[37]

He needed a way to weed them out. Not everyone was worth his time; not everyone was worthy of joining the fabled Lion's Den. What he needed was a test. Not of a young man's fighting ability; he would teach them those skills over time. Instead he would test their heart, their soul, and their capacity for pain. To produce the world's best fighters, the Den needed a steady influx of pain.

Ken's second student, Vernon White, said, "I started training with Ken in 1993, when he beat the crap out of me. I was a tae kwon do instructor at the time, and I had never done any wrestling or kickboxing, just tae kwon do and street fighting. I went to Ken's gym and I thought, 'Oh, he's a big guy, he's going to be slow, I can beat him.' I had fought plenty of guys who were bigger than me and beat them because I was faster. Ken beat me down for half an hour and I knew I had to learn what was in his head. I could not leave without learning. He made me do 500 push-ups, sit-ups, leg-lifts, and squats, and then I had to clean the gym. Then I came back and had to kickbox with him, and again he made me do 500 push-ups, sit-ups, leg lifts, and squats, and after that I was in."[38]

Ken's initiation was borrowed from Japan, where he spent his formative years as a fighter. In many ways it was like joining the army. The Den was much more than a fight team. The good schools always are. It was a way of life, a family. The fighters passed Ken's grueling initiation, had their head shaved, and came to live in Lodi.

"Marine boot camp is not fun. It is not pretty. That's because they are preparing you for war. I am preparing my fighters for war," Shamrock said.[39] That preparation covered the full spectrum of his fighters' lives. They followed a strict diet and trained all day, five days a week, letting loose on the weekend. Ken was instilling the mental and physical discipline they needed for success.

INSIDE THE DEN

When he started with Pancrase and real shoot fighting, Shamrock knew he needed regular training. Hard training. Without it, the Japanese fighters would rip him to pieces. Ken had spent time training in Japan and knew that while he was home in the States, they would be working.

"Ken started training people out of his garage. I drove an hour and a half there and back every day, and it was rough," White said. White was Shamrock's second professional protégé, coming to the Den after fellow Pancrase veteran Scott Bessac. "I'd have to work, get off of work, drive an hour and a half to go train, come home, but Ken didn't give up on me. He told me, 'You could have a life here.' I was lucky enough to stick with it. God's brought me a long way."

World-class fighters can't be built in a garage, and the gyms in Lodi weren't going to cut it. Shamrock needed his own space and rented a warehouse on the shady side of town. This wasn't Gold's Gym or Dana White's Boxercise studio. It didn't have even what most people would consider essentials. No showers. No water fountains. Just weight machines on one half and a boxing ring and mats on the other.

Frank Shamrock said, "It was pretty primitive. Basically we had a room with some mats in it. It was an industrial building behind a car stereo shop. We met up every day and trained. We trained mostly in submission wrestling, catch-as-catch-can wrestling. We did very little stand-up, a lot of muscular weight-based exercises with our own body weight and very little cardiovascular training. For Ken it was kind of like a fighting session combined with a training session. He had two schools of thought. One was the Japanese, kind of beat you down, overwork you mentality, and because he was a wrestler he had that dominate you and wear you down, beat you down mentality. It was pretty hard-core."

The training was as hard as the concrete floors the mats rested on. Shamrock didn't believe in doing anything half way, and the fighters went hard all the time. It was the Pancrase way, and it may have been, in retrospect, too much. "Back in the day we may have trained too hard," Lion's Den student and former UFC star Jerry Bohlander concedes.[40] Outsiders were often shocked by what happened inside the Den. Ken had a notorious temper and would often take it out on his students.

"He was an animal, he was crazy. He was 30 years old and a different creature from the guy I talk to today," Lion's Den star Mikey Burnette said. "His motto was 'win or you die trying.' And it was a literal thing. I'd never been choked unconscious, and the first day I was there I got choked unconscious twice. I thought he was going to have to call home and tell them he'd killed me. We were doing well, but looking back at it you could see it really wasn't going to stand. Ken was pushing us over the edge a little bit. And we were more than willing to jump. I don't know if he was pushing us or just showing us the edge."

Shamrock pushed everything to failure, even the brain. In a memorable passage in his first autobiography, *Inside the Lion's Den,* co-author Richard Hanner described a typical day training at the gym. Shamrock had Vernon White down, had his back, was choking him out. White tapped out, a concession of defeat. Shamrock wanted to push it further. It was commonplace when Ken was in a bad mood or had a point to prove. He was going to choke White into unconsciousness. The other fighters in the gym were not disturbed by this breach of decency. "Vernon go night-night," Bohlander said. When White recovered, the punishment continued, both physically from Shamrock and in the form of verbal taunts from the others. "Hey Vernon, you've been sleeping on the job." Just an average day at the Lion's Den.

"When we were grappling and got caught in a choke, we were getting choked out. You didn't even need to waste your time tapping," Burnette said.

"A lot of nights we would do MMA and the only instruction would be 'Hook it up. Get out there and let's see what you've got.' I went 15 minutes one time with Bohlander [200 pounds], got a one-minute rest, and went 15 minutes with Pete Williams [250 pounds]. I was 170 pounds and that was MMA. His philosophy was 'expect everything, but expect nothing.' That's what his mindset was. At the drop of a hat I was ready to go, to die, whatever."

Shamrock said, "I didn't coddle or pamper them. I put them in an extreme amount of pain every day in training. They were young and they needed to know what they were getting into from the get-go. I didn't want them to step into the ring and go, 'I didn't realize it was going to be this hard.' I showed them how hard it was going to be in training. I showed them on a regular basis. I paid for their room and board, but I took control of their lives. I told them when they could eat, when they had to work out, and when they could go out and have fun. I wasn't trying to be a dictator; I was trying to get them ready for the hardest thing they would probably ever have to do — climb into the ring with a Japanese submission master and engage in full-out hand-to-hand combat. When they stepped into that ring, I wanted their fight to be easy compared to what they had gone through in training."[41]

The fighters seemed to understand that Ken had their best interests in mind. There is an almost fanatical devotion to Ken among some Lion's Den alumni.

"When you see your guys, who can do so much better, slacking off and not listening and who should be training harder than they are, it makes you angry. I can see that now. I understand why we were making Ken so angry. I can't justify some of the actions that were taken, but that's him and that's how he dealt with it," White said. "We're in his camp. We have to learn to deal with it and get to the point where he doesn't have to get that angry. If you put your heart out and get knocked out, Ken is going to look at you and go, 'Good job.' If you go out and you do your job halfway and you get knocked out, Ken is going to be angry. It's always justifiable homicide when you're working with fighters. You say to yourself, 'Did I deserve that?' I've been in fights where I remember the beatings I took for not doing my best in training. And the guy that I'm in the ring with, he's almost got to kill me in order to get me to tap out. So it was justifiable treatment from Ken, because there are guys out there who are going to do that to us. It's just you and that guy in the ring and the referee. But when you're working with Ken he teaches you, I don't want to say to weather the storm, but how to avoid the storm. If you can avoid it from him, you can avoid it from anybody else."

In many ways, he probably went too far. It's telling that in a sport that still features many veterans from the early years, most Lion's Den students no longer compete or even train. Shamrock broke people, physically, but also mentally.

"Ken was probably the biggest mind trip. It was all mental," Burnette said. "He would come in in the morning, sometimes 4:30 or 5:00, and wake you up by whispering 'I'm going to kill you tonight.' And sometimes he would show up that night and tear into you and sometimes he would show up and not even look at you. He just totally screwed with your head until you got to the point that there was no fear of death after leaving the guy's place because they would tell you they were going to kill you as they were choking you out. You learn not to fear, but that's a dangerous thing. I don't think any of the guys feared any repercussions in life at all. I knew coming home I could never run a gym that way. I'd never run a gym the way Ken did."

Most of the earliest stars of the Pancrase promotion burned out quickly, as did the earliest stars of the Den. There is only so far the human body can be pushed, but Ken Shamrock was willing to go there and beyond. And his students followed.

"When you've got five guys there, and they're all in the world title hunt, and one guy says, 'I'm going to run 30 sprints' and the next guy says, 'I'm going to run 40' and it keeps going and going," Burnette said. "And it didn't matter what we were doing, whether we were training or drinking, we pushed each other. We were young and weren't always pushing each other the right way. There was a running contest to see who could be the most extreme, and I think all of us got pretty out there for a while. Some of it's ego and sometimes you push each other too much. It gets to where it's overboard. It didn't just end with working out. It carried over to the bar, it carried over to every aspect of life. I don't think what we did was normal by any stretch. The downfall was, you can sprint for a certain amount of time, but you can't sprint forever. And some guys, after they got through sprinting, never learned how to jog. It's difficult."

"He is very inspiring. He's able to push guys past what they think they're able to do," Ken's adopted father Bob Shamrock said. "He's like the captain of the football team or the sergeant in the foxhole with the troops because he can get people to do things they normally can't do. Most people who don't know him think he's just a dumb fighter, but he's not. When you're around him, you either love him or hate him. There is no in between because he's an inspiration to them. But he doesn't push people beyond what he does himself. That's one of the things that makes him great. He takes exactly what he dishes out."[42]

Many of the Lion's Den fighters came in search of Ken. Or at least came in search of a way into the UFC. "I'd never met Ken Shamrock. I was a Royce Gracie fan to be honest with you," Burnette said. "But the Gracies would only train you in jiu-jitsu. They weren't training people to fight. Ken was the way in Ultimate Fighting. I flew in on a Friday and the tryouts were on Sunday. I thought going in that I was going to go down there and show these guys who I am and what I'm made of. Then you go down there and get a wake-up call."

Others, like Jason DeLucia and Guy Mezger, Shamrock found on the UFC undercard. Unlike the other guys, who were being molded from fresh clay, Mezger already had an extensive combat background. Mezger was a top kickboxer when the UFC was still in the style versus style mode. The UFC needed someone to fight Canadian jiu-jitsu fighter Jason Fairn, and Mezger got the call.

Into the Fire

More than most of the limited stand-up stylists of the day, Mezger was ready for UFC competition right away. He wasn't just a top kickboxer; he was also a former Texas state wrestling champion and the Texas judo champion. None of this mattered to UFC announcer Jim Brown, who ridiculed Mezger's and Fairn's pretty boy looks and long hair. In a competition that featured toothless tough guys like Harold Howard, these guys not only owned a hairbrush, but had also entered into an agreement not to pull each other's hair. Brown was incredulous.

"I always find it amusing that people comment on it because you don't really pull hair. Pulling hair is kind of a bitch thing. The two times I've seen hair pulling I thought they were both bitch situations," Mezger said. "Me and Jason Fairn both have long hair, and I go, 'Hey dude, we could both cut our hair or we could make a gentleman's agreement that we'll have a good clean fight.' My background was sport. I like to keep the fighting sport. I don't like to make it personal, and when you have no rules, the inclination is, when things go bad, to make it a personal thing. One thing about Jason Fairn, he was taking a whupping the whole time and he never once pulled my hair, so he's at least a man of honor."

After the fight, Shamrock invited Mezger to come down and try out for the Lion's Den. He had the skills and the good looks Shamrock was interested in. Shamrock's pro wrestling background made him acutely aware of a fighter's marketability. He wasn't taking any ugly or unmarketable fighters over to Japan. Only pretty boys need apply. Mezger would later be named Dallas's most eligible bachelor, and other Den members made their living with their looks before they made it with their fists.

"I used to be a stripper and a bartender for maybe four or five years. Ken used to dance, too. I'm blowing the horn. The cat's out of the bag," Vernon White said. "It's a fun job. I see why the girls like it. You've got people screaming your name. It's funny because I went by the name Tiger when I danced. So I'd have girls screaming, 'Tiger, come here Tiger.'"[43]

When Mezger passed the test and became an official member of the Lion's Den, he didn't go to Lodi and live in the fighter's house with the other fighters. He was too well established in Dallas, Texas, where he had his own gym. He would travel up to California though, especially when he had a fight coming up. The lessons in the Lion's Den were priceless.

"It was a pretty good exchange of information. After I realized these guys [the fighters in Pancrase] couldn't take me down, I was a big fan of stand-up fighting. I was really pushing the ability to block the takedown and use the strikes. None of the guys [in the Lion's Den] really agreed with me about that for the longest time. But as I started having more and more success and they were having some mixed success, then a lot of these guys suddenly started really taking up the mantle," Mezger said. "I had to learn the submission game, and we learned the catch-wrestling style of submission, which is a very fast-moving style. It was something new to me at the time. Fighters today don't really have to go through what we did. I was a wrestler and a karate fighter, then a judo player, and then I learned kickboxing. I learned the whole gamut of stuff I didn't need to learn. Today we take a little bit from here and a little bit from there and we make ourselves an MMA fighter."

Mezger was immediately propelled right to the top. His second match was with Funaki, who liked to see what the new boys were made of right away. At that time, Mezger still had more balls than brains.

"I'm not afraid to fight. It's not really bravery. It's that I know it's a sport, and short of something tragic happening I'll be able to walk away from this. He wasn't known for being a smasher; he was mostly known for his submissions. I figured I could out-kickbox him, and I knew I was a better wrestler than him and I thought maybe I could hold him off that way and try to knock him out," Mezger said. "I was doing pretty good, but Funaki in his day was very, very slick. He broke my leg in that fight. He had an Achilles lock on me, and it didn't break my ankle; it gave me a three-inch fracture in my shin. I could feel the pressure and thought, 'Oh shit, it's going to break,' and sure enough. Not one of the wisest decisions I've ever made to let him break it."

Like all Lion's Den fighters in Japan, after this initial setback Mezger would go on to earn glory and riches with Pancrase. Ken was also building an army of fighters to compete in the UFC as well.

Success Breeds Success

Shamrock did more than teach his students to fight. He used them liberally to train for his own fights, the fights that were paying the bills. Ken was frustrated by Royce Gracie's win at UFC 1. Just when he thought he knew it all, it was back to the drawing board, this time with the Den's help.

"The day I got back to the Lion's Den, I dressed up all my training partners in uniforms and proceeded to learn everything about the gi. I learned how it could be used against me and how I could use it against the person wearing it," Shamrock said. Shamrock hated the Gracies and the sport of jiu-jitsu with an intense passion. He was bound and determined to prove that he was the better man and that jiu-jitsu was a fraud.

"It was us against the world. He tried to build that and I don't think it was very hard," Burnette said. "All of us had a chip on our shoulders and were looking to be antisocial anyway. We didn't want to fit in. We were going to do our own thing. We were pretty naive. We thought jiu-jitsu was stupid, but we were doing jiu-jitsu. We just didn't call it that. Submission wrestling, jiu-jitsu. It's all the same shit."

Shamrock was constantly angry as he prepared for the Gracie fight. He wasn't used to losing, and his students, more than any opponent, bore the brunt of that anger. Mikey Burnett explained: "I think he hurt people intentionally sometimes. It's hard to say. He was so fucking crazy. Obviously a crazy man still has a thought process. . . . He taught me a lot of mental things. Ken never worked with you too terribly much on technique. He was more 'come over here, I'm going to beat the fuck out of you.' And it shows. Frank's a way better technician. Ken's just big and strong."

THE DEN DOMINATES

Shamrock was gaining not just fans, but also students. The continued success of the Lion's Den and especially Ken Shamrock brought more and better students to the training facility, including the man who would become Ken's top student, Jerry Bohlander. Bohlander had been impressed with Shamrock's domination of Gracie in their second fight and was surprised to learn his gym was just an hour away. Bohlander took self-defense classes with Shamrock for three months before being allowed to try out for the Lion's Den team. And after beating Pete Williams in an inter-squad challenge match, Bohlander would be the first of the Lion's Den's young boys to get a shot at the UFC, making his debut at UFC 8, February 16, 1996, in Puerto Rico.

White said, "The competition was pretty fierce. There were guys that were going for the same fight. I always thought that if it's my fight, I'm going to get it. If it's their fight they're going to get it. There's no reason for me to be sitting here having harsh thoughts toward my training partner because he got a fight when I didn't. If I was ready, Ken told me. If I wasn't ready, he let me know. For one fighter to get angry because Ken thought another fighter was better equipped is childish. It's selfish. It's not for us to choose. Ken is the leader, let him choose. Jerry was and is very aggressive. Jerry was, 'No, I'm going in, I'm taking you down, I'm gonna beat your face in.' Until Ken found that in you, he wasn't going to let you go in. And I thank him for that, because I could have gotten hurt. He did the smart thing, which was not to protect me, but to guide me until I was ready."

Many of the original UFC stars brought in protégés to fight on subsequent shows. Ken had every opportunity, as the promotion's biggest star, to load the shows up with his guys. But he wasn't going to put them in the cage until they were ready. Bohlander was ready.

"I was a poor kid and I didn't have anything," Bohlander said. "I almost cried, and I had a lump in my throat that I was the first one he asked to fight, to represent the Lion's Den."[44] Bohlander exceeded all expectations in the "David versus Goliath" tournament that was the brainchild of SEG programmer Campbell McClaren. The 185-pound Bohlander had his first fight in the Octagon with the mammoth 350-pound former college football player Scott Ferrozzo. The feisty Bohlander was able to withstand his opponent's huge size advantage and lock on a guillotine in the final seconds of the fight for the submission win. Technique had again scored a decisive victory over size inside the unforgiving Octagon. But size would have its revenge. Bohlander's semifinal opponent was the Canadian strongman Gary Goodridge. Goodridge had not only beaten a thousand Japanese in a row at arm wrestling, he had just used those powerful arms to smash Tank Abbott training partner Paul Herrera into unconsciousness with a series of brutal elbows. Goodridge proved too big a task for Bohlander, but Jerry had shown heart. It was all Ken would ever ask from his fighters.

INSIDE THE LION'S DEN

In Japan, young men training for a life in the martial arts are called "young boys." They live together in a house and focus only on training and appeasing their masters. As they move up the totem pole life gets better and better, but initially they are expected to do anything and everything for their leaders. Ken Shamrock was there, training with the young boys and learning from the hard-nosed catch wrestler Karl Gotch. He took many of the ideas back to California with him when he formed the Lion's Den.

Shamrock said, "When I first started going to Japan, I was really impressed with the way they set up their dojos. They actually had fighters who lived there, cooked their food there, trained there, slept there. So it was kind of a lifestyle. That's kind of the way the Lion's Den was when I first started. It was more of a family and more of a lifestyle than just coming in and training. I didn't live in the house, but we'd have one guy there who'd be the head guy for a while with four or five guys in the house. They'd take turns cooking and of course they all had cleaning chores. They trained twice a day. Most of the time, Monday through Friday, it was in bed, food, cleaning, training, in bed, and that was their way of life. They didn't come in saying, 'Oh I didn't know it was this way.' They knew exactly what it was like living in the fighter's house. You'd have to put up with a lot of different personalities. And being 'the young boy,' you would have to do all the dirty chores, and once another young boy came in, you could pass that off to him. It was a really strong foundation."[45]

Being a young boy was about more than doing the dishes or mopping the gym floor. The young boy was also the low man on the totem pole. And most didn't make it.

Burnette said, "We lived in Napa Valley, and there were all these white stakes holding the grapes up and I would call it the young boy graveyard. I'll bet you when I was there we had 30 young boys. And they would stay about a month. Some of them snuck out in the middle of the night. You'd wake up and their ass would be gone. Most guys didn't stay. I was a young boy for about a year and a half. They had tryouts every three or four months and I'd be really happy, thinking I wouldn't have to do this shit anymore. But then we'd get these new fighters in and the guys would just torture them. They'd decide to leave and I'd beg them not to go. I think they tried to run everybody off. Because if you wouldn't go, they figured you were tough and crazy enough that you were going to be a good fighter."

Many people who watched the hit television show *The Ultimate Fighter* were shocked by the antics of the testosterone-charged men living together in isolation, focused only on their fight training. No one from the Lion's Den was surprised, or if they were, it was surprise at how tame things were.

"The UFC reality show, although it makes good television, is certainly nothing new. I think the Lion's Den was the first real one," Frank Shamrock said. Frank was the first head of the fighter's house and remembers the crazy days like they were yesterday. "Jerry Bohlander had, God, what must have been an eight-foot python that lived in his sock drawer and used to roam the house freely. Which was kind of cool but put an awful fright in you when he popped his head up."

Just like the trials, the fighter's house was another initiation. And not everyone made it. If you weren't tough enough, or couldn't get along with the established guys, you might be out the door.

White said, "I never lived in the fighter's house. I was always fortunate enough to have a woman who loved me. With a lot of these guys, the testosterone is flowing. We started what you see on TV nowadays, but without the cameras. It's worse without the cameras. Ken had this idea, and I'm glad people finally get to see what fighters go through now and they can kind of feel for us. They know now that for every nice guy you see on TV, if he's in a fighter's house, he's got to come up with a jerk. And sometimes those nice guys finish last and those jerks end up making all the money. They would sneak up on each other and choke each other out. If you really weren't liked they would make you do all the dishes, clean the house, cook all the food. It was horrible. They treated some of the guys like they didn't belong and those guys left. And the guys that they liked got to stick around."

"If you lived in the house, it was open game. And you knew it was going to be hell, at least until you proved your worth," Burnette said. "Until you got into that clique with Jerry [Bohlander], Pete [Williams], and Frank [Shamrock], life was not good. The choking out was difficult, and we had to make a rule that you could only be choked out three times in one day. Frankie choked somebody out who was on the phone, and they had a BB gun, pointing it at the kid when he woke up. The guy was out of his mind when he woke up, and obviously he left shortly after that."

The pecking order didn't end inside the fighter's house. In training, the fighters could be cold to each other. Ken was training fighters, not citizens. Like John Kreese's Cobra Kai dojo in the classic '80s movie *The Karate Kid*, inside the Den, mercy was for the weak. "I was the butt of a lot of those jokes between Frank and Jason [DeLucia] and Guy sometimes," White said. "But you know what? You have to have that one dude that you talk down to to make yourself look better. That's cool if I was that guy for a while."

According to his teammates, White was super-sensitive and a natural target.

"We loved to pick on Vernon because he did really goofy things. Like, he was always dating a fat chick and doing stuff that made him a target for having fun," Frank Shamrock said. "He always dated these big chicks, and we were like, 'Vernon, you're a good-looking dude with a great build, and you kick ass. What's with the big chicks?'"

To make it in the Lion's Den, you had to survive the gym, the house, and the notorious nightlife. Fighters would be cooped up like monks for weeks at a time, preparing for fights and training. When they were finally released into the wild, the fighters were like wild animals.

"We tore up a lot of shit. It was build and release. We'd go six weeks without seeing the outside world and then get turned loose at a bar? Fuck, it was on. Wild times," Burnette said. "We went to a bar in some fucking Podunk town and Ken made me strip on stage. The bouncers were going, 'Get down.' And I wasn't getting down. Everybody else was sitting there making me dance. I don't know what the guy who owned the bar was thinking. It was all of us, Maurice Smith, and I think Mark Coleman was with us. I went behind the bar and grabbed a fucking bottle of Jack Daniels, a big chocolate birthday cake they had back there for some reason and just helped myself. We were retarded. One of Ken's brothers got arrested and I was supposed to be watching him. Then Frank beat up one of Tank [Abbott]'s guys. He threw a pickle or something at Frank when we were coming out of the hotel and getting into a cab, and Frank beat the fuck out of him. Later that night we were on the top of the hotel throwing full beer bottles out of the window. Out of our fucking minds."

It was a great time to be a fighter. The sport was growing both in the United States and Japan, and the Lion's Den was leading the way. "It was a good experience and a lot of fun. It was like camping with all of your cousins," Mezger said. "Some of my best memories, camaraderie and buddy-type memories come from those training experiences."

The bonding was between the fighters, never with Shamrock himself. Close friendships grew because the Lion's Den fighters all had something in common: a lunatic instructor pushing them to the limit.

"He was difficult and it created a bond among all of us. I don't think he ever really knew how to let anyone get close to him. With me and Jerry and me and Pete and me and Frank, there were times we were close and bonded like a family. But I never really felt that way with Ken," Burnette said. "When I had my son, he did some things for me that I'll never forget, but he just never had any warmth about him. He didn't develop any family bonds with us, and I don't know that he can. Him or Frank. I know Frank's struggling to put some pieces back together in his life. Some guys get to a point where they've had so much disappointment, that there's not going to be any fixing them."

THE END OF THE DEN

Ken was the Den leader; no one disputed that. But Ken was busy, focused on his own career, and maybe not so good at explaining the concepts and techniques that came so easily to him.

Frank Shamrock said, "Ken had knowledge that nobody else in the world had. He'd had wrestling experience and he'd had Pancrase experience, and at the time the Pancrase fighters were the best athletes and mixed martial artists around. It was the best of the best for a long, long time. They were some of the greatest times of my life. What everyone forgets is that after I trained for eight months at the Lion's Den, I became the lead instructor. I trained Jerry Bohlander, Guy Mezger, and Tre Telligman. I trained all these guys. Because while Ken is a wonderful leader and he has a lot of power, I was the guy who learned to articulate and break things down. I learned how to teach and how to replicate. That's why I realized, after a while, that what we're doing is not right. It needs to be better and it needs an update. I just started training people differently, because that's what I believed the truth to be. My mission, as Ken had put it to me, was to train the guys and run the school. So I was implementing the things that I believed were correct. And he didn't want that. He wanted something different."

Ken's MMA career was slowly coming to an end. He had been fired from Pancrase after a disagreement with his longtime partners.

"Ken had a dispute with the Pancrase guys over fights. They had encouraged Ken to fight in the UFC, but then later on Ken was supposed to work as the exclusive contact for the American athletes in Pancrase, meaning anyone from the U.S. who wanted to fight in the Pancrase had to come through Ken. It was a way of helping to pay him back for building Pancrase, along with Funaki and Suzuki," Mezger said. "They were kind of upset with Ken about wanting to fight more in the UFC and spending less time in Pancrase. So they made a deal behind Ken's back with Phyllis Lee to bring athletes into Pancrase, so Ken stopped dealing with them. They ended up getting real pissy about it and started dropping all the guys that were associated with Ken. They were punishing Ken, but ended up punishing a bunch of good fighters who didn't deserve it. They wanted to drop me, but I just kept winning, and to be honest I was popular enough that it just wasn't a good move. If I wasn't quite as popular as I was at the time, I probably would have been dropped."

It was a huge blow to the Den's income. Not only did they lose Ken's contract, but Frank Shamrock and Vernon White were also dropped from the promotion. This was important, not just to Ken and his family but to his fight team as well. He was funding the Den out of his own pocket and had been for years.

"I paid for the house and the food and all that stuff, and when they'd go to a fight I think we'd get five or ten percent of whatever they earned, which would go right back into the house for food, electricity, and other things like that," Shamrock told *Full Contact Fighter.*

Not only were they losing their Pancrase revenue stream, but the UFC was cutting back as well. The politicians were watching closely from Congress, with an eye out for easy prey. When they pounced on the UFC it had major repercussions, not just for the Lion's Den, but for the sport in general.

6
THE TOURNAMENT

The UFC was suffering from a public relations problem. Royce Gracie demonstrated with grace and skill the beauty of jiu-jitsu. But there were still significant criticisms of his level of opponent. These weren't real athletes. At worst they were bar fighters. At best they were the guy who had been a pretty good high school football player and now taught kung fu at the local YMCA. Gracie and Shamrock were world-class athletes but they didn't have any legitimate credentials that didn't involve no-holds-barred fighting. The UFC needed someone with more gravitas. Enter Dan Severn.

Severn was a three-time all-American at Arizona State University and twice an Olympic alternate. He was a great wrestler and an elite athlete. There was no question of his ability, and he brought a lot of credibility to the organization.

Campbell McClaren said, "I brought Dan in because he had legitimate credentials and would start to make us look like a real organization. My sensibility is to always stage the wildest, most outrageous show I can. David's [Isaacs] sensibilities were that it's got to be real, it's not the circus. And between the two of us, we found Marco Ruas [an early UFC star and one of the Gracie family's top rivals in Brazil]."

Severn had failed to make the Olympic team in 1992 and had put amateur wrestling behind him. He was wrestling professionally in Japan for the UWF-I, shoot-style wrestling that was intended to look like a real fight. The UFC seemed tailor-made for a man with his skills, but Severn wasn't even aware the new sport existed.

Severn said, "I had never heard of UFC, because Coldwater,

Michigan, didn't have pay-per-view. A friend of mine watched the first two, and it was pretty wild stuff. My friend told me I ought to think about doing this, even though it was people getting stomped in the head and hit in the groin. Of course, he pointed out this skinny guy doing this Brazilian jiu-jitsu, beating all the competition; of course I'm talking about Royce Gracie. And I thought, okay, well for anybody to kick and punch me they have to have distance between us. I thought that I could avoid getting struck by moving fast enough, getting the clinch and takedown, and not allowing them any space once on the ground. The plan was to just smother them and then work my magic from there."[46]

Severn had applied for the UFC like hundreds of other potential fighters and never heard back from Art Davie. His manager, Phyllis Lee, talked Davie into watching Severn perform in a pro wrestling match, and he got the call to do UFC 4 on December 16, 1994. Someone had gotten injured and Davie needed a last-minute fill-in. Severn would make his UFC debut with just five days' worth of training. Severn trained with pro wrestler Al Snow, who put gloves on some wrestling students and had them try to hit Dan as he shot in for the takedown. Davie was skeptical about Severn. He didn't look like a fighter, more like someone's mustached uncle who works at the plant and plays softball. At the pre-show meetings, the other fighters were convinced that Dan's trainer, Al Snow, was actually Dan Severn.

"From the minute we got off the plane, everybody was sizing everybody else up," Al Snow said. "Everybody had their game face on. At the rules and regulations meeting, we're sitting there and three or four guys are staring at me. I'm thinking, 'What are these guys staring at me for? They don't think I'm fighting, do they?' They had these ace bandage wraps for the knees and elbows and Dan said, 'Why don't you get me some?' So I went up there, and two guys came up and said, 'Good luck Friday night.' I said, 'Well, yeah, thanks.' I went back to Dan and told him, 'These guys think I'm fighting.' He said, 'Yeah, I've watched about five guys sizing you up.' I said, 'Well, great, that will work to our advantage. They'll think I'm fighting, and then you'll come walking out.'"[47]

Severn wasn't the only wrestler making his UFC debut at the sold-out Expo Square Pavilion in Tulsa, Oklahoma. Jeff Blatnick, a 1984 Olympic wrestling gold medalist, would join new play-by-play man Bruce Beck and the legendary Jim Brown in the broadcast booth.

The first two fights were ammunition for future UFC political opponents. Royce Gracie easily dispatched of "The Black Dragon" Ron Van Clief,
who was a whopping 51 years old. After trotting out the old man to fight
their unbeatable champion, SEG then sent poor Joe Son out to fight karate
man Keith Hackney. True to the promise of karateka in *Black Belt* magazine, the Kenpo master Hackney punched Joe Son in the testicles seven
times in a row. Despite having founded his own martial art, called Joe Son-
Do, Son had no answer for the brutal attack and was forced to tap out.

By the time Dan Severn hit the ring, it was a relief to see something
resembling sport on the screen. Blatnick had an opportunity to use his
wrestling knowledge as Severn launched 190-pound Anthony Macias into
the air with a "straight back suplex." And then he did it again. In the three
previous UFCs, fans had seen men kicked, punched, and submitted. But this
was something new.

"The UFC had never seen anyone picked up bodily and launched
around," Severn said. "I arched up and bang! Launched him onto his head
and shoulders. He came back up again and I threw him harder yet, and he
hit so hard his own knee came up and split his eyebrow open. That's the
kind of impact that he hit with."[48]

The semifinals saw Severn beat alternate Marcus Bosset in less than a
minute to advance to the finals. There he faced the legendary Royce Gracie.
Severn took Royce to the mat. And that was all he did for 15 minutes.

"I tried a lot of things," Severn said. "But Gracie reacts to everything
instantly. I wanted to get a choke on him, but Gracie tucked his neck so I
couldn't get to his windpipe. I messed him up pretty good but I could never
get past his legs. He always kept me barely away from him. I got in punches
here and there, but never a strong punch. I never thought I could really
hurt him."[49]

Severn had created a new fighting style, one that would be used as a criticism every time a wrestler was involved in a boring fight: lay and pray.
With no submission skills and no striking to speak of, Severn could do little
but hope for a miracle.

"Dan is a real wrestler, but he's not a real fighter. And there's a difference. Dan couldn't end a fight, he wasn't a puncher. Dan is a very nice man,
but he reminds me of the horses on the Budweiser commercial," McClaren
said. "The Clydesdales? They can pull a wagon, but they're not going to win

any races. Everyone wanted him to be better and wanted to see what would happen next time. No one went, 'Bullshit, I'm never watching this again.' We still were presenting a more interesting thing than anyone else had."

Eventually Gracie caught Severn in a triangle choke from the bottom, choking Severn with his legs. Announcer Jeff Blatnick didn't understand yet what he was seeing and told the audience at home that Severn was in no real danger, that Gracie was just distracting him and was using the move to set up an escape. Seconds later, Severn tapped out.

Announcer Jim Brown was ecstatic. Blatnick was hardly an impartial announcer that evening, zealously promoting the greatness of American wrestlers generally and Dan Severn specifically. Brown was happy to shove the loss in Blatnick's face: "I don't ever want to hear about no rassler again." Blatnick had a lot to learn, but to his credit he made real strides as an announcer over the years as he fell in love with the sport.

"To see someone of that physical stature make Dan Severn tap was very impressive," Blatnick said. "When it was happening I didn't quite know that Dan was in trouble until I saw Dan trying to wiggle back out and that he couldn't breathe. Then I realized it. I hadn't really seen jiu-jitsu. That's when I started trying to study it."[50]

The fight was a dud, except for the exciting ending, another Gracie triumph. Unfortunately for the UFC, most of the fans watching had their feed cut off before the dramatic finish. SEG had booked only a two-hour time slot for the show. When the two hours expired before the fight was over, the show was cut off mid-fight. The UFC lost millions when fans demanded refunds from their cable companies.

THE BIG REMATCH

UFC 5, held April 7, 1995, was the biggest pay-per-view blockbuster in UFC history until the second Randy Couture–Chuck Liddell fight in 2005. That fight had an entire season of reality TV promoting it. UFC 5 had Campbell McClaren interviews and negative press all over the United States. But it featured the fight everyone wanted to see. It was the rematch between the two fighters who had captured the fans' imaginations more than anyone else who had ever stepped into the Octagon. Ken Shamrock would finally get his hands on Royce Gracie.

The show also featured the triumphant return of Dan Severn and the

Octagon debut of Oleg Taktarov, a former Russian soldier and sambo expert who had originally been rejected by the UFC. Most prospects had to have a tryout, usually a sparring session with a known quantity. Oleg worked out with the Gracies, holding his own with established jiu-jitsu player Pedro Sauer. Rorion Gracie, perhaps looking to protect his family legacy, told matchmaker Art Davie that Taktarov was a bum and not worth having on the show. Davie saw a tape of Taktarov's smooth grappling and thought otherwise. He would face Severn in the semifinals of the tournament in what was essentially the de facto finale.

This was a different Dan Severn, a Dan Severn who was not afraid to do bodily harm to his opponents. He was as ferocious in these fights as he had been timid at UFC 4.

"I didn't expect Dan Severn throwing knees and punches," Taktarov said. "Because I'd seen him fight with Royce Gracie and it was mostly grappling. Dan became a beast because he wanted to win."[51]

Severn had been unable to shake more than 20 years of strict wrestling rules in his previous Octagon appearance. This time he took a month off from his regular job as a professional wrestler to train properly and to get mentally tough enough to do whatever it took to win.

"I put a great deal of effort into it, knowing that if someone was going to beat me, by God they will be the best person. I trained hard cardiovascular wise, I trained hard in almost every position possible, going into submissions and how to counter submissions," Severn said. He had been disappointed by his performance at UFC 4 despite a $19,000 payday. He would not simply take his opponents to the mat. "Not this time. I simply knew, hammer strike right on that soft facial tissue. Bam. Got your attention now? I'm going to coil it back and hit again."

Severn used every extremity on the human body to turn Taktarov's face into hamburger meat. Oleg was bleeding profusely from the face when John McCarthy stopped the fight. Unfortunately for Taktarov, it was a stoppage that happened a few seconds too soon. He had been looking for an arm bar throughout the fight and had finally gotten into a good position to extend his body and Severn's arm when McCarthy decided he had seen enough blood and gore.

"Eventually I got the good position, where the leverage was so good, and I saw he was holding the fence with just two fingers. That was when the referee stopped the fight," Taktarov said. "I don't blame him. I probably looked horrible. My will was there, but when you get the cut and it's dripping into your eyeballs and people can't see you have eyes because of the blood, just for the good name of ultimate fighting the ref stops it."[52]

Severn went on to beat Canadian Dave Beneteau to win the tournament, in the process creating another main-event-level star for SEG.

"In the old days, the thought was, people don't know these fighters. And we had to get to know them," UFC owner Bob Meyrowitz said. "I thought by doing a tournament, by the end of the night when the last two fighters are left, everybody is rooting for one or the other. You've created an instant bond between the audience and those fighters."[53]

The producers of the UFC loved the tournament for its ability to create new stars in a single night. It told a story that appealed to whatever is inside us that craves tales of heroes and daring deeds. It's a visceral, subconscious appeal.

"When you watched someone go through the tournament and win multiple fights in a three-hour block, you saw their progression," McClaren said. "By the time the tournament got down to the last two guys, when you'd seen a man go through multiple fights he was the hero. Joseph Campbell wrote a book called *The Hero with a Thousand Faces* where he talked about how so many cultures' hero stories have similar setups. He thinks these are programmed into us, these archetypes; that our minds are literally wired for this type of story. And I think the tournament plays into our desire to see someone overcome huge obstacles, face adversity, and keep going."

GRACIE–SHAMROCK 2

Ken Shamrock had faced plenty of adversity in his life. His competitiveness was legendary. He couldn't stand the idea of losing, even in a training session. Losing to Gracie, and losing so decisively, had done a number on his confidence and self-image. Ken wanted the fight badly, and so did the promoters. But they weren't taking any chances with putting the two men in a tournament format, not after promoting the fight so heavily for UFC 3 only to see it fall apart when neither man made it to the finals. Instead, the Superfight was created. It was a one-on-one fight for two stars who transcended the tournament. Shamrock's place in such a fight was debatable.

He had never won a tournament and hadn't really beaten any top UFC fighters, like Keith Hackney or Dan Severn. But he looked good and drew money. And money talks.

The fight in the ring was one of the worst of all time. For 30 minutes, Shamrock lay in Gracie's guard, occasionally punching him in the ribs and hitting him in the head with glancing palm blows. He had planned for the long haul, to outlast the jiu-jitsu man at his own waiting game. When a 30-minute time limit was established to prevent the show from going over its allotted time like it had at UFC 4, he was unable to adjust his game plan.

"I wanted to wear him out and show I was in better shape than him and show my skill level was above his," Shamrock said. "I trained for a two-hour fight and I was working for a two-hour fight. When they changed the time limit, I couldn't really change my strategy."[54]

Shamrock had a strategy to outlast Gracie, he says, but it was clearly a strategy of self-preservation. Shamrock sought victory by not losing. He didn't want to win the fight, didn't even try. The UFC wanted a decisive winner and still had time remaining in their pay-per-view window. They decided to go to an overtime. In the most exciting moment of the fight, Ken hit Royce with a single right hand, swelling his right eye. To hear Shamrock tell the tale, this was the single most devastating punch in UFC history.

"I stuck him with the right hand. And as you see when he hits the ground, he's done. Right at that point in time, Royce Gracie's life will never be the same," Shamrock said in the *Ultimate Shamrock* pay-per-view special. "That punch has destroyed Royce Gracie's warrior mentality. Look at his eyes. Royce Gracie is done. Royce Gracie will never be the warrior that he used to be. Royce Gracie will never, ever be the same because of that punch."[55]

Shamrock got what he wanted. He didn't lose the fight. It was declared a draw. Shamrock raised his arms in triumph, but the Gracies were not impressed.

"He is looking for just one thing to chew on. He wants that thing. He doesn't have the ability that Royce has. He plays with one arm while he catches it from the other arm," Rorion Gracie said. "Before his match with Royce in Ultimate Fighting Championship 5, Shamrock practiced jiu-jitsu to increase his chances, even though he didn't publicize the fact. He fought Royce in a very defensive way, looking for a draw, which for him is like a victory. It's shameful!"[56]

Announcer Bruce Beck told the world that "Gracie is a mess. Shamrock looks marvelous." Shamrock always looked marvelous, except when the fight was going on. Then he looked timid and content to ride out the clock.

"In our second fight he came in not to lose! He came in to draw the fight. He knew there was a time limit, so he came in looking for the draw . . . and brags like it was a great achievement," Royce Gracie said. ". . . Can you imagine it? He was 50 pounds heavier than me! Now imagine, myself at 180 pounds fighting against someone 130 pounds. . . . Man, if I don't win this fight, I'll sink my head down the toilet and flush it down."[57]

Royce had now fought in five UFCs and amassed 11 wins and three tournament wins. This would be his last MMA fight for five years and his last UFC fight for 11 years. Although they had gotten worldwide fame and some hefty paychecks from their time in the UFC, the Gracies were disenchanted with the company's direction.

"I sold my interest in the company and stepped out exactly because rules were starting to be implemented, and it was against what I had created," Rorion Gracie said. "It's no longer the Ultimate Fighting Championship. The guy who wins the UFC is not the world's best fighter. It's just a tough guy who learned to use the rules."[58]

Royce was also unhappy with the changes to the rules, which he felt were to his detriment. Although Shamrock was publicly confident that he would have taken the fight eventually, Royce was equally sure he would have eventually finished the fight with a submission. "I don't like the time limit. I can fight for a long time. It is a question: who is the best fighter? In the streets there are no rules, there is no time limit, there is no weight division."[59]

Twelve days after UFC 5, Meyrowitz bought Rorion Gracie's and Art Davie's shares of the company. Davie stayed on board as the matchmaker. Gracie was cutting ties with the company for good.

Isaacs said, "We just couldn't do it the way he wanted to do it. I don't think Rorion ever misled anyone about his agenda. I always heard people say the Gracies were doing this sneaky thing and that sneaky thing to try to get an edge. The truth was Rorion preached Gracie jiu-jitsu as the best style in the world, and that is what he wanted to prove. And time limits don't work for his style. But you have to have time limits for TV. We just got to a point where it was tough because it was his brother who was our champion at the time." The Gracies were claiming their style was more realistic, that the fights needed to be given as much time as necessary to decide a true winner. "I've never seen a street fight last for six hours, which is kind of what they want to happen. We were really purists because we were not martial artists. I didn't really care whether a jiu-jitsu guy won or a kickboxer won. I cared about whether they were exciting fights and whether or not we had stars that fans wanted to see fight."

Royce Gracie was gone, but his legacy would not be forgotten. He and his family had played a huge role in changing the martial arts forever. But the show must go on.

Royce's draw with Ken Shamrock opened the door for the UFC to promote other fighters as the company's top stars. The next UFC would feature the new top stars in a one-on-one battle to crown a new champion for the promotion. The world's most dangerous man would do battle with the Beast.

STREET FIGHTING MAN

Dan Severn and Ken Shamrock do not like each other. At their pre-fight press conference before UFC 6, Severn had gotten up and walked out the door while Shamrock was talking. "Before I was going to beat him," Shamrock told Severn's manager, Phyllis Lee. "Now I'm going to hurt him." In Severn's mind, Shamrock didn't belong in the cage with him. "I thought to be in a super-bout, people had to achieve a level of success. I'd won a tournament and been the runner-up in another. What had Ken really accomplished? He was never even a runner-up."[60]

Severn was so confident in his abilities that he sent a letter to several close friends that would arrive after the show, detailing exactly how he was going to beat Shamrock. He probably didn't predict he would fall victim to a guillotine choke and tap out in just over two minutes. Severn claims he was sick, part of a pattern of excuses you hear all too often from MMA fighters looking to explain a loss. He hadn't appeared sick prior to or during the fight. He just looked like a wrestler who still hadn't taken the time to learn the submission game. The Severn-Shamrock fight was the titular main event, the Clash of Champions from which the show took its name. But the real stars of the show were the returning Russian Oleg Taktarov and a newcomer to the world of MMA, David "Tank" Abbott.

THE TANK

The Tank was a walking stereotype. If you pictured a no-holds-barred street fighter, his mug, or one like it, would come to mind. He looked like he had come directly from a biker bar, and he was the perfect antagonist for the company's stars, who were billed as skilled technicians and highly trained martial artists. Tank Abbott was the anti–martial artist.

Abbott said, "When I was stomping around in the streets, they didn't have anything like an MMA or cage fighting or anything like that. I showed up at Ultimate Fighting and said, 'Hey, I want to fight.' And they said, 'You have to be a black belt' or something like that. I said, 'I just got out of jail for beating somebody up. A cop's son, in fact. Isn't this supposed to be about fighting?' And they said, 'Yeah, but you've got to have some kind of black belt or something.' And I said, 'That's not what I'm about. I'm about fighting in the streets.' They called me a couple days later and said, 'We came up with this thing called Tank Abbott.' It's from the *Every Which Way But Loose* movie with Clint Eastwood. There is a guy in there who's a street fighting legend by the name of Tank Murdock, and Clint went and fought him. But that's where the Tank came from."

Abbott brought something different to the table, a unique charisma and presence that made him popular with the fans and dangerous to unskilled opponents. A clear pattern emerged in Tank Abbott fights. Fighters without great credentials or physical skills would get a merciless beating. Abbott made short work of his first opponent, John Matua, putting him down with hard punches and nailing his helpless victim with one uncalled-for right hand. As Matua lay unconscious on the mat, arms extended in what looked like rigor mortis, Abbott showed no concern for the fallen fighter. Instead he extended his own arms and mocked Matua's rigid posture. A star was born in just 18 seconds.

Abbott was as popular for his dry wit as he was for his powerful fists. After he beat Paul Varelans in the semifinals of the tournament, Jeff Blatnick interviewed him. Abbott said, "Varelans said earlier in his little preview thing that he likes to take people down and tickle them. Well I just wanted to tickle his brain a little bit." Blatnick made the mistake of asking Abbott to walk him through the fight replays. "I'm starting to get sexually aroused," Tank said. "You better get that off."

In the finals, Abbott would meet UFC 5 contestant Oleg Taktarov, who had trained with the Lion's Den and was ready to demonstrate his true skills. Unfortunately, his management wasn't as comfortable with his abilities as he was. When Pat Smith dropped out of his semifinal match, Oleg was set to face his stablemate Anthony Macias. Promoter Buddy Albin managed both, and Albin asked Macias to throw the fight with Taktarov. "I was in on the conversation with Anthony Macias, Oleg, and Buddy," UFC veteran Andy Anderson said. "Everyone knew that Oleg was going to need every ounce of strength he had to beat Tank." Macias lost in just 12 seconds. Abbott looked unstoppable, but he would be facing a fresh Russian submission master.

"You know the UFC has been riddled with that [thrown fights] the whole time. It is not rumor, it's fact. Don Frye and Mark Hall, Mark Hall took a fall for five grand. You can't keep a lid on that shit," Abbott told Jeff Sherwood from Sherdog.com. "What about that little pussy Anthony Macias. You know, to even be brought up in the same breath as those people, it's just a joke! Are you fucking kidding me? You think those guys are fighters? They're little fucking con men that suck your dick so you give 'em fights. That's a fact. You got a bunch of dumb fucks sitting around, and they want to be tough so fuckin' bad, but guess what? Money can't buy being tough. A real motherfuckin' warrior will not be a fuckin' pussy, and fuckin' con people like that."

Abbott is an interesting fighter. He talks a great game, has solid skills, and has fists like sledgehammers. But he lacks the heart and the stamina to compete with a world-class athlete or a fighter willing to put it all on the line. Taktarov was just the first to prove it. The fight took place in Casper, Wyoming, which has an average elevation of 5,100 feet. After a few minutes of fighting, the elevation wasn't doing much to help two already exhausted fighters. When you are tired, you rely on your heart and your desire more than your skills. And Taktarov just had more in reserve. After surviving the early Abbott attack, Taktarov bided his time and eventually secured a rear naked choke after 17 oxygen-starved minutes. The fight was every bit the equal to Gracie's dramatic win over the larger Dan Severn. It surpassed it when you consider that Abbott, unlike Severn, was actively throwing punches.

For Abbott, the fighting wasn't over yet. He and his running buddy Paul Hererra ran into Patrick Smith in the hotel elevator after the show. Still mad that Smith had dropped out of his semifinal, allowing Taktarov an easy fight with his training buddy Anthony Macias, the two beat Smith into unconsciousness.

"Pat Smith had his hands up and wanted to fight," Abbott said. "Paul nailed him with a perfect, straight right. Pat fell to his back. Paul mounted him and started delivering the spanking he deserved."[61]

Maurice Smith, the legendary kickboxer who was at the show with Ken Shamrock's group, happened upon the melee and was able to break it up. It was par for the course for Abbott, who, along with his entourage, would make a habit of causing as much havoc outside the cage as he did in it.

"Abbott, his guys were out of their minds. A lot of times the entourages are the bigger problems. At least the fighters have a way to consummate their rage," Isaacs said. "The entourages were just as hyped up and did not have a way to. You had these big gangs of guys and I felt like sometimes we were going to have a rumble to make every other rumble look like nothing right in the hotel lobby. There were a lot of times I thought there might be brawls, and they were intense moments. There were times when you could tell things were getting pretty serious. I think that goes with the territory. I thought Shamrock's guys and Abbott's guys were going to go for years. We would be in the hotel and we'd see those guys. You'd see them rumbling around, and Ken had that giant bodybuilder guy and the Lion's Den guys, and they'd be marching around. And Abbott had his guys and they were kind of marching around. You got the feeling if those guys turned the corner at the wrong time and kind of stood there looking at each other, it might get pretty hairy."

Abbott was a favorite of both the crowd and SEG owner Bob Meyrowitz. But Abbott was so wild in his younger days that he couldn't stay out of trouble. He was even suspended from the UFC for almost a year after an incident in Puerto Rico.

When he first started training for the UFC, Abbott went to jiu-jitsu fighter Alan Goes's gym to learn a little about submissions. When Abbott became famous, Goes started telling anyone who would listen that he had handled Abbott in the gym with no problems. When Abbott saw Goes in the stands, all hell broke loose. The UFC had struggled to get approval in Puerto Rico, and was just beginning what would become a losing battle with public perception and government intervention. It could hardly afford a scandal. Referee John McCarthy's wife, Elaine, tried to reason with Abbott's girlfriend and an enraged Abbott got in Elaine's face and threatened to kill her. It was more than McCarthy could tolerate.

"I thought John was going to kill Abbott. Or maybe John would kill me to get to Abbott," Isaacs said. "John's not normally that kind of guy, but you say something to Elaine and John responds. He was going after Abbott. John heard what he said to Elaine and was absolutely furious. John's a cop, he's not fucking around. And he knows fighting. I'm not saying he would win, but I don't think John would hesitate. I think he believes in the code, where even if you're going to get your ass kicked you've got to go in there."

Cooler heads prevailed. Instead of a violent ending, the McCarthys demanded that Abbott be let go. "You like him and I know that," McCarthy told UFC owner Bob Meyrowitz. "But I'm not doing anything else as long as he's around."[62] Abbott was suspended, with pay, for almost a year before Isaacs wrote an apology letter for him to sign and give to Elaine McCarthy. All was forgiven, and Abbott was allowed to return to the Octagon. He would remain one of the sport's most entertaining fighters, but would never win another significant fight in his entire MMA career.

7

THE GREAT UFC PR BATTLE

The UFC's political battle started as early as UFC 2 in 1994. It had to move to a much smaller facility at the Mammoth Gardens in Denver after the mayor found an obscure clause in the building deed and almost put a stop to the show. "It was really like being in a traveling circus all the time," Bob Meyrowitz explained. "Because you never knew from town to town what was going to happen. We never knew if the police were coming in or if a judge was coming in."[63]

The most vocal and most powerful UFC critic was Arizona Republican John McCain. McCain was a former POW and a legitimate American hero. He was also a politician in search of an easy political win. The UFC was an easy target in the much larger cultural war that McCain and his fellow conservatives were waging in an attempt to clean up the public airwaves and restore a sense of decency to the country — a decency that they believed had fallen prey to violence on television and in music.

"I said it will be some politically correct liberal who comes along and decides what we are doing is the victimization of fighters," UFC matchmaker Art Davie said. "I thought [Pat] Schroeder, because she's from Colorado and we ran our event in Denver. It didn't turn out to be her at all. It turned out to be a Republican POW and war hero. Very surprising. It shows you can't pick who your friends and enemies are going to be. He came out of the woodwork. He was a college boxer at the naval academy. He understands boxing. He doesn't know beans about the martial arts."[64]

McCain had a tenuous connection to the boxing industry that conspiracy theorists like *No Holds Barred* host Eddie Goldman like to trot out as an explanation for his push against the sport. McCain's second wife came from a wealthy family that invested heavily in Anheuser Busch/Budweiser. Budweiser, in turn, sponsored major boxing matches (and just about every other sporting event on television). Thus, in the MMA media's limited worldview, McCain had a reason to go after MMA. He was in cahoots with the sweet science.

"It's not in boxing's interests to have a show like *No Holds Barred* growing up," Rorion Gracie said. "So they get a guy like John McCain to go in and say, 'Look, this thing is too violent. There's no rules to this! It's crazy — let's stop this.'"[65]

In reality, that way of thinking is small potatoes for a national politician of McCain's stature. He didn't go after the UFC to help boxing. In fact, he went after boxing, too, in the form of stricter federal regulation. He was after violence on television, a much broader target. In 1996, Congress passed a sweeping telecommunications law that included introducing the controversial V-Chip, which helped parents censor violent shows, and also included a "voluntary" ratings scheme. Politicians were targeting smut. The UFC was simply in the wrong place at the wrong time.

"You had an America that was a little squeamish; you had McCain, who found a perfect thing," SEG's Campbell McClaren said. "No one stood up and said, 'No, we must have more violence on TV.' McCain found the perfect thing to come out against. Illegal immigration; that's a pretty tough subject. Abortion; that's a pretty tough subject. You've got to be careful how you answer questions about those things. But if you stand up and say, 'We shouldn't have people beating each other to death on TV,' pretty much everyone agrees with you."

McCain wrote a letter to the governors of all 50 states, particularly targeting Wyoming's Jim Geringer and New York's George Pataki after those two states hosted UFC 6 and 7. McCain took the fight to the airwaves as well, sparring with Ken Shamrock and UFC owner Bob Meyrowitz on *Larry King*.

"Some of this is so brutal that it is nauseating," McCain said. "It appeals to the lowest common denominator in our society. This is something I think there is no place for." The senator's problems with the sport in many ways stemmed from ignorance. He was talking about an event with no referees, no rules, and a local morgue filling up after every show. In fact, MMA seems to be safer than boxing, a sport McCain and most Americans have no problem with.

"The fact of the matter is it is intrinsically safer than even boxing, where you have removed all the defensive elements," Art Davie said. "In boxing, you mandate that people are continually separated and strike each other so they are hit 40 or 60 times in a round with a padded fist. Everybody in boxing and out of boxing knows that as soon as you put a boxing glove on a man's hand you turn it into a weapon. In the interest of safety, we ask our fighters not to wear gloves."[66]

The lack of gloves seemed to be one of the main sticking points for critics. It made the sport seem more brutal, more like a bar fight than an athletic contest. Eventually, starting with Tank Abbott at UFC 6, the promotion bowed to the pressure and started allowing, and then mandating, the use of open-hand gloves. For whatever reason, critics were sure this was safer. And it was, just not for the man being hit. A glove actually protects the striker's hand, not the recipient's head.

"People thought not having gloves meant you could get a head injury," Meyrowitz said. "I say to people all the time, when you're riding a motor-cycle you better put on a pair of gloves to protect your head. No! You put on a helmet to protect your head. The gloves are to protect someone's hands so they can hit harder."[67]

Clearly, many of the promotion's problems were rooted in perception. It just didn't seem very sporting to kick a man when he was down, or to punch him in the balls. The Octagon looked menacing, and critics often called for the fights to be moved into a ring, despite the ring being more dangerous because fighters could tumble out onto the ground. At first glance, the sport did seem brutal and repugnant. It took careful viewing before the beauty and efficiency of jiu-jitsu or the powerful athleticism of the wrestlers overshadowed the brutality. Most politicians were willing to give it only a glance. The UFC continued to add rules, attempting to appease critics by watering down its product. It didn't seem to matter. A district court ruling allowed it to run UFC 8 in Puerto Rico, but it would be the last event held in that territory. Local laws were changed to expressly prohibit MMA. UFC 9, held May 17, 1996, in Detroit, also required a tough court battle before it ever made it on the air.

DETROIT SNOOZE CITY

Detroit had to go back more than a century to find an 1869 law prohibiting unlicensed prizefights. No one, it seemed, wanted the UFC in their town. The show was set to feature hometown boy Dan Severn avenging his loss to UFC golden boy Ken Shamrock.

"Bob Meyrowitz, who was the head of the company, was very anxious to do that fight, because to him, it looked like a boxing matchup," Campbell McClaren said. "It was a guy that you knew with credentials against the current champion. It was programmable."

The fight was on. The UFC once again won the legal battle, but Ken Shamrock was not happy. Wayne County Circuit Court Judge Arthur Lombard had decided that the show could go on, but with some additional rules. There would be no head butts and no closed-fist punches. It was a rule in name only. The UFC told the fighters that using a closed fist would result in a nominal $50 fine. It was tacit permission to go about business in the cage as usual. But Shamrock was nervous about breaking the law. He had been locked up before, and didn't want to sit in a cell again.

"I wasn't going to do the fight. I was banged up, and they had just sent a rule down from Detroit saying we weren't allowed to punch. They told me these are the rules, you'll be fined this amount of money to pay at your leisure," Shamrock said. "They were going to let it slide is what they were saying. A week before that, these guys in Canada had gotten arrested for a NHB fight. I'm thinking to myself, I do not want to be on the cover of someone's 'Squash the UFC' campaign because I broke the rules."[68]

The UFC's success had spawned many copycat organizations, including King of the Cage, WFF, MARS, and Extreme Challenge. But the UFC's major competition was Extreme Fighting, a company owned by *Penthouse* magazine's Bob Guccione and agent Donald Zuckerman. The promotion's matchmaker was judo legend Gene Lebell's student, John Peretti — a man ahead of his time. Peretti introduced strict weight classes and rounds. He also brought in great talent like Ralph Gracie, Matt Hume, Kevin Jackson, and Maurice Smith. The company's first show lost money, partly because it had to be moved from New York to North Carolina after political pressure became too strong. But it was a tremendous artistic success.

The second show was held at a Mohawk Indian reservation in Quebec, Canada. The Canadian government was just as opposed to the event as its

American counterparts, but it had no control over the Indian reservation. Still, it did all it could to stop the event from airing. Production people were detained at the border; Bell Canada was prevented from carrying the signal; and Peretti and eight fighters were arrested the day after the fight.

Obviously, Shamrock and the other fighters had a lot on their minds before UFC 9. He wasn't comfortable, and was furious with SEG for putting him in a bad position.

David Isaacs said, "I remember Ken Shamrock screaming in the hotel room. Bob Shamrock told me, 'Once Ken thinks he's right, there's nothing you can do to change his mind.' And it can be about anything. I don't think he's a lunatic, but when he gets convinced that this is the way things should be, you just can't change his way of thinking. With Ken it was just hard. Once he kind of settled on a position on anything he was not flexible. He seemed to have a lot of rage at times. In Detroit, when the courts told us what the rules would be for his fight with Dan, Ken was just fucking furious. I just said, 'What are we going to do, Ken? What do you want to do? That's what the court said.'"

The end result was one of the worst fights ever, the "Dance in Detroit," which saw Shamrock and Severn circle each other for what felt like hours, neither man willing to make the first move.

"The problem was I didn't look for a way to win. I went into the fight with a meniscus tear, a cracked rib, and a broken nose. Back in the old days, none of that would have mattered," Shamrock said. "Instead of engaging, taking the fight to him, I stood in the center of the ring while he circled around me . . . that was the most boring fight in UFC history, nothing more than a 30-minute dance."[69]

NEW YORK, NEW YORK

John McCain enlisted a host of other powerful people against the UFC. Nevada State Athletic Commission Director Marc Ratner became a vocal opponent when he was urged to speak out, and American Medical Association President Lonnie Bristow also issued a statement in opposition to the company: "Far from being legitimate sports events, ultimate fighting contests are little more than human cockfights where human gladiators battle bare-knuckled until one gives up, passes out, or the carnage is stopped by a doctor or referee. The rules are designed to increase the danger to fighters and to promote injury rather than prevent it."

The UFC continued promoting its shows, undaunted by the gathering storm. It even made significant progress by getting the sport legalized in the state of New York. The UFC's lobbyist, James D. Featherstonhaugh, had worked wonders. The same state that had sent Extreme Fighting fleeing to North Carolina had legalized the sport. The UFC had a show scheduled in Niagara Falls on February 8, 1997. Its plan was to run upstate New York a few times, establish that it could operate under new laws, and then attack the New York City market. The UFC was flying under the radar. But a *New York Times* article changed everything, and soon politicians were scrambling to see who would be the toughest on the bloodsport.

"'The legislature basically said they would not adopt our bill [to ban extreme fighting]," Zenia Mucha, the governor's communications director, said. "The alternative was having nothing done last session or at least putting together something to regulate the industry. The governor finds this competition revolting and does not consider it a sport. We are going to reintroduce our bill, and we are going to keep doing it until we hopefully get it [extreme fighting] banned.'"[70]

The UFC emerged from under the radar when Extreme Fighting's Donald Zuckerman upped the ante by declaring that his company would run a show in Manhattan in March 1997. He didn't actually have a show planned; he was just piggybacking on Meyrowitz's free publicity.

McClaren said, "We had done one event in New York, in Buffalo, and were happily received by the city. Upstate New York is kind of a depressed area, and they were kind of happy to have us. We weren't talking about doing Madison Square Garden or any nonsense like that. We were keeping a low profile, we lived and worked in New York, and were very scared of the mayor, you may have heard of him, Rudolph Giuliani. We were actually more scared of him than we were of McCain, and we were pretty scared of McCain. So [Extreme Fighting owner Bob] Guccione does a press event and says he's going to do a show in Madison Square Garden. Which they didn't know about — no one had told the Garden. Giuliani went batshit. Everyone called everyone they knew. The governor was called, and Giuliani made his own press announcement, where he said, 'Not in my town, no way.' And we were like 'Oh, shit. . . . This is bad.' We felt like observers at our own funeral at that point, because we weren't doing anything. Guccione was making these crazy announcements — he was talking about MSG; we were just trying to go to Buffalo and do a nice little event up there. Everyone really jumped on the bandwagon, and they quickly passed legislation banning us. We later found out the commission never actually met, that it was done in a very illegal and bogus manner, but even though their procedures weren't in accordance with the law, we were still fucked. It didn't matter."

Extreme Fighting's announcement had awakened the sleeping giants of New York politics. It's one thing to showcase fights in Niagara Falls or Buffalo. Those UFC events had a lower profile and didn't draw the ire of powerful politicians. Promoting an event in Manhattan is a different matter. In New York City, the world is watching. Soon, Mayor Giuliani jumped into the fight over cage fighting with guns blazing.

"'I think extreme fighting is disgusting, it's horrible," Giuliani said. "I happen to be a boxing fan, have been all my life. And I know there are issues regarding boxing, and they are serious ones. But this is way beyond boxing. This is people brutalizing each other.'"[71]

The UFC had finally picked a fight it couldn't win. New York politicians were determined to ban the events, despite the law they had passed just months earlier. The law was going to be repealed, but a new 114-page rulebook was put in place to prevent any events from being scheduled in the meantime.

"I got a call from the *Daily News* asking if I would comment on the new rules that they set up for it [the UFC]," Meyrowitz said. "I said there can't be new rules. I didn't get them, and I'm the only one doing a show. If there were new rules, they'd have to give them to me. Then I get a call from the *New York Times* asking what I think of the new rules. I called the New York State Athletic Commission and I say, 'I understand you have new rules.' They say yes. I say, 'Since I am the only one doing a fight, can I get them please?' They said no. I said, 'What do you mean no? The *Times* has them, the *Post* has them.' We're not giving them out officially until tomorrow. So I called the *New York Times* and said 'I'll give you an exclusive. Send me those rules.'"[72]

The rules required headgear, banned kicking to the head, and required a 40-foot structure. The Octagon was just 30 feet. The law would effectively make it impossible to promote the UFC in Niagara Falls. The fights were just days away, and the UFC was committed to seeing them come to pass.

Isaacs said, "We kept thinking we were going to win. We had been through the legislature, and though you never know what's going to happen in court, the lawyers were telling us we had a very solid case. I was up in Niagara Falls and they were thrilled to have us. The economy up there was rough at the time, I suspect it still is, and they thought it was a great thing. There was no negative connotation at all."

Despite being confident that the show would eventually take place in New York, SEG was prepared to do what was needed to make sure the show made it on the air. "Because of all the legal trouble we'd had, we usually had backup venues. In case we couldn't pull the live event off, we knew we had to get it on cable. We always had so much pressure from cable, and if we ever didn't do an event we'd planned at the last minute, we really did think that would be the death of the UFC. So we were very focused on getting the events off."

Just the day before the show was scheduled to air, the UFC pulled the plug on the Niagara Falls location. Now it was a race against the clock to set the show up over 1,100 miles away, in Dothan, Alabama.

"It was not even a full 48 hours before the show and we were banned. David [Isaacs] chartered two 737s and loaded the Octagon onto them. The Octagon was a 20-hour build and we had 36 hours," McClaren said. "So we had to pack it up, put it on the plane, and then we had to find a venue. . . . We found that beautiful little theater in Dothan, but there was a question about whether we could fit the Octagon in the side door. We certainly had no time to sell tickets. The fighters were all warming up in New York, and they had to be shipped down there. They were all grumbling. Everyone was pissed off. The director sits in the truck and calls the camera action. He needs a day to prepare for that, at minimum. And he was going to be landing, going right to the truck, and starting. Logistically, it is amazing that it even happened. The fact that it went on live TV is just mind-boggling."

The fighters couldn't bring their entire entourages. Each could bring one person for their corner. The airport closed at midnight, and the UFC plane took off at 11:55 p.m.

Isaacs said, "I can remember the really dramatic moment, for me, was standing there with one of our production guys and literally throwing the fighters' luggage off the plane because the plane was overweight because the Octagon was so heavy. This is Thursday night, and it was a Friday event. This is surreal, you know? We went to breakfast at the Waffle House. I went around the group of people that were really in charge of physically putting the event together: the technical director, the lighting director, the guy who put the Octagon together. And I made them all sign up that they could pull it off. I really believe in having a strong team, and these guys all said 'I can do it.' That's when we made the decision to go. You tell people we moved a show that size in that amount of time and they'll tell you it's impossible. And we were painting the Octagon, literally, when the doors opened for the show. That tells you how tight it was."

To viewers of the show, there was never any indication of the behind-the-scenes turmoil. The organizers pulled it off because they had to. Politicians were waging war on the event, and the cable companies were waiting for their turn to open fire. Cablevision had stopped carrying the show after UFC 8, and others were starting to have second thoughts about the ultra-violent events. The UFC was operating in a zero-defect environment. A single mistake could see the show removed from pay-per-view forever.

"Everybody knew how important it was we pull the event off. The fighters included. Because it was a shitty way to do a fight," Isaacs said. "I think the fighters understood how hard we were working to pull this off. All of us understood that we were fighting for the survival of this thing. We were going to do whatever it took, and everybody had to do their part. It was my proudest moment as executive producer because the team pulled it off. We were fighting for the sport's life. We couldn't cancel and go on and do it some place else at a later date. If we didn't put that show on, cable would finally completely pull the plug and that would be that."

CABLE WOES

The UFC had proven that state governments could do little to stop the event from thriving. Even when the UFC was banned in one region, it could simply pick up the show and move to a more friendly state. As long as the pay-per-view profits kept pouring in, it made little difference where the fights actually took place. But cable companies were feeling the crunch. UFC critic John McCain had become the chairman of the Commerce Committee when the Republicans took control of the Senate, and it was clear that Congress would be taking a close look at violence and sex on television. The Commerce Committee has direct oversight of the cable industry, and companies were lining up to give McCain whatever he asked for.

"The cable companies are absolutely flabbergasting," UFC official John McCarthy said. "They are folding for no other reason than politics. We, and the subscribers paying for our event, have made the cable systems around this country millions upon millions of dollars. They are refusing to show our event, saying that they don't feel it is proper, while at the same time they are stepping up their pornography into the xxx category. I have no problem with cable systems putting anything they want out there for the paying customer to purchase. The point is, we cannot be viewed by anyone who does not want to view us. You have to pick up the phone and spend $21.95 of your hard-earned money to view our event. If someone does not want to see our show, it's not like they have to change the channel, it will never show up on their screen in the first place. I look at it this way: I am 35 years old and I don't need someone to be my daddy or mommy. If I want something censored in my home, I should be the one to censor it, not the president of some cable company."[73]

The day after UFC 12 took place, on February 7, 1997, Leo Hindery took over at TCI, a cable company with more than 14 million subscribers. Hindery was a major opponent of ultimate fighting, and was proud to announce to the *L.A. Times* that: "I came here, found out where the bathrooms are, and cancelled Ultimate Fighting." Meyrowitz had even met with Hindery to outline the rule changes and how the UFC would continue to adapt and present a more palatable product. But Hindery wasn't convinced and pulled the programming. This blatant act of censorship went forward in the name of morality. TCI felt an obligation to protect viewers from shows they shouldn't be watching.

Andrew Johnson, TCI's director of communications for the western U.S. said, "We have the right to make editorial decisions, and we provide a service to the community that carries with it a responsibility, just like the editor of a newspaper. Because of the level of violence in the programming, we choose to exercise discretion. The primary reason is that states where TCI is seen don't even allow these events in their jurisdictions. Our president, Leo Hindery, has met with the UFC, and hoped to get a long-term solution so we could televise them. It hasn't worked out."[74]

Time Warner quickly followed suit, taking another 12 million cable households with it. The two companies together controlled Viewer's Choice, so the UFC was out there, too. The potential audience had gone from 35 million homes to less than 7.5 million almost overnight. If you wanted to watch the UFC on pay-per-view, you needed satellite or Direct TV. It simply wasn't available on cable. This was the beginning of a dark era for the UFC, a time when only a few dedicated hard-core fans kept the sport alive.

"It's hard to be a success when nobody can order the pay-per-view. It was sort of a perfect storm for us," McClaren said. "The government was looking into the adult business on cable, which is like a third of their revenue. The cable industry went, 'Wow, that's a third of our money, maybe we should offer up this bullshit UFC thing and it will look like we're the good guys.' I don't think they thought, at the time, that this was their next big franchise. I think they saw it as a fluke. So cable offered us up as a sacrificial lamb. Video games and TV were pushing the boundaries, but we hadn't reached the saturation point with media violence yet. So the UFC looked very brutal and very real. All our arguments about face cuts versus brain damage didn't matter. America was just kind of turning a corner in terms of the level of violence in the media. I think, now, the UFC doesn't look as violent as video games and movies."

The cable ban changed the UFC's business plans considerably. It could no longer afford its most charismatic and popular fighters. Ken Shamrock, Tank Abbott, and Don Frye all left for more lucrative pro wrestling contracts. They didn't necessarily want to join the wrestling business — the UFC just couldn't pay them anymore, and fighters always go where the money is.

"I would have never been a pro wrestler until after the Ultimate," Abbott told Sherdog.com. He loved fighting, but the cable ban had changed everything. "The Ultimate, at no fault of their own, could no longer come up with the money."

Other fighters the UFC had developed, like Mark Coleman, Gary Goodridge, and Mark Kerr, left to fight for bigger money in Japan. The fighters that were left simply got what the UFC could afford to pay.

Isaacs said, "We cut costs and we cut costs dramatically. We pared down everything we could. Once we knew we weren't on cable, we could make a pretty good estimate of what the potential revenues were, and then we could build the event to fit that. From a personal perspective, it was really challenging. We fought a lot of battles in court, and I spent a lot of time making deals with fighters who just sucked. It's not fun to have to pay guys less money than you want to, and than they want. I remember one time I made Pat Miletich take a bus. That's the kind of numbers we were dealing with. We couldn't afford to fly people anywhere, we cut down the number of days people were there on-site, we cut down our own staff, we cut back our marketing. There was a point when we made a good deal of money at this, and then we kind of spent it all back on lobbying, lawsuits, and sustaining the events as best we could. We were looking for funding. Bob has money, but it isn't endless. He doesn't have Fertitta [the Las Vegas billionaires who currently own the UFC] money, and we just couldn't lock into other sources of funds. Not necessarily investors, but sponsors, advertisers, other ancillary revenues. People at major companies were always concerned that somebody was going to die. Despite the fact that we had all this information, that it was safer than boxing, and Budweiser continues to sponsor boxing. It didn't matter. The perception was so bad we couldn't get over the hump."

The UFC was still the big show, the "Super Bowl of Mixed Martial Arts." But fighters were often surprised when they finally made it big. When Chuck Liddell made his debut at UFC 17 on May 15, 1998 in Mobile, Alabama, he was less than impressed.

"They paid me $1,000 — including expenses . . . when we had the weigh-ins they used a bathroom scale, which made me laugh," Liddell said. "If you knew how to shift your weight right, the balance on the scale would change, and you could come in just over- or just underweight. . . . This was the UFC I had been training for? . . . All of it led to the Mobile Civic Center for a one-shot, $1,000 fight against a guy named Noe Hernandez in front of a couple thousand people? . . . So much for dreaming big."[75]

The UFC found several new stars during this era, fighters like Liddell, Randy Couture, Vitor Belfort, Frank Shamrock, Bas Rutten, and Kevin Randleman. They combined athleticism, charisma, and unmatched skill into a total package. The UFC had stars that could have attracted huge money on pay-per-view. They just didn't have a platform to showcase them.

The Ultimate Fighting Championship couldn't survive like this for much longer. But as the sport was placed on life support in the United States, it was exploding like never before in Japan. And a young Japanese star had attracted attention by challenging the most famous fighting family in the world.

8

PRIDE ARRIVES

In Japan, more than anywhere else on the planet, mixed martial arts and professional wrestling are inexorably linked. To the Japanese fans, the first major mixed martial artist of the modern era wasn't Royce or Rickson Gracie. It was Antonio Inoki, a professional wrestler who conquered legitimate martial artists across many disciplines and proclaimed himself the "World Martial Arts Champion." Inoki was hardly a martial artist at all, he was a track-and-field star that the most legendary Japanese pro wrestler of all-time, Rikidozan, had discovered in Brazil. But the fans believed. After Rikidozan was murdered at the hands of the Japanese mafia, the yakuza, Inoki became the biggest wrestling star in Japan.

Rikidozan had made his name fighting bigger Americans in front of huge crowds, giving Japanese nationalists something to be proud of in post–World War II Japan. Inoki sensed that his mentor's formula, though still drawing respectable crowds, was less resonant with Japanese fans in the '70s. But a Rikidozan match with famed Judoka Kimura, in which Rikidozan proved pro wrestling's superiority over judo, gave Inoki an idea. In his own wrestling promotion, New Japan Pro Wrestling, he, too, would prove pro wrestling was the strongest of all fighting arts, and he would do it by taking on the best fighters in every discipline.

"Many people criticize Inoki for constantly 'mixing up' pro wrestling and MMA. However, if you look back at the history, you just can't avoid the connection between those two sports . . . at least in Japan," wrestling historian Hisaharu Tanabe said. "Regardless, it can't be ignored that Inoki was the one who made the concept of mixed martial arts very popular in Japan."

He set the tone with his first match, an epic struggle with Dutch Olympic judo gold medalist Wilheim Ruska. It took Inoki over 20 minutes to beat the judo player at a sold-out Budokan Hall. Now he wasn't just the top professional wrestler, he was the top martial artist in the world. He continued beating champions throughout the '70s: PKA kickboxing champ "Monsterman" Everrett Eddie, boxer Chuck Wepner (who also had a pro wrestling match with Andre the Giant that inspired the Rocky-Thunderlips fight in the movie *Rocky III*), and, in the best match of all, Kyokushin karate champ Willie Williams.

These matches cemented Inoki's place in professional wrestling history. But it was another fight that cemented his status as a cultural icon in Japan, the biggest mixed martial arts fight of all time: Inoki versus Muhammad Ali.

THE CHIN VS. THE LIP

In 1975, Ali gave an interview to the *Sankei Sports Newspaper* bemoaning the lack of an Asian challenger. It was Ali being Ali, and he almost certainly immediately forgot all about it. Antonio Inoki, however, did not. He chased the boxing legend for a whole year, and accepted Ali's challenge at a press conference Ali held in Japan on his way to fight Joe Bagner in Malaysia. When nothing came of it, Inoki spread a pamphlet around everywhere Ali fought, stating: "Ali, Don't Run Away!" At the same time, Inoki was developing a relationship behind the scenes with Ali hanger-on Ronald Holmes. They signed the fight in the Plaza Hotel in New York. Both men got what they were looking for: Ali had a $6-million payday that he didn't have to get punched in the head a single time for, and Inoki got the worldwide attention he craved. Ali was a huge professional wrestling fan, and had even patterned his patter after legendary wrestlers Gorgeous George and "Classy" Freddie Blassie. Blassie was a legend in both the United States and Japan, and traveled around the country as Ali's manager, hyping the fight with pro wrestling–style interviews. "This will be serious," Ali said when the fight was announced as a nationwide closed-circuit extravaganza. "This will be a fight to the death. No boxing. This will be on the level." Ali even appeared on WWF TV, where the 400-pound Gorilla Monsoon picked him up like a sack of potatoes and tossed him with an airplane spin. Ali was going to earn his money.

Like the Monsoon confrontation, the Ali-Inoki fight was supposed to be a "work," a fixed fight. Ali would bloody Inoki up with punches and have so much concern for his battered opponent he would ask the referee, judo legend Gene LeBell, to stop the fight. This would allow Inoki to "pearl harbor" the valiant Ali and get the win with his trademark enzeguiri, a leaping kick to the back of the head. The fight would establish Inoki as an international wrestling star and fatten Ali's pockets. But along the way, something went wrong.

"Ali's fight in Tokyo was basically a Bob Arum [famous boxing promoter] thought-up scam that was going to be 'ha-ha, ho-ho. We're going to go over there. It's going to be orchestrated. It's going to be a lot of fun and it's just a joke.' And when we got over there, we found out no one was laughing," Ali's longtime confidant Ferdie Pacheco said.[76] Somewhere along the line, Ali had second thoughts about being involved in a fixed fight, or maybe he just didn't want to lose. Criticism of the fight may have changed his mind. The press was brutal. "Boxing is show business," *New York Times* columnist Red Smith said. "Maybe it's unrealistic to expect more of a champion than a succession of pratfalls on the burlesque circuit. Nevertheless, some do mourn for the sweet science."

The martial arts community was equally disgusted, not that Ali was doing a mixed match, but that the promoters had chosen the wrong opponent. Martial artist and author Donn Draeger wrote to friend Robert Smith: "Inoki is a protégé of Rikidozan, who found him in the farm fields of Brazil. Inoki can't wrestle, but looked fierce and could be taught to roll around. . . . Inoki's recent 'defeat' of Willem Ruska was a farce. Ruska could murtilize him if he was allowed to do so; so could Anton Geesink. The whole thing with Ali is a promotion gimmick. Of course Ali will win the match; he can't be allowed to lose. But do you think Ali, or at least his handlers, are unaware of the fact that a good wrestler is advantaged over a boxer? [Former boxing champion Jack] Dempsey and others can attest to that, as you well know. Frankly, if Ali sticks to boxing, I feel that I could get him: if I could avoid his blow and make a clinch I am sure that I could win on the ground, just like any other good grappler. (Hell, I'd try it for less money, too!) . . . If this were a real go, I think that it would scare Ali away, and that if Inoki insists on it, the thing will never take place."[77]

Ali had more courage than Draeger imagined, but just. He went forward with the match, but imposed draconian rules on the wrestler. After a public sparring session, Ali's entourage called a meeting. The rules, which previously allowed Ali to box and limited Inoki to a pro wrestling rule set, were changed dramatically. It was either this or the match would be cancelled. Ali's people allowed no middle ground. Inoki was representing the art of wrestling, but could perform no throws, no locks, and no striking on the ground. He couldn't even kick unless one knee was on the ground. "I think Inoki versus Ali was a historical matchup that helped pro wrestling's popularity a lot, but it was not much of a match because the wrestler really couldn't wrestle," MMA star Josh Barnett said. "The rules were much too restrictive for Inoki and he was, in my opinion, handicapped by them. If the match was Pride rules, Inoki would have beaten Ali easily and quickly."[78] The rules guaranteed that the fight would be something worse than a pro wrestling farce — it would be boring.

THE FIGHT

For 15 rounds, Inoki avoided Ali's boxing prowess by dropping into a crab or onto his butt and scooting around the ring kicking Ali in the leg. Ali landed less than ten punches in the entire hour. Inoki never landed any solid blows, but did damage Ali with dozens of kicks over 15 rounds, destroying his legs.

Ali's trainer Angelo Dundee said, "It's very simple, Inoki knew that one of Muhammad's punches would have been enough to end the fight. Staying on his back, Inoki didn't run any risks, and he could kick Ali's legs. When the match was over, Muhammad's legs were full of hematomas, and he had to go to the hospital. I wouldn't have accepted the bout because Ali could make the same money and get the same worldwide publicity through boxing, but Muhammad wanted to do it badly. As a matter of fact, he helped sell the fight, putting up a great show at every press conference. I think Ali's claims that he would knock the Japanese wrestler out convinced Inoki not to get into a brawl."[79]

The fight was declared a draw by the judges, and was roundly criticized the world over as a boring sham. Not many understood that Inoki was hampered by the onerous rules, and he was considered a pansy who would not "stand and fight like a real man." It's worth noting that even with the rules in place, Inoki did enough damage to affect Ali for the rest of his career.

Bob Arum said, "Finally, at the end of the 15th round, the referee calls it a draw. So fine, okay. It was terrible. It was embarrassing. But Ali is bleeding from the legs. He gets an infection in his legs; almost has to have an amputation. Not only would the [Ken] Norton fight not have happened, but Ali could've been a cripple for the rest of his life."[80]

Ali may have suffered physically, but he benefited financially. New Japan Pro Wrestling and the other promoters couldn't say the same. People in Japan watched the show in record numbers. Over half of Japanese television viewers had their sets tuned to Inoki-Ali that afternoon, but that level of interest didn't translate internationally, and the closed-circuit broadcast bombed. The company ended up losing almost $3 million. Inoki would never again receive the worldwide attention he got for the Ali fight, although he would certainly try. He announced a match with Idi Amin, to be held in Uganda, that was cancelled when the brutal dictator was overthrown, and he even negotiated the release of prisoners with Iraqi strongman Saddam Hussein. But he will always be remembered for his match with Ali, which started the mixed martial arts boom in Japan.

TRAINING FOR A REVOLUTION

While Inoki was revolutionizing the business of professional wrestling in front of the cameras, a revolution was occurring behind the scenes, as well. Foreign stars like Karl Gotch and Billy Robinson, noted shooters who were sadistic and could go for real, were taking over the training of wrestlers in Japan. Gotch was a renegade who was considered too dangerous for American wrestling. He was obsessed with real wrestling, and couldn't always reconcile himself with losing matches to inferior opponents.

While shunned and blacklisted in America, the Belgium-born grappler was embraced by the Japanese as the "God of Wrestling." The matches in the ring were still as fixed as ever, but in the dojo, where the next generation of stars was being taught, they wrestled for real, learning techniques and holds that really worked. Gotch had been trained at the famed Wigan Snakepit in England and brought those methods with him to Inoki's New Japan Pro Wrestling.

Gotch said, "Over there, every matman knows Wigan as 'The Snakepit,' and believe me, that's the word for it. . . . I give any credit for success to Billy Riley, the 'Old Master' at Wigan. What a fantastic man! When Riley trained you, you learned to wrestle in the strictest sense of the word. You learned the basic moves first — really learned them — and then refined them. Nothing was neglected. When a man left Wigan, he took the imparted knowledge of Riley's thousands of matches and years of training with him. You know what a snakepit is — a dangerous place! And that's just what Wigan is if you can't take care of yourself. Billy Riley has no time for a man with no guts, to put it bluntly, so his training is on a 'kill or be killed' basis. In other words, you smarten up fast at Wigan and learn to defend yourself against any attack on the mat."[81]

Gotch prided himself on being just as tough on his students as his trainer had been on him. "He'd sit in the office, drink wine, and occasionally he would come out there and work us until we couldn't walk anymore," Ken Shamrock said.[82] Gotch's teachings sunk in, through sheer repetition if nothing else. "I never took one cent from a boy to show him how to wrestle, all I asked for is guts," Gotch once said. "I can make you strong, fast, agile, and train you for endurance and reflex, but guts you get when you are born."[83]

THE CREATION OF SHOOT-STYLE WRESTLING

The rise of the WWF in America changed wrestling in Japan, too. The comical and theatrical style of Hulk Hogan was becoming popular in the land of the rising sun, and that didn't sit well with a Gotch disciple named Akira Maeda. Not only was Maeda unhappy with the style, New Japan Pro Wrestling was actually losing money in 1983 and cutting salaries. This was happening thanks to some non-wrestling Inoki business ventures and despite a string of sold-out shows. The wrestlers were in full revolt, and when the dust cleared Maeda and other young stars like Nobuhiko Takada and the company's best legitimate wrestler, Yoshiaki Fujiwara, made their break from New Japan to form the Universal Wrestling Federation in 1984. Fujiwara was one of Gotch's first students, and his best. He had been a top Judoka in college, and collegiate judo in Japan is still heavily focused on ne-waza, or ground work. Fujiwara brought with him the submission holds of judo and combined them with catch wrestling to create a particularly effective style. When Inoki needed a tough guy to corner him in the Ali fight, he chose Fujiwara.

The wrestlers proclaimed themselves the strongest martial artists in Japan. When karate men or other martial artists came to challenge that claim, they sent them to Fujiwara. Wrestling always proved best, as Fujiwara cleaned house. He credited all of his victories to his teacher, whom he loved for his skills and his single-minded focus on the grappling arts. Fujiwara said, "One time during training Mr. Gotch got a very bad toothache. His toothache was interfering with his training. So he went to the hospital, or maybe the dentist, and asked them to pull all his teeth out. They said it's dangerous. He said, 'That's okay. Pull all my teeth out.' And he went back to training the next day with no teeth, because he figured if he has no teeth he's not going to have any toothaches getting in the way of his training. He's so crazy but I love him."[84]

Although Fujiwara was the toughest man in the building every night, the fans were there to see Maeda and Satoru Sayama, who would go on to found the SHOOTO promotion in Japan. Those two men couldn't get along, and when a wrestling match between them turned ugly, Maeda quit and the promotion folded just nine days later.

THE NEW, IMPROVED UWF

The UWF wrestlers went back to Inoki's New Japan Pro Wrestling, but they just weren't satisfied with traditional pro wrestling. Maeda hated wrestling opponents he didn't think were true martial artists, and his fans hated watching it. When he was booked into a draw with pretty-boy pro wrestler Kerry Von Erich, his fans stormed out of Korukean Hall. They had seen the UWF, knew it was real, and there was no turning back. Maeda's frustration exploded when he kicked New Japan star Riki Choshu in the face — for real. The infamous shoot kick was a total cheap shot. Maeda waited until Choshu, a former Olympic wrestler, had his hands tied up with his famous scorpion deathlock and then delivered the kick, breaking Choshu's orbital bone.

The kick heard round the world led to the formation of the new UWF, and this time the promotion caught on with the fans. Led by Maeda, Takada, and Fujiwara, the UWF was the hottest ticket in Tokyo in the late '80s. Shows would routinely sell out in mere minutes, and the group, in an homage to Inoki, would often bring in outside legitimate martial artists like Maurice Smith, Frank Lobman, and Chris Doleman to compete in their shows. The shows were revolutionary. There were no gimmicked finishes or count outs, no one ever ran into the ring unexpectedly. There were winners and losers in every match. In 1989, the promotion did the unthinkable, drawing 60,000 fans to the Tokyo Dome for a show that made over $6 million. New Japan hadn't sold out the Tokyo Dome, and neither had Mike Tyson. The UWF was in full boom.

The crowd had completely bought into the promotion's claims of legitimacy. Hisaharu Tanabe said, "A large number of wrestling fans in pre-UWF days didn't think the matches were completely worked, though they knew there was some sort of showmanship in the sport. Inoki's famous words, 'ours [New Japan] is a strong style, Baba-san's [All Japan] is showmanship' also helped the illusion."

Fans a generation before always thought Inoki's martial arts matches were real, even if his regular matches with Tiger Jeet Singh and others were not. This new generation of hard-core fans was convinced that the UWF style was real wrestling. "When the second UWF became a phenom, there were still many fans who didn't think wrestling was 100 percent work. It started changing once UFC and Pride came out, of course. Even today, the major organizations such as Pro-Wrestling NOAH and New Japan don't publicly admit that their product is a work."

As the promotion grew more powerful and influential, the turmoil behind the scenes continued to grow. The group's president and promoter, Shinji Jin, wanted to do cross-promotions with other wrestling groups. The cross-promotion with the kickboxers had worked wonders at the box office, and he thought the time was right to do battle with another wrestling organization. Maeda vehemently disagreed, and the group was disbanded in 1990. Maeda formed Fighting Network RINGS, Fujiwara's top young students Masakatsu Funaki and Minoru Suzuki eventually founded Pancrase, and Nobuhiko Takada found the most success with the UWF-I.

THE MATINEE IDOL

Takada had it all. The movie-star looks, the indefinable charisma, and the ability to really wrestle — or at least make it look like he could. He had the backing of wrestling legend Lou Thesz, and packed houses all around Japan feuding with former University of Nebraska star Gary Albright and pro wrestling world champion Leon White, aka "Vader." The matches, though more theatrical than RINGS or even UWF fights, were still convincing enough to fool the fans. "There was nothing worked about those kicks or those punches. I'm not trying to insult anyone's intelligence, it was a worked shoot," White said. "But there's no way that man could have kicked me any harder. After those matches I couldn't work, I couldn't walk for two or three days."[85]

The UWF-I couldn't last forever. Its air of legitimacy was severely tarnished in 1993, when fans saw the UFC for the first time and when Rickson Gracie came to Japan for a pair of similar tournaments hosted by Sayama's SHOOTO promotion. Royce had famously said Rickson was ten times tougher than he was, and fans flocked to see the Brazilian in action. Not only had Rickson beaten RINGS star Yoshisha Yamamoto, but Royce had beaten Pancrase's top fighter, Ken Shamrock. It was getting more and more difficult for fans to believe that the Japanese wrestlers from the UWF were really the strongest fighters in the world. Something had to be done. First, the UWF-I tried to buy Rickson, promising an astronomical sum to do a pro wrestling match with Takada. Rickson was not interested, having inherited from his father, Hélio, a hatred for professional wrestling that still burned strong in the Gracie family. Since they couldn't buy him, they would try to discredit him.

The toughest guy in the UWF-I, like the toughest guy in the old UWF, wasn't the main event star. Midcarder Yoji Anjo was a solid 220 pounds, and could really handle himself in the gym. "After having wrestled with Anjo in UWF International, I know better than anyone what his potential is," Takada said. "He and I share something in common. Everyone became strong by sparring with Anjo, including Kazushi Sakuraba and Hiromitsu Kanehara."[86]

In a brilliant idea that went horribly wrong, booker Yuki Miyato sent Anjo to challenge Rickson Gracie in his Los Angeles dojo on Pearl Harbor day. They expected that Gracie would refuse a confrontation on such short notice, and brought the Japanese media along with them to film the great man failing to meet the challenge brought forward by the UWF-I. Anjo was confident, both in public and in private. He would have 30 pounds on Rickson and had years of training from Fujiwara. He could handle himself. "There's no need for Mr. Takada to go. If it's just Rickson, I'm 200 percent confident I can beat him," Anjo told the media before making his way to Gracie's Santa Monica dojo.

If Anjo made a mistake, it was underestimating a Gracie's willingness to throw down. These are men who had spent most of the century defending their family's legacy. His second mistake was making Rickson angry. He was at home with his family when he got the call that someone was making trouble and threatening his students, demanding to fight him. When he saw the media gathered, Rickson thought it was Takada himself who had come to make trouble. Regardless which Japanese had come to challenge him, Rickson would make them pay for disrespecting his dojo and his family name. "They were from a UWF, which is more like the WWF. They are strong guys and well trained, and after the Japan Open they invited me to fight. I said that I had other projects, and that I just fight in legit matches. Nothing worked. I said thanks and maybe another time. Then the magazines started to say that I was scared. After that, the Japanese press wanted to know what position I would take. I said that I would fight for only two reasons, for money or for my honor," Gracie said.[87] When the challenge from Anjo went down, Rickson told them if the fight was for money, he would stop hitting him when he asked him to. If the fight was for honor, Rickson would only stop hitting him when he felt like it. When Anjo and his entourage called Gracie a coward in front of his wife and kids, the fight was on. They asked Rickson if he was ready. "I was born ready, motherfucker," he said.

Many times, the Gracies will respond to a respectful challenge by showing jiu-jitsu to be a truly gentle art. They would win quickly, with a choke or a lock, and even teach their vanquished foes a bit about jiu-jitsu. But Anjo had taken a different approach to making his challenge, so Rickson took a different approach answering it. He took Anjo down and quickly got the mount. But instead of looking for a choke, Rickson pounded Anjo mercilessly in the face with punch after punch. Photos of Anjo afterwards show a man who looked like he was in a car wreck. "I had never seen Rickson mad before. He is always the one to keep a clear head in every situation, always trying to reason, but not this time," Gracie confidante Todd Hester said. "He was really mad and it showed on the beating he gave Anjo."[88]

In Japanese culture, Takada, as the senior man and the main eventer, was expected to rise to the challenge and defeat Gracie to restore the UWF-I's honor. "My role at UWF International was to protect Nobuhiko Takada. Fighting, and losing, to such a great opponent as Rickson is a blemish on my life," Anjo said. "Because of my loss, the Nobuhiko Takada versus

Rickson Gracie match had to be fought. I didn't fulfill my role as protector. I couldn't bring myself to talk with Mr. Takada face-to-face for a long time due to my failure."

When the fight didn't happen, the company began to lose credibility and popularity. Anjo had lost, and the rise of the UFC and Pancrase showed fans that the UWF-I might not be as real as they had been led to believe. Because of the company's struggles, Takada had to further compromise his promotion's credibility by working with the pro wrestlers they had mocked for years. After drawing big box office crowds challenging the fake pro wrestlers of Inoki's New Japan, Takada's career was at a crossroads. The fans were once again demanding that he fight Rickson Gracie.

FIGHTING FOR PRIDE

Knowing Gracie wouldn't do a worked fight, it was time to commit to something Japan hadn't yet seen — mixed martial arts on a grand scale. This new venture, called Pride, would be as different from Pancrase and SHOOTO as night was from day. Pride would take MMA and give it some show, some flavor. The headline bout would be Takada looking to avenge Anjo's loss to Gracie.

FightOpinion.com founder and Japanese wrestling expert Zach Arnold said, "When UWF-International died, Takada wasn't going to quit the fight business . . . Hiromichi Momose, a famous yakuza, was a big backer of Takada. Momose ended up backing KRS [Kakutougi Revolution Spirits], which was the first shell company that backed Pride for its first four events. Nobuyuki Sakakibara [from Tokai TV, a Fuji TV affiliate in Nagoya] and Naoto Morishita, who came from a discount electronics company in Nagoya, were the main players in Pride with Momose. There was a built-in storyline for Takada to face Rickson, because of the Anjo incident. Given that New Japan wasn't going to pay Takada the same kind of money he had been originally making, he had to take the fight against Rickson."

Takada was paid $180,000 and Rickson a rumored $1 million by Pride. The fight was not the success that promoters had envisioned. In 1994 or 1995, Takada and Rickson would have been the hottest ticket in town. By 1997, it was past its expiration date and only filled two thirds of the Tokyo Dome. Takada disappointed his fans and put the nail in UWF-style wrestling's coffin by losing to Rickson by arm bar in just under five minutes. Takada was clearly outclassed, but even with the huge defeat, UWF fans were undaunted. The biggest cheers of the evening were for a non-combatant shown briefly on the big screen in the Dome. When Akira Maeda was on camera, the crowd roared. Takada had let them down, but surely Maeda could beat Rickson and restore the UWF to glory?

"Everyone in the Big Egg [the Tokyo Dome] knew that there were only two left. The two who still carried, at the time, what I would call an 'Illusion of UWF,' Masakatsu Funaki and Akira Maeda," Japanese MMA writer Shu Hirata wrote at boutreviewusa.com. "The fans wanted to believe their hero could be the best in the world, so they pinned their hopes on Maeda, the oldest member of the club and the most charismatic of the three. That's why the fans went crazy when they saw Maeda's close-up displayed on that gigantic monitor."

Maeda and Takada were clearly the UWF's shining stars, at least at the box office. Maeda had drawn monster gates main eventing for the UWF and then for RINGS. The shows in his RINGS promotion were sold almost exclusively based on his name. He was so valuable that WOWOW (Japan's first pay television station) gave him a television deal for an unnamed and unknown wrestling promotion based on his name alone. He was such a one-man show that the cable contract specified that RINGS would only get paid if Maeda fought.

Maeda was slowing down. He was 37, and years of injuries had caught up with him. He could barely walk to and from the ring, and his wrestling performance suffered. "I always fought with injuries," he said. "But ever since I lost the ability to kick high with my left leg [because of the knee injury] everything became different."[89] Maeda had one more match in him, and he wanted it to be against Rickson Gracie. The buzz was tremendous. Takada was always the better athlete, but to the fans Maeda was more representative of the budo ethos of the Japanese warrior. Unlike Takada, who had been afraid to fight Rickson for three years, Maeda responded to the fans' calls right away.

Maeda negotiated hard to bring Rickson into RINGS, and was surprised to see the announcement that there would be a rematch with Takada instead. Maeda would counter with wrestling legend Alexander Karelin as his final opponent, but would never get the chance to set things right with the Gracies.

Pride was struggling. Their headliner, Takada, had been exposed too badly for fans to really believe in him again. They were also paying foreign fighters princely sums to come over and fight on their undercards. It was already becoming the place to fight for American fighters who were struggling because of the UFC's political problems. Dan Severn fought on the Pride 1 undercard for $40,000 instead of keeping his commitment to fight Maurice Smith for the UFC title. Smith ended up fighting Tank Abbott and Randy Couture instead. Severn was making more underneath in Pride than he did headlining the UFC.

The early Pride shows were a mixture of legitimate matches and fixed fights. To rehabilitate Takada, Pride paid Kyle Sturgeon to lie down for him at Pride 3 on June 24, 1998. American fans on the Internet were incensed, furious that the sport they had grown to love was being tainted with a pro wrestling influence. They didn't like the ambiguity that Pride brought to their black-and-white worldview. But the inability to clearly determine real from fake was nothing new to the Japanese audience.

"When you look at the first year or so of Pride, with the worked matches, it's easy to criticize them as this horrible organization, but if Takada had just gotten smashed by everyone they'd have been out of business," *Wrestling Observer*'s Dave Meltzer said. "Their number-one thing was preserving the business, and their number-two thing was presenting a good product. They all came from pro wrestling, so they had that mentality."

With a win under his belt, Takada would get another chance at Rickson, but the result was the same. Takada could offer no resistance, and lost again to a first-round arm bar. The mounting losses were killing Takada's ability to draw fans. For years, the UWF wrestlers had criticized and mocked traditional pro wrestlers, decrying their fake sport and promoting themselves as the real thing. When Takada looked so out of his element against Gracie, there was a backlash.

"When he lost to Rickson, he became somewhat unpopular and was bashed a lot, most likely because the 'big mouth' promotional tactic of UWF-I wasn't yet forgotten [plus the Anjo incident]," Tanabe said. "However, I'm pretty sure he gained a lot more respect afterwards because, without his courage in challenging Rickson, Pride wouldn't exist today."

In the pro wrestling market, and Pride was being marketed like a pro wrestling promotion, you need a top native star that fans can get behind in a big way. Takada couldn't be that guy. Even after giving former UFC world champion Mark Coleman a big payday for taking a fall, Takada still couldn't regain his popularity. Pride reorganized under the DSE (Dream Stage Entertainment) banner, and looked to move forward and build new native stars.

Arnold said, "The thought process in appealing to Japanese fans is no different than that of a political strategist on the campaign trail. Appeal to core Japanese fight fans by using a pro wrestling tie in? Check. Appeal to casual Japanese fans by booking Japanese talent in the positions of being heroes? Check. It's all about marketing and segmentation. Plus, many yakuza gangs are very big into nationalism, despite the fact that there's a lot of North Korean and South Korean blood [zainichis] in the gangs. Foreign fight fans will never understand Japan's politics, and it's not because they aren't smart enough to understand, either. They're bored by it. They don't care. All foreign fight fans care about is fights."

In Japan, finding the best fighters is secondary. More than anything, Pride was a nice show for a hip kid to take a date to on a Friday night. The fights were less important than the spectacle.

"This is an entertainment package. We produce the events to appeal to a wide variety of people," former DSE vice president of marketing Yukino Kanda said. "We value a fighter on marketability. Of course, a championship belt means something, but we ultimately evaluate the fighters according to their popularity."[90]

Finding the fighters who could demand that the audience stand up and pay attention was difficult. Pride brought in the best foreign fighters in the world, including Mark Kerr, Maurice Smith, and Igor Vovchancyn. It also had former judo silver medalist Naoya Ogawa fight Gary Goodridge in a worked match, but Ogawa had too much to lose to be a Pride regular. His successful pro wrestling career required him to be an unbeatable juggernaut. He couldn't risk that reputation on an uncertain shoot. While Pride searched far and wide for the next big thing, the next big thing was on its undercard all along. Takada protégé Kazushi Sakuraba was becoming a fan favorite. And, unlike his mentor, he was also a hell of a fighter.

Mark Coleman had been eliminated from the 1996 Olympic trials in Spokane, Washington. His athletic career, briefly resurgent with a win at the 1995 Sunkist Open, including a decisive victory over eventual gold medalist Kurt Angle, was seemingly over. But there was a man in Spokane that day scouting talent, and there was plenty on display. Richard Hamilton had been Don Frye's manager before a falling out. He saw how well Frye, an average collegian, had done in the UFC. Imagine how well one of the world's best would do?

Three men caught his eye that day: Coleman, Mark Kerr, and Tom Erickson. Basically, it came down to who wanted it more. And Coleman wanted it bad. The Olympic trials were on June 10, 1996. By July 12, Coleman would be stepping into the Octagon for the first time. Like all fighters, Coleman was in it for the money.

"I saw the paycheck that Royce Gracie got and that's all it took. I was hooked immediately," Coleman said.[91] Money was always an issue. It is for all amateur wrestlers, and Coleman had been on the Olympic grind since 1988. It was time to get paid. "All of a sudden, I'm put in a position to make some money. In wrestling you don't make a dime. I put in thirty of the hardest days of my life getting ready for UFC 10. Fighting is a little different from wrestling — when you lose a fight, you don't lose by points, you lose by punishment. For the first time since '92, I really, really trained seriously."[92]

Thirty days isn't a very long time to go from the ring into the cage. But Mark Coleman wasn't your average athlete. Dan Severn had shown the world that wrestling was a force to be reckoned with, and Don Frye showed what a wrestler in his physical prime was capable of. But Mark Coleman was a different beast altogether. As good as Severn was, Coleman was a better wrestler, and had represented the United States in the World Championships and the 1992 Olympic Games. He was stronger. And he was a brawler.

Some wrestlers, like the legendary John Smith or Cael Sanderson, get by on their technical mastery. Coleman wasn't that kind of wrestler; he was the kind of guy who used his power and wasn't afraid to grind a forearm into your face on the mat. In wrestling they call that the "Big Ten style." Coleman was Big Ten personified, and he was about to be unleashed on Moti Horenstein.

Horenstein was an Israeli soldier with movie-star looks and a solid physique. It wasn't nearly enough, and his "Survival" style of fighting only worked for 2:43. In his next fight, with Gary Goodridge, a huge Canadian arm wrestler who would go on to become a MMA mainstay in Japan, Coleman unveiled the weapon that would make him the most devastating and intimidating fighter in the UFC's short history — the head butt. He beat up Goodridge for seven minutes before finally getting his hands on UFC 8 champion Don Frye.

This fight was personal for Coleman and his manager Richard Hamilton. Hamilton held a grudge against Frye, and had recruited Coleman essentially to seek revenge against his former client.

"He made Don Frye out to be an evil person. I have nothing against anybody, but the stuff he was telling me about Don made me want to go in there and kick his butt," Coleman said. The fight was brutal, with Coleman landing dozens of head butts, punches, and elbows to the face of the helpless Frye. "Mark just overpowered me. He came in as a superior wrestler, a more powerful wrestler, and just put the boots to me. That loss has haunted me," Frye said. "It was my only loss for so many years. It was the only blemish on my record for so many years. I just . . . it just bothered me, and I can't really explain it beyond that. I was just immature. Some people can't handle losses. Some people get angry if things don't go their way and they take their ball and go home. Basically, I sat around with my bottom lip stuck out for six years."[93]

For his part, Frye was either too stubborn or too valiant to quit. He took his beating and Hamilton got his revenge. Frye had to be taken to the hospital in an ambulance. Both his eyes were swollen shut because of the abuse he had taken, and he had fractured bones in his face. Hamilton was thrilled. "Hamilton was supposed to be some type of minister, but during the fight I heard a totally different person the way he was talking to me."[94] Hamilton would soon be down another client. He spent a ton of Coleman's money to pay friends to come to the arena and hold Mark Coleman signs. He started acting strangely and told Coleman he was in the witness protection program. Coleman thought this was odd, especially since Hamilton had just accompanied him on nationwide pay-per-view television. He was eventually sentenced to 78 years for sexual abuse and sexual conduct with a minor. Hamilton was gone, but Coleman was here to stay, becoming a UFC fixture. In a single tournament in this new sport, Coleman was finally the top dog.

"When I won UFC 10, I was overwhelmed. That was something I really only dreamed about, being the toughest man in the world," Coleman said. "Even in boxing, you can be the toughest boxer in the world, but being the toughest man is something you can kind of brag about. When I won the UFC, I felt like I was the toughest man in the world. It was overwhelming."[95]

Coleman's aura didn't just come from winning. It was the way he was winning. Just two months later, at UFC 11 on September 20, 1996, he beat Julian Sanchez and Brian Johnston in just over two minutes — combined. He was so scary that night in the eight-man tournament that both fellow finalist Scott Ferrozza and alternate Roberto Traven chose to drop out rather than face him. He was $75,000 richer, and ready to challenge Dan Severn. It was the tournament champion versus the Superfight champion for the title of undisputed king of the Octagon.

Severn knew he was in trouble. Before every fight, he broke everything down: his own strengths and weaknesses and those of his opponents. "I wrote down that he was not only younger and stronger than I was, but he was also a better wrestler than I was at that point," Severn said. "Since that was my biggest strength, it wasn't looking so good for me."

Coleman was able to take Severn to the mat and submit him with a neck crank in just under three minutes. The UFC had a new heavyweight champion, and he looked to be unstoppable. He had beaten Frye and Severn, two of the UFC's biggest stars and brightest talents at the time, and made it look easy. His first title defense was against Maurice Smith, a world-champion kickboxer who had been on a tear for the UFC's top competitor, Extreme

Fighting. It was no disrespect to Smith that Coleman was taking the fight lightly. He would have taken any fight lightly at that point. He was unbeatable and he knew it.

A MAN NAMED MO

Maurice Smith found MMA late in his fight career, after establishing himself as one of the best kickboxers in the world. He had been World Kickboxing Council champion and World Kickboxing Association (WKA) heavyweight champion. Of course, everyone who won a single kickboxing fight in the '80s and '90s was some promotion's "World Champion." This made kickboxing prowess hard to judge for people who weren't there to see the fights. Smith was no paper champion. He was one of a half dozen American kickboxers who really mattered in the '80s, a group that includes Benny "The Jet" Urqiduez and Don "The Dragon" Wilson.

When the WKA became popular in Japan, Smith was a big enough name to attract the attention of pro wrestling promoters looking to add some legitimacy to their contests. He knocked out Minoru Suzuki for the UWF in his pro wrestling debut in front of a packed house at the Tokyo Dome. The show, headlined by future RINGS promoter Akira Maeda, was one of the biggest pro wrestling events in Japanese history, drawing more than 60,000 fans. He headlined the Tokyo Dome against another future Pancrase founder, Masakatsu Funaki, in 1992 before making his debut with the two hottest new martial arts promotions in the country the following year.

Smith fought anywhere and everywhere. He was invited to compete in the first K-1 Grand Prix in 1993, joining the best kickboxers on the planet in a contest to find out who was the "Best of the Best." Smith was knocked out by Ernesto Hoost in the semifinals, and may have realized his best days as a kickboxer were behind him. Instead of returning to K-1, he immersed himself in the new sport of mixed martial arts. He fought in Pancrase in the first year of the promotion's history with mixed results. The promotion was emphasizing slick grappling and Smith just wasn't ready for the kind of ground skills he was facing.

"At the time I fought in Pancrase, I didn't have any real experience in grappling," Smith said. Not only that, but the Pancrase rules took away his biggest strength too, prohibiting punching with a closed fist to the head. "That was the main thing, it had to be open hand. But since that was the rule then, it wasn't in my best interest to do it at that point. There are certain differences you have in punching with a closed fist and with the palm of your hand."[96]

THE ALLIANCE

Smith fought future MMA legends Ken Shamrock and Bas Rutten in Pancrase, losing to both by submission in a combined 6:32. If Smith wanted a future in this sport, he knew he would need to revamp his game. Since his biggest problem was avoiding submissions on the ground, he struck up a friendship with Ken Shamrock and traveled to California to train with the Lion's Den. The UFC made Smith an offer to fight when it was preparing Shamrock for his first fight with Dan Severn. Smith knew he wasn't ready yet. "We did more talking than training, and when he went into the WWF, I got pawned off on Frank," Smith said. Instead, he ramped up his training with Frank Shamrock and prepared to make his debut on a smaller stage, in Extreme Fighting. Smith was being fed to the promotion's top heavyweight, a giant Brazilian jiu-jitsu star named "Conan" Silviera who could go on the ground and also liked to stand and bang on his feet. "We worked on defending the side and full mount on the ground and reversing the guy. If I did that, I could work to keep him against the fence and start punching him."[97] Smith would face Silviera in the semifinals of a four-man tournament that included pro wrestling stars Kazanuri Murakami and Bart Vale. In Smith's corner, for the first time, was Lion's Den star Frank Shamrock.

"Maurice and I got together because Ken made a deal with Maurice. Maurice would train Ken in striking, and, in turn, Ken would train Maurice in submission wrestling," Frank Shamrock said. "So after Maurice had trained Ken in striking, when it came time for Ken to train Maurice he said, 'Frank, go train Maurice.' Like he had me train everybody. So I trained Maurice, and during that time we realized that Maurice and I were way more alike and had the same ideas about fighting and the art of fighting. We developed a real close friendship that exists to this day."

After surviving Conan's ground assault in the first round, Smith went to work, landing some stiff, straight punches before putting Conan away with a high kick in the second round. Smith had exceeded all expectations. In 1996, it was a given that the superior grappler would win any contest. Brazilian jiu-jitsu was king, and strikers could expect nothing but a quick, ignominious defeat. Smith was the first fighter to turn the sport upside down and return the striking arts to prominence in the martial arts world. When he knocked out judo player Murakami in his next fight, he established himself as a legitimate player in the world of MMA. Murakami actually floored Smith with a palm to the head and nearly finished him. Only instinct saved Smith, and when he got back to his feet it was time for revenge. Smith normally plays a waiting game; he is a counter and defensive fighter by nature. Here, he went right after Murakami and knocked him out with one of the cleanest and hardest right hands you'll ever see. In the three years the sport had been on television, this was the best knockout, bar none.

"When he went down I was really concerned" Smith said. "I didn't find out until later that he was paralyzed for almost two hours and I was kind of nervous about it."[98] Murakami recovered and continued to fight in his native Japan, as well as carving out a niche as a pro wrestling wild man.

Maurice Smith had arrived, not as a kickboxer brought in to give grapplers a credible win, but as a mixed martial artist in his own right. "I showed that strikers could compete in this sport," Smith said. "What I brought to the game was what great conditioning could do for someone. If the fight goes to the ground, the fight goes to the ground. But if a striker can keep it on the feet and avoid the takedown, then he has the advantage. I feel I've opened the door for strikers in this sport."[99]

Smith's rise coincided with his promotion's fall. Extreme Fighting was in the middle of the great moral war against human cockfighting. Despite their great shows, shows that were better than the UFC's offerings at the time and featured great talent like John Lewis, Matt Hume, Pat Miletich, and Olympic gold medalist Kevin Jackson, the company was losing pay-per-view clearance and couldn't afford to stay in business.

"[Arizona Senator John] McCain was leaning on us the whole time. We just kept losing distribution," Extreme Fighting President Donald Zuckerman said. "First, we were in 100 percent of the pay-per-view hub markets and then Cablevision stopped carrying it, and this company stopped, and that company stopped. And finally we lost Time Warner and we were down to 50 percent. It just didn't pay to do it anymore."[100]

The death of Extreme Fighting invigorated the UFC's lineup of fighters. John Lober, Kevin Jackson, Igor Zinoviev, John Lewis, Pat Miletich, and

Smith all made their way to the UFC. It was a golden era, and it started at UFC 14 with a champion versus champion match, Maurice Smith would be challenging Mark Coleman for the UFC heavyweight title.

THE FIGHT

To say Coleman was the prohibitive favorite would be like calling New York a good-sized town. It was an understatement of epic proportions. Although Smith had established that he was a bona fide threat, he had done so against unproven talent. No one had heard of Murakami, and Conan was a lower level jiu-jitsu guy who made the mistake of staying on his feet instead of taking it to the mat. That wouldn't happen with Coleman, and people expected an easy victory. Reporters were talking about Coleman's expiring UFC contract and his rumored fight in Brazil with Renzo Gracie (boy, that would have been an epic beating). They were talking about everything but Maurice Smith. Everyone was confident Coleman would dominate Smith — everyone but Smith, who remained convinced that his growing skills would be enough to win. Smith and Frank Shamrock worked out a basic strategy, the same strategy they would use when Frank fought a dominant wrestler named Tito Ortiz years later. They would fight to survive until the overly muscled wrestler was running out of breath. Then it would be their turn to strike.

"It's a simple game plan: stay on my feet. I'm just going to jab, jab throughout for five or ten minutes. Then, as he gets tired, and he will get tired, then I start putting the pressure on with some kicks. I'm going to wear him down," Smith told *Full Contact Fighter*'s Joel Gold before the fight. Gold was filming a documentary, which was never released, and had unprecedented access to the fighter's pre-event training. "He's got 260 pounds to move around to my 200 pounds. He's going to blow up. He's not used to running, and I will literally run to make him chase me. I don't have to be a tough man right away. I can be tough a little bit later on."

Coleman was on top of the world and on top of his game. UFC 14, on July 27, 1997, was going to be the culmination of wrestling's arrival at the top of the MMA world. Fellow wrestlers Mark Kerr, who had beaten Randy Couture for the 1990 NCAA title, and Extreme Fighting veteran Kevin Jackson, who had won an Olympic gold medal in 1992, would join Coleman. He felt he had already learned all he needed to know. His training camp in Arizona consisted of him wrestling around with Kerr and Jackson for a week. They worked almost no striking and very little on submission grappling. While it was cool to watch two world-class wrestlers like Coleman and Jackson spar, it wasn't doing much to improve Coleman's overall game. On top of that, the wrestling did little to prepare Coleman's cardio for a 15-minute fight. Wrestling is all about short bursts of energy; Coleman was ready for several three-minute matches. He wasn't ready for ten minutes, and it showed.

Coleman was nonchalant about the bout, and more concerned about how he was going to win than about whatever Smith was bringing to the table. Smith was just another stand-up fighter for him to throw down and throw down on.

"Everyone's been a puncher or a kicker so far. I've got the same strategy I've had in my previous fights," Coleman said. "I'm gonna look for an opening, I'm going to change my level and blast him and take him to the ground. I think I'm going to throw some punches because I want it to be exciting this time. If I can't finish him off with the punches, I'll choke him out."[101]

Everyone Coleman had fought had been a little intimidated by him, but Smith was not timid at all. He'd been around the professional fight game for almost two decades, and decided to play a few head games with his opponent. When reporters asked him about being the underdog, he told them exactly what he thought of Coleman's game, especially standing. Which wasn't much.

"He doesn't know how to punch. He punches like . . . he punches like a girl, okay? He may punch hard, but it's not like a solid punch. It's more like scratching than hitting me," Smith said in his pre-fight interview, while making an incredibly effeminate clawing motion. "It's not a punch. When he sees this interview, he's going to get mad, but later on he'll know I'm right and he'll change his punching style because it's not going to hurt me. It may bruise me, but it ain't going to hurt me. Watch when I hit him and see the difference. See a boxer or kickboxer's punch and see a wrestler's punch. There's a big difference."

Smith was telling everyone who would listen that Coleman punched like a girl, including Joel Gold and other insiders. When word got back to Coleman, he was furious. During the fighter introductions Coleman did a lap around the Octagon and got in Smith's face. If looks could kill, Smith would have been a dead man. Coleman took his anger out on Smith early, taking him down in just 24 seconds and commencing a brutal assault. Smith, much to the surprise of the announcers and everyone watching at home, did more than survive on the bottom, he actually thrived. His guard was phenomenal, a combination of hand control, hip movement, and striking from underneath that made Coleman work constantly to keep up any offense. After just two minutes, Coleman was spent. Smith may have been on his back for much of the rest of the fight, but he was also delivering the more effective strikes, including some vicious elbows to the back of Coleman's head that would be illegal in today's UFC. Suddenly, Coleman was regretting taking the fight so lightly.

"After the two-minute mark everything fell into place," Coleman said. "And I realized how dumb I was for taking on a championship fighter of Maurice Smith's caliber and showing him absolutely no respect."[102]

Smith continued to wow the announcers with his prowess on the ground, including former wrestler Jeff Blatnick, who was notorious for favoring his fellow wrestlers in his not-so-subtle commentary. But Blatnick knew greatness when he saw it, even if his partner, Bruce Beck, was the first to realize that Smith was not just defending, but also wearing Coleman down, covering Coleman's mouth with his hand to slow his already ragged breathing and taking over on offense as well.

"A lot of composure by Maurice Smith on his back. A striker on his back, not panicking, and not getting frustrated. Staying cold, calm, and collected," Blatnick said. ". . . Smith is well versed in the guard. This athlete knows some good jiu-jitsu."

After nine minutes, Coleman had the energy for one last burst, a submission attempt with a modified arm triangle or head-and-arm choke. When Smith escaped, the fight was effectively over. Coleman was dog tired. Nights in the club instead of in the gym were hurting him bad, and he had to put his hands on his knees to catch a breather. After a weak shot attempt by Coleman, Smith was able to land a kick to the head for the first time, a glancing blow that prompted McCarthy to stop the fight to penalize Smith. Replays appear to show that Coleman was up off the ground before the kick landed, making it a legal blow. "I couldn't tell," Smith said after the fight. "Maybe he looked down, so they gave me the penalty? C'est la vie. I thought he was up."

Even intervention by McCarthy couldn't save Coleman, who was utterly exhausted despite the additional rest the penalty provided. Smith was ever cautious of the takedown and warily stalked Coleman around the ring, landing a leg kick here and a jab there. Coleman got a reprieve when Smith finally pulled the trigger on a high kick and was taken to the mat. Even in his own element, in Coleman's world as Joe Rogan might say, Smith took the lead, pounding away at Coleman's skull with devastating downward elbow strikes. "This is a championship fight," an excited Blatnick said. "A clash of styles is proving to be, really, an even affair now. Smith, despite being on his back, has been able to defend himself."

After surviving Coleman's desperate last-ditch attempt at a neck crank by countering with several hard knees from side control, Smith cruised to a unanimous decision. "The striker beats the grappler," Blatnick said. "It's the first time in the UFC that has really happened." The fight did more to change perceptions than any other in MMA history, with the exception of Royce Gracie's debut at UFC 1. It had become a given that the ground fighter would dominate. Conventional wisdom told us that there were strikers and there were grapplers. Maurice Smith threw conventional wisdom out on its ear. A striker could win in MMA, but he had to become a true mixed martial artist.

"It takes balls to stay out there in a situation like that and more heart when you know that you're going to take shots and you know you've given everything you can give," Coleman's training partner, Mark Kerr, said post-fight. It was obvious right away to perceptive fighters like Kerr that everything had changed. "It breaks my heart what happened to Mark tonight. I've got one more tournament and then I'd like a superfight. Change is what it's all about. If I don't evolve I become extinct."[103]

No one discipline, no matter how powerful or deadly, was going to cut it going forward. By combining their talents and skills, Frank Shamrock and Maurice Smith had changed the sport forever, creating the cross-trained fighter and making willingness to learn as important as physical ability in determining who would win a fight.

"It changed the course of what seemed to be a runaway train in that ground fighters had dominated the UFC completely up until that point, with Gracie winning with jiu-jitsu and Coleman and Severn winning with wrestling. In people's minds back then it was perceived that ground fighting could not be beaten by stand-up fighting," Pride announcer Stephen Quadros said. This wasn't a case of striking overcoming grappling. This was something much larger, but it took time for people to come to grips with the new landscape of the sport. "They had yet to realize that the hybrid athlete was soon to arrive, an athlete who had to know all styles rather than just jumping from system to system depending on what the flavor of the month was."[104]

Smith was 35 and his career as a fighter had peaked. He would never again reach the heights he achieved at UFC 14, and would soon lose his title to Randy Couture. But he had helped open the door for the first true hybrid fighter to dominate the sport and change everything. Frank Shamrock was on his way to the UFC.

10
FRANK SHAMROCK AND THE ALLIANCE

The computer monitor flying through the air got Frank Shamrock's attention. You'd imagine it would. Ken Shamrock was furious, which was nothing new. He spent much of his life angry and flying off the handle. But this was serious.

"He came into the gym all 'roid-raged out and threw a computer monitor at me and freaked out," Frank said. "He screamed at everybody, and screamed at me, and I realized then that nothing I could do or would do was going to make it work."

The Lion's Den had fallen apart when Ken left MMA to join Vince McMahon's traveling WWF circus. He had left things in the hands of Frank and his top student, Jerry Bohlander. Frank had been the lead instructor at the school for some time anyway, and was better than Ken at communicating the ideas they were trying to impart to young fighters. The problems started when Frank began questioning the techniques and training regime that Ken had installed years earlier.

"I was there that day. Ken can say whatever he wants, that was his fault. I walked in and Ken was freaking out on Frank because Pete [Williams] was a little bit heavy," Lion's Den fighter Mikey Burnette said. "But Pete had a tendency to be heavy. Frank had fought over in Japan against [Japanese pro wrestler Kiyoshi] Tamura, who didn't have the name as a real fighter that he has today. Frank went to a decision with Tamura, a draw, and Ken fucking flips out on him. That goes back to being on the road [with the WWF]. I don't know what all he was on, but he was crazy. He blamed everything on Frank, but I don't think that's what it was.

These guys [in the Lion's Den] were staying in the limelight and fighting, and Ken was battling with doing pro wrestling. And I think he took it out on Frank."

Several tough losses in Pancrase and a brutal battle with John Lober in SuperBrawl left the younger Shamrock doubting the Lion's Den method. Visiting fighter Maurice Smith was also opening his mind to the dedication and commitment necessary to be a true professional fighter.

Frank said, "I really believed in the art of fighting. It made sense to me after a few years, and I studied hard and trained hard. I didn't believe you had to be an arrogant asshole who beats everybody up. I really felt like it was an art form, and you could train in the art, and enhance your life, and help other people. It wasn't about being the toughest guy in the world; it was about being the best technician. And that's what I tried to teach these young guys at the Lion's Den. But with Ken being the leader, you know, everyone had to be tough; everyone had to be cocky and mean. I left because I wanted to prove, to myself and to the rest of the world, that you didn't have to be a knucklehead to be good. That's not what it's really about."

Having his authority questioned was not something Ken was used to or willing to accept. Ken had made Frank what he was, Ken and their adopted father, Bob Shamrock. Frank was never going to be anybody, and needed to content himself with training students in Ken's methods and doing his best to prepare others for big fights. Frank was never going to be a world champion in his own right, and had no business disregarding Ken's training regime.

Ken said, "He didn't like the way I ran things. I'm the boss and I built this on my blood, sweat, and tears. This is what I've built and he has to recognize that. He is where he is because I gave him that opportunity. My dad took him from where he was at and gave him an opportunity to live in my house for two years. Frank needs to step back and ask himself, 'Why am I so successful?' Yeah, he has good ability, but someone had to teach him, someone had to give him the opportunity, someone had to give him a new life to get where he is. I didn't ask for much from him, just that he would take responsibility and do what I asked him as far as running the gym."[105]

While Frank was planning an exit strategy, the UFC was planning a big show in Japan. They already had well-known names like Maurice Smith and some native fighters from shoot-style wrestling in Yoji Anjo and

Kazushi Sakuraba. But they needed another big name in Japan to make sure the audience there was primed and ready for their show. "I decided I was going to leave right around the time the UFC gave me a call," Frank said. "They said, 'We need somebody who's an established star in Japan, because we're going into the Japanese market.'" The UFC was crowning a new champion that night in the middleweight (now called lightheavyweight) division. On one side of the Octagon would be former Olympian and former Extreme Fighting champion Kevin Jackson, who had dominated the competition in a middleweight tournament at UFC 14. Former King of Pancrase Frank Shamrock seemed a perfect choice for his opponent, but Shamrock was coming off some high-profile losses. To earn his place in the title fight, he would first have to beat tough Japanese star Enson Inoue.

FRANK'S TOUGHEST FIGHT

Enson Inoue is a legend in his own right, not because of his modest 11–8 record, but because of the way he approaches the fight game. He's like Frank Shamrock in a way, interested in fighting for the experience he gains testing himself against another man. Fearless in the ring, Inoue never tries to avoid his opponent's strengths. He prefers to face them head-on. Shamrock said, "I knew quite a bit about Enson. We grew up in similar circumstances in the fight game. It was a big fight for me, not only for the fight itself, but because the winner was going to fight Kevin Jackson [to be the] first middleweight champion in the UFC. There was a lot riding on that fight. When I took it, I knew how difficult it would be."

It was a Gracie-trained black belt in Brazilian jiu-jitsu taking on the Lion's Den elite. The first matchup of its kind since Ken and Royce had put the crowd to sleep at UFC 5 in Charlotte. Everyone at the time expected a ground battle for the ages. Instead, it was a stand-up war.

Shamrock said, "I saw his style and I saw his game, but I thought I could beat him by way of attrition and also with my clinch fighting, which I had developed shortly before that [with Maurice Smith]. Enson is the toughest guy I've ever fought, and I say that because, at my best, he came the closest to beating me, or having the opportunity to beat me."

To be honest, the first round of the fight was less than scintillating. Scoring on points, Shamrock took the round with five minutes of tepid ground and pound and two minutes of leg kicks to the prone Inoue. It's in the second round that the feeling out process was complete and the action picked up. If you've never grappled, it may be hard to appreciate Shamrock's persistent defense in this fight. Inoue took the mount, and Shamrock held him close for five solid minutes, preventing Inoue from doing significant damage. Inoue tried every trick in the book, but Shamrock maintained an iron grip on Inoue's back. Looking back, it ranks with Maurice Smith's textbook hand control against Mark Coleman as the definitive ground defense of the '90s.

When he was finally able to reverse Inoue, Shamrock had the bigger, stronger man right where he wanted him. Although Inoue was a hard puncher with dangerous looping combinations, Shamrock's new training partner Maurice Smith had him ready.

"I expected and encouraged the stand-up fight. I was just getting my striking down, just starting to understand it," Shamrock said. "My distance wasn't correct yet, and Enson does have good, flowing combinations of strikes, but I noticed a weakness in his style in the clinch game, so I prepared pretty heavily for that."

Shamrock stayed true to his game plan, despite a withering Inoue attack. In the clinch, he looked to knee and kick the leg, never trying for the takedown that in the past would have been his first option. "All of my techniques were designed to neutralize the ground game, close the distance on the stand-up, and fight on the inside where I knew he lacked conditioning and power," Shamrock said. "When I fought Enson, he was 208 pounds and I was 190 pounds. Every time he hit me he knocked me all the way across the ring."

Eventually, the strikes in the clinch journeyed north, targeting the head instead of the legs and bodies. Sometimes it's the accumulation of blows that ends a fight. On this night, it was, instead, the proverbial shot on the button. Inoue toppled to the mat, unconscious and unaware of the chaos that followed.

The referee began a ten-count, but it looked to be perfunctory. Inoue was out cold. But the count never made it past two, because Inoue's younger brother Egan came sprinting across the ring to tackle a stunned Shamrock to the ground.

"That was straight out of pro wrestling. I had never seen or experienced anything like that. I understand his position, he was scared for his brother and it happened," Shamrock said. "That was another eye-opener. I was ready for a second fight. I thought it was going to keep going, and I was going to keep fighting, because I was in that mode. Maurice came in and kind of settled it down, TK [Tsuyoshi Kohsaka] came in, Enson's team spilled in there, and I thought we're going to have us a good old-fashioned melee. Luckily we didn't, and everybody calmed down. There was so much energy in that fight, and so much emotion, that I think everybody just sort of lost their minds for a minute."

THE END OF AN ERA

Lion's Den teammate Jerry Bohlander was crushed when the news leaked out that Frank would be fighting Kevin Jackson for the title in Japan. It was a fight he thought he was going to be offered due to his UFC 12 tournament win. He felt betrayed. Frank wasn't just his training partner — the two were actually roommates. "It wouldn't have been such a big deal, but he was doing it behind my back," Bohlander said. "I was loyal to the UFC, but they weren't loyal to me . . . when one of your best friends stabs you in the back, that's always tough, but when they take something you've earned, it's tough to deal with that."[106] Shamrock says it was in the UFC's best interest to use him instead of Bohlander. He had the bigger name in Japan. Besides, he didn't swoop in to steal Bohlander's shot, the UFC came to him. "I don't know if Jerry believes that, or that's his story, or whatever the heck it is," Frank said. "I was his trainer and coach for years and years and years. I gave anything and everything I could for those guys."

It wasn't Jerry's reaction that Frank had to be concerned about. Bob Shamrock handled all the business arrangements for the Den fighters. When he called the UFC to check on the status of Frank's contract for the Jackson fight, he was told that Frank had asked that the contract be sent directly to him. Like all Den fighters, Frank paid Ken 15 percent of all his fight income. Now he wasn't just questioning orders, he was trying to take his career into his own hands. When Bob called Ken, his son was almost beside himself with rage.

"I said and did things I shouldn't have, as everyone else did, but I hoped it would be a stern wake-up call for all of us. We needed to get back to how things were, reacquire the fire," Ken said. "Instead of that happening, Frank left the next day. He packed up his stuff, threw it into the back of the car I had given him, and was gone."[107]

Frank said, "When I left, Ken was really unhappy and he told them all that they couldn't train or associate with me. They made me leave my family, my entire community, and everything else behind. What's funny about the whole Shamrock family is that it's like they're a little cult or a little mafia or something: 'If you leave the family you can no longer talk to anybody.' I come from a broken home, so I didn't think that was how family and life and relationships worked. It was really hard for me to leave, but, in hindsight, when I left I realized it was the best thing I ever did. Because you can't live in weird communities like that, where people threaten to take their love away from you and not recognize you as a family member anymore. That's just weird."

"I felt really bad for Frank because for the first time in his life he had a family: us. The Lion's Den," Mikey Burnette said. "When he left, I know he went through some hard times, and I know he went through some bad situations. He asked me to leave with him, but I was in a position where I just couldn't. I was fixing to have a kid, fixing to have a UFC fight."

Frank wasn't just walking away from a gym. He was walking away from his whole life. Guys he had spent his best years with weren't allowed to mingle with him because Ken had forbidden it.

Frank said, "They were the best years of my life. But nobody asks me how good those times were because no one cares. Everybody asks me why I left, and how bad those times were. Truth is, Guy Mezger slept in my bed and I cooked him breakfast every morning when I trained him. And Guy Mezger was my brother; somebody I would have laid down my life for. But when I left the Lion's Den, Guy Mezger turned his back on me, too. You can look at it any way you want to. The way I look at it, they're all a bunch of wussies under Ken's thumb, and if they had the nuts they would have stood up and said, 'Wait a minute. Frank gave me a part of his life. We owe something to Frank.' Instead, they all turned tail and ran and pretended like, 'I can't do anything, woe is me.' It's all or none. You're in or you're out. And I think, for a lot of people, what's the basic human desire? It's to be a part of something. Ken's a force of nature. He's a star. He has an enormous ego and an enormous drive and will to win. A lot of people appreciate that. And I appreciated that. He was my leader and my mentor. I thought the truth was a little askew in that world. It was just a little bit off. I felt like I had to go find the truth."

THE CHAMPION

The truth was that Frank Shamrock was the best fighter in the world. "Frank was probably the best of all of us; he had the most potential," Burnette said. "Very strong, very athletic, very strong mind. No one would have ever known that if he hadn't left. Ken would have never let him fight in the UFC. It was an ego thing. Ken had problems with everybody who was doing well with their career if it got to a point where they might be doing better than he was. He was weird about it. He wanted everybody to do good, but not better than him."

Ken had told Frank that he would never be a champion. That couldn't have been further from the truth. He beat Olympic gold medalist Kevin Jackson by arm bar in only 16 seconds to become the first light heavyweight champion. What followed was as dominant a run as the sport had ever seen. Shamrock was thriving in his new alliance with Maurice Smith. He was learning to grow, not just as a martial artist, but as a man.

"For me it was a lifesaver, because I was really depressed. I came from a broken home, and I've always had problems retaining a family and losing family figures, so it was really, really hard for me," Shamrock said. "The thing about Maurice is that he's an open book. He is who he is. He was always forthright and honest, and he never asked me for anything. He never asked me to sell my soul in any way, or to be a different person because of what he believed in. He tells me, 'Frankie you are what you are and you do what you do. Don't worry about it.' So it was huge for me. I think it really saved me as an athlete, because you need a teacher and a mentor to guide you properly, and he was that guy."

Inside the ring, Shamrock was becoming something special. He already had the base in submission, and he was adding striking skills every day in the gym. He beat Extreme Challenge champion Igor Zinoviev in 22 seconds at UFC 16, rising star Jeremy Horn by knee bar at UFC 17, and beat a submission out of John Lober at UFC Brazil to avenge a loss. Shamrock was head-and-shoulders above everyone else. He was the best.

"Oh yeah, bar none," Shamrock said. "I think I had a competitive edge on everybody. I was studying the arts. Everybody else was out there fighting and trying to get tougher. I was truly studying the art form, and seeing where the weaknesses in the technical and structural systems were. I was just a student. I came at it from a student's standpoint. I could just look at

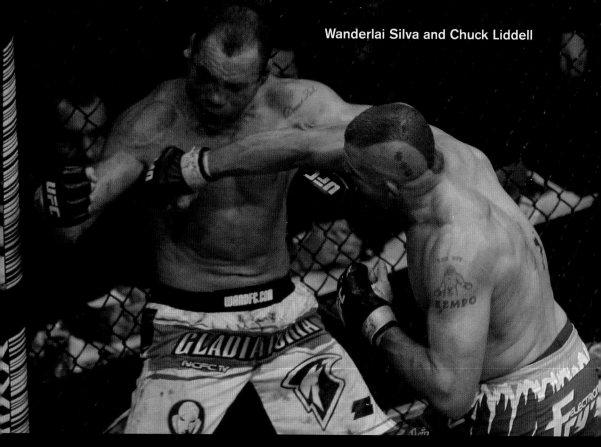

Wanderlai Silva and Chuck Liddell

Carlos Gracie, Sr.

Hélio Gracie

Rickson Gracie and
Masakatsu Funaki

Karl Gotch and Masahiko Kimura

Tae Kwon Do's Choi Hong-Hi and
black belt Chuck Norris

Ernesto Hoost (right) and Semmy Schilt

Art Jimmerson stepping into the ring

Ken Shamrock and Tito Ortiz

Bob Shamrock (standing)

Ken Shamrock and Don Frye

Frank Shamrock
and Cung Le

UFC founder Bob Meyrowitz (left)

Former UFC commentator
Jim Brown

Minoru Suzuki and Takashi Iizuka

Bas Rutten

Frank Fertitta III, Dana White and Lorenzo Fertitta

Big John McCarthy
refereeing

Akira Maeda

Muhammad Ali and Antonio Inoki

Tank Abbott and Hidehiko Yoshida

Carlos Newton and Pat Miletich

a guy, watch him move for like five minutes, and go, 'Okay, that's how you beat him.'"

TITO VS. THE LION'S DEN

Tito Ortiz had run roughshod over Frank's former Lion's Den teammates. Wins over Bohlander and Mezger made Ortiz the top contender, but his screaming match with Ken Shamrock made him a star. The UFC was pushing his title fight with Frank at UFC 22, on September 24, 1999, as a grudge match. Frank is all about business, so he played it up. But this was not a bitter battle. As the two filmed a tense stare-down, there were plenty of laughs behind the scenes, especially when the smaller Shamrock needed a stool to get eye-to-eye with Ortiz.

"I didn't care. I thought it was a great study for me, tape-wise," Shamrock said. "My personal opinion was that they should have changed their training. After a while, they were easy to beat. Everything works, but nothing works for long. Their training became commonplace, and the specialness of knowing the information went away. Tito and I were actually friends; we talked about the match beforehand and how we could play it [the feud] out."

Inside the Octagon, Shamrock knew that Ortiz would be the biggest challenge of his career — literally. Shamrock was a natural for the 185-pound or even the 170-pound division. Walking around, he was well below the then 200-pound limit. Ortiz, on the other hand, was monstrous. He was 6'2", a good four inches taller than the champion, and his weight once he rehydrated would be closer to 225 pounds than 200. His size was a challenge in itself, and he knew how to use it to keep his opponent down and beat him until he quit. Shamrock knew that he would be at a disadvantage physically, except for his lungs and his heart. He would have to win this fight with his work ethic and willpower.

"I felt at the time that there was a huge misunderstanding of vascular conditioning. And I also knew that, in his heart, Tito was a bully," Shamrock said. "He was getting by on being the bigger, stronger, bullying type of fighter. I knew that if I picked the pace and set it, and had vascular conditioning above and beyond what he could maintain, I could really just wear him out."

Shamrock was training for a long fight. If he couldn't submit Ortiz early, he knew he could beat him in the later rounds. For all his skills, Ortiz had never had to fight in those two extra championship rounds. The difference between 15 minutes and 25 minutes was going to mean everything in this fight.

Frank's training partner, Bob Cook, said, "At that point in time, Frank's game plan was to go out and put some pressure on him [Ortiz]. He'd either submit him real early when they were still dry, or keep him working constantly, never let him rest, and try to break him in the later rounds by upping the pressure. Get his cardio to fail and break him mentally. Which is eventually what he did. At the time, he was probably the most well-rounded, highly trained professional fighter in the world, regardless of weight. From a technical standpoint and everything else, [Frank] was extremely impressive."

The fight went as expected. Ortiz wore himself out in the early rounds, while Shamrock focused on spurts of action at the beginning and end of each round.

"The rest of it was just stylistic. I never used moves that cost energy, and I never resisted his power or strength. I flowed around him and let him run the race," Shamrock said. His was a victory of the arts and of physical science over physical strength. "Fifty percent of that was done in the gym, the other half was done on the track and field, and on the tread-mill, with plyometric conditioning. I knew I had to be faster and more explosive so I could push the pace without staying in front and taking the damage."

In the end, Ortiz lay exhausted in the middle of the Octagon, unable to find the energy to defend himself from a relentless Shamrock attack. At 19:42, the referee stopped the fight. Frank Shamrock had defended his title in the Octagon for the last time. He retired in the ring after the fight. There were no more hurdles to leap, at least none that he would be willing to con-quer for what SEG could pay him.

"They had their financial problems, and Bob [Meyrowitz] was very up front about them. I took a pay cut to fight Tito," Shamrock said. "I also saw the future of the sport, and at that time the future was that the sport was going to die. And I knew it. When I fought Tito, I put in the 'retirement clause,' as it is now known, and I retired at the end. Because I knew we weren't going anywhere. There's no sense in me going out there and crippling myself and jeopardizing my brain when no one is going to see it and no one is going to care."

He left his belt behind, and a legacy as one of the greatest champions in the sport's history. Shamrock had a falling out with the current owners of the UFC, and President Dana White, and you rarely hear his name on UFC programming. Like many of the older fighters, Shamrock is being erased from official UFC history. But no one who saw him fight could ever forget: Frank Shamrock stood alone in the late '90s as the best fighter in the sport.

11
GRACIE VS. SAKU

Pride fighting had been built by betraying the myth of the unbeatable Japanese pro wrestler. These fighters had long represented themselves and their art as the strongest in the world. The Gracies had shown them to be liars. And one young pro wrestler wanted revenge.

Kazushi Sakuraba had started as a protégé of Pride's founding star, Nobuhiko Takada. Sakuraba was a gifted young wrestler, a technical wizard both in the professional ring and in the dojo when the grappling matches were real. Sakuraba had an amateur pedigree. He had finished fourth in the All-Japan Collegiate Championships during his senior year at Chuo University. "I was an amateur wrestler before becoming a pro wrestler. In the case of amateur wrestling, there was no spectator. All I had to think about was my win and my team's win. That's all," Sakuraba said. When he graduated, he intended to follow in the footsteps of the legendary Satoru Sayama, better known as Tiger Mask. "I joined U-Inter [UWF-I] as a pro wrestler, where I had to think about attracting a lot of spectators to make a living."[108]

Sakuraba seemed to lack the necessary charisma to make it as a pro wrestling headliner, and wasn't destined for stardom. He toiled on the undercard of the UWF-I, and later, Kingdom. Shoot-style wrestling was dying in Japan, but his time spent as a pro wrestler, and, more importantly, his involvement in failed organizations, helped to form his fighting style. It was a style that focused more on entertaining than winning.

"It was good for me that the fans were gone and I lost the group I belonged to," Sakuraba said. "I always keep that experience in mind, and try to give the fans a good show, a fight that remains, in their minds, the most impressive fight compared to other fights. Otherwise, I can't establish my name in kakutogi [fighting] and I can't make a living, either."[109]

Sakuraba made his fighting debut with the UFC when it journeyed to Japan in December 1997. It was a tremendously controversial fight. Sakuraba was on the receiving end of some strong punches from former Extreme Fighting champion Conan Silviera. When he suddenly dropped, referee Big John McCarthy thought he had been knocked out. But replays showed that Sakuraba was clearly dropping down for an ankle pick. It was a bad stoppage, and Sakuraba didn't handle it with grace. He camped out in the Octagon, and refused to leave for almost an hour. The fight would eventually be ruled a no contest. When Silviera's scheduled opponent for the tournament finale couldn't continue, Sakuraba was simply inserted in his place. In this impromptu rematch, Sakuraba beat a deflated Silviera by arm bar.

With his strange debut behind him, it was time for Sakuraba to join Takada in Pride. While his mentor struggled, Sakuraba excelled. He won a series of exciting fights, beating Lion's Den mainstay Vernon White and the ever-exciting Canadian up-and-comer Carlos Newton.

"That is what's so cool about being in Pride from the beginning," Pride announcer and MMA legend Bas Rutten said. He had seen Sakuraba from the very beginning of his rise to the top. "It started when he knee-barred Carlos Newton [at Pride 3 on June 24, 1998]. And it was actually funny, because before the fight I went to Newton in the dressing room and interviewed him. I'd never met him, but for some reason we had a good connection right away. So we started rolling around, and he suddenly attacked me from the back. While he held me from the back in a bear hug, I rolled over and got him in a knee bar. He looked at me and I said, 'You better watch out, because Sakuraba is really good with knee bars.' Then he got caught in a knee bar. A week later, Carlos Newton moved into the dojo and lived with us for three months."

Sakuraba was innovating a new style of fighting, wowing the crowd with cartwheel guard passes, flying stomps, and pro wrestling–style chops. After dismantling a number of Brazilian fighters, like Ebeneezer Braga, Alan Goes, and Vitor Belfort, Sakuraba was ready for his first main event. The fans were starting to get behind him, and other fighters were studying his matches to try to copy his innovative techniques. Mark Kerr said, "I think Sakuraba is the best technician in the world. It seems that he is doing technique from a different point of view than ordinary people. For example, in the fight with Vitor Belfort his motion was new to me. Sakuraba held Vitor's leg from above and kicked it, at the same time preventing him from counter kicking. That was ingenious . . . I think Sakuraba is a perfect fighter who is creative, doesn't depend on power, and is fighting with intelligence."[110]

The Belfort win really put Sakuraba in the spotlight, especially in Belfort's native Brazil. But he would need all of his intellect and creativity for his next fight, against the technical sensation Royler Gracie, the first of many Gracies he would face. The fight took place at Pride 8, on November 21, 1999. It was the first in a series of battles that would help Pride explode in popularity and profitability.

"The Sakuraba–Gracie rivalry is bigger than mixed martial arts. It goes back further than mixed martial arts, to when Kimura went to Brazil and fought Hélio Gracie," Pride judge and MMA trainer Matt Hume said. "There's been a Japan–Gracie rivalry since before Pride was around, and before the Gracies that are currently fighting in Pride were born. So when Sakuraba fought the Gracies, that was a continuation of things that had already been going on."[111]

THE GRACIE CHALLENGE

Royler Gracie was just 150 pounds, but on the mat he was as skilled as any man alive. He won his weight class at the prestigious Abu Dhabi grappling tournament three years in a row, and was a former Brazilian jiu-jitsu world champion. More importantly at the time, he was also a member of the legendary Gracie family. That alone would have earned him his spot at the top of the card. Despite revelations that Hélio and Carlson had lost matches in Brazil, the modern-era Gracie fighters were still undefeated. They had an invincible aura, and even though he outweighed Gracie by 30 pounds, Saku (Sakuraba's nickname in Japan) was a decided underdog. He was a grappler himself, so his strengths were Gracie's strengths, as well. And who could be stronger than Royler Gracie on the mat?

"I have nothing to prove to anyone. I have, however, a great desire to test myself," Royler said. "I really wanted to fight Sakuraba, not only because he is heavier than me, but also because he is such a good fighter and strategist.

I wanted to find out how I was going to behave against a larger opponent of such high caliber."[112]

Gracie was unable to get Sakuraba to engage him on the ground. Instead, Saku used his superior striking and legendary kicks to the leg of his butt-scooting opponent to punish Gracie. After 26 minutes, Sakuraba was able to lock on a Kimura hold (the arm lock made famous by Japanese judo legend Masahiko Kimura). It was the ultimate indignity. Royler became the first Gracie in the modern age to lose, and it was due to the same hold his father had fallen victim to in his famous fight with the Japanese Judoka Kimura 50 years earlier. The Gracie corner was livid. Royler had never actually tapped out. The referee stopped the fight when it appeared that Gracie's arm would break. Gracie and his corner were convinced that he would have never quit the fight of his own volition. Gracie's flexibility was incredible, and apparently he wasn't even in pain because of the hold.

"That son of a bitch hits hard," Gracie joked after the fight. "Some of his kicks to my shin sent an electric current up my body. And they stopped the fight because of my shoulder? I hurt everywhere except my shoulder!"[113]

He could joke about it over time, but the Gracie family had suffered its first significant loss in decades. No one was smiling.

"I am really disappointed in the referee's decision over that, because it was inappropriate for the referee to stop the fight without Royler giving up and with only one minute left," Rickson Gracie said. Rickson was unimpressed with Sakuraba's cautious game plan, feeling he was not fighting with everything he had. "Every time Sakuraba asked him [Royler] to stand up, he got up and got beat up like a man. And every time Royler called Sakuraba to the ground . . . Sakuraba stayed up, like a chicken. So that shows no heart for Sakuraba. I'm disappointed in Sakuraba's spirit."[114]

As the Gracies continued their protest in the ring, Sakuraba took the microphone to address the crowd. Sakuraba said, "I kind of suspected he was going to complain after the fight. But I didn't know what to say or do, or how to react . . . I was thinking, 'Okay, you didn't tap out, but how come you couldn't escape?' So I told the audience I would like to fight his brother Rickson, please."[115] Sakuraba was normally very respectful of his opponents after a fight. But Rickson's critiques had angered him. The Gracies were making excuses and trying to take away his glory.

"If the enemy rejects the ground, I would take him down by tackle," he

said at the post-fight press conference. "Why didn't he do so? May I intro-
duce him to a good coach? His tackle was . . . like a girl's one . . . Mr. Royler,
how are you feeling? I took no damage, so I could restart training
tomorrow. Please say hello to your brother."

Pride Grand Prix

Rickson wasn't interested in fighting Sakuraba, despite the taunts. Not
only was Saku really good, he was also not the money draw Rickson
wanted in an opponent. He would fight Pancrase legend Masakatsu
Funaki instead. It would be up to Royce Gracie to settle the score for the
family at the Pride Openweight Grand Prix, held on two nights, January
30 and May 1, 2000. Royler's loss lit a fire under Royce, who was returning
to MMA action for the first time in five years. The Gracies had been the
top MMA fighters in the world for decades, and they were not willing to
yield the crown to the young Japanese star just yet.

Pride was putting its best fighters, regardless of weight class, into a 16-
man single-elimination tournament. Royce and Sakuraba were on the same
side of the bracket. Gracie advanced by beating Nobuhiko Takada in a list-
less match that featured Takada in full Ken Shamrock mode, simply
fighting to survive. Gracie would get a chance at Sakuraba if the Japanese
star could get past Lion's Den fighter, and former King of Pancrase, Guy
Mezger.

Mezger said, "Pride has their own agenda. They brought me in there to
lose to Sakuraba, and he'd enter the tournament to fight Royce Gracie. I was
a fly in the ointment, because I beat him and the best they could do was
make a draw out of it." Guy had proven a tough task for Sakuraba, outwrestling him and winning the striking battle standing. "I had been out of
action for four months because of a kidney problem. I actually hadn't
trained much, so originally I told them I wouldn't fight. But they threw so
much money at me that I finally said 'Okay, I'll fight.' For that much money,
I could have two broken limbs and I would say, 'Throw me in there.' But
because I had literally only been training for two weeks, I said, 'I can't go for
more than 15 minutes. I can fight anybody for 15 minutes, but I can't go further than that.' So the contract was for 15 minutes, and they would have to
render a decision one way or the other. But since I beat him, they couldn't
do that. So they called it a draw and wanted me to do another round. But

that wasn't in the contract. That's the way they rolled, I guess."

In Mezger's corner, Ken Shamrock threw a fit that made the Gracie conniption after Royler's loss look tame. Pride officials were demanding another round, even though the contract called for a single 15-minute round and then a decision.

Mezger said, "There's a side of me that's a smart guy who can figure things out and is a good business man; and then there's a side of me that's a blockheaded, egotistical fighter who thinks he can fight anybody. And that guy was telling Ken, 'Listen, I can knock this guy out.' But he was like, 'Nah, dude. They're fucking you and we're not going to put up with it. You made an agreement, it's in the contract, and that's the way it is. It's their fault, not yours. You did what you came here to do, and they need to honor their end of the deal.' And I listen to my coach. We've dealt with the Japanese on a lot of this kind of stuff, and they have an interesting sense of honor. It's not quite the way we think of things. It's not right or wrong, it's like comparing apples and oranges. They would turn around and screw you out of money or something like that, and then, when you'd get upset and threaten to leave the company, they just couldn't understand it. . . . It would totally shock them that you would want to do that. Sometimes, it was just differences of society. It was weird, and dealing with them was often a frustrating experience."

THE 90-MINUTE MAN

When Mezger decided to refuse to fight another round, Sakuraba moved on in the tournament by way of forfeit. He would get a shot at the undefeated Royce Gracie in a tournament match with special rules. The Gracies were still upset about how the Royler fight had gone down and insisted on special rules for Royce's fight with Sakuraba. There would be no time limits, just an endless number of 15-minute rounds. The referee could not stop the fight. Only the corner or the fighter himself could stop the contest.

The Gracies were prima donnas, but their demands seemed reasonable. Royler's loss was unacceptable, and Royce, more so than Rickson or Renzo, needed time for his style to be effective. "I think Royce has great potential. What he needs is time to 'cook' his opponents," Rickson said before the fight. "Royce doesn't have the aggressive style to maintain the pressure, impress the judges, or make a quick fight. . . . So if he has the time he needs. . . . I don't see a problem for him."[116]

Sakuraba set the tone for the evening with what would become one of his trademarks — a flashy entrance. Three masked men entered the ring and faced off with Gracie. When the announcer finally yelled out, "Sakuraba!" he pulled off his mask and revealed his red-dyed hair. The crowd went crazy, and his bravado made it clear that he wasn't intimidated by Gracie's fearsome reputation. Now he just had to live up to his entrance.

"I thought it would be embarrassing if I lost so easily after such an extravagant display," Sakuraba said. He was angry that the Gracies had insisted on special rules for the fight. Why, he wondered, did Royce Gracie deserve such special treatment? "They made a lot of demands about the rules before the fight. It annoyed me, so I tried to make fun of them a little bit."[117]

Gracie started the fight very aggressively, showing he had used his five-year layoff to improve his striking technique. Sakuraba was unimpressed, and often looked to the camera and mocked Gracie's efforts.

"I went in to beat him [in the first round] and it didn't happen. When I got to my corner I got pissed and it became a personal thing for me," Gracie said. "I knew we were going to the end. He was brave, and so was I, and we were going to see this through, no matter how long it took."[118]

Both nearly secured submissions early, with Sakuraba grabbing a knee bar and Royce a guillotine choke. But the key to the fight was Royce's ineffective stand-up and inability to get Sakuraba on the ground.

"Royce was standing on the left side, so I knew powerful punches would only come from the right. I didn't suffer any damage from his punches," Sakuraba said. When Gracie came out so aggressively and Sakuraba found his punches to be weak, he was more confident than ever that he would win out over the long haul. "He was so excited, and he just pushed me to the rope. I hoped he would run out of stamina. The brain doesn't work properly without stamina because of a lack of oxygen. I was saving energy to avoid that condition."[119]

Sakuraba was using Gracie's own modified rules against him. Ironically, had there been a time limit and a judge's decision after 30 minutes, Gracie would likely have been declared the winner. It was only after he had tired Gracie out that Sakuraba turned up the pressure. He was able to use Gracie's gi as a weapon against the Brazilian, pulling it over his head and grabbing him by the seat of the pants to control his movement.

"It was Royce's mistake in strategy. It is ridiculous to fight in gi in Vale Tudo. It is to Sakuraba's advantage. Moreover, he shouldn't have fought with Sakuraba in a standing position," former UFC middleweight champion Murillo Bustamante said. "If I were him, I would have fought in a different way. Royce should focus on more weight training, to build up his muscle so he can get power. He has good technique, but he should build up more muscle and enhance his body function. If his body was stronger, he could fight better."[120]

Sakuraba put on a clinic for the last hour of the fight, landing punches and Mongolian chops from the guard and blasting away at Gracie's legs with standing kicks. The kicks would be the turning point of the fight.

"There was no problem until I got hurt on the left instep. In the sixth round, when I was lying on my back, he kicked my left instep twice in exactly the same place," Gracie said. He had a fervent conversation with his corner between rounds. "I just told them about the pain. I wanted to make them understand that my leg was in so much pain that I couldn't move as they demanded."[121]

True to their word, the Gracies did not need the referee to decide that their fighter had taken enough punishment. "Royce said that his leg was in pain, so my father and I discussed it and came to the decision [throwing in the towel]. If I had asked him to fight in the next round, he would have done it, I am sure. But it is not right to make him do it in that condition," his older brother and coach Rorion Gracie said. "The Gracie family won't give up, but at the same time we are not stupid. . . . It was not the right decision to continue the fight more than that. We temporarily did 'give-up' that day for a further fight at a different time. You shouldn't mix courage with stubbornness . . . there is no excuse. Sakuraba was the winner."[122]

When the towel came flying in, the crowd exploded with joy. The normally docile Japanese fans were riotous. They had just seen history made, and they knew it. The two men met in the center of the ring and exchanged a few words. The torch had been passed, and Sakuraba was now the king of MMA.

Pride announcer Stephen Quadros said, "Gracie–Sakuraba was almost biblical in proportion: a 90-minute match, Kazushi defiantly turning his back on the Brazilian in the fight, ignoring Royce's up-until-then feared jiu-jitsu and a vocal reaction and tribute from the audience after the Gracie camp threw in the towel that I have yet to see matched." After fighting for 90 minutes, Sakuraba actually had to return to the ring later that night. He faced one of the most feared fighters on the planet, Russian striker Igor Vovchancyn and actually won the first ten-minute round. Then exhaustion set in, and Vovchancyn advanced to face Mark Coleman in the final fight. Coleman knocked the Russian silly with 17 knees to the head. He won the tournament and took home the $200,000 prize. Coleman was back on top as the very best heavyweight in the world. But it was Sakuraba who came out of the tournament as the consensus best fighter on the planet, regardless of weight.

"If he had not met me in the first match, he would have been the champion of the tournament," Royce Gracie said.[123] It was a sentiment shared by many.

THE GRACIE HUNTER

Sakuraba would become known as the Gracie Hunter. He had hunted down Gracie disciple Vitor Belfort, Royler, and now Royce. "That was fantastic," MMA star Don Frye said. "That was electrifying. Not for the Gracie family, but for the rest of the world and Japan. You had the greatest name in submission fighting against this unknown Japanese kid. He came to fight, and fight he did. And the Gracies all fought, but a couple of them just couldn't keep up with this kid."

The fans were intrigued, and Sakuraba became a star who could fill buildings with people and get them to tune in on television. "Sakuraba took a couple of years [to become a star in Japan]," Dave Meltzer said. "Really, beating Royce is what put Sakuraba on the map."

Next on his list was Renzo Gracie, a very different kind of fighter. While Hélio's sons Royler and Royce relied on a traditional jiu-jitsu attack, Renzo adopted a different approach. He was more aggressive and incorporated more striking in his arsenal.

"Renzo attacks with not only jiu-jitsu and amateur wrestling but also a mix of other kakutogi. I am looking forward to the fight, because he is one of the fighters I have been eager to fight with. To my knowledge, we are the same weight. I am satisfied with him as my opponent. By comparison, based on an attack, I think a fighter who can do anything is stronger. In this sense, Renzo is stronger than Royce, I think. He is versatile and doesn't stick to one thing. He tries to take a lot of things in and turn them into his own," Sakuraba said. "I want to have an interesting fight with him. It will be fine, of course, if I win as a result. I really feel that we will be able to have a good fight. But it will be embarrassing if it becomes a boring fight, contrary to expectations. So come and see the fight without any expectations! You will feel as if you have gained an extra bonus if the fight is interesting."[124]

Renzo was thrilled at the opportunity to re-establish the Gracie name as the preeminent name in all of MMA. "Kazushi Sakuraba was a stone in our shoes. He was one of the most amazing fighters who came from Japan, and most amazing was his ability to play smart," Gracie said. "He was able to adapt himself and to figure out ways to break his opponents. He was very successful at what he did."[125]

The fight, at Pride 10 on August 27, 2000, was an even and fast-paced exchange of techniques. With time almost expired, Sakuraba caught Gracie in his favorite hold, the Kimura. Gracie refused to tap, and the referee stopped the fight after Gracie's arm was dislocated. Through it all, he never screamed out or even grimaced. It was an amazing display of heart and will. "To be honest, I even enjoyed that moment. Because I was plenty conscious of what was going on and I didn't give up," Gracie said. "I saw the ligaments going and I heard them, one by one, giving way. And I embraced that as punishment for the mistake I had made. I really believed I could keep fighting, even without the arm."[126]

Although Gracie hadn't tapped out, he understood the reason for the stoppage. The officials couldn't allow him to continue with a badly damaged arm. He handled the loss with grace. "Many people make excuses when they lose," he told the Japanese fans. "I have only one. He was better than me tonight."

The Final Challenge

Sakuraba had only one more Gracie left to defeat. Ryan Gracie was the Gracie bad boy, a street brawler who would later stab a man in a bar fight. Ryan was most famous for sucker punching jiu-jitsu fighter Wallid Ismael in a nightclub.

Brazil was a divided country. There were people who had money and influence, and there were people who didn't. This divide was also the source of many conflicts between the rich and privileged jiu-jitsu players and the street kids who practiced *luta livre*, literally translated as free fighting, a style that relied more on stand-up fighting than on submission grappling. The

Gracies had a history of lawlessness, starting with Hélio Gracie himself. Hélio considered himself above the law, and with good reason. When he almost killed luta livre champion Manoel Rufini dos Santos in a street brawl, he was sentenced to two and a half years in prison. But he was a Gracie.

"I was never in jail. Two hours after the Supreme Court confirmed my sentence, Getúlio [the president of Brazil, Getúlio Vargas] pardoned me," Hélio said. "One of our students, Rosalina Coelho Lisboa, whose brother was an ambassador, was very close to Getúlio and intervened, saying that it was unjust for such a youngster to go to jail because of a street fight. He was a good person and pardoned me. The Supreme Court was demoralized."[127]

Ryan was continuing a long Gracie tradition of street brawling. He would also continue their tradition of losing Pride fights to Sakuraba. Ryan had blistered pro wrestler Tokimitsu Ishizawa in just two minutes, and Sakuraba paid tribute to his fallen friend by wearing his mask into the ring. Sakuraba had promised a big surprise to start the fight. "Honestly speaking, I was thinking of doing it, a pose of *The Karate Kid*, in the fight with Ryan . . . but I forgot to do it. I wondered if Ryan would be scared by my *Karate Kid* pose, wondering what would happen next."[128] Inside the ring, Sakuraba struggled to finish a defensive-minded Gracie, who was claiming an injured shoulder, but Sakuraba wasn't buying it. Whatever the reason, Ryan was fighting to survive. Sakuraba had forgotten his Daniel LaRussa impresson at the beginning of the fight, but showed his sense of humor by spanking the bad boy.

Sakuraba said, "He put his hand between his thighs. I was thinking to spank him so hard in the end, but I changed my mind to chop his butt, because it might cause trouble later if I spanked him. I thought, 'Oh, here is the butt! This guy is doing something bad.' There were only 30 seconds left at the time, so I thought it was impossible to tap him. Instead, I came up with the idea that if I spanked him, everybody would enjoy it. But I chopped him, not spanked, in order to avoid a complaint possibly coming up later like, 'Are you making a fool of me?'"[129]

The Gracie Hunter had beaten the last Gracie willing to challenge him. Rickson Gracie never agreed to a fight with the man who had forever rewritten his family history. But other challengers from Brazil would emerge. Two hungry fighters, one from luta livre and one from jiu-jitsu, would replace the Gracies in Japan as the top foreign fighters on the planet.

12

ENTER THE FERTITTAS

Bob Meyrowitz was wearing down. Five years of constant battles with cable companies, politicians, and the underpaid warriors he promoted had left him exhausted. David Isaacs said, "We were assailed on all sides. We're fighting this legal battle. We're fighting with fighters because we had to say, 'We can't pay you that, we can only pay you this.' We're fighting with cable companies because they don't want to put us on. It just felt like a fight. And we're big boys and Bob's a tough guy, but after a while you feel like you're in the fifth round of a championship fight. I had to explain to people what I did for a living, and they really looked at me like I was a pornographer. Seriously. People really were, 'You do what?' I went to Harvard and Harvard Law School, and I have to explain to those guys what I do? Barack [Obama] was in my class. I used to play basketball with Barack. Think I should tell him about Ultimate Fighting?"

seg was still confident that the ufc had hit potential. But to be a hit, the show needed to be available to the masses on pay-per-view. And to make it on pay-per-view, it needed to be approved by the two leading sanctioning bodies in the country: the New Jersey State Athletic Control Board and the Nevada State Athletic Commission. Nevada was the most powerful and influential of all the state commissions, and seg aggressively promoted the sport there.

Isaacs said, "I think the one thing people may not know is that when cable took us off the air the big thing they used as the rationale was that the event was not sanctioned by what they considered the most prestigious commission, the Nevada State

Athletic Commission. "So we were focused on Nevada. We were willing to discuss rule changes, we had other commissioners, who were pretty knowledgeable, who had already backed what we were doing. Cable told us, in no uncertain terms, that was what we needed to do to get back on the air."

Many of the recent stories from mainstream media outlets focus on the idea that the new UFC ran to sanctioning, while the old SEG-owned UFC tried to avoid it. Nothing could be further from the truth. SEG knew it needed to get sanctioned to get back on pay-per-view. They devoted thousands of dollars and significant time and mental resources to getting the sport cleared. The Nevada State Athletic Commission's executive director, Marc Ratner, had been an early and vocal UFC opponent. "They advertised no-holds-barred. No rules. Anything goes," Ratner said. "I knew as a regulator that it would never be in Nevada. You can't regulate a sport with no rules." The sport had changed significantly since those early days. They would need to prove that to convince three of the five Nevada commissioners to give them a chance to get the sport sanctioned.

On April 23, 1999, SEG made the trip to Nevada to appear before the commission. They were prepared to make their case. Isaacs said, "I remember Marc Ratner driving me around in his car. I don't mean a chauffeured limousine, I mean Marc's personal car. We were going state-to-state with a good idea of what we were trying to do and a strategy to get it sanctioned in those states. It didn't always work. In Nevada, we spent a lot of time lobbying, and there was a big discussion; if we got turned down, that would be it. We'd never be able to get into Nevada."

This meeting is especially controversial. One of the Nevada State Athletic Commissioners was Lorenzo Fertitta, a casino owner who would eventually buy the UFC. Meyrowitz has suggested that Fertitta opposed sanctioning the UFC in order to drive the price down.

"The fact is, we were scheduled to go before the Nevada State Athletic Commission," Meyrowitz said. "As we did with every athletic commission, we worked very hard to make sure everybody understood it, and everyone knew what we were doing and what we were talking about. And there was a new, young commissioner who seemed to like it, and it looked like we had all the votes we needed. And the night before, at midnight, I got a call telling me that this young commissioner decided this was just wrong for Nevada, and that it would be a big mistake for Nevada to approve it. So that commissioner changed his mind and decided to vote against it. For anyone who doesn't know, that commissioner's name was Lorenzo Fertitta."[130]

Current UFC owners Zuffa and Fertitta have attacked these claims head-on. Their contention is that there was never a vote scheduled with the NSAC.

"As far as the commission was concerned, there was never supposed to be a vote; it was only an agenda item for discussion," Fertitta said. "We had never even discussed mixed martial arts. We had never talked about it. We knew nothing about it. All of a sudden it showed up on our agenda, and, for whatever reason, people were expecting a vote, and that is just not how the process works. What you have to understand is that the reason Nevada is seen as one of the premier regulatory bodies throughout the world is because they do their homework. And that was not necessarily the time for a vote, but the time that got the ball rolling to start doing the homework. What that means is me, a fellow commissioner, and the head of the medical advisory board flew out to a UFC fight in Iowa and started collecting data relative to mixed martial arts; watching videos, reading publications, and trying to learn as much as we could about it, but I think that is where there was a little bit of a miscommunication. There was never supposed to be a vote regarding mixed martial arts."[131]

Though the agenda for the meeting included a "Presentation by SEG Sports Corporation and filing of the rules and regulations of the Mixed Martial Arts Council," current Zuffa (Italian for "scrap," Zuffa is the name of the company that purchased the UFC) vice president Marc Ratner remembers things a little differently.

"I certainly remember the meeting very well," Ratner said. "It was at city hall. Fertitta was on the commission at the time. There was no vote taken that day. It was on the agenda, but was taken off the agenda. . . . It was taken off the agenda because if they would have turned the sport down, it might have affected the sport for a long time. I think Mr. Meyrowitz and his advisors decided they'd rather not risk a vote and not get a positive result, so they took it off the agenda. There was never a vote. I can't tell you who was for or who was against, or even if it would have passed or not passed. I don't know."

Wrestling Observer editor Dave Meltzer, the sport's preeminent investigative reporter, also believes a vote was scheduled. "As the hearing approached, Meyrowitz believed that he had the votes [3–2] for sanctioning, but the night before the hearing he was informed that one of the commissioners had switched his vote," Meltzer reported in the *Observer*. "Meyrowitz withdrew his request for sanctioning because he was told that he could only ask for one vote, and a negative result would doom the company's future on pay-per-view. I don't know which commissioner it was, but the commissioner who had the 11th-hour change of mind that caused Meyrowitz to pull out was not Fertitta."

When they met with the commission, Meyrowitz and SEG, according to the minutes of the meeting, "addressed the commission regarding item number 13 on the agenda. They asked that the item be deleted from the agenda. They also invited the commissioners to attend their next live event, and then they would ask to be placed on a future agenda. Both Mr. Meyrowitz and Mr. Chwasky stated that they felt viewing a mixed martial arts event would answer some of the questions that the commission might have."

The meeting may not have ended with the UFC being sanctioned in Nevada, but it did pique the interest of Commissioner Lorenzo Fertitta. "I thought it was very interesting, but I was also a little uncomfortable with some of the brutality of it," Lorenzo Fertitta said. "After meeting [Frank Shamrock] and talking with him for a few minutes, I realized that these were not guys stepping out of a bar trying to hurt each other. They were professional athletes."[132]

Fertitta began studying jiu-jitsu with MMA fighter John Lewis in Las Vegas and continued to keep a close eye on the new sport. "He said to me, 'If you really want to learn, take the time to understand what we do,'" Fertitta said. "We met, got down on the mat, and he started showing me the different submission techniques and fighting techniques. I was intrigued. Before I knew it, I was taking private lessons in Brazilian jiu-jitsu."[133]

NEW JERSEY

Meanwhile, SEG continued its efforts to get the UFC back on television. These were dark days, indeed. Not only were the shows not available to most Americans on pay-per-view, but they also weren't available on home video. Hard-core fans would send tapes to friends in the mail. Knowing someone with a satellite dish or Direct TV was a must for any devoted fan. Fans called it the "Dark Ages," and the UFC seemed like a dying company. The sport was huge in Japan, with the emergence of Pride and the continued popularity of kickboxing promotion K-1. But it just couldn't seem to gain any traction in the United States. Then the sport found a new friend, New Jersey State Athletic Control Board Chairman Larry Hazzard. The first sanctioned event in the United States wasn't held by the UFC. It was Paul Smith's International Fighting Championships (IFC) that paved the way for MMA's big breakthrough in North America.

Hazzard said, "I met with representatives of the IFC. They gave me tapes of their events. They gave me copies of their rules and regulations. I know some of the history of the IFC. Having a background in martial arts, I understand what they're all about. I think that this form of competition got a bad rap early on, when it was being billed as 'no-holds-barred.' You know, perceptions are very real. The perception at the time was that it was street fighting for street fighting's sake. I don't think the public appreciates that kind of competition. Since they went back and really refined what the sport was about, I think it has reached greater levels of acceptance — not only in New Jersey, but also in other states. I think this is a very crucial step for them, because New Jersey has status in the combative field. If they make good here, I think this will give them a great opportunity to go other places. I simply think that people have the right to self-expression. The martial arts are a very formidable form of competition, and this is nothing more than the evolutionary stage of karate as it evolves into a more sophisticated level of competition. I think, as a public servant, we have an obligation to give the people what they want as long it fits within the framework of health, safety, and welfare being uppermost in our minds. Here in New Jersey, we take great pride in putting the competitors first. The IFC has demonstrated to us that it also concurs with our mission. It has met all of the standards as they pertain to health and safety."[134]

The show went off without a hitch, and the UFC was next in line. It ran its first sanctioned show, UFC 28, in New Jersey in November 2000. The pre-fight press conference felt like a victory party. After years of toiling before small crowds in the deep south, SEG had finally made the big time. The UFC drew a sellout of 5,000 fans, and New Jersey would become the promotion's new home territory.

"Mixed martial arts is a relatively new type of athletic competition, which I personally endorse," Larry Hazzard told the press and fighters prior to the event. "I endorse it mainly because I am very familiar with the martial arts, but this form of competition has not been accepted universally . . . I am an advocate of it, and I am an ally. So you should take it as a personal challenge to help promote this sport, because we are in the infancy stages."

A returning Randy Couture, who would take on UFC champion Kevin Randleman, headlined the show. It was a unification bout of sorts. Couture had never lost the title before departing the UFC in a contract dispute. "They actually called me and asked if I would be interested," Couture said. "I was a little leery about getting involved again . . . the UFC is still probably the most prestigious event in the United States to fight for. And therefore it's good for me to get back in there and compete."[135]

Kevin Randleman was a tough opponent for anyone. He was a two-time NCAA wrestling champion at Ohio State before running into some trouble in his senior year. Randleman was as gifted an athlete as the UFC had ever seen: explosive, fast, and powerful. He had won the UFC heavyweight title when Bas Rutten retired, but was feeling a little disrespected. Couture's opponent was initially going to be Pedro Rizzo, whom Randleman had beaten decisively. Why was the UFC looking to promote a Couture–Rizzo fight? Why wasn't the heavyweight champion contacted to fight in the promotion's major arena debut, except as an afterthought? Randleman was fired up.

"I'm not here to promote or anything. This fight is for no one but my family, my friends, Hammer House [Mark Coleman's fight team], and myself," Randleman said. "I don't want to be their champion. 'Cause the way I've been treated, I don't need a belt to prove I'm the champion. I don't need a belt to prove my worth. . . . I don't plan on doing no dancing around with Randy Couture. And I know that Randy Couture is not trying to dance around with Kevin Randleman. I know that Randy knows that I'm dangerous. I know that he knows that I'm tough, I'm strong, I'm young, and I'm in shape. We wrestled together in college. That's what people don't understand. I'm gonna watch Randy Couture, but I don't think people's styles change that much, because he pretty much already had the attributes."[136]

Couture knew Randleman was a great wrestler. He prepared to confront his own biggest weakness, a lack of skill on his back. As a champion wrestler, Couture had rarely been taken down in a fight. But if anyone could do it, it would be Kevin Randleman. So when the fight went to the ground, Couture would be ready.

Randleman put him on the ground in both the first and second rounds. The second round saw Randleman land several hard punches on his feet as well, but although Couture was losing points on the scorecard, his practice on the ground was allowing him to stay alive, to stay in the fight. In the third round, he turned the tables. When Randleman went down, he had no way to protect himself.

"It seemed apparent that Kevin didn't spend a lot of time on the bottom, and wasn't really sure what to do or how to respond to that," Couture said. "I think that was the biggest difference. I was able to maintain position and neutralize him from the bottom and force him to work a little bit. . . . When he was on the bottom, he wasn't as successful at protecting himself."[137]

Couture was once again the heavyweight champion of the world. Randleman, for all of his physical tools, had peaked. Like his mentor, Mark Coleman, he never developed into a well-rounded fighter. The sport was evolving to the point that you needed more than one skill. At the very least, you needed the ability to neutralize your opponent's offense, as Couture had done with his guard.

"He's a very smart warrior," Randleman said. "He got inside and got me down. I was not expecting to be on my back. I was like a turtle on its back."[138]

The matchup between two former collegiate champions had impressed Larry Hazzard, as had their show of respect after the fight. The future of MMA, still in a provisional status, was looking good in New Jersey. But it was too little, too late for SEG. The bigger and more prestigious venue cost more to book, and without pay-per-view clearance, the company simply couldn't afford to run the quality shows it needed to attract a large crowd. Meyrowitz was looking to sell at least a portion of the promotion, and opening the doors in New Jersey had made that possible.

"I think there were a lot of times Bob would have entertained offers," Isaacs said. "We had a lot of lows, and we absorbed a lot of blows. For me it just got too hard. We were constantly under siege. We weren't getting a lot of mainstream coverage, and the coverage we were getting was all cockfight stuff. And the mixed martial arts press were constantly looking for the bad."

Promoting MMA seemed like it was now a potential moneymaker. New Jersey could open the door to pay-per-view, and the UFC had the most recognizable and respected name in the business. Potential buyers were coming out of the woodwork. "A lot of people wanted to buy this company," Dana White said. "I was the one who originally contacted Bob, because I heard he wanted to sell. Once Lorenzo got involved, I think Bob stepped back and said, 'You know what, this is something I've thrown a lot of money at, I've spent a lot of time with, and I don't want to see it die.' He sold it to the right people. You gotta give him credit for that."[139]

ZUFFA SAVES THE SHOW

Dana White was a former boxer and boxercise instructor who had started managing fighters, including the UFC's Chuck Liddell and Tito Ortiz. He had orchestrated a holdout for Ortiz, and had guided Liddell into title contention.

"It felt good to have Dana on my side," Liddell said. "He loved the sport, he loved fighters, and he loved fighting. He was as confrontational outside the ring as any of his clients were inside it. And he was also fiercely loyal, especially to me. . . . He had an innate sense for calculating the value of a match, what his fighters were worth in that fight, and how much the entire UFC enterprise was worth."[140]

When he learned Meyrowitz was interested in selling the UFC, White contacted his old friend Lorenzo Fertitta.

White said, "He was down in Miami, and I said, 'You know what? I just found out the UFC is for sale. What do you think?' And he said, 'That's interesting.' A month later we owned it. . . . Three guys bought the UFC when it was dead. It was over. The sport was dead and no one cared. We didn't buy this to make billions of dollars. We saw something in this sport, and in the fighters, that we thought was incredible."[141]

Meyrowitz tried to get Fertitta to buy into the UFC as an investor. The Fertittas, however, were only interested in buying the promotion outright. Lorenzo Fertitta had come a long way since 1999, when he was unsure whether the UFC was right for Nevada. He was now an unabashed fan. He was not just a fan, but also a fan with enough money to not blink at a $2-million gamble.

"When me and my brother decided to buy the company, it was clearly a gamble. The UFC was literally on its last breath," Fertitta said. Fertitta, his brother Frank Fertitta III, and their brother-in-law Blake Sartini formed

Zuffa to purchase the UFC for a reported $2 million. "We had a crazy idea. I think it was all in the approach. We thought this sport would really resonate with men 18-34. And if presented the right way, they could really grasp it, and it would be this generation's boxing."[142]

Fans and the MMA media were thrilled with Zuffa's purchase.

"The mixed martial arts press was constantly looking for the bad," Isaacs said. "When Zuffa took over, there was a big switch. Whatever Dana said, they were like, 'Thank God those guys bought it and are going to do something with it.'"

For many in the industry, it was like a dream come true. UFC announcer Joe Rogan said, "Could you ask for anything more? When we were doing the old UFCs, I used to have conversations with my friends, and I'd say that all the UFC needed were some billionaire dudes to come in that love the sport and pick it up. And that's exactly what happened! Some crazy rich dudes who just love the UFC came in and started shelling out shitloads of cash. Not only are these guys crazy rich, but they've been involved with the Nevada State Athletic Commission. They're guys that know business, and can get the UFC into markets that it could never get into before. You couldn't ask for a better combination. . . . Finally, there is a light at the end of the tunnel."[143]

The attitude toward Zuffa would change over time. People didn't understand how Zuffa operated yet. To understand the Fertittas, you had to go back to Galveston, Texas — back to the time when it was the gambling capital of the southwest.

THE WILD WEST

In Galveston, Texas, the wine flowed and the crooners sang their love songs at the Balinese Room. The club was truly unique, built on a pier and stretching out into the Gulf of Mexico. Everyone who was anyone during the '40s performed there. I'm talking the cream of the crop: Frank Sinatra, Bob Hope, and George Burns. But the Balinese Room was more than a nightclub. It was also a gambling hotspot, run with the full knowledge of the town's law enforcement and legitimate businessmen. *Texas Monthly* said in a 1993 retrospective that 10 percent of the town worked directly for the Maceos, and everybody in town had a taste. Salvatore "Sam" Maceo was just that powerful. His brother Rosario was just that dangerous. Sam's money and influence made the law turn a blind eye. Rosario's gun made the other mafia families keep their distance. Besides, the bad guys constantly outsmarted the good guys. "The B-Room hosted the biggest names in show business and highest-rolling gamblers. It was almost impossible to raid because the casino area, where the illegal activity took place, was situated on the T-head of the long, narrow pier," wrote Gary Cartwright in *Galveston — A History of the Island*. "When raiding parties of Texas Rangers appeared, someone up front pushed a button, the band struck up 'The Eyes of Texas,' and the gambling paraphernalia folded into the walls like Murphy beds."

Not many wanted to see the illicit casinos shut down. Galveston was a tourist town, and the Gulf Coast could only entertain them for so long. "If I closed down all the joints, they'd have to close all the hotels in Galveston," County Sheriff Frank Biagnne said.[144] Former Police Commissioner Walter L. Johnson was even more blunt: "Galveston was wide open before I was born. It was wide open when I came into office, and I left it wide open. The people of Galveston want an open town."[145]

It was natural that the Maceos would be involved in the nightclub business. Sure, they were into prostitution, extortion, and drugs too. But they had made their mark during Prohibition, selling liquor for "Dutch" Voight and Ollie Quinn, the leaders of the Beach Gang.

Tens of thousands of cases of booze would make their way up from Cuba and Jamaica. The Beach Gang would sell it. The Maceos would make sure it got to where it was going. They did such a good job of it that they were given other opportunities. Nightclubs like the Hollywood Dinner Club, the nation's first air-conditioned nightclub. If the conditioned air, Duke Ellington on stage, and the drinks with umbrellas in them weren't enough, the Maceos were happy to provide other distractions, like roulette, craps, blackjack, or any other game of chance you could imagine. Their various enterprises all collided in the club. Drugs shut down the Dinner Club. No problem, they would just build another, with the legendarily pleasant Sam Maceo smiling through it all. Soon, the Maceos were running the whole town, and in the mind of the mafia, who better to trust with your expanding empire than your own family?

The expansion of family power helped put the Maceos' nephews, the Fertittas, in the game. Anthony and Victor Fertitta ran the Balinese Room. Victor was in charge of the club, while Anthony took care of other things.

Rosario was getting old, and a family needs younger, vibrant men to do the things that needed to be done. Radio disc jockey Harry Martin, who got his start emceeing the Balinese Room for Maceo, said, "He was a large, muscular man with black slicked back hair, dead eyes, and white, glistening teeth that appeared about to bite your head off, even when he smiled, unless you were a high roller. Then he was all charm. He warmly smiled on me, mirroring the Don. In his youth, he had been the Maceos' enforcer under Papa Rose. It is a legend that during the Prohibition era, news of the Maceo empire's success reached Chicago's boss, Al Capone. He dispatched Frank Nitti, the notorious thug, to Galveston to deliver the message to the Maceo brothers that he was muscling in. Fertitta met Nitti at the train station, ostensibly to take him to Rosario and Sam for a council. Instead, he spirited Nitti far down the island, where he pulled off onto a remote beach and 'broke' Nitti, a notoriously evil man himself. No one knows what Fertitta did or said to Nitti, but he fled back to Chicago and warned his boss to lay off the Maceos."[146]

By the '50s, the elder generation of Maceos was slowing down. The rackets were a young man's game. They had expanded their empire into a wide array of legitimate business enterprises, which made the family a fortune. Sam was in the oil business, the import/export business, and was moving into the casino business in Las Vegas. He would pass away in 1951. Rosario was sick, and finally succumbed to his illness in 1954.

It wasn't just the loss of the family patriarchs that slowed business. Galveston was a dying town. The military base, Fort Crockett, closed up shop and there were suddenly fewer customers for the red-light district's famous madams and gaming parlors. The once untouchable Maceo syndicate was now being investigated by the law, the "Little Kefauver Committee." Like many of the nation's most prominent gangsters, the family didn't take a hit for murder or extortion. It was the IRS that did them in. The Maceos had been making $3 million or $4 million a year on the books. But when their accountant, aptly nicknamed "Books," flipped, the truth started coming out. Rosario had secret bundles of cash at his various clubs. He'd pull out a bundle and start counting it out, always sharing with his brother. "There's $600,000 here," Books testified he had told his brother Sam. "Three hundred grand for you, and three hundred grand for me." When Sam passed away, the gamers kept gaming and the lawmen got bolder. On the day of his funeral, just after Monsignor O'Connell said, "The angels in heaven will welcome this good man," Sheriff Frank Biagnne said the gambling establishments were also welcome to accept good men. Just so long as the payoff was good.[147]

The Galveston rackets were sold to the "junior" Maceos, led by Anthony Fertitta. But Anthony didn't have Sam's winning way with people. If *Life* magazine had come snooping around in Sam's day, they would have been charmed and dined and left with a positive story to tell. If Sam Maceo was the carrot, Fertitta was the stick. After *Life* photographer Joe Scherschel and reporter Hank Suydam took pictures of the Fertittas' gambling operation, Fertitta followed the pair back to their hotel room and smashed Suydam in the face. Fertitta says he barely touched him. Then, in a scene right out of *The Godfather* when Sonny Corleone throws some money on the ground to pay for a camera he's broken, Fertitta tried to make things right by stuffing a twenty in the reporter's pocket. Real life isn't the movies. Instead of a memorable scene, although it was certainly that, charges were filed, and a negative article appeared in *Life.*

More than that, the tide of public opinion was shifting. Galveston didn't seem like a great place to take your family anymore. People were ready for change. When outsider Jim Simpson ran for county attorney on an anti-Maceo campaign in 1954, he wasn't laughed out of the state, and fell just eight votes short. "I had always had a pride in the town in which I lived," Simpson said. "I didn't have that feeling here. I could walk down the street and see a gambling joint within sight of a grammar school. I just wondered: how is that affecting the children who are growing up in that environment? Are they going to adopt the corrupt practices they see around them?"[148]

When Will Wilson was elected attorney general in 1956, Simpson saw an opportunity to strike. Wilson was a crusader and crime buster who had cleaned up Dallas. Now was their chance to take on the mob in Galveston. Instead of old-fashioned busts led by the notoriously corrupt Texas Rangers, Simpson convinced Wilson to use the power of his office to file injunctions against the gambling houses. Every time an undercover agent saw gambling on the premises, a temporary restraining order was filed. When the gambling continued after the restraining order, the courts could put violators in jail for three days. All this went down with no jury trial and no interference from corrupt judges. The plan worked, partly due to the bravery of undercover men James D. "Buddy" Givens and Carroll Yaws. Neither were professional lawmen; they both worked for oil companies in the area. But Simpson insisted on using these outsiders, and they were effective, taking copious notes and risking their lives to put the mob out of business. Wilson wanted to continue using the Texas Rangers, but Simpson had been around the block a few times and insisted that they needed to function outside the established law-enforcement mechanism.

"Will Wilson was a good man, totally honest," Simpson said. "But he was fundamentally naive. I had a different view. I'd been an FBI agent in Chicago, and I understood corruption."[149] This innovative law-enforcement approach essentially shut Galveston down. But there was a new city further west in need of men who knew how to run a gambling establishment. The Fertittas were heading to Vegas.

Frank Fertitta, Jr., started as a bellman, graduated to dealer, and was soon running his own casino. That's the rags-to-riches story the Fertittas like to tell. In reality, Frank was a man who knew how to run an illicit gambling organization. His family had spent years perfecting the art in Galveston. So he was a natural to help run a Las Vegas casino for the Kansas City mafia.

The Civella family ran Kansas City. Their main asset was an ability to tap into the Teamsters Union pension fund for loans, which they would use to finance Las Vegas casinos, including the Star and the Fremont. They didn't control the Teamsters because of their clever PowerPoint presentations or their business model. Roy Lee Williams, president of the International Brotherhood of Teamsters, was shoved into an automobile after a meeting, blindfolded, and told in no uncertain terms that he had better start co-operating with the Civellas' requests to tap the pension fund. If not, he'd watch his wife and children be murdered before his eyes.

The Civellas couldn't invest in Las Vegas casinos directly. They needed an intermediary, because they were well-known gangsters. Of the eleven people on the original Vegas black book, two were Civella family members. Officially, Las Vegas wanted no part of the mafia.

"The first 11 men were placed in the black book without any formal notification or hearing. All were reputed to be notorious associates of organized crime. . . . Without the apparent sanction of the commission, the board, and its chairman, former FBI agent R. J. Abbaticchio, Jr., decided that these individuals presented a threat to the industry, and instructed the enforcement agents to distribute the List of Excluded Persons to all state-licensed gaming establishments."

Since the mob wasn't directly invested in the casinos, it needed a way to make a profit. A lot of cash passes through a gambling establishment, and it was easy enough to set some aside now and again. This was called skimming, and nobody was better at it than Carl Thomas. Thomas ran the hotels for the Civella family, including the Fremont, which was featured in the Martin Scorsese movie *Casino*. Here's the lowdown from Nicholas Pileggi's book of the same name: "What almost no one in the state knew about him — was that in addition to his impeccable reputation as the first of the new breed of Nevada casino executives, Carl Thomas was also the greatest casino skimmer in America at the time . . ."

In 1963, Thomas met the man he was skimming for at a party, Kansas City mob boss Nick Civella. Soon, the two men were meeting every time Civella came to town. Thomas was the front man for the Civella crime family, and Thomas's right-hand man was Frank Fertitta, Jr., who was the president of the Fremont and ran the show for Thomas and Civella. In 1976, Thomas and Fertitta even invested in their own casino together. It was called The Casino, and later renamed the Bingo Palace, and finally Palace Station. The two kept working for the Civella casinos, and the skimming operations continued. In 1979, the FBI put a stop to the whole operation. Phone taps had provided evidence to arrest Carl Thomas, the Civella brothers, and a dozen others. Despite being recorded by FBI wire taps and implicated by other defendants, Fertitta was never charged with skimming the Fremont, even though he was the hotel president.

Fertitta escaped prosecution, but not punishment. He was investigated by the Nevada Gaming Control Board and stepped down as the chairman of Station Casinos. The new head of the family was his son, Frank Fertitta III, better known to some as "Three Sticks." And when Three Sticks Fertitta wanted to get into the fight game, he made Bob Meyrowitz an offer he couldn't refuse.

13

THE UFC SURVIVES

Zuffa took over two weeks before UFC 30, in February 2001. After the show, promoters and New Jersey officials sat down to hammer out a final set of rules to govern MMA in the state. The UFC was now on the road to nationwide legitimacy. Not only was the sport cleared in New Jersey, but Nevada's Marc Ratner was actively involved in the process of putting the rules together. "We formulated what it is now called 'The Unified Rules of Mixed Martial Arts.' I was on the phone for almost four hours," Ratner said. "That's how we came up with the rules. Once they had rounds and rules and weight classes, it became something you could regulate."

The Unified Rules of Mixed Martial Arts created nine weight classes, banned wearing shoes or the gi, and outlawed knees on the ground. The regulators were focused on things that were unlikely to happen, like pro wrestling style pile drivers, and for the most part left the rules of the sport unchanged from the SEG days.

"It turned out better than we thought it was going to. We went in there nervous about a lot of things," Dana White said. "Maybe they were going to try and take slams out. Who knows what they were going to do? You know what? They were so open-minded."[150]

Zuffa's first real show was at UFC 31, on May 4, 2001, and it was one of the finest cards fans had ever seen. Zuffa was committed to putting on the best show possible, and had plenty of money to burn.

"When me and my brother Frank bought the Ultimate Fighting Championships in January, we sat down with Dana [White] and we said, 'In every one of our shows, we want every fight to be a significant fight. We want only the best fighters in the world — no one else," Fertitta said. "And we want even our preliminary matches to be of the level that they would be main events in other shows. . . . I think you would agree that we have accomplished that. . . . You can expect tons of entertainment. Hold on to your seats — there's going to be a lot of pyro, there's going to be a lot of lasers, a lot of smoke. But the most important thing I think you're going to see is the best mixed martial artists in the world competing in the Octagon in action-packed fights."

The show delivered everything Zuffa promised. On the undercard, Chuck Liddell knocked out former champion Kevin Randleman, Shonie Carter made a dramatic comeback to beat Matt Serra with a spinning backfist, and Carlos Newton upset longtime 170-pound champion Pat Miletich. But the highlight of the night was Randy Couture's title defense against Pedro Rizzo, in what many consider one of the best UFC fights of all time.

COUTURE

Before he was a title contender, Randy Couture had been unsure about stepping into the Octagon. But when he stared across the ring at a 300-pound behemoth, he wasn't nervous in the least. He had always been nervous before big wrestling matches, but the idea of this monster punching him in the face didn't seem to concern him.

"It struck me as odd, but later I realized I had a lot of expectations from myself in wrestling. I had a lot of goals and things I wanted to accomplish, such as making the Olympic team," Couture said. "But fighting was just something I wanted to try for fun. I didn't have any expectations, and that took a lot of the pressure off my shoulders."[151]

His muscular opponent was Tony Halme, better known as professional wrestling's Ludwig Borga, and he meant business. His hilarious promo before the fight left little doubt as to his intentions: "My greatest strength is I'm not afraid of anybody," Halme said. "I have balls of iron. I go in there to rip the head off or die trying."

Competition wasn't new to Couture. As a two-time runner-up in the NCAA wrestling finals and twice runner-up for a spot on the Olympic team, Couture was used to burly men trying to toss him on his head, if not tear it off. When he first started MMA, Couture was still training full-time for the Olympics. He had just missed an opportunity to represent the United States in the 1996 Atlanta Olympics, finishing second in the trials to Army

Sergeant Derrick Waldroup. Although still committed to international wrestling, the $25,000 he made as an assistant wrestling coach wasn't paying the bills. He needed something else to support his family. The success of fellow wrestlers Mark Coleman, Mark Kerr, and Don Frye had intrigued Couture, and he had even sent SEG an application to become a UFC fighter.

Couture said, "In the summer of '96, I lived in an apartment complex in Corvalis and was coaching at Oregon State. One of the athletes lived in the same complex and brought this tape over and plugged it in my VCR and was like, 'You've got to see this!' So the UFC comes up on the TV, and lo and behold one of the competitors in the tournament we were watching was Don Frye. And I was like, 'Dude, I know this guy.' I went to college with him. My freshman year was his senior year, he was a heavyweight and we wrestled each other. So I was immediately intrigued by the sport."[152]

Thanks, but no thanks, the UFC told the man who would become the most beloved figure in the sport's history. We already have enough wrestlers on our roster. Undaunted, Couture joined the RAW (Real American Wrestlers) team, and waited for his name to be called.

"They had this brainstorm to get a bunch of world-class wrestlers, both in freestyle and Greco, and form a fighting stable," Couture said. "Having been friends of theirs through wrestling, I was one of the athletes they approached about being a member of the RAW team. At one time they had several of the top fighters [including Tom Erickson, Frank Trigg, and Dan Henderson]."[153]

When he got the call from the UFC as an injury replacement for the May 30, 1997 UFC 13 heavyweight tournament, Couture was in Puerto Rico training for the Pan Am Games. The UFC event was in just two weeks, but Couture was ready to fight. After finishing up in Puerto Rico, and with the fight just days away, Couture turned to RAW trainer Ricco Chapirelli for help. "Ricco showed me what the guard was and how to pass it, and what an arm lock was and how to defend it," Couture said.[154]

With no MMA training, he would rely on his amateur wrestling background to sustain him. In this case, amateur wrestling was able to trump pro wrestling, and Couture dispatched Halme in less than a minute. He won the tournament by choking out 290-pound Steven Graham.

As it would later in his UFC career, the promotion had Couture in mind as a stepping-stone for an exciting young striker it was grooming for the heavyweight championship. Vitor Belfort was lean, jacked up, and pretty; exactly the kind of teen-idol poster boy SEG had traditionally put their promotional muscle behind. Despite being listed as a Brazilian jiu-jitsu expert, Vitor was actually a heavy-handed puncher with lightning-quick strikes. To the fans and experts, Couture was a heavy underdog, just another pin for Belfort to bowl over on his way to the championship.

Couture said, "Nobody really gave me a snowball's chance in hell of beating the 'Phenom.' Going out and proving everybody wrong was certainly a defining moment for me as an athlete. I've always had this innate ability to rise to the occasion when people count me out. In that underdog situation is when I perform my best."[155]

Couture was able to study Belfort and pinpoint his weaknesses. This would become a Couture trademark, the cerebral game planning and fight preparation that would separate him from fellow wrestlers who never really evolved beyond the ground-and-pound phase. What Couture saw on tape surprised him. Belfort had quick and accurate punches, but he just wasn't a very good boxer in the traditional sense. His technique involved plowing straight forward with straight punches, and Couture was ready. His strategy, taken from his wrestling days, was to close the distance and keep Belfort close to his body. This would allow Couture to use his Greco techniques and keep Belfort from landing any big punches. The goal was to put Belfort on his back and test his stamina and heart. It wasn't to win the fight standing, but that was an added bonus.

Couture had just three weeks of boxing training from his army days at Fort Rucker, in Alabama, but was able to combine that training with his world-class Greco skills to control Belfort and pepper him with punches. This dirty boxing clinch, using a single collar tie instead of the more traditional Muay Thai clinch, allowed him to keep his opponent off balance while circling him and landing dozens of uppercuts.

The win over Belfort gave Couture a shot at the UFC heavyweight title in just his fourth professional fight. It was also an opportunity for Couture to re-establish wrestling at the top of the stylistic pyramid. The champion was kickboxing legend Maurice Smith, who was once even referenced in the John Cusack film *Say Anything*, and was famous by kickboxing standards, as famous as you could be in the insular and nearly invisible sport. He had recently established the template for strikers everywhere by stalemating Mark Coleman on the ground and dominating him on his feet on his way to the UFC title. It's not hyperbole to say that Smith's win had shocked the MMA world. Having spent years learning that grappling arts were the key to success, fans had to be retrained to understand that a dominant striker could ply his trade if he gave himself the tools to stay in the fight. It looked like Smith had the magic formula for success, and Couture was again the heavy underdog.

Unlike the fight with Belfort, Couture had no interest in standing with Smith, who didn't have any identifiable weaknesses in his standing game. But unlike Smith's last wrestling conquest, Coleman, Couture wasn't going to gas out and get tired. When Couture stepped into the cage in Yokohama, Japan, the game plan was the old wrestler standby: ground and pound with a mixture of lay and pray. At the time, the format called for a single 15-minute round with two three-minute overtimes. Couture put Smith on his back three times, executed some tepid ground and pound, and took home the title with a decision.

Despite winning the world championship, Couture and SEG parted ways over a contract dispute. Facing money troubles of its own, SEG offered Couture just one quarter of his guaranteed purse to fight Bas Rutten at UFC Brazil. Couture was willing to fight, but only for the amount they had previously agreed upon.

This made a hard decision easy for Couture. He was struggling to balance his training schedule between his continuing Olympic dreams and his MMA paydays. Now he was free to train for wrestling full-time, and he wouldn't fight again for almost a year. When he returned, like many of the sport's most prominent stars, he tested the waters in Japan. They were a bit hot for his liking. Even though he was the UFC world champion, Couture was still an MMA novice, and had yet to face a real submission expert on the ground. He learned his lessons the hard way — in the ring — with live competition. His first opponent after leaving the UFC was Japanese tough guy Enson Inoue. Inoue was one of MMA's most unique characters. A Hawaiian of Japanese descent and a former world-class racquetball player, Inoue had embraced the Japanese culture and its budo spirit. He bested Couture by arm bar. After additional losses to Valentijn Overeem and Mikhail Ilioukhine, both by submission, the Couture that returned to the

UFC to fight Pedro Rizzo was battle hardened. And he was not prepared to make the same mistakes again.

UFC 31

"Every fight tonight was just amazing. The heavyweight bout was — I've never seen anything like it," UFC President Dana White said. "It was unbelievable. Toe to toe, you know they both wanted to quit, and they didn't. It was unbelievable."[156]

Couture and Rizzo fought tooth and nail for all five rounds. It was an amazing back-and-forth fight that saw Couture almost finish the fight in the first round before Rizzo came back with a series of hard leg kicks.

Couture said, "The first Pedro Rizzo fight was definitely the toughest fight I have been in to date . . . five rounds of just brawling . . . I was so tired at the end of that fight . . . I was just like, 'Oh my God.' My leg swelled up. I couldn't walk for about three weeks . . . I have a big divot in my quad where he kicked me."[157]

The battle was so tough to call that there was legitimate tension in the air when the judges came back with their decision. When the decision was announced for Couture, Rizzo was devastated. After a slow start, he thought he had done more than enough to win the decision. "Inside my head, I won that fight. . . . People ask me, 'Why did they give him the win?' and I say, 'Well, he's American and the USA is one of the most nationalist countries in the world,'" Rizzo said. "I was crushed. I was even pissed with Couture for taking so long to face me again. Because if I could, I would have fought him again the following week."[158]

Rizzo would have to wait until UFC 34, in November, to get his rematch. The first fight, though, was the perfect ending to a great first show. It was the kind of fight that fans would be talking about for years. "I have had a lot of favorite fights, I mean, there have been a lot of great fights that I have really, really enjoyed," Dana White said. "Randy Couture versus Pedro Rizzo one was an awesome fight. I mean, those guys went at it. I mean, you want to talk about two warriors with heart and the will to win; that fight was awesome. Afterwards, Couture had to have rehab done on his legs, he got kicked with so many leg kicks. Controversial decision, it was just bell-to-bell an awesome fight."[159]

UFC in Demand

Putting on great fights was easy enough. seg's ufc had plenty of great fights. But what good were great fights that no one could see? The ufc needed to get back on cable. Pay-per-view had made the company, and it could play a huge role in making the show profitable again.

"I think Bob [Meyrowitz] burned a lot of bridges and had a lot of conflicts. That's what made it tough for him to move forward with it," Dana White said. White had done business with Meyrowitz, so he knew firsthand how difficult he could be. "Very confrontational. You have to look at it like this: he had a company that was doing business with the cable companies, and he lost cable. And it was just a constant fight to get it back. That is our goal: to get it sanctioned in the state of Nevada and get it back on cable."[160]

Both would happen in the first year of Zuffa's reign. "Lorenzo has a lot of credibility. He's a stand-up guy and a great businessman, with a lot of respect from a lot of people," White said. "Rather than butt heads with the commissions, we went in and sat down with them and said, 'Hey, listen.' And they listened."[161]

After a three-year cable blackout, in demand announced in early July 2001 that it would make the ufc available to its 28 million customers. The pay-per-view business was reeling from the loss of two major professional wrestling companies. in demand needed a replacement for wcw and ecw shows, and it was ready to give the ufc another try.

"The ufc had been in an ongoing dialogue with the cable industry to examine the progress, diligence, and upgrades of the rules and sanctioning of the states," in demand vice president Dan York said. "Over the long term, we think this event . . . has a terrific mix of action, athleticism, marketable stars, promotional support behind it . . . to make it a very successful pay-per-view franchise."

It seemed like a tremendous victory for the ufc. Zuffa had put a lot of money into its first two events, significantly upgrading the lighting and presentation, trying to make a good impression.

"We lost $2.4 million on that show [ufc 32]. We put billboards up all over New York and New Jersey. We gave away a ton of tickets. We invited a lot of people from the cable systems. We had the press down there, other key people who we were making business deals with. When they showed up that night, the ufc looked like a big fucking deal," Dana White said. "The place was packed, the music was rockin', and the fights were great that night. Was it the right decision? Look where we are today. Had it not worked, you would have said we burned $2 million that night, and it didn't make a difference."[162]

The new-look UFC had indeed impressed the cable companies. It looked ready for prime time, like a big-league promotion. A huge show in front of more than 11,000 fans in the Continental Airlines Arena in New Jersey looked more like a pay-per-view show than fights in front of 1,000 fans in Louisiana or Mississippi.

Lorenzo Fertitta said, "We just sat down and said, 'We want to work with you, not against you.' Tell us where we need to be and what we need to do to get back on. The sanctioning by New Jersey helped. . . . The increase in the production value of the show helped. . . . We needed to put the cart before the horse in order to get where we needed to be. We did it, and put on a first-class show that was deserving of cable, because if we ran a rinky-dink show they wouldn't want to put it on."

PAY-PER-VIEW

The first pay-per-view show would also be the first show sanctioned by the state of Nevada. Fertitta's connections had helped pave the way for the UFC to go to Vegas. The show was held at the Mandalay Bay hotel, and there was a quiet confidence that the company was finally on track. The UFC brought in Carmen Elektra to be its new spokesperson, and was looking to re-establish the brand in the mainstream media.

"People have no idea what Carmen Elektra has done for us," White said. "If you went to UFC 30's press conference, there was nobody there. Now, fast-forward to the UFC 33 press conference at the ESPN Zone with Carmen Elektra. *Entertainment Tonight, Extra* — all the Hollywood press was there."[163]

The UFC also launched an aggressive marketing campaign, which aimed to let fans of the old shows who had lost track of the sport know that the UFC was back on cable.

Frank Shamrock said, "My first meeting with them was the wrong meeting. First of all, they flew me out to consult and asked me, 'How do we do this?' And I told them the truth, which, of course, they disregarded and did something else." Shamrock had been SEG's brightest star in the dark era of the UFC. His win over Tito Ortiz had been the last UFC show released on home video. He knew full well that the sport had a long way to go. Getting on television was just the first step on a long journey.

"Their first approach was to launch a $2-million marketing campaign aimed at an audience that didn't know what we were and thought we were a bad, dirty thing. My advice to them was, 'Look, this is a waste of money.' The sport has to be rebranded, reintroduced, and the audience re-educated before you can just start showing up in *FHM* magazine and *USA Today* and everything else. Basically, they were politely arguing with me while trying to get me to sign a very long-term contract. I got the feeling that they didn't know what they were doing, and they were only focused on taking that brand and maximizing it in the short term. I played it safe and watched from the sidelines to see if it was true and, unfortunately, it was."

The branding was a part of the new pay-per-view deal. The UFC had committed to spend millions advertising the shows. Former SEG executive David Isaacs said, "Remember the advertising campaign they ran in *Sports Illustrated*? I thought it was the most homoerotic ad campaign. These guys were wasting money. They did a terrible deal with pay-per-view when they got into it. . . . But they could absorb that. For us, it was hard to absorb any kind of mistake. We just didn't have that give."

Tito Ortiz was headlining the show. He was supposed to fight the former "Phenom," Vitor Belfort, but Belfort pulled out with an injury. Vladimir Matyushenko was a last-minute replacement. Still, it seemed almost destined for success, regardless of the fighters in the main event. It was supposed to be a night to celebrate the long road back to prominence. Instead, it was one of the biggest disasters in UFC history.

The show was unspeakably boring. Every fight went to a decision, and Zuffa had plenty of fluff and filler on the show, as well. At the end of the night, they simply ran out of time. Like UFC 4, where the Dan Severn–Royce Gracie fight was cut off, the show went off the air before the end of the main event. "It was the one thing we said we could never do again, come hell or high water," Isaacs said. "And then the Zuffa guys did it at their first event.

Fans demanded refunds and the show, which drew 75,000 buys (about the same as UFC 1) was a money loser. "It was devastating. I don't know how it happened, but it will never happen again," White said. "First of all, they bomb us on September 11. Vitor gets hurt, pulls out. Then they put the

Hopkins-Trinidad fight the night after us. There were just so many things that went wrong that were beyond our control, it was insane — and things that were within our control!"[164]

The bad first impression did incalculable damage to the new UFC. UFC 34 was a great show, everything the previous blunder wasn't. There were great fights, including a now legendary battle for the welterweight title that saw Matt Hughes dethrone Carlos Newton by knocking him unconscious with a powerbomb while Hughes himself passed out from Newton's triangle choke. But the damage had already been done. Only half as many people ordered the show on pay-per-view. The new stars just weren't resonating with people the way the SEG stars had. People knew Ken Shamrock, Don Frye, Tank Abbott, and Royce Gracie. No one was quite convinced that the new era fighters were really the top dogs. Fighters like Tito Ortiz had potential, they just needed to be introduced to the audience properly.

"Tito's a great face and can be marketable, but he's sitting on a broken foundation," Ken Shamrock said. "Who's he beat? Nobody. And they're shoving him down the fans' throats. What they need to do is bring somebody like me in to fight Tito Ortiz, somebody who has built a reputation already. If Tito Ortiz beats him, now we can build on this."[165]

Zuffa came to the same conclusion. Ken Shamrock would be back for the ultimate grudge match.

There are actually five cities in the Midwest's Quad Cities, one for each of the Miletich Fighting Systems (MFS) world champions the area has spawned. The region grew up as the home of John Deere and ALCOA (The Aluminum Company of America), and thrived as a manufacturing center. The farm crisis of the 1980s changed all that. Today, Iowa's best exports are its fighters, and its leading exporter is Pat Miletich. Thousands of fighters have crossed the I-74 bridge to Bettendorf, Iowa, to work with MMA's best trainer.

Like just about everyone in Iowa, Miletich started as a wrestler. But he also had a passion for the sweet science. Before Miletich, the Quad Cities were a Midwest boxing hotbed, and the home of middleweight boxing champion Michael Nunn. Miletich, too, dreamed of being a world champion, but was merely good as a wrestler and passable as a boxer, not world class. But MMA was tailor-made for a man who had a black belt in karate, a wrestling background, and a boxing and kickboxing pedigree. After seeing the early Ultimate Fighting Championships, he got his hands on a Renzo Gracie video, set after a seminar, and taught himself jiu-jitsu.

Miletich said, "I was in college wrestling and my father had died when I was a senior in high school. Then, during my second year in college, my mom got sick with heart problems, so I had to leave and go home and hang out with her. I was working three jobs trying to help her pay the bills, because she couldn't work for a while. A friend of mine got me started in kickboxing, and then I went from that into jiu-jitsu and Muay Thai and everything like that. Then I decided I had always been pretty good at fighting, so I decided to start fighting boxing and Muay Thai matches, and I did well. I won a U.S. Muay Thai title, and then the UFC started and I saw my chance to start making some money quickly, and in fairly large chunks at a time. I started fighting to make money to pay off my mom's house and bills and things like that."[166]

Soon he was fighting all over the Quad Cities, and all over the world. And winning. In just two years, he racked up a 17–1–1 record, often fighting guys much heavier than his 170 pounds.

Former opponent and subsequent student Rick Graveson said, "I fought Pat twice. He was my first fight ever, and then I fought him again a month later. He easily beat me both times. Back then, Pat Miletich beat all of his opponents easily. He was light years ahead of all the other fighters. There were no weight classes, no time limits, and the only rules were no biting and no eye gouging. Pat was 170 pounds, and I watched him fight guys that were 270 pounds and just throw them around the ring like nothing. He was, and still is, a good kickboxer, as well as a good ground fighter. When he put it all together in the cage, he was incredible."[167]

Along the way, he gathered the best fighters in the region to work together and improve their games. The foundation for what would become Miletich Fighting Systems was being formed.

"Pat had a group of guys and I had a group of guys, so we'd fight each other pretty regularly at the Quad City Ultimate," Jeremy Horn said. "When we ran out of guys — all our guys had fought all of his guys — we said, 'Look, we're done fighting, so how about if we start training together?' I'd come up once or twice a month and train for the weekend at Pat's. Eventually I got sick of driving, and I figured I'd just move there [to Iowa]."[168]

Eventually the UFC came calling, and Miletich, the "Croatian Sensation," was on the big stage at last. His opponent that night, at UFC 16 on March 13, 1998, was Olympic silver medalist Townsend Saunders, the kind of superb athlete Miletich would never be. But Miletich was tough, battle tested, and as hard as they come. Even at 30 years of age, the best way to describe Miletich was grizzled, and he won a hard-fought 15-minute decision, going on to submit alternate Chris Brennan to become the first UFC lightweight tournament champion.

To many fans, the real standout lightweight fighter that night was Mikey Burnett of the Lion's Den, who, in true Lion's Den tradition, bowed out after breaking his hand on the thick skull of luta livre fighter Eugenio Tadeu. It was a great fight, one UFC matchmaker John Peretti thought was among the best he had ever seen. Burnett was the star who emerged that night, not Miletich, and Pat was ready to prove his critics wrong. He was ready for Burnett, and would get him at the next show, UFC Brazil.

Burnett was a powerhouse, a weightlifter who was incredibly strong for his 170 pounds. Miletich wanted to keep the heavy puncher close to him at all costs, and on his back if at all possible. The two spent 21 minutes, mostly in a clinch, alternately grabbing each other's shorts and throwing knees to the body. A potentially great fight became interminably dull, and prompted the UFC to create a rule preventing the shorts grabbing that had marred this matchup. Still, someone had to win, and the difference in the fight ended up being a low blow that referee Big John McCarthy penalized Burnett for. In a fight that was too close to call, the foul made Miletich the first UFC lightweight (which later became the welterweight division) champion.

His success brought fighters from around the country to train with Miletich and Jeremy Horn, who was quickly establishing himself as one of the most cerebral fighters in the game. Miletich was the lightweight champion, and Horn had nearly beaten UFC middleweight champ Frank Shamrock. And both were succeeding without the benefit of superb athleticism. Clearly, they had plenty to share with others not gifted with the world's best physical tools. Soon the gym was packed with top fighters, including Joe Slick, Tyrone Roberts, Matt Hughes, LaVerne Clark, Bobby Hoffman, and Andre Roberts. Besides the fighters there was also the support staff, men who didn't fight professionally but did their best to help the guys develop. Steve Rusk was a Division III wrestling champion, and worked the guys hard in grappling practice. Professional boxer Ted Muller helped them work their hands.

"I come here for their benefit and for my benefit. I get some great sparring from Pat and some of the others," Muller said. "Pat is open-minded enough to know that other people may know more about some things than he does, and he knows what can benefit his fighters."[169]

The UFC has a certain glamour associated with it today, but when it was in its early years there wasn't much money involved in the fight game, and the training conditions were sparse. Today's MFS fighters train in a great facility in Bettendorf. This wasn't always the case.

"We were training on a racquetball court for years. I rented a space from a fitness club, rented the racquetball court. Eight hundred dollars a month and put mats on the floors and turned it into our own little battle box," Miletich said. "Gym members were constantly complaining because we were stinking up the gym, but they needed my rent there. It was really intense. Those were some really hard days. Everybody in the room was hungry and wanted to make a name for themselves."[170]

LITTLE EVIL

The rough conditions didn't stop Jens Pulver from calling after his camp, Shamrock 2000, closed down. The conditions in Bettendorf were tough, but he had seen tougher. Like many fighters, Pulver came from a broken and abusive home.

"I'm just not afraid to get punched. I'm not afraid to get hit. I grew up getting punched and hit. I mean, I've never died from it," Pulver said. "Being around my father hurt more mentally than physically — physical beatings are nothing. They go away, they heal. The bruises, they're gone. I didn't get into fighting because I was abused. I have just always loved the whole aspect of being in a sport where it's all on you. It's all left up to you. Your hard work, your heart, your skill."[171]

Pulver found a new home at Team Miletich, and the guys were soon calling him "Little Evil" and "The Pulverizer." Nothing was wrong with his personality, it was his wicked left hand that was causing his partners problems. After spending time with Lowell Anderson and Bob Shamrock, Bettendorf, Iowa, was a wake-up call for the future champion.

Pulver said, "I moved out to Iowa, and that's when I was just blown away. I was like, 'Holy cow, I just met a whole room full of guys and all they did was hand me my butt on a platter.' Just beat me silly, choked me out left and right. I was in heaven. When I moved out there I had two duffle bags, quit my job, left the house, gave up everything, and took the train for two and half days to come to Iowa. [MMA manager and promoter] Monte Cox let me stay in his house. I can't thank him enough. A lot of guys were in it for the same thing. They were in there to fight, train, and be the best they could be. We had a great group of people. We all trained hard every day. You never walked in that room by yourself going, 'Hmm, nobody showed up today, what am I gonna do?' It was never like that. They trained extremely hard, day in and day out. My worst beatings to this day have come in that practice room, never in the fights. I have taken lumps and bruises in that practice room, and that's what made us work. We all got on each other, we all pushed each other, and it was everything I ever wanted. It was like a wrestling room with all this boxing, MMA, jiu-jitsu, lifting, and running. The support group was massive. I mean everybody there, that's what they did. They all gave up something. They did whatever they had to do just to be around the rest of us who were doing it, and we pushed each other. That was the key to success. We just pushed each other so hard in the room that it was a day off to go in the ring."[172]

Pulver had already been discovered by UFC matchmaker John Peretti at the Bas Rutten Invitational, and had already made his UFC debut. He was not a raw lump of clay, but he was still new enough to the game for Miletich to mold him into a complete fighter. Pulver was an excellent wrestler, a starter at Boise State before injuries ended his grappling career. He would use that wrestling skill, just not the way Mark Coleman or Randy Couture did.

Pulver wasn't about the ground and pound. He was innovating a new way to use his wrestling skills: sprawl and brawl.

"It's not me that's shooting the takedowns! I don't take it to the ground. I've never done anything other than to try and stand up as long as the guy will allow me," Pulver said. "Everybody I fight shoots in and tries to take me down. I think I've done a real good job of taking the highlight off the fact that I was a college wrestler, and that I am a good grappler with submissions and stuff. But I just choose to try and stand up and punch because I hit hard — and I hit real hard. I have a better chance of ending the fight standing than I do on the ground."[173]

Peretti was trying to create a lightweight division in the UFC, patterned after the successful SHOOTO promotion in Japan. Led by the dynamite Rumina Sato and Caol Uno, the little guys in Japan often had the energy to keep fighting hard when bigger men started tiring. Peretti hoped Pulver could be one of the linchpins of his new division, and Pulver was on a tremendous roll, running over opponents in the UFC and on the independent scene. At UFC 28, on November 17, 2000, he knocked out the highly regarded John Lewis in just 15 seconds, looping a left hook over the top of a lazy jab. The victory over Lewis put Pulver in line for a title shot, and he beat tough Japanese fighter Caol Uno by decision over five rounds to become the first UFC lightweight (155 pounds and below) champion. "It was five rounds and a really good fight. Today it would be raved about, but it didn't get over to the live crowd. It was ahead of the tastes of the people," *Wrestling Observer Newsletter*'s Dave Meltzer said. After avenging teammate Matt Hughes's two losses to Dennis Hallman, Pulver would face his toughest challenge in the main event of UFC 35 on January 11, 2002.

HILO HOMEBOY

B.J. Penn grew up fighting. It's what people in Hilo, Hawaii, did. It was a part of life for kids growing up.

"Like Beef?"

"Give 'um."

And just like that, the fight would be on.

"Hilo is such a small place, you're going to see everyone again and again. If you've got a problem with somebody, you can't escape it."[174]

Penn was a rich kid, something his opponents never fail to mention, since most fighters grow up in less idyllic environments. But he still loved a good scrap. His parents were prominent real estate investors in the Pu'ueo neighborhood of Hilo who taught him the importance of a solid work ethic and to strive to be the best that he could be. What Penn wanted to be was a fighter. As a teen, fighting was his life, as it would be as an adult, but he was only interested in street fighting, not traditional martial arts. That changed when a Ralph Gracie student named Tom Callos moved into the neighborhood and wanted the rough-and-tumble kid down the street to spar with him. Penn was initially skeptical. How could this rolling around help him settle business in the street? But a few arm bars and chokes later, he was curious, indeed. Soon they were rolling on the wrestling mats every day, and when Callos took a trip back to California, a 16-year-old B.J. Penn went with him, searching for an upgrade in competition. Penn was no match for the more experienced students at Ralph Gracie's school, but he caught Gracie's eye. Gracie made an offer for Penn to come and train with him full-time in California. Penn was flattered and horrified when his father accepted the offer.

"At the time, I was spending a considerable amount of time hanging out with my friends at the beach. I had no direction, and my father was concerned," Penn said. "He thought it would be good if I got off the island for a spell, but the question of where to send me presented a problem. When he heard I had a talent for jiu-jitsu, it solved that problem. By sending me to California to train, I would not only be getting away from the late nights and street fights, but I would also be doing something constructive that took drive and determination. I would be doing something to better myself."[175]

What he would be doing was carving out a place among the most legendary jiu-jitsu practitioners of all time. He started entering jiu-jitsu tournaments in 1997. By 2000, he was the first non-Brazilian black belt to win his weight class at the Mundials, jiu-jitsu's Super Bowl.

"It was a dream for me, so when I was finally there, I didn't even think it was that big a thing. I guess it didn't hit me then. Maybe I was in shock. I don't know. But as every day goes by, I start to feel like I did something good. But at that time, I was just glad I didn't lose. Winning's not that great, it's just that losing sucks," Penn said.

Even as he achieved glory in Brazil, Hilo was on his mind. "When I'm out there, I really don't think about it as much. But after I win, 'right on!' I come from Hilo, a small town that not too many people know about. But there's a lot of talent out there I see in Hilo itself. . . . I am happy knowing that I'm from Hilo, a small place. There are not too many people in Hilo who know what I'm doing, you know what I mean? There are a lot of people in Brazil who know what I'm doing, though. It's kind of weird in that sense."[176]

Penn was nicknamed "The Prodigy" for his prodigious rise up the ranks of Brazilian jiu-jitsu. Soon, people in Hilo would know all about Baby Jay Penn. He was moving from the hidden niche of Brazilian jiu-jitsu into the public eye of Ultimate Fighting. Penn took the UFC by storm, much as he had the world of jiu-jitsu. His brother J.D. Penn had been training with John Lewis in Vegas, and Lewis was willing to make some calls for the talented youngster who Frank Shamrock was calling one of the world's best fighters before he had ever stepped in the cage.

Penn said, "I got into the UFC through John Lewis. He pulled some strings and got me in and I owe him for that. He knew Dana White and Lorenzo Fertitta before they bought the UFC. I met those two and rolled around with them, so they knew my ground and pounding. But they didn't know how I would do as a fighter. Nobody really knew that I was really fighting all my life, all the time. So it translated pretty well for me. No one knew how it would translate because they all thought of me as a jiu-jitsu guy."[177]

It translated pretty well. Penn was the hottest prospect the UFC had showcased since Frank Shamrock, and, like Shamrock, Penn made his UFC debut against a wrestler. But instead of catching Joey Gilbert in a quick submission, Penn took it to Gilbert standing, using his strikes to set up the opportunity to take him down. There, it was all Penn, and he showed no remorse, landing 11 unanswered punches to the head, forcing referee John McCarthy to intervene. Before the fight, Penn was so nervous he wanted to break down and cry, but he had stepped into the Octagon anyway, and would never have those kinds of nerves again.

"I can honestly say it was the most important fight of my life. There was no belt on the line, but it was the first time I had fought in front of that many people. Listening to the music and the cheers of those in attendance ran a chill up and down my body," Penn said. "I had just lost my MMA virginity, and I knew I would never experience a moment like that again. I had discovered my destiny, the place I belonged, and I realized I would be in the sport in some fashion for a long time."[178]

Penn continued his rise to stardom with wins over the world's top-ranked contenders at 155 pounds, Din Thomas and Caol Uno. Thomas had beaten the current champion, Jens Pulver, in WEF, but Penn had knocked him out easily with a knee. Thomas said, "I wish I knew [what happened]. But after the fight, I didn't even remember fighting. I just got caught, fell asleep you know?"[179] Penn had gotten the crowd going with his unusual ring entrance — instead of the standard jaunt out to the cage with his entourage, Penn ran to the fight in a dead sprint.

"I just get mad. Once I go in the ring, I'm not messing around," Penn explained at the post-fight press conference. "As soon as I walk in, a million things are going through my head. 'Walk out, look good, but then it's like, no way, forget about that. Let's go to fight now.' I really don't have an explanation for that. When I used to fight in the streets I'd be calm and once you're ready it's boom! That madness. I just click that on as I'm about to walk up."

Uno had taken Pulver to the limit in a five-round war. Penn knocked him out in just 11 seconds. "I trained for a fight that was going to be a war.

I was gonna take it to him and I expected it to go a while," Penn said. Instead, after a wild flying Uno kick, Penn knocked the Japanese star unconscious with a flurry of punches. Penn hopped the fence, and just as he had sprinted to the ring, he sprinted to the back. "I had only knocked out one guy in a street fight, and then I knocked out Din and Uno. Frank Shamrock and Javier Mendez said that I have the most powerful punches and was the hardest puncher in the division. . . . Frank was telling the UFC, 'This guy's got knockout power,' and I was saying, 'Okay, whatever you guys think.' Then I just started knocking guys out, and I was like, I guess I do have knockout power."[180]

During the Penn-Uno fight, Pulver was ringside doing commentary. The fight was going to crown a number-one contender for his UFC lightweight title. UFC play-by-play man Mike Goldberg remembers Pulver's vivid reaction: "Jens Pulver doesn't get intimidated by much, but he sat back and said, 'Wow. This kid's good.' And since that day, I think Jens Pulver knew he was going to meet 'The Prodigy.'" It was a fight that captured the imaginations of UFC fans. Penn was the hottest newcomer around, and Pulver had established himself as a dominant performer in the new weight class. For the first time, lightweights would headline a UFC pay-per-view.

THE FIGHT

Prior to the fight, Jens Pulver was furious. He had been entrusted by the UFC, first by former UFC matchmaker John Peretti and then by the new Zuffa owners, to help create the lightweight division. He had shouldered that responsibility and become the first champion in that division. And now a newcomer, a kid with just three fights, was getting all the attention. Not only was the B.J. Penn hype machine out of control, the kid from Hilo was actually favored in their fight.

"He was very mad that he was the underdog," UFC announcer and Hook and Shoot promoter Jeff Osborne said. "A three-to-one underdog — and that's a big spread." Pulver was motivated like he had never been before. He was literally beating his sparring partners up. Even venerable coach Pat Miletich, who almost never got the worst of stand-up sparring, was dropped by a body punch and had his nose broken. Pulver was fired up and ready to fight.

"I'm fighting against all those people who said I'm going to get trucked over, that I'll be helpless, that he's too good standing, that he's too good on the ground, that I've got no chance," the champion said before the fight. "I've trained to fight hard. I've been beating my teammates up day in and day out. I'm throwing harder than I've ever thrown in my life." What he said next was prescient, a criticism that would follow Penn throughout his career: when the going got tough, Penn would collapse mentally. "I look at B.J. as a momentum fighter. If things are going in his favor, he gets looser and looser and feels better and better. At the same time, if he gets in trouble, he's never been there. You can train for trouble, but it's not the same thing."

Penn came in to Phil Collins's "In the Air Tonight," making it, by proxy, the most manly moment in Phil Collins's career. The champion entered to a dazzling display, a WWE-style entrance that was part of the new Zuffa promotional strategy: if it looks major league, it must be major league. Penn was nervous, as always, and when the bell rang he moved away from his game plan to stand up with Pulver to start the fight. Instead he went for, and got, a takedown. Despite Pulver's wrestling pedigree, the jiu-jitsu champion had no problems putting him on his back. "B.J.'s got a better takedown than I ever imagined," Pulver said after the fight. But on his back, Pulver defended well. When Penn got a standing guillotine, Pulver seized the opportunity for a big slam, winning the round and putting the pressure on Penn.

Penn responded with his best round of the fight, faster to the punch on his feet before getting a takedown and the mount. Pulver said, "I knew how much time was left, but when he got the mount I was like, 'Oh, man, there is still two minutes left, how am I gonna keep this guy off me, how am I gonna get him off me, what am I gonna do to let John [the referee] know not to stop it? Don't let this guy do these little pity-pat flurries and stop this fight.' So when John said, 'Hey, let me know you're in it,' I was throwing punches. I threw everything, like, 'Hey, I'm in a bad position but I'm not done, I'm here,' and I remember Jeremy [Horn] yelling 'six seconds' when he went for that arm bar. So I was trying to get that time off, and I remember him getting that arm straight with about two seconds left and I'm like, 'Oh, dear lord,' and I was just like, you know, 'Snap it if you have to, whatever you got to do, break it, but I'm not tapping with two seconds left,' and that's when people were yelling, 'Oh, he tapped, he tapped.' No, I just knew when the bell was gonna ring, and as soon as it did I said all right, he didn't get it. Hey, he almost got it, almost, but luckily the round ended and I had another chance to come back and try again."[181]

On the replay, it looked like Pulver did tap out just after the bell rang to end the round. "I wish there had been a little more time left, but the bell sounded and I got the arm bar a little too late," Penn said. "I had it extended and pulled, but the round was up. I wasn't going to be unprofessional and try to hurt his arm. It would be unsportsmanlike."[182]

After the second round, Pulver was better able to counter Penn's take-downs, but Penn did well standing, often beating Pulver to the punch, throwing combinations while Pulver searched for one knockout punch like the one he landed on John Lewis's chin at UFC 28. "Hey, if I've got to take three to get one so be it. I always had that in me, and I had the confidence. If they hit me with a shot and the lights go out, so be it, but I had the con-fidence," Pulver said. "I had a love for standing up, and no matter what it took I was gonna make it work, and that's all it was. I mean, he hit me with a hook that swelled my eye up, swelled my nose up. Hey, that's just one shot, let's keep going. I'm still here, I'm still standing, let's keep fighting."[183]

Penn was game but not as aggressive as he'd been in the past. Pulver was able to counter his takedowns in the fourth round and do damage on the ground. When they were standing up, Penn was sharp with jabs and weak kicks, but never went for the kill. By the fifth round, Penn had given up on the takedowns and fought Pulver standing the whole round. Despite 20 minutes of hard fighting, Pulver looked fresh and got into a groove. When Pulver finally landed that big left hand, guest commentator Randy Couture knew why. "He threw the jab to set up the left hand, instead of just throwing the bomb." The announcers knew they were watching a classic title fight. "For those who thought B.J. couldn't stand, or that Pulver couldn't survive on the ground — they've all been proven wrong," Osborne said.

With 45 seconds left, Pulver erased any doubts that Penn was winning the fight, staggering him with a multi-punch combination. Penn survived thanks to an inadvertent low blow and the two battled to the bell. Pulver won a majority decision and was vindicated. "Sometimes, hype isn't enough. This is my fucking cage. Mine," the champion said. "Without a doubt the hardest fight of my life. A rematch is going to be inevitable because the guy can't be stopped."

Lightweights had just made history. After the fight, Penn looked both battered and spiritually broken. He would later say that it was a huge mistake to fight in two UFCs in a row. Six months of constant training had taken the fun out of the sport, but Penn was gracious in defeat. "My hat goes off to Jens Pulver," Penn said in the post-fight press conference. "I've never been in a fight like that in my life. I just wish it went another way, but Jens is the man."

Pulver was on top of the world. He was a UFC star coming off his first main event, and had won a fight the world had expected him to lose. "I just want to thank Lorenzo, Frank, Dana, Joe, and Zuffa for making the fight happen and believing in me and B.J. and giving us the main event," Pulver told the press after the bout. "Tito, I know what you go through — that's hard being the main event." But Pulver's new status as a main eventer would lead to his departure from the company. When he couldn't reconcile his championship status with his meagre paychecks, Pulver moved on to fight in Japan. It was the first of what would become many champions leaving Zuffa without losing their titles. It was a rough road to prosperity — luckily the Fertitta brothers had the money to see it through.

TITO VS. THE LION'S DEN

At UFC 40 in November 2002, Zuffa took another shot at mainstream success. It was always assumed that when the UFC made it back on pay-per-view, its financial woes would be over. That's what SEG had been fighting for when it owned the UFC. But even when the Ultimate Fighting Championship made it back on cable, things turned out to be a little more complicated.

"Our expectations were too high," Lorenzo Fertitta said. "They were not on par with where we thought we would be. Going back and looking at the great numbers that the UFC did in the early days, the thought process was that we'd get back on cable and be doing those numbers. The miscalculation was that it's not the same product as it was before. Unfortunately, it seems that [the fans] were more interested in tuning in to a spectacle or a car wreck than a true sporting event. I think we had to do everything we could to turn this into a sporting event for its mere survival. What we have to do now is re-evaluate, take the product we have, and make it as good as we can."[184]

Pay-per-view buys that had once surpassed 250,000 for Ken Shamrock's second fight with Royce Gracie were well below expectations. The new UFC, headlined by wrestlers Randy Couture, Matt Lindland, and Matt Hughes, had averaged around 50,000 buys. A closer look made things appear even worse for the UFC: in 1995 there had been only half as many homes wired for pay-per-view as there were in 2002. Way fewer people were watching the shows, but way more people had access to them. The UFC just wasn't able to attract an audience.

Hard-core fans of the sport were convinced the new breed of UFC fighters were superior to their pioneer counterparts in every way. They were in better shape, more skilled, and more athletic. But they weren't stars. Fans who had flocked to see the likes of Andy Anderson fight John Hess weren't as interested in the sanitized UFC. The emphasis for years had been on sportsmanship and respect. That was important when the sport was fighting for its life and every show was a battle with media critics and politicians. But those days were gone. And the casual sports fan wanted to see more than a genetically gifted athlete do battle with another respectful fighter no one had heard of. They wanted to see a fight, an old fashioned slug out, and they wanted to see someone they recognized. The UFC could promote the newer fighters as being better, but fans wanted to see them prove it in the ring.

Ken Shamrock was the biggest name in the history of the sport. Shamrock had left the company when SEG started struggling and joined Vince McMahon's WWF for a contract that paid into the mid six figures. Unfortunately for Shamrock, he made some bad investments and left control of his finances in the hands of the wrong people. "I lost my house, my gym, everything," Shamrock said. "After fighting all over the world, entertaining thousands upon thousands of fans on a nightly basis, I didn't have a penny to show for it. I was in my mid-thirties and back to square one."[185]

Shamrock had lost almost everything — not just all of his money, but his job with the WWF, his marriage, and his relationship with his father. He needed to start again, and returned to the only thing he really knew how to do: fighting.

"Fortunately, I started when the UFC first came out," Shamrock said. "And there are a lot of die-hard fans out there who still think the old UFC fighters are the greatest things that lived. It's great to have that."[186]

Shamrock made his return in 2000 for Pride. This was before the UFC was sold to Zuffa, and Bob Meyrowitz just couldn't afford to match what Pride offered — a three-fight deal for a rumored $350,000 a fight. So Shamrock went back to Japan, where his MMA career had started. After beating pro wrestler Alexander Otsuka, Shamrock lost two fights in a row. Against Kazayuki Fujita, his body let him down. Against former UFC 8 tournament champion Don Frye, he ran into a fighter with more guts than brains. Frye had gutted out a Ken Shamrock leg lock to win a decision. Frye won the fight, but battled a crippling painkiller addiction for years because of the damage Shamrock had done. Still, it was two losses in a row. Ken Shamrock had never lost two in a row, and seriously considered retiring. But Tito Ortiz still lingered in his memory.

TITO ENTERS THE LION'S DEN

Tito Ortiz was Zuffa's poster boy. He had grown up on the rough streets of Huntington Beach, California, the son of a Mexican father and an American mother. His parents had fallen into drugs, and Tito had fallen into the gang life. Wrestling took him out of the gangs and gave his life focus. He finished fourth at the state championships in his senior year of high school, and had won a junior college championship. His high school coach was Paul Herrerra, a former University of Nebraska Cornhusker who was a UFC fighter and good friend of Tank Abbott. When Abbott needed a big wrestler to spar with, Herrerra thought of Tito Ortiz.

"Tank needed a guy to train with, and I was 215–220 pounds and my wrestling skills were really good. I helped him out a lot," Ortiz said. "Tank was actually a really cool guy when you got to know who he was. His problem was alcohol. When I would speak to Tank, he was a very caring person. But when that Tank Abbott persona started happening, he was a force not to be messed with. I remember him singling people out in clubs and bars. He'd find the biggest guy he could and punk him in front of everybody. It's just one of those things. You don't have to be like that, man. I came to realize that the way to grow and become a better fighter and a better person was to keep myself away from people like that, who are so negative. And I did."[187]

Ortiz was focused on wrestling, and didn't really commit to MMA until he saw Jerry Bohlander win a few fights in the UFC. He had beaten Bohlander in high school, had wiped the mat with him. If Bohlander could do it, Ortiz knew he could, too. He made his Octagon debut at UFC 13, winning his first match as a tournament alternate before being submitted by Guy Mezger of the Lion's Den. Mezger had years of professional experience, and Ortiz had more than held his own with less than six months worth of training. Ortiz had been winning the fight, and had Mezger cut and reeling. Mezger was gushing blood when referee Big John McCarthy stopped the fight to let the ringside doctor check the cut. When the action started again,

Ortiz was immediately caught in a guillotine. He went from thinking he had won the tournament in his debut to being just another Lion's Den victim.

"I thought Tito got a raw deal. I thought he had Mezger in a lot of trouble, and Guy was not going to be able to get out of that position," UFC matchmaker Joe Silva said. "If it had to be stopped because he was bleeding, then it's over. I think Tito thought he won. And he didn't. They restarted it, he got caught, and Guy won. I felt bad for Tito. I thought he was winning the fight. And certainly he came in and had something about him. He had that extra quality, so I wanted to see him back. And then he just never was back."[188]

Tito had competed in the UFC for fun. But he still intended to follow his wrestling dream as far as he could take it.

"I fought as a complete amateur, just so I could keep my scholarship for wrestling. I wanted to keep competing in wrestling because my idea wasn't really to be a fighter, it was to see what this stuff was about, to have fun. Really, my dream was to make it as a coach," Ortiz said. He continued his college wrestling career at Cal State Bakersfield, but struggled with a new coach and injuries. Just when he was questioning his future plans, the UFC came calling again.

"I took a huge chance. It was either continue and get my degree or fight. I took a chance and I got out of school and I continued fighting. When I fought again, it was against Jerry Bohlander. . . . I stopped him in 15 minutes and I think a star was born right there. It was something I really loved doing — being on television. I got my 15 minutes of fame and it became my career."[189]

After the Bohlander fight, Tito put on a T-shirt that said "I Just Fucked Your Ass." It became his trademark. "It was nothing against Bohlander at all," Ortiz said. "A porno company was sponsoring me and helping me out, so I wore the T-shirt for them. From that point on, people were like, 'What are you going to wear for another T-shirt?' I thought, 'I'm going to roll with this ball right here. This ball is rolling really well.'"[190]

SEG saw potential in Ortiz and brought him back on the very next show, UFC 19. It was a rematch with Guy Mezger, a chance for Ortiz to avenge his loss and for Mezger to get revenge for his teammate Bohlander. Mezger was an established star, the King of Pancrase in Japan, and was confident in his chances. His pre-fight talk about Ortiz being a boy in a man's game just made Ortiz mad.

"Tito's very brash and cocky," UFC President Dana White said. "He did a lot of stuff that pissed people off, which made him very popular, very fast. It really started to blow up when he had the confrontation with Ken Shamrock. Tito fought Guy Mezger, who was one of Ken's best fighters. Tito won the fight, jumped up, and flipped off the Lion's Den, which was Ken's training camp. And Ken Shamrock freaked out, jumped up on the Octagon, and started screaming at him."[191]

It wasn't just the middle fingers that had enraged Shamrock. Ortiz put on a new T-shirt that said, "Gay Mezger is my Bitch."

"Obviously I wasn't real happy with it," Mezger said, "Tito at that time was a kid, kind of a punk, actually. He's matured a lot over the years, and I can have friendly conversations with him. I figure if I'm still upset about it this many years later, I probably need a counsellor more than anything else. At the time, it irritated me. My ego was a little busted up."

Shamrock was more than irritated. He was already angry at what he saw was an early stoppage. The middle finger and the T-shirt pushed him over the edge. He jumped on the cage and started yelling at Ortiz, who yelled right back. Shamrock was still with the WWF at the time, but looked ready to go at it in the Octagon right then. He was wagging his finger in Ortiz's face like a 250-pound schoolteacher. McCarthy had to physically remove Ortiz to prevent a donnybrook. "Don't let me catch you with that shirt, Tito," Shamrock warned.

Shamrock continued his tirade backstage, breaking a table and laying in wait for Ortiz, who was unapologetic. Mezger had started it, and Ortiz had finished it.

"Ken Shamrock's a big boy. I don't know if I want to tangle with him," Ortiz said. "His guy talked a bunch of shit before the fight. I let my fight do the talking. You saw what happened. . . . I guess he got a little pissed because I beat up on Jerry and I beat up on little Gay Mezger."[192]

Security was everywhere, and UFC officials were scared a brawl might break out. Shamrock had the whole Lion's Den backing him up. Ortiz had Mark Coleman and Kevin Randleman in his locker room, and they were down for whatever. "Nobody's getting jumped," Randleman said. "I'll fight anybody, anywhere." Order was restored and violence was prevented. But the incident was far from forgotten.

"Do whatever you want before the fight, during the fight — but when the bell rings and your hand is raised or not raised, you show a little respect," Shamrock said. "And if you don't want to show any respect at all, don't show any disrespect. To me, that's lowering our event to where it doesn't need to be. We're trying to elevate ourselves to a professional organization. And in order to do that, we have to have professional athletes. I take nothing from Tito Ortiz's ability, but I do have a lot to say about his attitude and what he did to me and the Lion's Den. I did say I would not leave the mixed martial arts world until I got in there and got the opportunity to knuckle him up."

UFC 40

The Fertittas and Dana White were thrilled to have Ken Shamrock back in the fold. Not only could they match their biggest modern star against their biggest star of all time, but there was also a compelling storyline driving the fight. It was a potential matchup that fans had been debating for three years.

White said, "The reason we did so well on UFC 40 was because of Ken Shamrock and the fact that everybody knew who he was. . . . I think the sad part is that those guys [the older stars], at the end of the day, are the only guys anybody knows about. My thinking is that if we bring these guys in, maybe we'll bring back a lot of old fans. When they tune in to see [them], they will see the awesome athletes we have now. They will see Chuck Liddell and Robbie Lawler and Carlos Newton, and hopefully they'll want to come back and watch them again."[193]

If any fight could get the UFC back on track, this was it. Shamrock and Ortiz hated each other, and even the fighters were intrigued by the possibilities. While it seemed that Ortiz would have a wrestling advantage, the same had been true of Dan Severn. Ortiz had run over the Lion's Den students, but everyone knew Ken Shamrock tapped everyone right and left in the training room. Could he overpower and submit Ortiz as well?

"Everyone wants to see this fight," UFC matchmaker Joe Silva said. "I think it is a huge matchup. It has even captured the interest of most of the other fighters. . . . It has had more buildup than those other fights because people have known for a long time that they don't like each other. . . . It's not exaggerated at all, especially on Ken's side. Ken is a proud guy, and he really feels that Tito has disrespected him and his team, and he is out for some payback."[194]

The press conference set the stage for what was to follow. The promotion had emphasized sportsmanship and respect for so long, the theatrics seemed out of place.

"Tito Ortiz is going to find out what Ken Shamrock is all about. I guarantee you that," Shamrock said at the pre-fight press conference. "So if I was you, I hope to God you come ready. 'Cause if you don't, I'm going to beat you into the living death."

Shamrock stared at Ortiz long and hard. It looked like an over-the-top act, but it was not. If you've seen Shamrock's pro wrestling career in the wwe, you know that he's not nearly that good of an actor. He was fired up, and Tito Ortiz fanned the flames when he laughed out loud. Welterweight champion Matt Hughes could barely keep his composure onstage. Shamrock's intensity was funny, and a little scary too, especially when he kicked a chair right into a surprised Dana White's arms.

"I might have overreacted by laughing hard," Tito said. "But it was all I could do. It was either I was going to get up and punch him in his face, or I was going to laugh about it. I figured I'd be the bigger man and I'd laugh about it. He flipped out like Ken Shamrock always does. He can't handle the pressure."

Shamrock wasn't done. He had three years of pent-up aggression. Three years of thinking about the T-shirt. Three years of hard time on the road with the wwf that had amounted to nothing. This was his chance to finally let it all out.

"You think this is all fun and games, but when that cage shuts and the bell rings, you'll find out it's not fun and games," Shamrock said. "This ain't the wwf, boy."

Tito Ortiz stayed calm and collected. Ken Shamrock looked spent. He'd wasted all of his energy and emotion before the fight. It was certainly a more impressive performance than he put on in the ring. You could almost sense the defeatism in his corner. They were saying the right things, but their eyes told another story.

"A month ago, he was fired up and ready to go," Lion's Den teammate Tra Telligman said. "And now he's saying, 'Let's just get this over with.'"

Shamrock had an incredibly difficult time cutting the weight for this fight. He battled a knee injury that kept him from running it off; instead he went on a crash diet. He crashed too hard. By the time the two weighed in, Shamrock was only 201 pounds, four pounds shy of the light heavyweight limit. Ortiz would go into the cage with a significant weight advantage. Still, Shamrock's disciples held out hope.

"I've never doubted Ken. Even when Ken has gone into fights where he couldn't lift his arm above his head, I never doubted him. He's family, and family's something," Lion's Den fighter Vernon White said. "Even when you know there's a chance they won't win, you're still behind them 100 percent, and you give them all the love and positive attention. You give them every-thing. Even if it meant I got hurt, I still went out there and worked with him, knowing he was hurt, knowing he could still hurt me, because he's hurt. When people are hurt, self-preservation comes in and they hurt other people. I've gone out there and gotten ribs broken. We have both sacrificed a lot for each other. We've broken bones, bled, sweated, and cried for each other. We're family. I never doubt Ken."

The crowd at the MGM Grand was electric. A full house of 13,370 fans had packed in to see the old collide with the new. Fans were pretty sure Ortiz would have too much for the old man. But even at 38 years of age, Shamrock had that charisma, that aura and name that meant something. No one would be too surprised if the legend taught the younger man a lesson in humility. It was "the greatest night in Mixed Martial Arts history," Mike Goldberg said. And he was not far wrong. It was the best night in MMA history for Zuffa. They drew a live gate of more than $1.5 million and doubled their previous best pay-per-view sales. One hundred fifty thou-sand homes paid $29.95 each to watch the fight.

Zuffa had finally found what would become its permanent broadcast team, adding comedian Joe Rogan as the color man. He had done backstage interviews for SEG's UFC thanks to his manger's lifelong friendship with Campbell McClaren. Rogan was a sharp fan of the sport and had a back-ground in both tae kwon do and Brazilian jiu-jitsu. He knew the fight game and had infectious enthusiasm. His newfound celebrity status as the host of *Fear Factor* was icing on the cake. "Fans of the UFC know Joe is a regular at our events. So when I asked him to be the color commentator for UFC 40 with Ken and Tito in the main event, I didn't know if he could do it with his busy schedule. But I knew with all of his experience, he was the right man," Dana White said. "Joe and I have become friends over the years, and his intimacy with the sport and his knowledge of the fighters is going to be a huge benefit for the viewers at home."

Rogan had a great fight to start his broadcast career in earnest. Shamrock came out aggressively, showing an improved stand-up game. His last fights in Japan were marred by cardio problems that had even caused him to drop out of a fight he was winning with Japanese star Kaz Fujita, famously telling his corner to stop the fight with an audible "Petey, my heart!" He was determined to end this one before that could happen. But Ortiz was too much for him, even standing and punching.

"I dominated Ken like everybody didn't think I would," Ortiz said at the post-fight press conference. "I grabbed a hold of Ken and . . . he ain't that strong. He was not that strong. It amazed me. I grabbed a hold of him, he felt like a rag doll."

Ortiz was known strictly as a ground-and-pound wrestler, but he had been working diligently on his Muay Thai kickboxing. He outpowered and outpunched Shamrock, even landing a knee to the chin that rocked him.

"[Tito's] being pushed by the best guys in the world," Rogan said. "Guys bigger than him, like Ricco Rodriguez. Better jiu-jitsu guys, better kick-boxers. He is in tremendous condition and totally prepared for this fight."

Ken Shamrock showed a warrior's heart. For three long rounds he was demoralized and decimated by Tito Ortiz's well-rounded attack. His face was a bloody and bruised mess. "Look at Ken Shamrock's face," Rogan said. "It looks like he got hit with a howitzer." It was an extended and one-sided beating. But Ken took it like a man before retiring to his stool for the evening. Tra Telligman stopped the fight by throwing in the towel.

Shamrock was classy in defeat, embracing Ortiz and saying he was the better man. Only later did he claim that he had a severely damaged ACL going in to the fight. There was no doubt that Shamrock had been banged up for some time. But his physical tools didn't seem to be what hampered him that night. It was Ortiz's complete game that hurt the "World's Most Dangerous Man," not his knee. Ortiz was just better than Shamrock in every phase of the fight game.

Zuffa was thrilled with the fight and the night. It had given this event the full-court press and it had paid off. It had failed miserably the first time it reintroduced the UFC at UFC 33. UFC 40 was a triumph. "We had such high hopes for our first big show in Las Vegas," Silva said. "And anything that could go wrong went wrong. . . . I begged, I pleaded, 'Please, fight your hearts out. Make me look good.' And they did. These guys are the best fighters in the world."

They announced that another UFC legend would be making his return. Tank Abbott would headline the next show. Silva was furious, sure that Abbott was more trouble than he was worth, and had never drawn a crowd. Although the fans popped for Abbott, the buy rates did not.

Abbott would headline the next show, but the buzz was about another future fight: Tito Ortiz taking on his number-one contender, Chuck Liddell. "The Iceman" Liddell had already earned the number-one contender slot with a string of victories in the Octagon, but risked it all against tough Brazilian fighter Renato "Babalu" Sobral. "Chuck Liddell and his manager called me and said they wanted to fight on this card," White said. "I said, 'What are you, nuts? What do you mean you want to fight on this card? You've got an automatic shot at the title. Why would you do that?' Chuck said, 'I don't care about that. I want to fight. I'm not concerned about losing. I'm not going to lose. I don't lose.' I fought with them forever, and I didn't want this fight. Chuck wanted it . . . Chuck was right. I was wrong. I admit it. Chuck is unbelievable."

By the end of 2002, everyone was excited about the possibility of Ortiz–Liddell. . . .

Everyone but Tito Ortiz.

Chuck Liddell wasn't handed stardom. He fought for it in the cage. After a loss to Jeremy Horn at UFC 19 in 1999, Liddell had strung together ten wins in a row, including solid victories over star fighters like Vitor Belfort, Guy Mezger, Murillo Bustamante, and former heavyweight champion Kevin Randleman. He was building a fan base, and his former manager Dana White was the new UFC president. Big things were in the Iceman's future. The only thing standing in his way was Tito Ortiz. And Ortiz didn't want to fight.

After Ortiz's win over Ken Shamrock at UFC 40, the build for Ortiz and Liddell was officially on. "I can't even begin to fathom a match between Tito Ortiz and Chuck Liddell," UFC announcer Joe Rogan said. The UFC brought Chuck into the ring to promote what was going to be its next blockbuster main event. It didn't take long for Ortiz to put a damper on the crowd's enthusiasm.

"I don't know. I'm not really thinking about that right now," Ortiz said. "Me and Chuck, I guess we gotta sit back and look at it. I guess we gotta renegotiate things, because our friendship is not worth the money we're getting paid, if you ask me. If we're gonna get in here . . . I'm gonna make it worthwhile for me and him. So I don't know, I guess we'll be going to Japan to fight, possibly. But that's the last thing on my mind right now."

Dana White had created a monster. He had orchestrated a holdout for Ortiz when he had been his manager. He was a tough negotiator, and SEG owner Bob Meyrowitz hated dealing with White. The tough negotiating posture had stuck with Ortiz, and now White was on the other side of the bargaining table. Ortiz was coming off the UFC's greatest success in the Zuffa era, and was demanding a fairer shake. In his mind, Tank Abbott and Ken Shamrock had altered the pay scale.

"When Tank Abbott gets paid $150,000 to lie on the mat and get tapped out in 30 seconds, and I am only getting paid $80,000, there's a big difference there," Ortiz said. "In my mind, it didn't make sense. Why am I sacrificing [and not getting] what this guy is making?"[195] Ortiz had just finished the second fight in a six-fight contract, paying him $80,000 to fight and $80,000 to win. He wanted a significant raise to fight Liddell, and the UFC wasn't blinking.

"A lot of fighters, these guys just don't understand. All they care about is fighting. They don't care about their future," Ortiz said. "I think the fighters should be getting paid the right amount of money, and someone needs to make a stand, and I think a lot of us fighters need to come together. Possibly create a union. If there was a union for us fighters, then everybody would get paid the same salary cap and everything. . . . When guys are getting paid $1,500, $2,500 just to show up and compete in the UFC, that's just ridiculous, man. Money like that shouldn't even be thrown around. It takes anywhere from $5,000 to $6,000 for a training camp for a fight. How are you going to live off of $2,500 or $5,000?"[196]

There was another reason for Ortiz's reticence in fighting Liddell. The two were former training partners and casual friends. When both were managed by White, Liddell helped Ortiz prepare for his fight with Evan Tanner at UFC 30 in February 2001. He hadn't come away impressed with the champion.

"One day we decided to spar one-on-one," Liddell said. "I leveled him with a shot to the body. . . . It happened a few times. I finally put my hands down, looked at Dana, and said, 'I am not going to hit him anymore. He drops every time I hit him.' Dana was so mad that Tito was so soft he started screaming at him, 'Get back on your feet, motherfucker.' But he wouldn't."[197]

Ortiz wasn't denying that Chuck was a tough opponent for him. "He's pretty difficult to take down," Ortiz said. "I mean of course him being a former Cal Poly wrestler. I mean the guy has a lot of education in wrestling, of course. I think there's scrambling positions, a lot of them I could win. I mean, that's a fight you've just got to get down."[198]

Still, sparring and fighting are two different things. There are plenty of fighters, like Ken Shamrock, who are legendary in the gym when they work out. Their performances in the Octagon are less stellar. In baseball, they call them five o'clock hitters; guys who are amazing in batting practice but can't get it done in a live game. Ortiz wasn't convinced that Liddell could take it to him when it counted. But as the days turned to months, the usually laid-back Liddell started getting restless. He had waited patiently while the UFC brought in Shamrock to usurp his number-one contendership. Now he wanted the title fight he had earned.

"I think he's worried about losing, obviously," Liddell said. "He's been coming up with a lot of excuses. Excuses are a dime a dozen. He came up with all of them. He bruised his hand in what? November [five months earlier]? Come on. In the UFC, Gan [McGee] broke his hand in September and was training with me in October. He was helping me get ready for my fight. Whatever. He is going to have to step up sooner or later."[199]

Ortiz continued to have a myriad of excuses. He had several nagging injuries, movie commitments, and a friendship to consider. Liddell admitted that he and Ortiz had been friends. Ortiz was a guy he knew and was friendly with. But they weren't tight. Ortiz wasn't a close friend, like Scott Adams or Gan McGee. He would fight Ortiz. Ortiz had once felt the same way. The whispers that Ortiz was yellow, scared to fight the Iceman, became louder and louder.

"Go back and watch the interview after I fought Vitor [Belfort]," Liddell said. "[Tito] said, 'All friendship aside, I'm going to have to give Chuck a loss.' That is exactly what he said after I fought Vitor. It is kind of funny when he changes his tune when I am his next fight. Not Ken Shamrock, but me."[200]

Eventually, Zuffa had to act. It had dozens of fighters under contract, and legal obligations to each one. Liddell needed a fight, had earned a title fight, and it didn't look like Ortiz was going to step up.

"The only correspondence we've had from Tito's guys is that Tito is hurt and that he had entertainment commitments," UFC President Dana White said. "That's why he couldn't fight. Per Chuck Liddell's contract, he was guaranteed a title shot. We also owe Chuck so many fights during his contract. He had to fight this time, and it has to be for the title."[201]

When Zuffa had a contractual dispute with lightweight champion Jens Pulver, it eventually just dropped the title. When welterweight champion

B.J. Penn signed for a big-money fight with K-1, he was stripped of his title. With Ortiz, the biggest name in the business, Zuffa tried a different tactic. Instead of waiting Ortiz out or releasing him outright, the UFC would crown the first of what would become many interim champions.

THE NATURAL

Liddell's opponent for the interim light heavyweight championship was a legend thought to be in the final stages of a great career. Randy Couture was three weeks shy of 40 years of age, and had just lost convincingly to two heavyweight behemoths.

Couture had won two amazing fights with perennial contender Pedro Rizzo, and showed unparalleled skill and grit. What Couture lacked was size. This didn't hinder him against average-sized heavyweights like Rizzo or bigger heavyweights who lacked athleticism and skill. But it spelled trouble when he was matched with a 260-pounder who could move with the speed and grace of a much smaller man. Couture lost his heavyweight crown at UFC 36 to one of these new-era heavyweights, Josh Barnett. But when Barnett was later suspended for steroid use, Couture was given a reprieve. The title was returned to him.

His next fight wasn't any easier. Grappler extraordinaire Ricco Rodriguez was also just a little too big for Couture to handle. Couture had won the first round in both the Barnett and Rodriguez fights. But eventually, the larger challenger had gotten on top of the champion, and Couture had, each time, been unable to escape. Rodriguez had overwhelmed "The Natural," and left him beltless and with a broken eye socket.

Couture was clearly overmatched by his bigger challengers, and was looking to make a change. He was still in great shape, and didn't think he was done with the fight game. He just needed to pick on someone his own size. He looked down to the 205-pound fighters and liked his chances.

"I had friends who said, 'You need to go down to light heavyweight . . . these guys are too big . . . you used to wrestle at 198 . . . you should be fighting at 205. Somebody needs to shut Tito up. . . . Why don't you go down and do it?' All that kind of stuff from my friends. And after the Ricco fight, it made a lot of sense. The guys were just getting too big in the heavyweight division. And they're not just big guys like the first guys I fought. They know how to fight. And weight becomes a huge advantage."[202]

Couture would end up in the cage with Liddell, however, while everyone waited for Ortiz to make his highly anticipated return. "I presented the scenario to them," Joe Silva said. "Randy Couture. . . . He's a two-time heavyweight champion. He's a popular guy who's recently lost his title. But he was always a very small heavyweight. I knew he was small enough that, if he wanted to, he could fight at 205."[203] Couture looked like the perfect opponent for Liddell. He was a well-known name, but didn't seem like a big threat to defeat the rising star. "Everyone pretty much assumed I was being fed to Chuck to build him up," Couture said.[204] He was filling in for Ortiz, a placeholder until the real marquee main event of Liddell and Ortiz could be negotiated.

INTERIM CHAMPION

"I've always had the feeling that Randy knew this was coming. We had been working out together for a few days before the fight was announced," Liddell said. "His coach asked me how I set up certain moves, especially for getting out of trouble when I am in the bottom position. But Randy was a heavyweight; I didn't see us fighting soon."[205]

Couture trained with his former opponent Maurice Smith to prepare for Liddell. Like when he faced noted puncher Vitor Belfort, the wrestler was able to outstrike the striker. Couture was one of the most studious fighters in the game, and had closely analyzed Liddell's fights. He knew that to beat Liddell you had to keep the pressure on him. Couture used his aggressive stand-up to put Liddell on the defensive, and then used his superior wrestling to put him on his back. It was a dominating performance against a fighter who had looked unstoppable.

"The biggest thing we worked on was cutting off the ring and basically hunting him down," Couture said. "He likes to back up, then come in and make his attack, then back out and make you kind of follow him. And the guys who follow him and allow him to have that space allow him to control the tempo. So we worked on cornering him, cutting him off, and I think you saw that a lot tonight."[206]

Couture was in Liddell's face all night long, slamming him hard to the mat and amazing everyone with his boxing prowess. "He was just better than me that day," Liddell said. "I didn't condition right for it, and about three minutes into that first round I was tired."

Liddell had injured his MCL before the fight, but would make no excuses. He had been beaten by one of the UFC's all-time greats. The company was still having trouble negotiating with Ortiz, and this great fight between two respected fan favorites gave the interim title legitimacy and gravitas it might have otherwise lacked.

"The way the interim champion works is basically this man right here [Couture] is the light heavyweight champion of the world until Tito Ortiz comes and takes it from him," White said. "If Tito wants his belt back, he has to come and take it back from Randy."

Captain America Triumphant

The holdout was a turning point for Ortiz's career. He claimed he wasn't afraid to fight Liddell, but his tough negotiations with the company were less about his overall salary and more about getting more of his money guaranteed up front. Instead of being confident that he would win and collect his bonus, Ortiz wanted his money win or lose. He was estatic not to have to fight Liddell, and was willing to fight Couture. Ortiz stepped into a title shot at UFC 44 in September 2003 that was originally meant for Vitor Belfort, who was looking to avenge a loss to Couture at UFC 15.

"I don't think Tito deserves to fight for the belt," Vitor Belfort said. Belfort had faced both Couture and Liddell in the past, and was hungry for redemption. "He doesn't want to fight Chuck. Chuck is up there. He's a warrior. Tito dropped down. Everybody knows he pulled out to avoid fighting Chuck . . . Randy came, and, like I said, this 205-pound light heavyweight division is tough. I want to fight my idol. Randy, I'm sorry, but I want that belt."

Belfort would get the next title shot. But first Dana White and Zuffa would unify the interim and light heavyweight titles. Ortiz brought not just his title belt to the table, but also his unique ability to promote a fight and get under his opponent's skin. Even the unflappable Randy Couture was drawn into the verbal combat.

"Tito kind of brings a certain intensity and persona to the pre-fight hype and it's not my style," Couture said. "It's not what I like to do. It's not how I like to represent myself or the sport. And he kind of forced me to stand up and do a few things I'm not used to doing — talking back a little bit, and, fortunately, I didn't have to make up a lot of what I felt. I pretty much said what I felt about the situation, and was able to do that with conviction, so that made it easier for me. Generally, I would have kept those thoughts and feelings to myself and just gone out and done my job."²⁰⁷

Ortiz had been out of action for nearly a year. In that year, he had gone from being the dominant champion to a fighter people were mocking for a lack of courage. He wasn't happy — with the media, the promotion, or the interim champion. "I am afraid of no man, let me tell you that, for one, I am afraid of no man," Ortiz said. "I felt really disrespected. All of a sudden, Tito out of the picture . . . it seems like I am now the challenger. Of course I am the champion, but there is a little feeling of being the underdog, and I love being the underdog."

The UFC and Zuffa were put into a strange situation. They truly disliked Ortiz — vehemently by this point. Even though White had been a manager, he didn't have any natural empathy for the fighters he was negotiating with. He couldn't understand why Ortiz was being so demanding. The company was losing fistfuls of money, and one of the only guys who could staunch the flow was demanding more and more.

The pay-per-view numbers were back in the toilet without the top star. After Shamrock-Ortiz drew the big number at UFC 40, the shows were back under 70,000 again. Matt Hughes had drawn less than 40,000 buys for his UFC 42 main event against Sean Sherk. Even Couture's win over Liddell had netted less than 50,000 buys. The show needed Ortiz and his star power.

"I suppose I should thank Tito for creating this situation in the first place, and allowing me to come down from heavyweight and compete against Chuck," Couture said. "Undisputed is a great name for the title of this fight coming up. I look forward to the opportunity to compete against Tito. I don't know about calling this championship I hold now an interim title. Because I was willing to step up and fight the guy Tito really didn't want to fight. . . . But Tito is a great fighter, well rounded, a lot of great skills, and I think this settles the dispute once and for all, and unifies this weight class. I savor the opportunity to get in there."

Couture was being diplomatic as the two went back and forth in front of the media. Ortiz wasn't convinced there was a dispute about who the real champion was. He had earned the title and had never lost it. Couture's was bogus.

"Wait, wait, wait, wait, wait . . . last time I looked at my bedroom, I think there was a belt next to my bed," Ortiz said. "And it is still there, too, and it does say light heavyweight champion on it, and the last time I remember, I got through beating up Ken Shamrock."

The banter went on. The painfully polite Couture was getting drawn into a feud with the brash Ortiz. "It doesn't change the fact that you weren't willing to fight Chuck for whatever reason and I did," Couture said.

"I have no problem with that at all, your beating is going to come soon enough," Ortiz said. "But at the same time, last time I looked I was still the champ."

Ortiz may have succeeded in drawing Couture into the pre-fight hysterics that go along with any Ortiz match, but it didn't help him inside the cage at all. Ortiz was confident that he would easily beat Couture. Even though Couture had better wrestling credentials on paper, so did Vladmir Matsushenkyo. And Ortiz had easily outwrestled him. But Couture turned out to be a completely different animal. The freestyle wrestling Matsushenkyo specialized in was more technical than tough. Couture was a veteran of the more rough-and-tumble collegiate folkstyle and world competition in Greco-Roman wrestling. He put Ortiz on the mat for five rounds and kept him there.

"It was everything I didn't expect. Randy Couture caught me totally off guard," Ortiz said. "He outwrestled me in every aspect, as a wrestler and as a fighter. It was his night. I couldn't take anything away from him. Randy Couture showed me a weakness that I should have never looked past, and that was wrestling."[208]

Couture even got a final blow in on the Huntington Beach Bad Boy. Toward the end of the fight, with Couture dominating Ortiz on the ground, he reached down and gave him a spanking. It was a memorable moment, and Ortiz hated being the butt of the joke. He was sure that his extended pre-fight media campaign had hurt his performance. Ortiz was demanding an immediate rematch.

"Well, you know, I had a lot of PR stuff as well, so I think that excuse is as solid as water," Couture told mmanews.com. "I would fight Tito again, but I think he needs to fight Chuck Liddell first."

FRIENDSHIP ASUNDER

In an MMAWeekly.com interview, Liddell said, "I'm convinced he [Ortiz] won't fight me. He'll never fight me. The guy is a coward; he's not a real fighter. He doesn't want to fight someone who he thinks can beat him. And he knows that's true, not only today but back when we used to train together and I used to pound him. I haven't talked about it that much because training is training, but you can ask Dana White. If he originally stepped up to fight me, then it would be just like any other fighter, whether I won or lost. But when he talks all this shit. He just has a big mouth. If he would fight me, if he would really fight me, this would be a non-issue. Instead, he just talks shit about how much he wants to fight me even though he knows it's not true. I'll be shocked if he ever actually does step up and fight me."

Ortiz had gotten inside Liddell's head. They called Liddell "The Iceman" because he was cool, calm, and collected going into a fight. But Ortiz had gotten under his skin. Normally, an opponent was just an opponent, an obstacle in his way. But this was getting personal. Ortiz had focused in on Liddell's losses to Couture and to Ortiz's training partner Quinton Jackson, in Pride, like a laser beam. It was yet another chance for Ortiz to talk trash.

"I'm going in there to try to hurt him. I'm going to show him no respect, and I'm going to go in there and try to take his head off," Ortiz said. "He leaves himself open to shots. He might throw one or two shots really, really hard. They'll catch average guys and knock them out. But I'm not an average guy."

The promotion for the fight was pure pro wrestling. At UFC 46, they called both fighters to the ring. Ortiz had record amounts of swagger, and the two stared bullets at each other. Joe Rogan moderated as the two men did their best "Stone Cold" Steve Austin impressions.

"The Iceman? With that belly, you look more like the snowman," Ortiz said. "You think I was ducking you? I just didn't want to give you a beating. But now it's going to happen." Liddell was not impressed. "This guy's been talking all this shit for a long time. He's the one who started talking shit. . . . He better have been practicing his wrestling, because I know he's not man enough to stand in the middle of this ring and strike with me. . . . If he's man enough to stand in the middle of this ring, I'll knock him out. And he knows it."

Although the UFC had toned down some of the pyrotechnics and elaborate ring entrances, as a cost-cutting move for the most part, it was still promoting WWE-style feuds. UFC President Dana White wasn't happy with the comparison.

"I don't tell the fighters what to do or how to come out or what to say. As far as WWE goes, they control every aspect of what those actors are doing. Those guys are actors. They have scripts that are written by the WWE, and they have personas that are created by the WWE. We don't do any of that kind of stuff. These guys are real fighters," White said. "The thing with Chuck Liddell and Tito Ortiz — we just got them both in the Octagon and they did an interview with Joe Rogan. None of that was scripted. They knew they were going to come in there, so I'm sure they thought about what was going to be said. But none of that is scripted or planned out or rehearsed. None of it."[209]

It was a fight that was years in the making, and a matchup that captured the attention of the global media. The two men promoted the show on Fox Sports's *Best Damn Sports Show Period* and on the *Carson Daly Show*. It was one of those matchups that intrigued fighters as much as it did fans. Vitor Belfort, who had just defeated Randy Couture thanks to a fluke cut, was particularly interested, as he might be defending his new light heavyweight title against the winner.

"Tito can surprise with his strikes. Chuck is not scared of punching at all. He goes forward," Belfort said. "Tito has much more to lose than Chuck because he's talking all the crap. I think Chuck is very humble right now. He learned a lesson, I think. When you talk, you have to prove, and it's bad when you don't prove. That's how life is. The more you talk, the more responsibility you have to do it. So the less you speak, the less it matters whether things go bad or good. People always respect you, which is a good way to live, I think."[210]

It's On

Ortiz, after all the delays and all the talk, almost didn't make the fight. "About three months ago, I had a little scare. I was wrestling a guy and I was going to inside trip him and my knee popped," Ortiz said. "My ACL, I had a little partial tear in training, but it hasn't hindered me at all." He was ready to get in the Octagon.

It was a true grudge match, and the crowd was amped. Everything seemed a little bigger. The weigh-ins saw Chuck Liddell looking as lean as he ever had for a fight. When Ortiz tried to make him flinch, he didn't move an inch. He stepped back and shot Ortiz a double-bird salute. Liddell was enjoying himself. "I knew it bothered him that he didn't intimidate me at all," Liddell told MMAWeekly.com's *Sound Off Radio*.

After losing his last fight in Pride to Ortiz's training partner Quinton Jackson, Liddell went back to basics. No more all-star camps. He was back at The Pit (John Hackleman's famous, bare bones training facility) with his usual crew, and was feeling very relaxed and confident. Unusually so, even for a man nicknamed "The Iceman."

"I've seen him more animated for this fight than I've ever seen him," Liddell's trainer John Hackleman said. "He's much more upbeat. He's laughing and dancing around. That aspect is going to play in our favor in this fight. You're going to see the emotion come with the power."[211]

With the crowd at a fever pitch as the fighters made their way to the Octagon, Rogan set the stage for what announcer Mike Goldberg called the biggest fight in UFC history. It was a funny way to describe a contest between two men coming off devastating losses, but it really did feel that way. If this wasn't the best matchup in MMA, it was certainly the most anticipated.

"The biggest grudge match in the history of mixed martial arts is about to occur," Rogan said. "These guys truly hate each other. They started out as friends, started out as training partners. How close were they as friends? Depends who you ask. Tito says they were great friends, Chuck says they were acquaintances, at best. Just training partners, and he would have fought him at any time."

As Ortiz circled the ring, he threw his hat to the crowd. A Liddell fan threw it right back into the Octagon. The fighters had set the tone. It seemed even the crowd was in a fighting mood. When the fight began, so did the chants of "Tito, Tito." Ortiz was true to his word, standing with Liddell and even beating him to the punch on several occasions. Liddell was moving forward, more aggressive than usual and not content to counter Ortiz. He normally waited for his prey to come to him, but he was actively hunting Ortiz down.

"Tito has always said that he'll go toe-to-toe with Chuck, and Chuck has contended that he will not go toe-to-toe," Goldberg said. But Tito was standing in there, making only two attempts at trying to take Liddell to the mat. "I don't know if it's guts or a lack of a good game plan." Goldberg said. It was an even exchange until Liddell took the round with a flurry of punches and a kick in the final 15 seconds. Ortiz was undaunted, screaming in Liddell's face, telling him to bring it on. Liddell had said that if Tito stood on his feet and punched with him, he would knock him out in the first round. That didn't happen.

Early in the second round, Liddell's hand opened up on a punch and he gouged Ortiz in the eye. As Ortiz checked his eye and staggered backwards, Liddell exploded into action, landing a barrage of punches that sent Ortiz down and sent referee John McCarthy into action to stop the fight. The thumb in the eye would become a Liddell trademark. It was a common technique in Kenpo karate, which was Liddell's base, and a tremendously effective tactic. It was also against UFC rules, although he was never punished for his repeated use of the technique. He would use it again in tough fights with Randy Couture and Vernon White. It happened enough times that it couldn't have been coincidence. "I think I was going to knock him out sooner or later anyways" Liddell said. "But if he thinks that's what did it, fine. He always looks for excuses, anyway."[212] Although he would mention it later in interviews, Ortiz made no excuses for his loss that night.

"I did what I said I was going to do," Ortiz said at the post-fight press conference. "I stood in front of him. I'm a stubborn person; I'm a very stubborn person. It's kind of like my way or no way. Liddell did what he does best — overwhelm people. He was in good condition, he's strong. Can't take anything away from him. He was the winner tonight."

The show was a tremendous success for Zuffa. For the first time since Ortiz had fought Ken Shamrock, the company drew more than 100,000 buys on pay-per-view. That success would continue at UFC 48, in June 2004, with Ken Shamrock versus Kimo in the main event. But subsequent shows failed to reach the 100,000-buy mark.

"Buy rates have been an issue for us since day one, and that's the part of the business we're trying to build. There's no doubt that the buy rates are pretty low," White said in an MMAWeekly.com interview. "We're basically a start-up company. You know, that's the way we looked at this company when we bought it. If anybody thinks that when we got into the UFC we thought we were going to be making huge amounts of money right off the bat, there's no way. This is an uphill battle, but let me tell you something. This is going to be a battle long after Zuffa is gone and somebody else owns the UFC. This sport is decades and decades away from being at its highest point of popularity. Everybody's waiting for us to become mainstream tomorrow, but it's not gonna happen. It's going to take years and years and years and years, and this is a battle that will be fought long after I'm gone and Lorenzo's gone. It's a battle that will take decades and decades. This isn't something where we think we're going to make millions of dollars in the next few weeks. We're trying to build the sport."

The UFC was struggling to make ends meet, and couldn't sustain an audience. Quietly, despite the public confidence, the Fertittas asked Dana White to begin shopping the company around. It looked like the Zuffa era might be coming to an end.

17
THE GROWTH OF PRIDE

The Kazushi Sakuraba era was short-lived. The charismatic wrestler had run through four members of the famed Gracie family and made himself a superstar. But his next opponent wasn't a technical ground fighter. He was a menacing striker with a fearsome glare and a tattoo on his head.

Sakuraba's opponent was almost Pride announcer Bas Rutten, but the money just wasn't right for the charismatic Dutchman to return to the ring. "I'm not going to fight for $50,000," Rutten said. "They wanted me to fight Sakuraba. I say that's good. I think the first offer was $60,000. This is just not what I had in mind. I made more money in Pancrase." Pride then turned to its next option.

Wanderlei Silva had beaten opponents in Brazil into bloody pulps in bare-knuckle Vale Tudo matches. He got the attention of hard-core fans and UFC promoters with a win over world-class American wrestler Mike Van Arsdale. Silva absolutely brutalized Van Arsdale, who was thought to be a top performer. That earned him a match with Vitor Belfort in the UFC, which didn't go quite as well. Belfort displayed his hand speed and hit Silva dozens of times as the two flew across the Octagon. The loss did little but galvanize his spirit. Silva went 9–1–1 over the course of the next two years, his only loss a controversial decision against Tito Ortiz that saw Ortiz do nothing but hold Silva down for 25 minutes to win the UFC light heavyweight title. Silva had wowed Pride fans with a knockout win over the highly regarded Guy Mezger and a great back-and-forth decision win over Dan Henderson. Silva was undefeated in Pride and hungry for the big game. And the biggest game of all in 2001 was Kazushi Sakuraba.

"I am always aiming at the top. And if there is a chance, I am eager to fight with Sakuraba," Silva said. "I will win without any doubt, and I promise to send him to the hospital. I am very honored to participate in such a big tournament like Pride, and it was my ambition. Now that my dream has come true, my next dream is to fight with Sakuraba."[213]

Sakuraba had never been in the ring with an opponent like Silva. Silva was hyperaggressive, a killer. Sakuraba had spent the last several years engaged in tactical battles with grapplers. Silva would take a different approach and come straight forward. "Sakuraba is weak at Muay Thai. I am better than he is at striking. If he comes to me with punches or kicks, he will crumble. . . . I am totally superior to Sakuraba, and I will defeat him without a doubt. I want to show the world who I am with my defeat of Sakuraba," Silva said. "If Sakuraba comes at me with striking, I will meet him head-on. I intend to attack with striking, and I hope Sakuraba will, too. If it happens like that, it will naturally be a good fight, won't it?"[214]

Sakuraba was sitting on top of the sport. He was confident in himself, and rightfully so. He was the favorite, and would have been against almost anyone on the planet, but a new rule allowing kicks and knees to a downed opponent seemed to favor his challenger. Sakuraba paid the new rules no mind, and didn't seem to do much at all to prepare for Silva.

"Basically I train only wrestling, as usual, and sparring for striking a little bit. As I've said many times before, a key to success is not to adjust to the pace or rule of an opponent, but to get him into my own world at my pace," Sakuraba said. "I think his physical ability is great. But no matter how great his physical ability, he doesn't stand on four legs, so he falls down without any exception. He doesn't have eyes in the back of his head; he is off his guard without fail. So I will watch for that chance and make it somehow."[215]

Although Sakuraba was primarily known for his grappling, he was ready for a stand-up exchange, as well. He knew that to beat Silva he would need to survive his angry flurries of punches.

"Even if I am knocked out, it won't hurt me. But I don't want punches to the body, which are so painful to me," Sakuraba laughed. "If he knocks me down, I want him to do it with a blow on my chin without giving me any pain. Chin, or around here [pointing at the back of his head]. A blow from somewhere I can't see is very effective, isn't it? Look at the fight between Mr. Uno [Kaoru Uno] and Mr. Rumina [Rumina Sato]. When Mr. Rumina tried to stand up, he took a punch without noticing it coming. So he was on queer street, although it was not a strong punch. But I think Mr. Rumina felt good with it. I want Silva to knock me down that way. If so, I will accept it. But if he gives me pain, I will give it back to him without fail."[216]

Silva gave Sakuraba plenty of pain. The fight almost ended early, and was nearly another amazing Sakuraba win. Sakuraba hit Silva with a beautiful right hook that dropped the Brazilian to the mat. Silva had been knocked down before, and had always gotten off the canvas to win the fight. This was no exception. He got back to his feet and sent Sakuraba down with his own punching combination. And then the new rules came into play, as Silva kneed him in the back of the head and then landed two brutal kicks to the scrambling Sakuraba's head.

Former Pride announcer Stephen Quadros said, "When Wanderlei clashed with Sakuraba the first time [at Pride 13 in March 2001], Pride had changed back to the 'old' rules, which allowed knees and kicks to the head of a downed opponent. And these weapons would prove to be the loser's undoing in the fight. Surprisingly, Sakuraba stood toe-to-toe with Silva early and dropped him in a wild exchange. But in the end it was 'The Axe Murderer' smashing the Japanese fighter into oblivion with the knees and stomps that had just been reintroduced."

In less than two minutes, Pride had a new top dog in the middleweight class. "The first time Sakuraba got dethroned by Wanderlei Silva — Jesus! He lived up to his nickname, 'The Axe Murderer.' He came in and was so devastating," Pride announcer and former King of Pancrase and UFC champion Bas Rutten said. "It was just insane. Sakuraba was undefeated at the time and had beaten four Gracies."

The crowd was in shock. So were fighters around the world, who were in awe of Sakuraba's skill. Royce Gracie said, "Sakuraba should have clinched and taken Wanderlei down. You can't exchange blows head-on with a guy like Wanderlei. Wanderlei is better at striking on stand up, after all . . . but on the ground Sakuraba's level is several steps higher. I can't say why Sakuraba lost, but what I can say is that Sakuraba disregarded that point too much. As I said before, Sakuraba didn't take Wanderlei down, did he? If I was Sakuraba, I wouldn't even try to think about exchanging strikes with Wanderlei. He has terrifying knees, punches, and kicks. Sakuraba surely must have forgotten that the rules had been changed."[217]

SAKURABA–SILVA 2

Sakuraba was a true warrior and wanted an immediate rematch with Silva. He got his wish at Pride 17, in November 2001. The Japanese fans were just as keen to see the fight. The first fight had drawn 27,000 fans to the Saitama Super Arena. The rematch attracted more than 50,000 to see Pride crown its first middleweight champion.

The fight saw an outstanding performance from both men. Sakuraba survived an early Silva barrage of knees to take control of the battle with his wrestling. He secured a tight guillotine choke and almost had Silva out. Only a desperate body slam broke the hold. It also broke Sakuraba — his collarbone, specifically. His corner threw in the towel after the first round, and Silva was the first-ever Pride champion at 205 pounds.

Silva said, "As I thought, this time it was a tough fight. Sakuraba is a great fighter. I knew that. Both on the ground and in stand-up striking, his punches landed on my face. Actually, I was lucky to win. Therefore, I think I fought my best fight ever. Sakuraba dislocated his shoulder. Things like that happen in a fight. But I won. I'm really terrifically happy. I trained for this day with all of my heart in order to get this title, and I got it. This Pride is the biggest of all events in the whole world, so I'm thrilled to have this title. What I'm happiest about is that the fans supported me with all their hearts, and I could win. I really appreciate all the fans."[218]

Sakuraba was in tears as he apologized to his Japanese fans. His shoulder was popped out of its socket and grotesque, and yet he still apologized for his valiant performance. Sakuraba was a gifted fighter who was a natural for the 185-pound weight class. Instead, he was fighting huge 205-pound monsters like Silva — and holding his own.

"What I think is that Sakuraba is a great fighter. Of course, for someone who had been the champion to lose twice to the same opponent could make anyone bitter," Silva said. "Fighters like us, who don't fight for money but because we love fighting, for us, it can really be bitter to lose. But what doesn't kill us makes us stronger."[219]

MINOTAURO

At the same event that saw Silva take the first-ever middleweight championship title, another Brazilian made his mark in the heavyweight division. Antonio Rodrigo Nogueira (known as Minotauro or Nog) was Silva's polar opposite. Silva was all brawn, Nogueira all technique and heart.

"I like the fans who admire my technique," Nogueira said in an interview with adcc.com. "I go to Japan and I just fight technically, I do not fight with strength. When I face fighters who are heavier and stronger than me, I do not trade strength with them, I try to put my technique over their strength. And I think the fans appreciate it when fighters fight looking for submissions. This is like the boxing fans who love to see a great KO."

Nogueira was a Brazilian jiu-jitsu black belt training with legendary jiu-jitsu players Murillo Bustamante and Mario Sperry at Brazilian Top Team. "I consider Minotauro to be like my younger brother. I always give him a lot of advice, not only on the ring, but also in his private life. We respect each other as close friends," Sperry said. "We have had good results in the ring so far. I am trying to pass all the experience I've had on to him. He learns so fast. Indeed, he is an all-around fighter and a model for 21st century. He is good at both standing and ground work. He is in good condition, and besides, he can hold on against punches."[220]

Nogueira had made his name in Japan in Akira Maeda's RINGS promotion. In 1999, he was the runner-up to Dan Henderson for the promotion's King of Kings tournament, and in 2000 he won the $200,000 prize as the champion. He had wins over legendary wrestlers Kiyoshi Tamura and Volk Han, and had beaten crowd favorite Gary Goodridge by triangle choke in his 2001 debut at Pride 15.

His next victim was Pride Grand Prix champion Mark Coleman, the powerful wrestler whose struggling career was revitalized by his move to Japan. To the Japanese, it was Pride versus RINGS, tournament champion against tournament champion.

"It is the fight between two Vale Tudo kings," Nogueira said. "The winner will get big attention from the media, too. This is the fight I want all the fight fans to watch. I will show you my best."[221]

Nogueira was peaking as an athlete and a fighter. He also had many tools at his disposal. Coleman was a one-trick pony, strong in his wrestling but almost nothing else. Nogueira was confident that his jiu-jitsu would beat Coleman's grappling. Nogueira's faith was in technique, and he knew technique would conquer pure strength.

Nogueira said, "It was long my wish to enter Pride. It is one of the best Vale Tudo competitions, and it is great to be able to fight with the best Vale Tudo warriors. Of those, Coleman, one of the best fighters, was chosen as my opponent. That is indeed what I really wanted. I am ready physically and mentally. I can fight with anybody. I have already studied Coleman's fighting style. I am looking forward to fighting with him. He is a very tough fighter. He possesses important elements for Vale Tudo, such as strong power and quickness. But he'd better train very hard to fight with me, because I am going to drive him into a corner many times. He is a great fighter, but not invincible. He sometimes makes mistakes, like anyone else, and I am going to attack when he does. I am studying his strategy well. He has excellent takedown technique. But if he depends on his explosive power and quickness from the beginning, he will get tired and make a mistake."[222]

The fight went exactly to plan. Coleman was shocked by Nogueira's stand-up prowess, eating several hard punches. When Nogueira slipped on a kick attempt, Coleman engaged him on the ground. It was all Nogueira there, and Pride's top heavyweight was forced to defend submission after submission. A triangle choke/arm bar combination ended Coleman's night in the first round. Nogueira had established himself as one of the top fighters in the world and earned the right to take on Heath Herring for the Pride heavyweight title.

The Champion

"It was a very overwhelming experience fighting for the championship in the Tokyo Dome," Heath Herring said. "Cor [Hammers, Herring's kick-boxing coach] did not feel that I was ready, but my manager really pushed for it. We had the wrong game plan going in. I was going to try to keep the fight as a stand-up game. However, looking at the fight in retrospect, I was able to get out of everything that he tried on me on the ground and I should have been more aggressive on the ground. However, you live and you learn, and Cor has more respect for what I can do on the ground after that fight. Nogueira is the best heavyweight submission guy on the ground, and I was able to hang with him. I am proud of that."[223]

The fight has been called the best heavyweight MMA fight of all time.

Herring was expecting Nogueira to be good off of his back in the submission game. He wasn't expecting the jiu-jitsu artist to do more than hold his own standing. The two stood toe-to-toe, trading wild punches, with Nogueira getting the best of most of the exchanges. On the ground, Herring was busy escaping submission after submission. The pace was insane for a heavyweight fight, and the action was nonstop for all three rounds. Nogueira took a unanimous decision and became the first Pride heavyweight champion.

The new champion looked unstoppable. Nogueira was more than a match for fighters from a variety of disciplines. He beat two Japanese grapplers, Enson Inoue and Sanae Kikuta. He beat strikers, too, submitting former King of Pancrase and eventual K-1 world champion Semmy Schilt and the enormous Bob Sapp. As Christmas 2002 approached, Nogueira also avenged his sole defeat, catching wrestler Dan Henderson with an arm bar at Pride 24 in December 2002. It was as impressive a string of victories as the sport had ever seen. People definitely believed Nogueira was the greatest fighter in the world. Little did they know that a quiet and slightly puffy man from Russia was ready to knock the entire sport for a loop.

RUSSIAN NIGHTMARE

Like many of the best fighters throughout history, Fedor Emelianenko grew up poor. He calls Stary Oskul, Russia his home. It's a mining town located as far west as you can get in Russia, and still constructed very much in the Soviet fashion. His mother was a teacher and his father worked in construction. Together, that afforded them one room in a communal apartment. There, Emelianenko and his three siblings grew up in abject poverty.

"We were a very poor working family with four kids," Emelianenko's brother and fellow fighter Aleksander Emelianenko said. "Our mother was a teacher and our father had a number of industrial jobs. When Fedor came back from the army, things were very hard. There was a time in the late '90s when we had to share one jacket between the two of us."[224]

Fedor was not a natural athlete, but he trained hard from the age of 12. He had a goal of making it onto the Russian national judo team. Unfortunately, the money was not there for him to survive as a judo player. There was a time when this would not have been the case, when the Soviet Union would fund hundreds of young men in a search to find the best athletes for international competition. But times were changing, and his talent wasn't such that he was tabbed for athletic training. Instead, like many young men in the incredibly nationalistic and proud Russian Republic, he joined the army.

"I, of course, had the desire to go into the army. . . . Let me put it like this: it warms my soul that I went through it. I grew up. I developed my character there, toughened. I went in as a boy and came out as a man with a hardened resolve," Emelianenko said. He joined a firefighting unit and later spent time as part of a tank crew. Unlike many top athletes, who were transferred to special athletic units where they spent all day training, Emelianenko was a real soldier. "In the army I was never disrespectful, never cocky, though I could always stand up for myself. And I always tried to help those younger than me. I did have to fight a lot, but only at the very start."[225]

After his time in the army, Emelianenko returned home and rededicated himself to training. "I entered my first competition, literally, a week out of the army," Emelianenko said.[226] He was soon on the national judo and sambo teams. He saw some success, finishing third in the 1997 Russian Judo Open, but judo wasn't going to earn him a living, not by the late '90s.

"I was a Master of Sports. Right after the army, I completed the require-ments for judo and sambo, and a little later I became an International Master of Sports in these sports. I was on the Russian national team, but there wasn't enough financing," Emelianenko said. "That's very simply why I had to start MMA fighting. I was really in a dead end. I had to leave every-thing — I had already, let's just say, made a name for myself, but I had to leave it all and start from zero. After I started MMA fighting, I realized that I had to study striking technique."[227]

Emelianenko got an education in MMA, like Nogueira before him, in Akira Maeda's RINGS. He became the RINGS world champion, winning nine fights and losing only to Tsuyoshi Kohsaka after an illegal elbow forced a cut stoppage. By the time he got to the Pride promotion in the summer of 2002, he was a well-rounded and dangerous fighter.

"Fedor and the trainers work together on developing techniques and have done so for a long time," Emelianenko's trainer Vladimir Mihailovich Voronov said. "We try this variation, that variation until we hit upon tech-niques that work. Talking specifically about what goes into the training is long and probably boring, filled with technical terms. Of course, a great portion of our time goes into training just with Fedor. When he is resting, we work with the other fighters."[228]

Emelianenko beat Pancrase champion Semmy Schilt and Nogueira nemesis Heath Herring to earn a title shot. At Pride 25, in April 2003, Minotauro battled the Russian.

THE LAST EMPEROR RISES TO HIS THRONE

"In what was the greatest heavyweight fight thus far in MMA, Fedor Emelianenko defeated a man who was widely regarded as the best fighter at the time, Antonio Rodrigo Nogueira, at his own game," Stephen Quadros said. "Most pundits thought it would be suicide for Fedor to even get close to 'Minotauro's' guard. Every other opponent in Pride who had ended up there had tapped. So what happened? Emelianenko dove right into Nogueira's guard and stayed there the whole match, brutalizing Rodrigo and snatching the gold."

Fedor was fearless, and he engaged Nogueira where the Brazilian was most dangerous — on the ground. Fedor survived Nogueira's submission attempts. It was like he knew exactly when and where they were coming.

"Fedor studied Minotauro very well," Mario Sperry said. "Minotauro was not his usual self, because Fedor, who was not tired yet, landed a punch on Minotauro's face with 100 percent of his power and a dry glove in the early stages of the fight, and the damage continued through 20 minutes."[229]

Emelianenko was as complete a package as anyone had ever seen in MMA. He was equally good at striking and grappling and moved like lightning.

"I'm a big Fedor fan. I like my own record for the same reason I like Fedor," Bas Rutten said. "I submitted people in all different fashions, all different submissions, and knocked people out in different fashions. Fedor is one of those guys. If you give him an arm, he arm-bars you. If you give him a leg, he leg locks you. If you give him a punch, he knocks you out. I enjoy the mixed martial artist who can win fights by submission and knockouts, and that's why I'm a big Fedor fan."

The package was deceptive. Emelianenko didn't look like a bodybuilder and was even a little dumpy. But the outside was misleading. This was an incomparable athlete.

Nogueira said, "For sure, he defended himself successfully. He was fast, too. Moreover, he kept a good position and didn't try to pass my guard as long as there was no chance. It doesn't mean he was passive there. He kept moving. But I watched the video of the fight three times and got some ideas on how to defeat him. I could understand his strategy; that is, to focus on punches on the ground and avoid submission. I was on top of him two times in the first round, but it took a long time to sweep. If I had been on top, I think I could have done things differently. But when I was on top of him after a sweep, it was almost the end of the first round. I wanted to take time to change the position after that, but time was short. So I tried a pass-guard anyway, and I could make it. But it ran out of time. And I tried a sweep in the end of the second round, and it was successful, too. But time was short again."[230]

SAKURABA–SILVA 3

Nogueira had a plan for beating his conqueror. At the same time, Kazushi Sakuraba was game planning for a third and final shot at Pride middle-weight champion Wanderlei Silva in August 2003. Silva had continued winning, battling, and destroying a series of Japanese pro wrestlers like Kiyoshi Tamura and Hiromitsu Kanehara, while Sakuraba had struggled. He lost to the highly regarded Mirko "Cro Cop" Filopovic and the lightly regarded Nino Schembri. Sakuraba's best days as a fighter seemed done. But he was still booked in the main event. There was criticism from the U.S. MMA media, who didn't seem to understand that this was the match the fans in Japan wanted to see.

Silva said, "I found it a very good choice, 'cause all the Japanese fans want to see me fighting him again. And every time I fought Sakuraba we made a good showing, so the public will have a good showing once again. This is usual in Japan, fighters face each other a lot of times there, and they believe Sakuraba can beat me. I don't think so, and I fully trust my potential, so I think I'll beat him for the third time."[231]

Sakuraba came out striking, surprising everyone by taking the fight to Silva. He didn't think he could actually win a prolonged standing battle. He was trying to use strikes to help secure a takedown, the same way Randy Couture had against Chuck Liddell at UFC 43.

"I punched too much," Sakuraba said with a laugh. "He was able to get out of my takedowns, so I was looking for a way to break his rhythm. . . .

He didn't come straight out like he usually does. He would get away from all my takedowns, so I thought if I punched him, he might come forward."

Sakuraba was knocked out in devastating fashion. He threw a low leg kick that Silva countered with a giant left-right combination. Sakuraba fell to the mat in what looked like slow motion. It was the third tough knockout for Sakuraba in less than a year, and the announcers openly speculated about a possible retirement.

"I don't remember talking to Silva in the ring or even the ride home after the fight. After the fight, I kept asking everyone what day of the month it was. Every time they said 'August 10,' I would say 'What about the fight with Silva? I lost?' I saw the actual fight when I went home and watched the television broadcast."[232]

Silva had defeated Japan's most popular, and best, fighter for the third time in a row. He was becoming a star, even getting the television commercials and other perks usually associated with only the biggest names. He was also learning that fighting was about more than merely winning, especially in Japan, where entertaining the fans and showing your fighting spirit was even more important.

"It is very important in fights to not only win but also to attract people. So I think each fighter has to perform an attractive fight, as if he himself becomes a promoter. It will make spectators happy, too," Silva said. "He himself will grow up by doing it. . . . The strength of heart is very important, too. It is difficult to make a living from only sport in Brazil. That's why we are fighting with a spirit of 'never give up,' no matter how hard a fight would be."[233]

With Sakuraba declining, Pride desperately needed a new star. It had tried a number of pro wrestlers, like Alexander Otsuka, Kiyoshi Tamura, and Kazayuki Fujita. And while they had some success in the ring, and were able to attract large crowds, they weren't able to compete with the very best fighters in the world the way Sakuraba had. For the next big MMA star, Pride had to open its pocketbook and reach out to another combat art. It would look to the national sport of judo to find its next champion.

18

THE ULTIMATE FIGHTER

In many ways, Mary Ellis-Bunim saved the UFC. She's never been inside the ring, or even to a dojo, but *The Real World*, her story of seven strangers picked to live in a house in order to find out what would happen when people "stopped being polite and started being real," changed the face of television. *The Real World* was a huge hit for MTV, and the era of reality television was upon us.

Soon there were reality shows in every conceivable genre and every conceivable locale. Hot singles cavorting on an island? Check. People starving and conniving on an island? Check. Viewers found out what it was like to be a professional wrestler on *Tough Enough*. The audience followed the trials and tribulations of up-and-coming boxers on NBC's *The Contender*. Why not Ultimate Fighting?

Before *The Ultimate Fighter* (TUF), the UFC was floundering. The losses were mounting, and Lorenzo and Frank Fertitta III had 44 million reasons to call it a day. Despite getting the sport cleared by the Nevada State Athletic Commission, the Station Casino owners were losing money by the fistful. The promotion could either get on television or get out of the fight business.

"Yeah, we were nervous a few times. One day I'm sitting in my office and Lorenzo calls me. He says, 'This is crazy, and this thing keeps losing money. Why don't you go out there and see what you can get for this thing right now,'" UFC president Dana White told *Entrepreneur* magazine. "So I got on the phone and started calling around, and I found someone to buy it for $6 or $7 million. So I called Lorenzo back and said, 'I think I got about $6 or $7 million for this thing.' He says, 'All right, I'll call you tomorrow.' The next day he calls me, and he's like, 'Fuck it; let's keep going.' And here we are."

Zuffa needed television and Spike TV needed young men to watch its fledgling network. It already had a solid hit with the wrestling show WWE *Raw*, and was looking to continue to add programming for the young-adult male. The idea was to go with a boxing show, but that seemed too old, too much like your father's television programming.

"The UFC appeals to a younger guy, whereas boxing is having serious trouble because it doesn't have any stars," Spike TV senior vice president of sports and specials Jim Burns said. "The UFC exudes stardom and it's a younger, quicker, legitimate sport."

Spike wanted the UFC and the UFC wanted Spike. But first they needed a format. White, a former amateur boxer and boxing promoter, wanted a show like the one he grew up with, the USA Network's *Tuesday Night Fights*. The television executives were more interested in the proven reality-television format. White wasn't happy with the reality show, but the UFC wasn't in a position to be choosy. Spike TV's instincts were on the money. The combination of reality TV and mixed martial arts action would be irresistible to the coveted 18-49 male demographic. But there was real concern that advertisers wouldn't bite. The UFC was still a risky proposition, even for an edgy network like Spike TV. The brand was damaged, and had dangerous connotations.

White said, "When we bought the company [in 2001], we took a whole different approach. We didn't run from regulation. We built it as nothing but a sport with great athletes. It's just an education process with the public, and it took us almost seven years. Here's the thing, and it's not to take a knock at the old owners, but this thing started in 1993 when a bunch of TV guys wanted to answer the question, 'Which fighting style is the best?' 'Would a boxer beat a wrestler?' And so on. These guys never knew they were creating a sport at all. They just sort of fell into it."[234]

In order to give the UFC a chance, Spike asked Zuffa to fund the first season of *The Ultimate Fighter*. Already down $30 million, another $10 million could have seemed like throwing good money after bad. Zuffa swallowed the bitter pill and decided to fund the show, confident that Ultimate Fighting was still the sport of the future, and still had the chance to be boxing for a new generation. They brought in one of the big guns in the reality television field to help put their show together, *Survivor* co-executive producer Craig Piligian. *Survivor* was one of the most successful television shows in history. When Piligian signed on with *The Ultimate Fighter*, *Survivor* had just finished its tenth season in a row in the Nielsen top 10 television ratings.

"As someone who knows something about *Survivor*, I can tell you that nobody knows more about survival than these 16 young men," Piligian said. "Viewers will love the hearts and souls of these guys, and how much their lives are placed on hold in pursuit of this dream."

The format had been decided on, and some of television's top professionals were onboard. Now it was time to cast the show. It would necessitate a delicate balance. The show would require entertaining personalities, but the participants would also need to be able to fight. The roles for the show's producers were easy to assign. Piligian would look at the fighter's personalities and White would concentrate on whether or not they could fight.

"First and foremost, what we care about is if the participants are good fighters," White said. "Personality is important, of course. We don't want a bunch of boring guys who don't talk or hang with each other. But I'm more interested in getting guys who really want to fight."[235]

The casting process was designed to immediately separate the wheat from the chaff. If you weren't comfortable with the cameras, or they weren't comfortable with you, you were out.

"The guys who we are interested go through such a comprehensive interview process that it is insane," White told *Ultimate Grappling* magazine. "They are interviewed over and over again. They are locked in rooms, they cannot go anywhere, they cannot take any calls, and it goes on for days and days."

Many of the fighters from the first season were not the kind of young unknowns the show would feature in later years. There was a healthy mixture of up-and-comers like Diego Sanchez and Josh Koscheck and veteran journeymen like Bobby Southworth and Forrest Griffin. Some of the fighters had to be coaxed back to the sport.

"I had been retired, and when they called me about two weeks before the show I was 251 pounds and hadn't done very much training in the last 14 months," Bobby Southworth said. "There wasn't a lot of money involved, and I was struggling to make it as a full-time fighter and instructor. I'd had enough of the heartache and heartbreak and decided to go back to being a working stiff."

Forrest Griffin had also left mixed martial arts behind him. After suffering a dislocated shoulder and a shattered hand, a broken arm was the final straw.

Griffin said, "That was a big one. And then, of course, there's the little stuff. But those were the three big ones that, when you add them up, I've been training since 2000, you add that up and that's two years without training. A little over, actually. Sitting there for three months, you can't get a job because you've got a fucking cast on. That's the third time that's happened in three years. You can't get a job, you can't train, you've got no way of making a living, there's nothing you can do. Thank God I was still in school and I lived off student loans. It's just not worth it. The benefits, the perks, don't outweigh the downtime."[236]

But the dream died hard. He was working a steady job as a police officer and was moving on with his life when the UFC called. He was ready to sacrifice the mundane, average life for a chance at greatness. He was willing to fight, no matter the physical cost. He was in. Joining Griffin and Southworth were Diego Sanchez, Josh Koscheck, Stephan Bonnar, Jason Thacker, Chris Sanford, Josh Rafferty, Sam Hoger, Nate Quarry, Alex Schoenauer, Lodune Sincaid, Kenny Florian, Alex Karalexis, Mike Swick, and Chris Leben.

The 16 fighters were cast, the production team was in place, and it was time to shoot the show. Everyone associated with TUF signed a confidentiality agreement that included a $5-million fine for divulging the results. Spike gave the show a perfect lead-in, one of cable televison's most popular shows, WWE *Raw*. It was up to the UFC to keep a portion of that primed audience. "When you talk about the first season of *The Ultimate Fighter*, those are wrestling fans that stayed the extra hour," *Wrestling Observer*'s Dave Meltzer said. Shows had been notoriously unsuccessful in their attempts to keep wrestling's large audience tuned in. TUF would need to get out to a fast start and set the tone early. Television viewers had seen a lot of shows that featured young twenty-somethings living and working together. They had seen plenty of arguments between cast members on reality TV shows, but this offered the potential for real fireworks. Arguments in this show could be settled with flying fists and feet. In fact, at least one fight a night was a virtual guarantee. The show started with a bang. In the very first episode, Chris Leben urinated on Jason Thacker's bed. The tone was set, and things only got crazier from there.

The fighters were divided into two teams, a blue team coached by Chuck Liddell and a green team coached by Randy Couture. For the fighters, this was an opportunity to train with some of the sport's true legends. For the UFC, it was a chance to promote not only a generation of new fighters, but its upcoming pay-per-view as well. Couture and Liddell were always portrayed in a positive light, but the true stars of the show were the fighters in the house. The two teams shared a house together, and the tension was high. The fighters weren't allowed any distractions. There were no televisions, no books, no phone calls, and no trips outside the house, except to the gym.

Griffin said, "I didn't know going in that it was going to be like that. That's not how they told me things were going to be. I was sort of misled about the whole premise of the thing. And when we got out there I was like, 'Whoa, I'm what?' You know what, the way they kinda sold it to me was like, 'You're going to get these opportunities' and 'We're going to take you out and do stuff for you.' It was like a dream come true. 'Work with these coaches. You won't have TV or books, but we'll take you out and let you do stuff.' And they took us out one time during the whole thing."[237]

Griffin wasn't the only one who felt misled by *The Ultimate Fighter*'s producers.

"They told us we weren't going to be fighting unless we were in the finals. When we got there, I was told we weren't going to have to make weight. So a little bit into the show, when it came out that we were going to have to make weight in five days, that upped the stress level, for me in particular," Southworth said. "I had no idea what to expect, and I think a lot of the time those people [the producers] were just winging it. They had a format for what they wanted to do, but, at the same time, as different rivalries and different personality clashes occurred in the house, they tried to tweak things for the show."

Being stuck in the house for weeks was one thing. Being stuck in a house that wasn't fit for human habitation was something else.

"They put us in a house with a septic system designed for four people. There were 16 people living in the house. So two times raw sewage flooded both of the downstairs bathrooms and was left there for up to three days," Southworth said. "Several of the fighters got pretty sick. Stephan Bonnar had some kind of mutated impetigo, and Sam Hoger got a flesh-eating virus. I got some kind of weird respiratory infection that caused me to cough up blood."

Feeling misled and living in a germ factory was bad enough. Living with 15 other guys was worse. The star of the early episodes of *The Ultimate Fighter* was indisputably the vocal and obnoxious Chris Leben. Leben came from Randy Couture's Team Quest, and had already established himself as a rising star with a series of flashy wins. He didn't hesitate for a moment in making sure everyone else in the house knew all about how he "put the stamp on kids."

"Chris Leben, most of the time, was just this asshole. Messed with people, talked shit, just went nuts every time he could," Kenny Florian said. While the fighters in the house couldn't stand him, the audience and the camera loved him. He was featured so prominently on the show that hard-core fans online started calling it *The Ultimate Leben Hour*.

Riding the strength of Leben's personality, the show was an immediate hit. The first episode did a 1.42 rating, including a 1.49 in the extremely coveted 18-49-year-old male demographic. In the cable industry, a 1.0 rating is a success, a 1.5 is a hit, and a 2.0 is a tremendous success. The UFC executives were thrilled, and if fans thought the show was focused on Leben before, well, they hadn't seen anything yet. Watch Leben argue with Mike Swick. Watch Leben get drunk and leave the house to look for a pay phone. Watch Leben complain about his "lackluster teammates." He was the center of attention, and was loving every minute of it. He was annoying everyone in the house, it seemed, but no one more than Josh Koscheck. Leben and Koscheck were like oil and water.

Koscheck said, "At times, Chris and I were very cool in the beginning, but then something just clicked and the conflict started. Then we just didn't like each other. I think that, even now, if they put us back on that show together, the same thing would happen again because some people just don't get along. I mean, when you put 16 guys in a house and you've heard each other's stories ten times, you get annoyed and tensions run high. Add alcohol to that, you know, crazier things could have happened in that house."[238]

Koscheck, who looks remarkably like a kangaroo with a blond Afro wig, was a former NCAA champion wrestler who had the best physical tools of anyone in the house. He had an undefeated junior year in 2001, winning the NCAA title at 174 pounds, and had a legitimate shot at making the Olympic team in 2008. Instead, fight manager "Crazy" Bob Cook talked him into giving professional fighting a try.

"One of the reasons I left wrestling is because there wasn't a big fan base following it, and there wasn't a great payday," Koscheck said. "You can train your butt off just as hard as most guys in MMA train, you train the same way for wrestling, and there was no reward. The reward was getting my hand raised, and that wasn't paying my bills and feeding me. So wrestling got very stale; I was at a point where I thought I knew everything about wrestling, and I didn't think I was getting better. Plus I didn't have the training partners I needed, and I was just like, 'What am I doing? I think I'm wasting my time.'"[239]

Leben was going stir crazy in the house, and was ready to fight. He demanded a fight with Koscheck, but Team Liddell went with Diego Sanchez taking on an overmatched Alex Karalexis instead. Sensing the guys in the house were under enormous stress, Dana White was ready to take them out on the town for a relaxing evening. The guys primped their hair and carefully selected their evening's ensemble, acting more like high-school cheerleaders than stereotypical Ultimate Fighters. Leben's plan was for everyone to get equally hammered. In retrospect, this was probably not a good idea for 16 young men who were sick and tired of seeing each other's faces and already had a propensity for violence.

Southworth said, "They had had us cooped up for about four and a half weeks. All you could do was go from the house to the gym and then back to the house. So then they took us out to a nice dinner, open menu, and open bar, and the Chris Rock concert at the Hard Rock Casino, also with an open bar. If you let a bunch of crazy people out from the loony house and they can do whatever they want, well, there might be trouble. We drank so much that night. There were never more than five minutes when I didn't have two drinks in my hand. I felt that drinking binge for two to three days afterward. Those alcohol-fueled evenings we all have, they come back to you in flashes. And by the time the show aired I could remember a lot more."

The drinking led to the kind of boasting and trash talking common to locker rooms and frat houses nationwide. The main target was Leben, who went berserk after Southworth jokingly called him a "fatherless bastard." He was inconsolable, and ended up sleeping it off on the lawn, desperate to get far away from Southworth and his friend Koscheck. The seemingly benign insult was anything but. Everyone in the house knew Leben's father had left his family when Leben was a young boy, and had only recently come back into his life. It was a sensitive area, and Southworth was pushing all the right buttons. He came to apologize, but Leben was beyond consolation.

Leben's Team Quest teammate Nate Quarry said, "You don't dig down deep and call someone horrible names and then have a sudden change of heart five minutes later and come out and apologize. That was the most transparent apology I've ever seen in my life. All the respect I had for Bobby was completely gone in that moment." Most people in the house called it a night. It was late, and everyone had to be ready for training in the morning. But the night was far from over. Southworth and Koscheck turned a water hose on the sleeping Leben, and the fireworks really exploded.

The eternally smirking Koscheck said, "Our intention was to just spray around him, but that didn't happen. I kind of went overboard. I'm an instigator, you know, and I instigated it. When you have a couple of cocktails, of course, you want to see how far you can push somebody, to see what they are going to do next. We did it, it was bad judgment, so what? He didn't have to flip out. He schizzed out and he couldn't handle the pressure. Bottom line is, I'm not going to regret it."

Leben ended up putting his fist through a window and knocked a door off its frame looking for Koscheck, who had wisely (or perhaps cowardly) fled the scene.

Forrest Griffin said, "All of the sudden I'm having this dream and God's yelling at me. But it turns out it's not really God at all. It's Chris Leben, and he's busted through my door. There are pieces of my door in my bed. He's like, 'Hey, where's Koscheck?' And I look at him and say, 'Are you out of your fucking mind?' Chris likes to dish it out, but he can't really take it. Now, should Bob and Koscheck go and spray water near Chris when he's trying to sleep outside because everybody inside was making him crazy? No."

The three nearly came to blows. It was an ugly and scary scene, but Southworth is unapologetic.

"Chris had a really abrasive personality and was rubbing everyone in the house the wrong way. He was always cool when he was the guy that had the leg up on someone, but we were all drunk and having verbal wars that night, and he was losing," Southworth said. "It was a poor decision, but if everything happened again, that night would probably still happen the same way. It was payback for all of the stuff he had been doing in the house. If you're going to dish it out, you have to be able to take it."

The next morning, it was time to pay the piper. Dana White was awakened by the news that there had been a fight at the house. He called the coaches into his office to figure out what to do with the three guys involved in the incident. The coaches agreed that Leben had a screw loose, but Chuck Liddell said they were Ultimate Fighters, so they all had issues. White thought Southworth was the main problem, but, to Liddell, Leben had it coming.

"From what I understand, Leben had been messing with people the whole time. It's no surprise that they were doing that to him," Liddell said. "You're talking about a kid who had already gone and pissed on someone's bed. You're going to throw pranks out at people, you better damn well be able to take it."

In the end, they decided the best way to settle this score was inside the steel cage. "This is a fight show. This isn't one of those shows where, 'Oh, we're going to gang up on them and vote them off the show,'" Dana White said. "The way you get eliminated from this show is by fighting." It was going to be Leben versus Koscheck in a loser-leaves-town match. Koscheck looked less than thrilled when Liddell told him the news. Leben was downright giddy, and ready to commit violence on an epic scale: "I'm going to be able to crush his skull in and not go to jail for it."

The stage was set for *The Ultimate Fighter*'s first legitimate grudge match. Unfortunately, as so often happens, the fight couldn't live up to the hype. Koscheck was only four fights into his MMA career and had very limited skills. He was scared of being hit, and completely clueless when it came to submissions on the ground. His only hope was to use his superlative wrestling skills to hold Leben down and blanket him for a decision win. It was a game plan he executed to perfection.

Unlike regular three-round fights in the UFC, these exhibitions were scheduled for two rounds. In the event of a draw, the fight would be decided by a third round. Everyone was ready for Dana White to announce the third round, but he instead announced a unanimous decision for Koscheck.

"I thought for sure they'd at least give me a third round. This is TV, it's intense. They're going to say it's a tie and go to the third round for the drama. I was putting my mouthpiece back in; I was ready to go for the third round. I was back on my feet. I had my chance to knock him out again. Then all of the sudden they just called it over. That's just one of those things. The UFC kind of favors wrestlers, the way the rules work. Bottom line, I should have gotten out from under him or I should have submitted him," Leben said. "I only saw it once, and I was so wasted when I watched it that I can't really remember the fight because it was frustrating to know I was going to have to watch myself lose on TV. I was pretty bummed when I watched it, and I haven't had the guts to watch it again because it angers me so much to watch that fight. All I wanted to do was knock that guy's jaw off. It just didn't work out that way. It wasn't in the cards that day."[240]

The show had peaked early. The episode leading into the grudge match drew a 1.7 rating and the big fight between Leben and Koscheck was the most watched MMA fight in United States television history, drawing a 2.0 rating and 2.2 million viewers. MMAWeekly.com called the show a "breakout ratings hit." *The Ultimate Fighter* was looking like a tremendous success, and Spike TV was getting it for peanuts. And the UFC's controversial nature meant that other networks wouldn't be knocking down Zuffa's door to steal the UFC out from under them.

Unfortunately for Zuffa, the boring Koscheck–Leben fight seemed to turn viewers off, and the show settled back down into the 1.5-rating range. It didn't help that the most exciting thing on the post-Leben shows was an argument between Dana White and Bobby Southworth after Southworth lost a controversial decision to Stephan Bonnar.

"If I had a green shirt on, a pink shirt, a blue shirt, if I had a fuckin' tie-dyed Hawaiian shirt from 1952, Bobby still won that fight," Forrest Griffin said, referencing the different colored shirts the teams wore. The judges didn't see it that way, and Bonnar would be the guy who went on to fame and fortune. Southworth was going home. And he was pissed off. Dana White came to give him a pep talk, and Southworth was in no mood to hear it. The conversation was heated. "I don't really want a pep talk right now," said Southworth.

"Too bad," said White, who lost his cool and started screaming, accusing Southworth of being a psycho.

"Why are you yelling at me?" asked Southworth.

White had a point to make, and he made it on national television. "I'm not one of his buddies he's hanging out with in the house," White said. "He ain't gonna talk to me like that, because at the end of the day, when this whole thing is over, if this is really what Bobby wants to do for a living, I'm the boss. I'm the boss. It's my way and no other way. End of story."

With Southworth gone, the show was stuck without any real catalysts to keep things lively, and, more importantly, no one to keep people tuning in to Spike TV. So the producers brought back Chris Leben, the show's breakout star. Teammate Nate Quarry had injured his ankle when coach Randy Couture accidentally ran into him from behind. Quarry needed surgery, and the team was allowed to bring an eliminated fighter back to take his place. Although I'm sure it was hard for Quarry to choose between Jason Thacker and his real-life teammate, it was no surprise to see the Ultimate bad boy come strolling back into *The Ultimate Fighter* house. Leben was going to be given every chance to prove himself and win the contract. Opponents in the house called foul. Leben had been eliminated already. How fair would it be for him to continue forward and win the tournament?

Dana White said, "Basically, what everybody has to understand is that this is a game. It's like playing *Fear Factor* or any other game show. There were rules that were set before this thing even got started. The rules don't change throughout. It is what it is." Leben wasn't the only one making himself into a star. With his obscene mouth and confrontational personality, White was quickly becoming the UFC's Vince McMahon. White claims it wasn't by design, but he certainly seemed to enjoy hamming it up on camera. "Originally, I wasn't supposed to be on this show that much. As the show started to progress, the producers wanted to me to be on more and more to act as a kind of bridge and be the guy to tell the story of what was going on. So this thing really evolved, and it ended up that I became a participant on the show. A lot of the time I didn't know what was happening, either, until they told me. The producers would tell me, you know, 'This is what's going to happen next, this is what you need to let the fighters know.' I more or less became the host of the show, but that was never the intention."[241]

With Southworth gone, there was time to focus on some of the other fighters in the house. Soon a new bad guy emerged, a different kind of scoundrel. No drunken brawls or obnoxious taunts, just old-fashioned villainy. Sam Hoger was already in hot water with his Team Liddell mates for skipping out on practice to bond with Team Couture on a long-distance run. Tensions were high, and he received a drubbing in practice as his repentance. That was fine with Hoger, who trained with the Miletich Fighting Systems team, where brutal beatings were an initiation into the fraternity. But it went from bad to worse when he was accused of stealing gear from his teammates. Not money or jewelry or anything of value at all, really. Beanies. Grown men almost came to blows over beanies bearing the UFC logo.

Hoger said, "I never stole anything. What you didn't see was the part where Forrest [Griffin] said, 'I took some stuff, and Diego [Sanchez] you're the worst. You've taken more than anyone.' But I was the one they wanted on the witch-hunt. They're trying to make a TV show. In order to continue doing that, they have to keep creating characters. We all play good guys, and we all play bad guys. When my teammates turned on me, I declared war on everybody in that house."[242]

The show had hit a low, but after weeks of being cooped up together there was still plenty of steam to let loose. There were only eight fighters left in the house when Dana White made the surprise announcement that the semi-finals would be teammate versus teammate. It seemed designed, in part, to make sure Chris Leben made his way to the finals. Instead of facing Koscheck in a rematch or the tough Diego Sanchez, Leben got an "easy" match with the unheralded Kenny Florian. Florian wasn't even supposed to be on the show. White had found him by accident while scouting another fighter.

"Drew Fickett had like 23 wins and only two losses, and he had already beaten three UFC veterans," Florian said. "Not knowing any better, I said, 'I'll take the fight.' It was at 175 pounds, and I was only 165 pounds. Dana White was in the crowd that night, and he was actually scouting Drew Fickett for the show. We, absolutely, had a war. I lost a split decision. It was a close, close fight. Dana White was so impressed that he went back to my dressing room and told me about this new show, *The Ultimate Fighter*."[243]

Florian was scrappy, but he was a natural 155 pounder fighting in the 185-pound division. Leben was a true 185 pounds, and was expected to walk over Florian. This was before anyone knew about Florian's deadly elbows. Up to this point, he had primarily been a Brazilian jiu-jitsu artist. But he was learning quickly under the expert tutelage at the UFC training center.

He used his developing Thai skills to open a huge gash on Leben's skull, and the fight was stopped. The UFC's golden boy had been eliminated again. Florian would go on to the finals to take on Chuck Liddell's representative, Diego Sanchez, who had easily beaten Koscheck and shown himself to be on a different level than the other guys at 185 pounds. "Kenny's not even supposed to be here," White said. "He wasn't supposed to be in the finals, and he's not supposed to beat Diego Sanchez. He's been the underdog this whole time. I'm sure he wouldn't have it any other way."[244]

Bonnar and Swick were unhappy that they had to square off in a light heavyweight semifinal, but their position seemed sentimental and juvenile. This was a fighting game show, and ultimately there was only going to be one winner. Under any system, teammates would have met in the finals, so the bellyaching seemed unwarranted. But it did seem to throw them off their games. "I couldn't really get aggressive, and I was put in a weird situation fighting like that. I had to change my strategy two days before the fight," Swick told *Ultimate Grappling*. "I am not sure either one of us gave 100 percent or fought our normal fight, but we went out there and did what we could do." Swick has since dropped two weight classes, down to the 170-pound class, so Bonnar had more firepower as he fought his way to the finals.

The other teammates had no problems fighting. There was some drama about whether a bad cut Griffin received in a tough fight with Alex Schoenauer would heal sufficiently for him to participate, but it did, and he did. He was all too happy to fight Sam Hoger. "You know, I don't really like not getting along with people. I tried my best to get along with the guy. I realized that I personally didn't like him, I was never going to like him, but, you know, you function with people," Griffin told Sherdog.com. Animosity didn't change Griffin's approach, but he didn't have any second thoughts about punching Hoger in the face. "It didn't make it easier or harder. Man, I just don't give a fuck. You know, for me, it's just a fight. It's not about friends or enemies. I'm going to hit you just as hard if I love you as if I hate you." Griffin hit Hoger enough that the referee stopped the fight. The finals were set: Griffin versus Bonnar, and Sanchez versus Florian.

19
POST-TUF

It was like looking in a mirror. Both men were gifted on the ground, but preferred to bang. Both were highly intelligent and shared a sly sense of humor. And both men would give anything to win the six-figure UFC contract. Before the fight, there was a palpable tension in the air. It was expected that Diego Sanchez would win the contract in the middleweight class, and he did, despite a valiant effort by the undersized Kenny Florian, who had gone in relishing his role as an underdog and had let it all hang out. But no one really knew what to expect from Griffin and Bonnar. They were too evenly matched and too well-rounded to be pigeonholed into a particular fighting style. Griffin, in particular, had impressed everyone with his attitude and work ethic on *The Ultimate Fighter*. Even though he was on Liddell's blue team during the television season, he would go on to accept an offer to train with the green team's legendary coach, Randy Couture.

UFC announcer Joe Rogan said, "He really enjoys the physical-combat aspect of it. He enjoys fighting. He likes getting in there, he doesn't mind getting cut. He likes to bang. He's got incredible endurance. He's a diligent worker. You're talking about a guy who got his arm broken and knocked a guy out with his other arm. If you look at Forrest Griffin's left forearm, he's got a huge lump on it. And that's because a guy snapped his arm in an arm bar, and instead of tapping he knocked him out with his right hand. That's a tough dude."

Within the first minute, the tone of the entire fight was set. There was never a thought about going to the ground. These guys were trading punches. Bonnar scored with a precision jab, and Griffin countered with big haymakers and short counters when he could. Halfway through the first round, the fight was out of control.

"I worked on my footwork a lot, my feints," Bonnar said. "And sure enough, after a few minutes I bagged all that, and we were just swinging bolos for the fences. And that's pretty much how it went for the next 12–13 minutes."

They call boxing the sweet science, but there was no science on display in this fight. The pace was unbelievable for 205-pound men, and every punch was thrown with the intention of ending the fight. No one set up their shots; they didn't have to. They were throwing enough that something would eventually land.

"I would hate to have to score this fight," Rogan said, echoing the thoughts of everyone at home and the three ringside judges. "What a round! That's the most exciting round I think I've ever seen. That was the Hagler–Hearns first round of the Ultimate Fighting Championship's history."

In the second round, Griffin got hit with an inadvertent head butt, opening a big cut on his nose. He just smiled as the blood poured down his face. The crowd was becoming rabid, driven into a frenzy by the blood and the pure action. "This place is erupting. The crowd in here is on its feet," Rogan said. The punches continued to fly, and Bonnar began to take control as Griffin grew weary from the incredible pace. He looked up to the clock, looking for a friend, but instead found that the round was only half over. "Forrest is in big trouble here," Mike Goldberg yelled. It was gut-check time. Instead of slowing down, after a brief lull the action actually picked up. Goldberg didn't even have to see how the fight would end up: "One of the greatest moments in UFC history . . . in the over 40 events I've done in the Ultimate Fighting Championship, I don't remember two men going toe-to-toe as diligently as these two have for ten straight minutes." And he set the stage for what was to come: "There might be three contracts given out tonight, not two, buddy."

The third round continued in much the same way. Bonnar concentrated on his boxing, landing some nice chopping right hands and counters to Griffin's continued aggression. Griffin looked to work his Thai game, hitting knees from the clinch and throwing a series of effective low kicks. The action continued all the way to the bell, and the fight was too close to call.

It ended the same way it had started, with both guys punching each other in the face simultaneously.

"You have just witnessed three rounds of the greatest action seen inside the Octagon in the history of the UFC," ring announcer Bruce Buffer said before naming Griffin the winner with unanimous scores of 29–28 across the board. The crowd exploded with a mixture of boos, cheers, and an audible "bullshit" chant. Not everyone was so sure that Griffin was the best man that night. Fellow cast member Sam Hoger was sure Bonnar would get the contract. "I mean everyone knows that Stephan Bonnar won that fight versus Forrest. I feel like I need to bare my soul; I must tell the truth, and the truth is Stephan Bonnar won that fight! Every fighter and every fan knows that."[245]

Bonnar, of course, agrees that he won the fight. "I thought I had him in deeper water than he had me in, I think I had him more hurt and more damaged. At the end of the day, it was a close fight. With a close fight, it could go either way, so it is not something I am bitter about."

After the fight, UFC president Dana White was ecstatic. "Oh my God, that is what it's all about right there." There was no loser in a fight that good, and White did the right thing, offering Bonnar a contract, as well. The UFC had delivered one of the all-time best fights when it needed it the most.

"Dana gambled millions on *The Ultimate Fighter*, and the season's excitement built to a finale in prime time," MMA journalist Kirik Jenness said. "When Griffin and Bonnar delivered a bloody, overwhelming display of all the sport can be, instead of Dana chasing the mainstream, it had now finally come to him."[246]

Griffin was at his self-effacing best after the fight. "There were a couple of times I was like, 'Man, I wish he would land one of those so it can be over. I'm so tired.' I love a fight like that. I love to just swing for the fences and see what happens." Looking back on the fight, it's easy to be critical. The striking wasn't as crisp as it could have been. Both men fought fatigue as much as each other. It wasn't a technical classic. It transcended that.

Future Griffin manager Bob Cook said, "Maybe it wasn't the most technical fight in the world. Mostly it was stand-up, and I heard people say, 'Oh, their boxing wasn't the greatest, their kickboxing wasn't the greatest.' But it wasn't about that. It was about those two guys having so much heart, standing in there toe-to-toe and just putting everything they had out.

Trying to win at any cost. That was really the appeal there. The biggest thing was that you could see that those guys fought with all their heart. They used everything they had, and I think that's what made such an impression on everyone."

The fight was just what the UFC needed. *The Ultimate Fighter* had been a self-financed test run. Although the ratings looked good, Zuffa was still looking to impress Spike TV with the sport's potential. Not only did Griffin-Bonnar blow the roof off the Cox Pavilion in Las Vegas, it also drew a record 3.3 million viewers.

"We didn't have a television contract [after the finale was over]. So the card was going along and nothing was standing out. . . . Then, Diego Sanchez destroys Kenny Florian in about ten seconds [actually 2:49] to win the contract we promised, and I'm thinking, 'We need a blow-your-mind fight or Spike is going to tell us to get lost,'" Dana White said. After the show, Spike TV was thrilled. "That has so much to do with Stephan and Forrest and what they did that night. They had fans in the building screaming and stomping, and during a six- or seven-minute stretch we had millions of new viewers."[247]

The show brought the UFC some much-needed mainstream attention in *USA Today* and the *Boston Globe*. It also helped secure a new deal with Spike TV that ran through 2008. And this time, Zuffa wouldn't have to foot the bill. They had a bona fide hit on their hands. White would get not only *The Ultimate Fighter*, but also his personal *Tuesday Night Fights*, called *Ultimate Fight Night*, and a show that would dig into the UFC's archives to show classic bouts on commercial TV for the first time. "We think we're on to the next big emerging sport," Kevin Kay, Spike TV's executive vice president of programming said.[248]

The Ultimate Fighter was a multi-purpose promotional tool. The show itself was the perfect platform for introducing the next generation of stars. But it could also be used to promote a pay-per-view fight between the two coaches. "Really from the beginning that was the formula," *Wrestling Observer*'s Dave Meltzer said. "Because Couture and Liddell were on the first season. But they didn't really have a grudge. They were very respectful of each other."

Couture was 41, but his conditioning was as good as ever. He was struggling in his personal life, going through a tough divorce, but was as physically ready as he'd ever been. Not only was he defending his title against a top fighter, but he was in the main event of a sport that was growing quickly. Ten million viewers had seen Stephan Bonnar and Forrest Griffin duke it out a week prior to UFC 52. The underground was now going mainstream.

"I think the show in general, and certainly that fight in the final, couldn't have been any better," Couture said. "More people have watched this sport in the last two to three months than have ever watched it before."

The MGM Grand Garden Arena on the Las Vegas strip was sold out. A sport that had long struggled for recognition was now the belle of the ball. There was unprecedented media coverage, and the nation was now aware of what hard-core fans had known for years — the UFC was the home of some of the best athletes in the world. For the third time in the Zuffa era, the UFC was getting the chance to make a good impression on a new group of potential fans. At UFC 33, it had set the sport back years. At UFC 40, it had delivered. This was another opportunity to shine when the spotlight was brightest. And Zuffa delivered a knockout show.

The undercard featured a classic matchup between welterweight champion Matt Hughes and his voluble opponent, Frank Trigg.

The main event had the air of a big boxing bout. "I have goose bumps. For real," Joe Rogan said. "This place is electric right now." Couture had the same game plan he employed in the first fight. He wanted to strike with Liddell just long enough to get him in a clinch and take him down. Liddell hadn't changed his game much for this fight. He was more concerned about his gas tank than his toolbox. "The biggest thing in the last fight [with Couture] was my conditioning," Liddell said. "My conditioning helped him implement his game. He was able to force his will. I wasn't. I changed my training after that. By trial and error, we went through a lot of things. By the time we got to Tito, we had it down."

Couture was boxing well in the beginning of the first round, and had managed to put Liddell up against the fence. He was one step away from a takedown when Liddell poked him in the eye. When the action restarted, Couture lost control of his emotions. His trainer, Robert Follis, preached a controlled aggression, but Couture spun out of control, pursuing Liddell with a vengeance. Liddell patiently sidestepped a charging Couture and landed a vicious right hand right on the button. It was something he had specifically worked on to prepare for this fight. The last time Couture had surprised Liddell with his aggression and his willingness to exchange punches. This time, Liddell was ready. "I think a lot of it had to do with game-plan stuff we learned from the first fight," Liddell said at the post-fight press conference. "John [Hackleman, Liddell's trainer] had me move. We kept moving. I think any time I got flat-footed I was risking getting taken down. So, if you noticed, I was moving side-to-side and forward." For the first time, Randy Couture had been knocked out. For the first time, the Iceman was the UFC champion.

"He came out striking a little better than usual," Liddell said. "I was able to catch him on his chin. There aren't too many people who can stand up after that. I've been waiting for this [winning the title] my whole career. Randy is a great champion and a great guy."

THE NEW UFC

Chuck Liddell would go on to become the face of Zuffa's UFC. He assumed the role once occupied by Ken Shamrock, and later Tito Ortiz. He was the go-to guy for media interviews and television appearances. Liddell was the perfect amalgam of everything that made up the new UFC fighter, and an amazing representative for the new sport. He was a fierce-looking brawler, sporting a Mohawk and a tattoo on his head. But he was also a college graduate and a soft-spoken, laid-back guy.

The other fighters suddenly thrust into the spotlight were the stars of *The Ultimate Fighter* reality show. Zuffa had big plans, and these fighters came with an added bonus: they worked cheap. While stars like Tito Ortiz were more interested in their next contract than their next fight, these young men were becoming just as well-known, and would perform at a cut rate. Dana White liked to say that more people had seen Forrest Griffin and Stephan Bonnar fight than knew of Tito Ortiz.

When the UFC aired its first live-fight special, *Ultimate Fight Night*, on Spike TV in August 2005, the card wasn't focused on returning stars or established names. The new stars were the fighters who had been featured for weeks on reality television. It was a sign of things to come. Although some of the TUF fighters were solid professionals with the potential for legitimate stardom, like Stephan Bonnar and Chris Leben, others were not ready for such a grand stage.

"I mean these guys are . . . 'C' fighters to me. Even 'B' fighters. I don't see them as really that good. All of a sudden they're put on a pedestal, but don't take nothing away from them. These kids are young, and there are guys who'll fight in the UFC for free, it seems," Tito Ortiz said in an MMAWeekly.com interview. "They just want to be in the UFC, and that takes away from a lot of the bigger fighters who've been in here for a long time. You know, this is our living. It's not a hobby. This is our living. This is our career. This is what we do for a living, to make money, and guys come in and pretty much fight for free. I mean, fight for $1,500? Are you kidding me? What if they get hurt? I mean, that's not even going to take care of training, let alone paying for food for the two months they're training. These guys are pretty much fighting for free, and I don't even have to say anything myself. You can watch *The Ultimate Fighter*, and each and every one of those guys says, 'I'll do anything the UFC tells me to do.' You know what it comes down to? These guys are just cronies it seems like, man. They're just programmed by the UFC. But you know what? More power to them. I mean I wish them nothing but success. It just seems like the fighters now aren't the fighters that there once used to be."

While established names like Ortiz may not have liked the concept, or the glut of hungry young men willing to fight cheap, the UFC brass loved the show. Its popularity soared, just as they'd hoped. The first post-TUF pay-per-view, UFC 52 in April 2005, set a new buy-rate record of 280,000. This is where Zuffa had envisioned the company all along. Now, it seemed like a modest beginning — the potential was clearly sky-high.

For the second season of *The Ultimate Fighter*, the UFC tabbed welterweight standout Matt Hughes and the winner of the Rich Franklin–Evan Tanner fight (Rich Franklin) at UFC 54 to be the coaches. Hughes should have been thrilled. This was a life-changing proposition. But getting Hughes off the farm to train for a few weeks was hard enough. Getting him to Las Vegas for several months seemed next to impossible. "He [Dana White] called me up and said, 'Hey I need you to come out and be on *The Ultimate Fighter*' and I said, 'Well, I'll have to see.' I really didn't want to do it, but I said, 'Let me talk to my wife about it' and I did, and my wife said, 'go ahead. . . .' So I called him back the next day and said I'd do it."

Things immediately went awry when Hughes and Franklin told Dana White that they wouldn't fight each other. For a show built around promoting a pay-per-view showdown between the coaches, this was a significant problem. And clearly, the show wasn't nearly as successful the second time out. While ratings in the first season steadily increased all season long, the second season saw a complete collapse after a successful debut. With no big battle between the coaches in the offing, Hughes and Franklin would be forced to face second-rate opponents at UFC 56. Season two was a failure on pretty much every score, but it did accomplish one very significant thing: it made Matt Hughes a star.

A COUNTRY BOY CAN SURVIVE

Hughes was a farm boy from Hillsboro, Illinois, who had grown up fighting and wrestling with his twin brother Mark. He rode wrestling all the way to a Division I scholarship at Eastern Illinois, and was a two-time all-American. He fell into fighting while he was an assistant wrestling coach at Eastern. "I had a friend come to me and say, 'I'm going to fight in a couple of weeks.' I started to train with him, and I became as good as he was, so I went to fight as well, and won. It just took off from there."

Hughes benefited from the guidance of promoter/manager Monte Cox. Cox was a former boxer and newspaper reporter who had gotten involved in the MMA game early. He had his hands in every company and every show around the world. If you were a fighter who needed fights, Monte Cox was the man to know. If he couldn't get you booked in another show, he could always put you in his own Extreme Challenge shows, which he ran throughout the Midwest.

"I'll be honest, when I got a hold of Monte I didn't know anything. I didn't know a good manager from a bad manager, I was just lucky enough that my manager was the right guy," Hughes said. "It wasn't that I chose Monte Cox, Monte was the only one to really approach me, and I took him up on it. Without a good manager, you don't really know which fights to take. I was pretty new to the sport, and I didn't know which fights to take and which fights to stay away from. A good manager is gonna keep you on a good line."

Cox sent Hughes to train with UFC champion Pat Miletich in Iowa. Wrestling skill like Hughes possessed could take you a long way, but NCAA and Olympic champions had failed at MMA because they hadn't added to their games. Miletich could teach you everything you needed to know to thrive. "Pat's taught me everything, from my best submissions to my stand-up. Pat's been awesome for me. Half of what I know comes from Pat, and the other half comes from Jeremy Horn and everybody else," Hughes said. "We're always trying to get as well-rounded as we can get. If we can do that, that's what were looking for. We're always working on our stand-up, our striking, our takedowns."

In 1999, Cox got Hughes booked on the undercard of UFC 22. He had been fighting in Extreme Challenge and in Japan for SHOOTO, but now he was finally in the big show. Cox was close to John Peretti, who had become the head matchmaker for the UFC.

"They called a couple of times and nothing came from it. Something would happen, and I wouldn't end up on the show. Finally it happened, and I got into UFC 22. That's when my career really took off, when I fought and won in the UFC and people started to know who I was," Hughes said. What really sent his career skyrocketing was his mentor Miletich's loss to Carlos Newton at UFC 31. For the first time since he had been a professional fighter, the world welterweight title was up for grabs. But the title didn't motivate Hughes, revenge did. "I didn't like that a bit, the guy beating my coach and mentor. It was very important to me to go out and avenge that loss and come back and beat Carlos."

HIGH VOLTAGE

Canadian Carlos Newton was one of the most exciting and charismatic fighters on the planet. He almost always had the best match in the show, win or lose, and his first title defense against Hughes was no exception. The fight progressed with dizzying speed. Hughes would secure a takedown, and Newton would immediately reverse him and look for a submission. It was the best kind of back-and-forth grappling match, and after one round it was too close to call.

In the second round, Hughes got another of his trademark big slams. When he got a hold of an opponent, the only direction he was going was down — to the mat — which was fine with Newton, because it was where he was most dangerous. He secured a triangle choke, cutting off the blood flow to Hughes's head with his legs. In a moment that will live forever in UFC history, Hughes picked Newton up over his head like a rag doll. Newton was suspended in midair, but refused to let go of his choke. And then gravity took over. Hughes dropped Newton to the mat, and the shock of the impact sounded like a gunshot. Newton was out cold, and Hughes was the new welterweight champion.

Monte Cox, Hughes's manager, said, "What other decision could there be? [Referee] John McCarthy has to make the call. It's gotta be made inside the ring. McCarthy, he comes in, Newton is on his back and unconscious, No one is disputing that he is taking a nap. He was there for a minute, taking a nap. Matt is on one knee, and obviously you can't see his face. You can't tell whether he is out, he is dazed, he is spinning, who knows? I think when you have fight like that, that is the closest fight in MMA history. How can it be any closer? Someone has got to get lucky and someone has got to get unlucky. But the thing was, ten seconds later, Matt is jumping up on the cage, Newton is still taking a nap."[249]

Hughes was the champion, but his win was not without controversy. Hughes was also loopy from the choke, which was seconds from rendering him unconscious. Newton, and many of the fans watching at home, thought Hughes had been choked out mid-fall. Newton filed a grievance, arguing both had been knocked out and the fight should have been declared a draw. Or he should have been declared the winner.

Newton told maxfighting.com, "To say we both went out at the same time, that's like perfect timing. That's narrowing it down to a split second. That means either he's passing out on the way down or he's passed out while he's still standing. My legs opened the second I hit the mat, so logic would tell you that he went out first. At the same time, I understood how such a thing could have happened or such a bad decision could have been made. The referees and judges were in shock when they saw my head hit the mat. All the attention went to me, and everyone abandoned the situation at the time and tried to attend to my safety, which I do appreciate."

In the immediate aftermath, when the slam had just happened, Hughes looked confused and disoriented. He had to ask his cornerman, Jeremy Horn, what had happened in the fight. Only then did he celebrate his win. But Hughes maintains he wasn't out cold.

"I don't think I was out. I was dazed. In the first round I was winning pretty handily. I think all the judges had me winning the round. In the second, I came out and took him down and he slapped me in a triangle. To get out of the triangle, I lifted him up and he tightened the triangle even more. Now the triangle's starting to get to me a little bit, and I can feel pressure on my neck. So I take a step back and slam him down. The triangle was hurting me so bad it took me probably two seconds to know what was going on after I slammed him down. It was a couple of seconds before I realized he was unconscious. By no means was I knocked out. I was just groggy from him having a chokehold on me. Me hitting the floor and slamming him had nothing to do with the triangle. I jumped up and ran around for a little while. When I got done running around, he was still laying on the ground. He was hurting."

It was MMA's first photo finish, and it couldn't be resolved with words. The best way to settle the dispute was in the cage. "We're in negotiations with Carlos right now. . . . If we can come to an agreement, we'll see what I think will be a super fight," UFC owner Lorenzo Fertitta said. "The rematch will settle it once and for all. Carlos is an incredible fighter, Matt Hughes is an incredible fighter, and it needs to happen."

The rematch dispelled any doubt about who the better fighter really was. Newton had worked on his wrestling and planned to stand up and punch with Hughes. Hughes had other ideas, and took Newton to the mat and pounded him for four rounds before he surrendered. Combined with his win over the highly regarded Japanese star Hayato "Mach" Sakurai, the victory left no doubt that Hughes was the top welterweight in the world, and just maybe the planet's new best fighter.

He followed the Newton win with three consecutive title defenses. He was beating the best challengers the UFC could find, and beating them easily. He was well-respected by his peers and the hard-core fan base that closely followed the sport. But he wasn't becoming a star. In boxing, some of the top technical fighters, like Bernard Hopkins and Ronald Wright, aren't the biggest draws. People preferred the more charismatic performers, guys who weren't as good, but had more pizzazz. UFC fans were the same way. Hughes seemed bland, and his ground-based attack wasn't going to result in flashy knockouts or submissions. While the wins piled up, the pay-per-view buys did not. The shows headlined by the welterweight champion routinely attracted the smallest audiences. Matt Hughes may have been the best fighter in the world, but he wasn't a star.

In MMA, even the best are going to lose. The slightest mistake can end in a submission, and the four-ounce gloves can make any punch a potential knockout. Hughes finally met his match when he lost to his teammate Jens

Pulver's former rival, B.J. Penn. But after dropping the title, Hughes seemed more relieved than angry. Maintaining perfection can be a struggle.

"People don't realize how mentally tough this sport is. You've got to be just as mentally tough as you are physically tough," Hughes said. "After the B.J. Penn fight, I was a little bit relieved that I didn't have to defend my title anymore. It just kind of gets to you after a little while. After you've defended it so many times, you just don't care about it. So I was happy to not have to go out and defend the title anymore, but, on the same note, you wish you still had the title, so it's kind of a no-win situation."

Penn would end up stripped of the title when he took a fight with the Japanese kickboxing promotion K-1. K-1 was starting to run MMA shows, and Penn was offered a much better deal than he had made in the UFC to give the promotion instant credibility. Hughes fought up-and-coming Canadian star Georges St. Pierre for the now-vacant title, and after a first-round arm bar he was once again the world champion. But he still wasn't a star that fans would pay to see. That would soon change.

The Ultimate Bad Guy

When Hughes was presented to the public on reality TV, he went from being a bland and boring wrestler to a man fight fans either loved or loved to hate. He was cocky and extremely brash. Hughes was like Tito Ortiz's television character, only he was real.

Hughes was the ultimate jock, cocky to the extreme. When fighters won, it was a credit to their coaches. When they lost, it was their fault. He mercilessly taunted contestants like Jorge Gurgel, and told eventual winner Rashad Evans exactly what he thought of his showboating. There was no guessing with Matt Hughes, no subterfuge. What you saw was exactly what you got, at least to a point.

"Everything they show, I've said or done. That's me," Hughes said. "You actually forget the cameras are in your face after a day or two. You just do. The viewers have to realize they can show you the things they want and not show you the things they don't want you to see. They can paint an image of whatever they want. I can be a jerk five times over the course of that whole show, and be the nicest, sweetest guy 150 times and they can just show you those five times and not the 150 times. You can be a good guy and they paint you as a bad guy. There's a lot of editing to the show, and by no means is it the real thing. If I go on there and act like a jerk, it looks like I'm a jerk. If I go on and act like a nice guy, I look like a nice guy. But if I go out there and laugh and joke with my friends, well, that can pretty easily make me look like a jerk. I don't know if I'd say I got booed a lot. I think the cheers heavily outweighed the boos. I think I did take some hits because people didn't understand how well Rich [Franklin] and I get along . . . the camera only showed that I was teasing Rich, and they never really showed him teasing me. They've got to have a little drama on those reality shows, and that's what it takes."

If the UFC couldn't sell Hughes's all-American country boy image, it was going to turn him into the bad guy. There had always been a villain in UFC mythology, whether it was Tank Abbott or Tito Ortiz. Now they had Hughes, the best fighter around and obnoxious enough to tell you just how good he was.

Hughes said, "When Rich and I were watching season two [of *The Ultimate Fighter*], we'd call each other up and say, 'Man, they showed me having an easy practice this week when I really pushed the guys,' and we were always joking about how they showed me teasing him and never Rich teasing me." The show's numbers were down from the first season, but it was ultimately worth the loss of a marquee coaches' matchup to create a new star in Hughes.

The Zuffa UFC had been fruitlessly negotiating with Royce Gracie for years. Now they had him hooked. "It's not the matter of it being the right time," said Gracie. "There's a business aspect of fighting, as well, and the UFC has been working with my management for four years now to bring me back to the UFC, and they made a deal. I'm a fighter — I'll fight wherever. I don't care. They made a deal, so it's on."[250] Royce Gracie was coming back to the Octagon, and they had the perfect opponent lined up.

THIS IS MY HOUSE

Royce Gracie was a true legend. He was undefeated in the Octagon, winning three of the first four UFC tournaments. Since 1995, he had fought several times in Japan, helping to build new stars there in natives Kazushi Sakuraba and Hidehiko Yoshida. He had lost to both men, but most UFC fans didn't know that. To the fans, he was a returning champion, a myth who had done more to change the martial arts than anyone since Kano or Bruce Lee. His opponent wasn't just any champion, either. Hughes was dominant. It was a fitting challenge for Gracie, who only wanted to fight the best.

"I don't need to prove anything. I fought four fights in one night, with no rules and weight limits, I am the only fighter in UFC history to win three UFC tournaments," Gracie said. "I have the second-longest fight in MMA history. I fought a guy three times my size. I have nothing to prove. I look at this fight as another challenge in life, so the only one I have to prove anything to is myself."[251]

In Matt Hughes, Gracie was facing his toughest opponent since he took on Sakuraba in his prime. "Hughes is such a tough opponent. He is the current welterweight champion, and we do believe it will be a hard fight, but I have to tell you Royce is very confident and in very good condition. Physically and psychologically, I am sure he will be 100 percent ready on the day of the fight," Royce's brother Royler said. "His motivation is the best it can be, and I know him and I can tell you he is very motivated to fight Hughes. He is enjoying this situation of being 11 years away from the UFC, and he is treating this challenge as a good test, and he likes being tested."[252]

Gracie had defeated top wrestlers before, but this was different. Hughes knew Gracie's game and could defend submissions. And his wrestling background would mean that he would dictate where the fight took place.

"He is definitely the one who's going to set the pace and push the pace of the fight. If he wants to stand up, I am ready to stand up," Gracie said. "What I think is that it's going to eventually come back to his background. That's wrestling. He's going to try and take me down and ground-and-pound me. If he wants to stand up — sure. But I'm not a stand-up fighter, I'm a grappler. In the end, I always come back to my background. . . . I'm not thinking about staying up. If we get in a clinch, I'm either going to take him down or he's going to take me down. But I'm not giving him a chance to lock his hands and pick me up. I'm either going to pull guard or I'm going to do a takedown on him."[253]

The UFC was promoting the fight hard. There was a giant multi-story billboard in Times Square and tons of media coverage everywhere. MMA was finally legal in the state of California, and fans were rabid for any show they could find. Frank Shamrock and Cesar Gracie had drawn a North American record of 18,265 fans to the first show there in March. Hughes and Gracie put more than 14,000 fans in the Staples Center in Los Angeles at incredibly inflated prices. The gate would be the second highest in UFC history: almost $3 million. This was still a disappointment for Zuffa. The company intended to set an MMA gate record, but the fans weren't willing to pay an arm and a leg to make that happen. The nosebleed seats were priced at $400. If you wanted to be close to the action, you had to pony up four figures. There had just been too much MMA in the market to support this pricing structure. If this had been the first UFC in California, Zuffa may have reached its goals. But UFC 59 had taken place in Anaheim just two months before. It looked like California had reached MMA saturation.

The UFC didn't have the same problems selling the show on pay-per-view. The pre-fight barker show was tremendous. Gracie was the heavy underdog, but his calm assurance and quiet confidence were convincing. "This is my house," Gracie said in his heavily accented English. "I built this." Fans wanted to see if this old legend had a place in the new UFC. And they were willing to pay to find out. The UFC was in full spin mode as it attempted to portray Gracie as an undefeated fighter, despite his high-profile losses in Japan. "Royce's history was rewritten to where his most famous matches were suddenly no longer part of his story, and the term 'undefeated,' constantly being used, was not just misleading, but outright deceptive," Dave Meltzer wrote in the *Wrestling Observer*. "As much as the UFC wants to be taken seriously as a real sport, Major League Baseball doesn't erase its own history, make up team records or individual player records during the World Series, have commentators change the results of famous games, or claim sellouts that aren't so. Even boxing, a sport that the UFC compares itself to and talks about being the more honest version of, doesn't do that. HBO Boxing doesn't pretend fights that didn't air on HBO didn't actually happen. Even the WWE, with its decades-long history of dis-honesty, doesn't do that anymore."

Before a fight, Royce Gracie is supernaturally calm. His heart rate barely reaches 60 beats per minute and his face betrays no emotion. Hughes is equally relaxed, joking and clowning around with his Miletich team bud-dies. For these old warriors, there are no nerves.

"There's no pressure if you believe in what you're doing, and you grow up in an environment that's been competitive for the last 80 years," Gracie said. "If I were to put you in the middle of the war in Iraq, you would freak out. But if you spent ten years in there, you'd be like, 'Okay, the grenade just blew up, it's not a problem.' So this has been in my family for 80 years and we grew up with it, so there's pressure to be a Gracie every day, not just to walk into a fight. You do seminars and everybody wants to challenge you, so it's not a problem."[254]

The UFC had done such a great job promoting that it was easy to forget Gracie was horribly overmatched. Hughes was a different class of athlete, and Gracie couldn't compete with his speed and strength. Hughes took him down, passed his guard, and locked on a tight straight arm bar. Gracie's arm was in trouble, but he showed no indication of tapping. Hughes let the arm go, took Gracie's back, flattened him out, and pounded him out. It was a memorable match that looked like one of the Gracie Challenge matches that saw Royce and his brothers toy with overmatched opponents before tapping them out. Only this time, Gracie was on the opposite end of the demolition.

"I had no idea it was going to be that easy. When it hit the ground I thought, 'Royce Gracie is going to pull out a magical Gracie submission that I've never heard of and he's gonna submit me,'" Hughes said. "So as soon as I take him down you can tell that I'm just relaxing and not really doing anything, trying to stay tight so he doesn't submit me. It doesn't take very long before I figure out he doesn't have any submission moves what-soever. For the rest of the fight I never felt threatened one bit. I never felt threatened by a submission hold or any type of a strike from the bottom. It took me about 30–45 seconds to figure out he's not going to be able to do anything. I went for the straight arm bar and finally gave up on that because I didn't want to waste all of my energy, and so I thought I'd go to another submission. I do think I'm more of an athlete than anyone he's faced, but I think this sport has passed Royce Gracie by. It's evolved, and Royce has not evolved. He just hasn't kept up with the sport."

Matt Hughes had convincingly closed the book on the Royce Gracie story. "The past is the past and the present is the present," UFC announcer Mike Goldberg said. As profound as that is, it wasn't quite true. There was still one more legend that Zuffa thought could create even more of a stir than Royce Gracie. The Hughes–Gracie fight had drawn more than 600,000 pay-per-view buys. The UFC was confident that Ken Shamrock could do better. The "World's Most Dangerous Man" was coming back to the Octagon.

20
PRIDE BEFORE THE FALL

Nobuhiko Takada had been a failure. Kazushi Sakuraba was past his prime. Pride needed a new Japanese star, and found one in judo legend Hidehiko Yoshida. Yoshida's accomplishments in Japan's national sport were the stuff of legend. He was the 1992 Olympic gold medalist at 172 pounds. It wasn't just that he won the gold medal. It was the way he did it. Yoshida won every match decisively, by Ippon. The Ippon is the KO of judo, and results from a pin that lasts 25 seconds, a choke or arm lock that produces a submission or incapacitation, or a throw that places the victim on his back with power, speed, and control. He won six matches in the 1992 Games in just over 16 total minutes. While he was up in weight to 190 pounds for the 1996 Olympic Games, where he placed fifth with a bum knee that would trouble him for the rest of his career, he was far from washed up. He won the World Championships in 1999, and was the favorite at the 2000 Olympic Games before breaking his arm. He was still an elite athlete, and was still competing at the highest level. But he was 32 years old, and would be 34 before the next Olympics. It was time for something new.

"It was destiny. I was lucky that there was a stage like that [Pride] for me," Yoshida said. "I just wanted to show my fighting skills wearing a judo-gi to draw interest to judo. You know, you don't really start something unless there is a clue. I want to be a clue."[255]

It was destiny and a $250,000 cash bonus that drew Yoshida into the Pride ring. His debut was at Pride Shockwave, and his opponent was a legend of MMA — Royce Gracie. It was a modified rules match — this was Gracie, after all — but they were rules grounded in history. The battle between the Gracie family and Japanese Judoka had been waging for years, and Royce wanted to pay tribute to that history.

"This year will be the 50th anniversary of the jiu-jitsu match between my father, Hélio, and Kimura. I asked the promoters if we could have the same rules my father and Kimura fought under. No striking and only grappling. My father will turn 90 years old this October, and I would like to fight under those rules as a present to him," Royce Gracie said. "I don't want to use the word 'revenge.' Revenge is something you do yourself, not something someone else does for you. However, this year is the 50th anniversary of that fight. It's a historic year. I'd like to fight the same once-in-a-lifetime fight that my father did. I'd also like to get as many members of the Gracie family as possible to come to this event. I definitely want my father to come."

The two men played a large part in drawing a crowd of more than 90,000 to Tokyo National Stadium for a card co-promoted by K-1. The show is remembered today for the epic battle between Bob Sapp and Pride champion Antonio Rodrigo Nogueira. But it was Royce Gracie and Yoshida that brought in the fans. Many fighters are nervous about their first fight, about performing before such a huge audience. Yoshida, already a sports celebrity, seemed unfazed.

"When I was in the Olympics, there were a lot of people watching me," Yoshida said. "I think it will be even bigger this time. It'll be in the ring this time, not on the tatami, so I may be a little bewildered. I'm a little concerned about how slippery or hard it is. Other than that, I'll just do what I've always done in judo."[256]

The fight was a back-and-forth affair. Both men wore their gi, and did battle primarily on the ground. Yoshida had a strength advantage, and eventually secured a dominant position. As he tightened up an ezekial choke, known in judo as sode guruma jime, the referee stopped the fight. This was controversial enough, as after previous bad stoppages the Gracies had demanded a match where the referee wasn't empowered to stop the contest. So whether the ref thought Gracie was out or not, he had no power to stop the fight. It became especially controversial when Gracie immediately hopped up and protested, clearly not unconscious at all. "Royce was completely defending the choke," Gracie confidant Pedro Valente said. "Even though the newspaper wrote that he was KO'ed, unconscious, such a stupid thing could never happen. After all, Royce immediately got up, didn't he? If he had really been unconscious, he couldn't have been expected to have gotten up like that." The Gracie corner went crazy and stormed out of the arena. At the post-fight press conference, the tension had not subsided. Royce was too angry to address reporters, but his father spoke for him.

"We regret the hasty decision given by the referee. Moreover, Yoshida lacked courage and morality," Hélio Gracie said. "Yoshida didn't admit the misjudgment by the referee. Royce wasn't unconscious at that time. Yoshida understood that well enough. And that's why I say he has no morality. Unless the fight ends as a 'no contest,' I regret to say that we will consider the Japanese people to be unfair, just like the referee."[257]

Yoshida's career was seemingly off to a strong start. But to Gracie, it was a career built on a shaky foundation. "He was not successful at all! He faked the move, but he never completed the move or put any pressure," Gracie said. "I was never out! He faked the attempt, then told the referee I was out. He is a liar, a total liar."[258]

DON FRYE

The Gracie fight was a good MMA primer. Yoshida got a taste of the style without having to worry about being punched in the head or grounded and pounded. But his next fight was going to be pure, straight-up MMA.

Don Frye was the top American star in Pride. He had gotten his start in the UFC, and then moved on to Japan when the money in the U.S. dried up. Like Ken Shamrock, he had found fame and fortune as a professional wrestler. When he returned to MMA for Pride, he was a well-known commodity. His fight with Yoshida would follow a memorable fray with fellow Japanese pro wrestler Yoshihiro Takayama. The two men grabbed each other behind the head and just wailed away in what can best be described as a hockey fight.

"Don Frye versus Yoshihiro Takayama was a wild and entertaining match," Pride announcer Stephen Quadros said. "Takayama is a pro wrestler who fought MMA. Don Frye was the opposite. Because both guys knew the power of the buildup and Takayama was so much bigger than Don, it took on a life of its own. A little known fact is that Yoshihiro is a really mellow person outside the ring."

Frye was expecting a totally different fight from Yoshida. Although this was technically his first match, Frye knew this was a veteran warrior.

"Everyone says he's a rookie, but he's not a rookie. The guy's had 2,000 or 3,000 matches, plus training eight hours a day for many years. There's no rookie aspect about him. He's ready to go. He's a trained professional," Frye said. "He's the most decorated athlete to come into MMA. It used to be Mark Coleman. Coleman was on the U.S. Olympic team and the Pan Am champion. And now it's Yoshida, because Yoshida is a two-time world champ and an Olympic champ. Being the most decorated athlete, he's at the top level. He's not going to come in and start at the bottom. I really respect him. I'm glad he gave me the opportunity to fight him."[259]

Frye entered with a gi top on, but took it off prior to the bout. Although Frye was a judo black belt, the gi would have given Yoshida a significant advantage, and he would hardly need the help. Yoshida dominated Frye, taking him down, nearly choking him out, and finally securing an arm bar for the win. American fans immediately cried foul. In fact, despite later wins over Japanese stars Masaaki Satake and Kiyoshi Tamura (who had beaten top stars like Renzo Gracie, Jeremy Horn, and Pat Miletich), Yoshida was widely regarded as a fraud.

"There are two different versions of Yoshida — the Japanese and the American. The Japanese version has Yoshida as a submission expert, one of the best Judokas of modern times, anywhere in the world, using that skill to stop some of MMA's biggest names, like Royce Gracie, Don Frye, Masaaki Satake [while not a good MMA fighter, he is very well known in Japan from the glory days of K-1, and even as a karate star in the early '90s], and Kiyoshi Tamura," Dave Meltzer wrote in *Wrestling Observer*. "In the U.S., while not universal, there is a common theme among many people. He's a fake. A cheater. Someone who has never won a real match. A creation of Pride, which needs a Japanese top star because Sakuraba has taken too many beatings. The arguments are that three of his wins came over people who have done pro wrestling [Frye, Satake, and Tamura]. While the Gracie win is often misrepresented as a work and a cheat, it was controversial nonetheless."

While his wins created controversy, it was his first loss that would prove Yoshida was real. He gained more respect for standing strong in defeat than he'd ever received for a victory.

THE AXE MURDERER

Wanderlei Silva was the most dominant champion in MMA history. He was cutting through Japanese competition like it was made of tissue paper. "In the past ten years, I have come across many fighters," Pride president Nobuyuki Sakakibara said. "But personally I think Wanderlei Silva is a fighter who not only represents Pride, but symbolizes Pride."[260] Few thought Yoshida would be able to upset Silva, except, perhaps, for the more than 40,000 fans who packed the Tokyo Dome to watch the match. The crowd was beyond electric. Traditionally, Japanese fans are known for being quiet and respectful during fights. But these were not traditional Japanese fans. The building came alive when Yoshida shrugged off a Silva punch and took him to the mat. The crowd was crazy until the end of the fight.

It was a matchup that threw expectations out the window. Everyone knew Silva wanted no part of Yoshida's dangerous ground game. At least that was what they thought until he tried to submit the Judoka from the bottom with a triangle choke.

"I didn't expect him to try sankaku jime [judo term for the triangle choke]. The sankaku jime was not on tight enough to choke me, and the rope was in the way also, so it was a question of how long I could endure. I think he got tired, too. I practice sankaku jime often, so I know that doing sankaku jime consumes a lot of strength. Looking back at it, I think I should have been more active in that situation. I knew he would be tired at that point, so I should have attacked aggressively after the sankaku, but instead I let him rest. That had an effect on the decision."

No one expected that Yoshida would stand and trade punches with Silva. The champion had the best knees in the business, and everyone had seen what a well-timed Silva punch could do. But stand and trade is just what Yoshida did. He felt forced into it when Silva was careful to avoid his upper-body throws.

Yoshida said, "I couldn't do it because he studied my style well. I thought too much about Silva's strategy. . . . I was waiting for him to attack. That turned out bad. I shouldn't have waited. If I have another chance, I will initiate the attack myself." The judo legend had surprised the crowd with how willingly and successfully he engaged the Pride champion in the striking game. "His punches felt heavy, but they didn't hurt so much. His punches were very different from Kiyoshi Tamura's. Tamura's punches were sharp. Silva's punches just felt hard, but not to the extent that I was in danger of being knocked out. . . . Maybe because I can take a good punch."

Yoshida did more than survive Silva's onslaught. He was giving as well as he got, at least for a while. "A big surprise. I knew he was tough and very strong, too. I think he was also a great warrior," Silva said. "His power surprised me. I was really surprised. His punch was really strong. I am really honored that I could fight him."

At the end of the fight, Silva was throwing everything he had at Yoshida, grabbing him by the gi and landing punch after punch — even a kick to the head. But Yoshida refused to fall. The fight ended with Yoshida reversing Silva on the mat. It was a decision win for Silva, but Yoshida had made it close enough that there was some drama while the crowd and fighters waited to hear the verdict. "He was strong. I'm sorry that I lost," Yoshida said. "I took a lot of punches. . . . I wish there had been one more round. But whatever I say, it would just be an excuse." He needn't excuse that performance. In losing, Yoshida had proven to his critics that he was no company-created faux warrior — he was every bit the fighter he was advertised to be.

GRACIE 2

Yoshida had given his all in the Silva fight, but his year was not quite complete. First, he had some unfinished business with Royce Gracie.

Gracie said, "The first time Yoshida and I fought, the fight was unfairly stopped, and it left me with a very sick feeling. I was disgusted with MMA in general. If such a thing can happen to me, it can happen to any fighter, at any time. For the past year, my management and Pride have been trying to set things right, and Pride came through; they offered a rematch with Yoshida, and I accepted on the spot."[261]

Gracie again requested special rules. There would be two ten-minute rounds. If the fight went to the finish, it would be declared a draw. There could be no doctor stoppages and the special referee (Matt Hume) could not stop the fight.

"I never want anything special," Gracie said. "I got fucked once by the referee. I don't like to leave my destiny in the hands of others. I want the referee out of my way. I want nothing special. I'm not going to fly 12 hours to Japan and miss Christmas and New Year's with my family to get robbed."[262]

There would be no surprises from the referee, but Gracie provided a surprise of his own when he removed his gi and fought without it for the first time.

"I like to fight with a gi, but I am a fighter and have been doing jiu-jitsu all my life, so I can fight with the gi, I can fight without the gi," Gracie said. "I was not concerned with Yoshida's skills with the gi. The last time we fought, Yoshida spent a lot of time stalling by holding onto my gi. This time I did not want to give him a chance to do that, so I took the gi top off so he could not stall and hold onto me."[263]

Ironically, Gracie's demands for modified rules cost him a victory. He would have easily won a judge's decision after dominating Yoshida for 20 minutes. Instead, Gracie had to settle for a draw. He was in the same position as his rival Ken Shamrock at UFC 5: forced to celebrate a draw like it had been a glorious win.

"I don't like to make excuses. I just wasn't on," Yoshida said. He didn't want to make excuses, but the Silva fight had left him in no condition to perform. He took the Gracie fight anyway, out of a sense of obligation to his promoter and his fans. He said, "I feel frustrated with what I did in that match."[264]

RULON AND THE REMATCH

The next year's New Year's Eve show — the night was fast becoming the biggest night in Japanese sports — featured Yoshida's next mega-match. He had disposed of K-1's Mark Hunt in June. Now he would face fellow Olympian Rulon Gardner. Gardner had been the first man to ever defeat Russian legend Alexander Karelin in Olympic competition. Now he was training with Randy Couture at Team Quest for his MMA debut. Gardner had recently retired from wrestling after winning the bronze medal at the 2004 Olympic Games. He was disappointed after taking gold in 2000. He left his shoes behind him on the mat, a wrestler's retirement gesture. Now he was weighing offers from MMA companies and Vince McMahon's WWE. He was giving MMA a try, not just for the $200,000 Pride was paying him, but to prove something to himself.

"I wondered if I could defend myself . . . I knew I could wrestle, but I was apprehensive about the goal of hurting someone else," Gardner said. "As a wrestler, it's about respect. You're not actually trying to hurt somebody. I'm here for the test."[265]

Yoshida was an interesting choice for an opponent. He had won his

Olympic gold at 172 pounds. Although he was a plump 220 pounds for the bout, he looked like a child next to Gardner's mammoth 300 pounds. To Yoshida, it was less judo versus wrestling than big versus small. Could a superb little man beat a good big man?

"Well, I do judo and he does wrestling. Pride is a completely different sport than those two, so I don't feel anything particular about it being sport versus sport," Yoshida said. Still, the fans and the media were in a frenzy. For the first time ever, two Olympic gold medalists would fight in a professional ring. "It is the first time, so I do want it to be a fight that everyone will remember."[266]

The fight didn't live up to the hype. Gardner boxed the smaller man, using his superior size to keep Yoshida at bay. He won a lackluster decision and hasn't been back. While the Yoshida bout was uncharacteristically dull, the main event made up for it. The two best heavyweights in the history of the sport were set to collide. Fedor Emelianenko was fighting Antonio Rodrigo Nogueira for the third time.

FROM RUSSIA WITH LOVE

The rematch between Emelianenko and Nogueira almost didn't happen. Emelianenko had injured his hand, and had signed with the rival Inoki Bom-Ba-Ye show. There was a battle going on behind the scenes in Japanese MMA, not just between rival Japanese promotions, but between rival Japanese yakuza gangs as well. New Year's Eve MMA had become a big business, and 2003 was the apex. Three rival shows would go head-to-head on network TV: Pride's Man Festival, K-1's Dynamite, and Inoki Bom-Ba-Ye. Inoki's show was originally going to be headlined by Mirko Cro Cop, but he re-signed with Pride instead — for a big raise and a promised title shot. When he lost Cro Cop, Inoki's group stole Emelianenko from Pride. He headlined Inoki's show against pro wrestler Yuji Nagata, but the show was a complete bust, finishing a distant third in the ratings.

Since Emelianenko was unwilling or unable to defend his title against Nogueira, Mirko Cro Cop fought the former champion for an interim title. "It's going to be an amazing match that will be determined by technique and mental sharpness. Technically, Cro Cop's striking ability, especially his invisible left high kick, is among the world's best. Even top Pride fighters such as Heath Herring and Igor Vovchanchyn could not stop Cro Cop's overwhelming assault," Nobuyuki Sakakibara, president and CEO of Pride Fighting, said. "On the other hand, the Brazilian jiu-jitsu master, Antonio Rodrigo Nogueira, also known as 'Minotauro,' is just as talented fighting on the ground as Cro Cop is on his feet. Nogueira is among the elite submission fighters in the world, and has defeated such monsters as Mark Coleman and Bob Sapp. This matchup will show the world's best striker against the world's best submission artist in the heavyweight division. Mentally, it's tough to say who has the advantage. Cro Cop has wanted the Pride FC title for so long, and has been destroying his opponents, so I know he's going to take advantage of this opportunity to win. But, on the other hand, Nogueira has the heart of a champion and was our former heavyweight champion. Nogueira lost his title to Fedor Emelianenko, who is now injured, and his goal ever since has been to become champion again. I know Cro Cop and Nogueira are going to be ready to fight mentally, technically, and physically, and fans can look forward to an excellent match."

It was a classic battle between grappler and striker. Cro Cop landed fearsome punches and kicks, but eventually succumbed to a Nogueira arm bar. Emelianenko was watching intently, always looking to learn something to take into his own fights. With the failure of Inoki's show, he was back with Pride, and would eventually face the winner of this fight to unify the interim and heavyweight titles.

"I learned a lot from Mirko and Nogueira's fight. It was a great fight, and I didn't know who would win," Emelianenko said. "Nogueira won because he was able to skillfully bring the fight to the ground, but I'm sure that if Mirko had been able to stay standing, the result would have been different. I think they're both aware of my weak points, and I'm aware of theirs, too."[267]

Nogueira felt on top of his game going into his rematch with Emelianenko. "Every time you lose, it's good because you see something is amiss," Nogueira said. "The guy who's on top with no effort just settles."[268]

What could have been a classic struggle at Pride Final Conflict in August 2004 was cut short. The two butted heads as Emelianenko attempted to land a big blow; he wound up with a massive wound and the fight had to be stopped. Because the cut came from accidental contact, the fight was declared a no contest. Nogueira, who was performing much better in their second fight, would have to wait to attempt to take back his title.

Their third fight took place on New Year's Eve 2004, headlining a Pride show that also featured the Gardner-Yoshida fight. While K-1 won the ratings war that night, behind teen-idol kickboxers Masato and Kid Yamamoto, and foreign ratings machine Bob Sapp, Pride won the artistic battle with its epic title clash.

Nogueira was as good as he had ever been. Before the first fight, he was actually in bad physical shape. On the way to the arena, he had to sit down on a Tokyo street corner because his back was bothering him badly, but he fought anyway. What else could he do? At the end of 2004, he was physically prepared and mentally focused. Emelianenko was the Liddell to his Couture, the Ortiz to his Shamrock, the Frazier to his Ali. Every superstar needed a rival like that, someone who could make a good fighter great.

"He pushed me — I'm much better than I was two years ago," Nogueira said. "Before I had him, I felt like, I am going to train for what?"[269]

Fedor was going to be tough to beat. His former opponents raved about his ability. "He's got takedown skills, but sometimes just throws you down, using tremendous strength that he just doesn't look like he's got," Renato "Babalu" Sobral said. "But being chubby means nothing, and he is proof of it. Fedor is a modern-age fighter, a guy who knows how to do everything."[270]

Nogueira was equally skilled, able to perform in the striking and grappling phases of the fight. His trainer, Mario Sperry, thought his advantage would be his speed. Nogueira would have to move, outbox Emelianenko, out-think him. Emelianenko was at his best when he was able to get an opponent down and pound him out. Nogueira would try to make it a standing battle. When the fight went to the ground, he wanted it to be because Emelianenko was frustrated.

Not everyone was convinced that Emelianenko had a weakness for Nogueira to exploit.

"He can play true MMA, he trades standing, he takes down, plays on top, submits, he doesn't only play on the bottom. He is good at everything, so in order to beat him one must do everything, too," heavyweight contender Pedro Rizzo said. "Fedor is no excellent striker, no excellent wrestler, no excellent ground player, but he is good at everything. . . . And Fedor looks like a small refrigerator on top, with those little legs underneath. But he invests a lot in training; the same way Rodrigo goes to Cuba and I go to Holland, Fedor is now in Holland all the time training Muay Thai with Ernesto Hoost."[271]

If Nogueira's game was improving, so too was the champion's. Nogueira went to Cuba to train with the boxing team there. Emelianenko's time in Holland was spent with the best kickboxing instructors. His legendary calm and confidence only deepened.

"I think at this point of my career, I am ready for any fighter. I just adjust my training to focus more on one technique or the other," Emelianenko said. "I have now mastered ground grappling as it applies to fighting; my throws, I think, are good; my striking skills with arms and legs, in general, are on par with leading K-1 fighters. I've been through many training camps in Holland. So, at this point, I am ready for fighters of all martial art styles."[272]

He was definitely ready for Nogueira. Nogueira's belief that he was going to be faster and more explosive was shattered quickly. Emelianenko didn't mind standing and striking with Nogueira. In fact, that was his strategy. While Nogueira has technical skill, he doesn't have power. Emelianenko wasn't concerned about Nogueira's punches, and was able to let his heavy hands go. When Emelianenko threw Nogueira to the mat, he didn't let loose with his patented ground-and-pound offense. Instead, he allowed Nogueira back to his feet. Emelianenko had obviously decided that, as good as he was operating out of Nogueira's guard, that was also where the former champion was most dangerous.

It was a brutal beating.

"Technically, he may not have such a big advantage, but physically he is the fastest heavy guy in MMA history. He tries a punch, misses it, then immediately shoots again," Nogueira said. "He's the fastest I've ever seen. Much faster than Mirko. And he's got a great reaction."[273]

Emelianenko had emphatically proven himself to be the legitimate heavyweight champion and the best fighter in the world. He went on to beat Cro Cop to clear out the top contenders in the Pride heavyweight division. What he wasn't, however, was a top ratings draw. Pride had lost the battle for eyeballs to K-1. It needed a main event that could attract mainstream attention, and it found one for New Year's 2005.

THE GENTLE WAY

Naoya Ogawa had fought several times for Pride, but his post-judo career had been spent primarily in the pro wrestling ring. His series of matches with New Japan's Shinya Hashimoto had literally changed the face of the

Japanese wrestling business. He let loose with real punches and kicks, and overnight it was important for Japanese wrestlers to exude real-life credibility. Soon, pro wrestlers were pushed into real fights, with generally disastrous consequences. The wrestling business was in a downward spiral; what had worked for Ogawa undermined an entire industry. Ogawa had become the biggest star in a dying sport.

What pro wrestling had also taught Ogawa was how to build a match up and make the audience want to put money down to watch him fight. Pride knew that Ogawa would draw attention to himself in the media. And that would mean more attention for Pride.

"In MMA, all you have to do is to fight, win, and go home. Well, that's a walk. On top of all that, I value pleasing spectators," Ogawa said. "It's not only about winning or losing. I am looking at it dimensionally. That's why I belong to a different category."[274]

The best way to maximize Ogawa's impact was to give him an impact opponent. No one would have a bigger impact than an old rival, Hidehiko Yoshida.

Judo enthusiast Kendall Shields said, "Hidehiko Yoshida and Naoya Ogawa go way back. They both attended one of the best college judo programs in Japan at Meiji University, and their rivalry started there. It's been said that Ogawa, as the upperclassman, was particularly hard on the younger Yoshida, for whatever reason. MMA fans generally know that Yoshida won gold at the Barcelona Olympics, and that Ogawa won silver at those same games, and there's an assumption that Yoshida is, therefore, the more accomplished Judoka, but it's not that simple. Yoshida won the 1999 World Championship in Birmingham to go along with his Olympic gold, but Ogawa won four World Championship titles, the first while he was still a student at Meiji. In fact, in five World Championships, Ogawa won four golds and three bronze medals competing in both the over-95 kilogram [209 pounds] division and the open. Yoshida is one of the greats of his era, but Ogawa is one of the most distinguished judo competitors ever, even if you forget about the All-Japan Judo Championships — which no Japanese would. To the Japanese, the open-weight All-Japan Judo Championships are every bit as prestigious as an Olympic or World title, and Haruki Uemura, who has won all three, says they're the toughest. Ogawa won the All-Japan seven times, second only to the great Yasuhiro Yamashita's nine.

And Ogawa's seven probably would have been eight, and eight in a row, if it wasn't for Hidehiko Yoshida."

Because the All-Japan Championships were an open-weight tournament, they usually favored a heavyweight like Ogawa. Despite Yoshida's Olympic gold medal, it was the biggest upset in All-Japan history when he beat Ogawa 2–1 in the 1994 semifinals. "Yoshida was ecstatic. Ogawa was incredulous," Shields said. "There he was, the five-time defending All-Japan Champion, and the reigning open-weight champion of the world, beaten by a middleweight."

The Japanese public knew this history. Yoshida's win had been a memorable upset. Now the two would do battle again, this time in the Pride ring. The fight also featured the largest purse in MMA history, with both fighters paid $2 million to square off.

The fight was decided by relative experience. Yoshida had been fighting in MMA full-time. Ogawa was a professional wrestler. Neither wore a gi top, and Ogawa was lost without it. When it went to the mat, Yoshida broke Ogawa's ankle with a leg lock, even though Ogawa eventually broke the hold with stiff punches to the head. Finally, Yoshida caught the bigger man in an arm bar. Ogawa refused to tap. "He couldn't tap with his arms, and it was creaking already, so I wasn't sure if I should do it," Yoshida said. "It was completely in, so I left it up to the referee."[275] The referee wisely stopped the fight 6:28 into the first ten-minute round.

"Yoshida! In this ring, I want you to do well!" Ogawa said after the fight. "I am not making any excuses here, but my leg is broken. I wanted to fight you one minute or even one second longer, but this was the limit."[276]

Ogawa and Yoshida embraced, and Ogawa tried to get Yoshida to do the hustle, his silly pro wrestling dance. Even in defeat, and in agonizing pain, Ogawa tried to get a final plug in for his pro wrestling show. "I would like to save that for after my retirement from MMA," Yoshida said. The two had done big business together, beating K-1's top matches of Akebono versus comedian Bobby Olugun, and Kid Yamamoto versus Genki Sudo in the television ratings battle, and drawing a sellout 35,000 fans to the Saitama Super Arena. The two were happy to put their differences behind them.

"The mass media just invented the problems, but there really weren't any," Yoshida said. "There might have been a small gap between us, but it always felt like we were two guys who have walked the same path."[277]

The second season of *The Ultimate Fighter* (TUF) clearly failed to live up to the expectations established by the ratings juggernaut that was the first. There was more focus on the action in the cage — the fights were now three-round contests — and less focus on the in-house shenanigans. Because Rich Franklin and Matt Hughes had no real grudge and no fight in their future, they weren't as interesting as they could have been. But UFC president Dana White had held back his secret weapons. He had the most intense rivalry, the most charismatic performers, and the most recognizable faces in MMA chomping at the bit to get in the cage with each other.

"It was my idea to get Ken [Shamrock] and Tito [Ortiz]," said White. "Ken hates Tito, Tito hates Ken, I hate Tito and Tito hates me. As painful as it all sounds, it seems to make sense for television," UFC president Dana White told *Ultimate Grappling*. "When I asked Ken if he would be interested, he initially said no. Then I told him we got Tito. Then he was interested. He wants to fight Tito so badly . . . he agreed to do the show because it created an opportunity for him to fight Tito."

Shamrock initially seemed willing to put his long-running feud with Ortiz in the past, but it wasn't long before he could no longer contain his anger. Shamrock felt short-changed by their first fight — he had been injured in November 2002, when the two met in Las Vegas for UFC 40. With a healthy knee, he was confident that the outcome would be dramatically different. And there was still something about Ortiz that could push Shamrock to the brink. The two had a verbal confrontation at the UFC 48 press conference after Ken had beaten his UFC 8 opponent Kimo for a second time. After that, Shamrock was more vocal than ever in the MMA media about securing a rematch: "I dislike him very much, and I always have. He's been disrespectful ever since the first time we fought, as well as prior to our fights, so I have no love for the guy and I just want to hurt him . . . I truly think that inside, he's one who likes to live off other people's pain. He's a bully. He's all fine and dandy when he's winning, and he always wants to step on the guy when he's done winning — he wants to put him down and make himself look better. But when he's losing, he cries — literally, he cries in the ring — and complains about things, about why he didn't do what he needed to do, so he's a typical bully. When things are going your way, you put people down; when they're not, you want people to feel sorry for you."[278]

Ortiz's UFC contract was up, and it was looking like his fighting career might be over. He was pursuing acting and flirting with the fledgling pro wrestling company TNA. Tito loved the idea of pro wrestling, but thought the work was too hard on the body. He was negotiating with the UFC, but the two sides were far apart. Ortiz wanted to earn more than anyone else in the UFC, even fighters who had beaten him. They owed it to him, he believed, because of the money he brought in.

"I want to get what I deserve. I've worked a lot. A lot of the die-hard fans have seen the work I put in. I'm a fan-friendly guy, I never say no to a picture or autograph," Ortiz said. "I just want to get what I'm worth. I make the UFC a lot of money, and I plan on making them a lot more money. I'm trying to do my part, as much as possible, to build the Tito Ortiz name brand. It seems like making mixed martial arts as big as possible, putting it on the map and in the mainstream, is my job."[279]

Ortiz was asking for a guaranteed $200,000 a fight when Chuck Liddell was still making just $60,000 to show and $60,000 to win. This didn't sit well with many of the UFC's fighters, men who remembered how the Fertittas had saved a dying sport and made everyone rich.

"Dana and the Fertittas built this thing, and they were losing a lot of money, but they continued to run it as a first-class operation and never tried to cut corners. He was running around demanding $200,000 a fight, even though it was pretty obvious that the finances were in trouble, and that no one [in the UFC] was making money," manager Monte Cox said. Most of Cox's fighters, including welterweight champion Matt Hughes, sided with the company over Tito, even though a raise for Tito would have ended up being good for their bottom lines, as well. Cox went on: "Matt called him a self-centered piece of [trash] and said, 'We don't need people pissing off the Fertittas.' It's a little different now, because they're starting to bring in a lot more money, but the fighters understand the business side of it a lot better than boxers do. That's why there really hasn't been a problem."[280]

Success was making it harder for the promotion to balk at salaries like $200,000 a fight. They were in the middle of the hottest year on record, and could easily afford to pay a main eventer of Tito's stature five times that amount per fight. He got his guaranteed money and a three-fight deal. He would fight the first *Ultimate Fighter* winner, Forrest Griffin, at UFC 59 in what would be the UFC's first show in Ortiz's home state of California. Then he would fight Ken Shamrock again after the third season of *The Ultimate Fighter*. If he won both fights, his third fight would be with light heavyweight champion Chuck Liddell.

"I'll be in my hometown in Orange County — there will be 18,000 Tito Ortiz fans screaming their heads off, and I've got to give them what they've paid for," Ortiz said. "But I can't look past Forrest; he's tough. I'm just gonna try to buzz saw through him and get ready for my next match."

Griffin had followed his TUF win with strong performances against journeymen Bill Mahood and Elvis Sinosic. Ortiz would be his first real test. There were questions about whether he would be a world-class fighter or a popular and scrappy, but not elite, competitor, like boxer Arturo Gatti.

"I'm going to learn how to become an Olympic-style wrestler before April 15, so don't be surprised if we both get a little banged up," Griffin said. "But, in all honesty, I am very excited for the opportunity to fight Tito — it's an honor to fight someone of his caliber."

Ortiz won a controversial decision over Griffin. It was a loss that gave Griffin more respect and proved he was a real contender. Despite the loss, he had hung strong with one of the UFC's top fighters. After more than a year off, Ortiz was going into *The Ultimate Fighter* on a winning streak.

"I think this will be one of the most exciting shows on Spike TV and in *Ultimate Fighter* history. This will be the best show they have done to date, and it will be the best one until I do another one," Ortiz said. "It's not just because I did it. I really put my heart into it, revealed my coaching strategies. I had two great assistant coaches with Dean Lister and Saul Soliz, and we really put a great game plan together to pick apart Ken Shamrock's guys. Each match was really, really tough."[281]

THE SHOW

Ortiz and Shamrock promised White they would be on their best behavior, but the tension was thick as the two went face-to-face in the season opener. Shamrock had a hair-trigger temper: it had been part of his wrestling character in the WWE — he would get angry and body slam the refereee as well as his opponent — but he was like that in real life, too. White was telling both men that he didn't want trouble, but everyone knew that the UFC was counting on conflict to sell the program and a subsequent pay-per-view bout. The top-rated episodes from season one revolved around Chris Leben's feud with Josh Koscheck. People expected that level of drama, at least, in every episode of season three.

"A lot of that will have to do with how Tito approaches the situation. If Tito comes in and tries to punk me out or be a smart-ass, I'm the type of guy who is going to face that head-on. I don't want to take away from *The Ultimate Fighter*, but at the same time, I am not going to be disrespected," Shamrock said. "If Tito concentrates on training his fighters and being a coach, that's great. If he thinks he is going to use this as a way to get into my head, psych me out, or get me riled up, then that's another story. I won't put up with it. We'll have to wait and see."[282]

Ortiz was just excited to be back. He was being programmed as the bad guy, had been ever since his relationship with Dana White had taken a turn for the worse. This was his opportunity, not just to sell a pay-per-view, but also to show America who he really was.

"The biggest thing I got out of it is that people got to see what type of person I am. I'm one person when I step inside the Octagon, and another person when I step outside of it," Ortiz said. "The picture the UFC painted when we were having problems with contract negotiations [in 2005] was that I was a bad guy who didn't want to fight Chuck Liddell. Now that I've made amends with everyone, and we're on good terms with each other, people are seeing the real person. *The Ultimate Fighter* proved that I am a humble person. I'm not cocky. I'm confident. People got to see my coaching side. I took all of the guys who competed in *The Ultimate Fighter* under my wing."[283]

The first episode exceeded all expectations. The show drew record ratings for Spike TV, and did better with men ages 18-34 than any other show that evening. The show soundly beat both NBA basketball on TNT and coverage of The Masters on the USA Network. Spike was thrilled. "It's a great start to season three, which promises to be the best one yet, with the intense rivalry between Ken and Tito and an incredible crop of fearless athletes," Spike TV general manager Kevin Kay said. The show continued to draw good ratings all season long.

Taking a cue from their coaches, several of the fighters had ongoing feuds with others in the house. Ed Herman and Rory Singer engaged in a running battle that included urinating in headgear, and Kendall Grove and Solomon Hutcherson created their own secret society, Team Dagger. But the most memorable feud was between the UFC's first disabled fighter, wrestler Matt Hamill, and its first prominent British export, Michael Bisping. Hamill was deaf, and that alone necessitated special treatment and extra attention. He was also an Ortiz favorite because he reminded the coach of himself. Hamill was an amazing wrestler and dominated practices with his strength and will to win. Others on his own team, including the eventual winners of the competition, Bisping and Grove, thought Hamill was taking liberties with his teammates. He was reckless in practice, and his hard-charging style put everyone in danger. The two taught him a lesson, Grove by delivering a hard shot to the head that rocked him, and Bisping by putting a little extra torque on an arm bar when the two were sparring.

"Day to day, he seems like a decent enough sort of a guy. He's just a very competitive person — he's a wrestler, and wrestlers are by nature, because to succeed in that sport, you've got to be," Michael Bisping said. "The problems were always in the gym. In the house, we never really had a problem. I'm competitive, he's competitive, so we just clashed in the gym, to be honest. I think that if we met in different circumstances, I think he'd be okay. We had a good chat toward the end of the show, and we cleared the air. That's basically all it was, we're just a couple of stubborn bastards."[284]

Bisping and Hamill was the classic TUF fight that never was. Hamill was hurt, and had to drop out of the competition. With his toughest opponent out of the running, Bisping cruised to the UFC contract. The drama and the attention shifted once again to the coaches. Shamrock was intended to be the good guy in the feud, a returning and respected legend who was going to teach the brash anti-hero Ortiz a lesson. Instead, Shamrock and the show's producers managed to make him the villain. Shamrock feuded with his own team, and often seemed out of touch and disinterested. Ortiz, by contrast, was an engaged and talented teacher. He was earning his team's respect and leading them to victory. Ortiz wasn't supposed to be winning. In the Zuffa mythos, he was the selfish maverick; Shamrock was the experienced coach who could mold champions.

"People always come up to me now and say, 'They portrayed you in such a bad light on that show.' That's always how they phrase it. They portrayed you that way. I guess that means people really know what I'm like. They wouldn't say that if they thought that was really me. It makes me feel better to know that people feel that way, but it does hurt me that the UFC and Spike TV did that," Shamrock said. "I've been in this business a long time, so it's basically a slap in the face from them, because I was a fighter for them for so long . . . I've trained dozens of guys to be champs in other organizations. . . . My reputation doesn't have to be spoken for or defended. The UFC and Spike TV did what they thought they needed to do for ratings, but, in the end, my fans, my family, and my God know exactly who I am."[285]

Ortiz believed the cameras were showing America exactly who Ken Shamrock really was. He had been prepared to leave the past in the past. But Ken Shamrock hadn't been able to let him get on with his life.

Ortiz said, "I thought there was reconciliation after the last fight. Shamrock said, 'The better man won, and I got to give it to Tito Ortiz. . . .' We settled our differences, and I thought the same thing, too. It seemed like after that fight all of a sudden he wasn't a hundred percent, he had a bum knee and he had all kinds of excuses for why he didn't win. He never gave me the credit for beating him. He wanted to do it again, and I didn't want to do it. But he kept pressing and pressing and pressing, and I was like, 'If you want a beating that bad, let's do it.' Luckily, *The Ultimate Fighter* came about. I get to beat him as a coach and I get to beat him as a fighter. . . . I really, really dislike him. It's like watching *The Karate Kid.* The guy in the Cobra Kai, he walked around like his shit didn't stink. Walking around, big shoulders, big chest, strutting his stuff. A lot of the fans asked him for autographs and pictures, and he denied them. . . . These fans are here for us. If it weren't for these fans, we wouldn't be here right now."[286]

Shamrock was losing at every turn and feuding with his own team. "I am the captain of this ship and I'll go down with it. I'll take full responsibility. Will you?" Ken asked his team. Shamrock said, "I failed them miserably, completely. So I have to figure out a way to get this back on us; get us back in the driver's seat." Team Shamrock was struggling, and Ortiz, being Ortiz, was plenty happy to rub it in. This was exactly what the UFC had wanted when it cast the two coaches, and the hubbub was drawing viewers.

"That was all real, that wasn't fake," former fighter and agent Bob Cook said. "With *The Ultimate Fighter*, you know you're being filmed, so you're going to play to the cameras. It's real life, but real life exaggerated a little bit. These guys know they're there to put on a show. They're going to be themselves, but I'm sure they play to the cameras. There's a little extra in there."

The show eventually exploded into violence. "Tito, keep smiling," Shamrock said when Ortiz's team chalked up another win. "I smile after every one of 'em, buddy," Tito retorted. Then the talk turned to their own fight, and Shamrock couldn't be controlled. He jumped at Ortiz, and everyone hustled between the two coaches. It was compelling TV, and great hype for the co–main event of UFC 61. The live finale drew 2.8 million viewers, making it the most watched UFC program in history — and the highest-rated Spike TV original telecast in the network's history among men 18-49. Most viewers tuned in for the middleweight war between Kendall Grove and Ed Herman, another fight so good that the UFC offered contracts to both fighters. While the two arguably wound up as career journeymen, on that night, at least, they put on a memorable show. "We have reached the point when guys across the country say, 'Did you catch the fight last night?' and they are referring to a UFC fight," White said.

Contracts were handed to Bisping, Grove, and Herman, but the true culmination of the show was UFC 61. Ortiz and Shamrock drew a record 775,000 pay-per-view buys, grossing more than $30 million. Not everyone, however, was thrilled with the fight.

"I didn't like seeing Ken Shamrock fight Tito Ortiz the second time. It is a very difficult thing for a great athlete to, perhaps, comprehend that their time is past," former UFC owner Bob Meyrowitz said. "And it's hardest of all for a fighter. Boxing is full of stories where somebody just fights when they really shouldn't any longer."[287]

Shamrock had been dominated at UFC 40, but at least he was game. Here, he offered no resistance. Ortiz slammed Shamrock to the mat and rained down elbows. Referee Herb Dean jumped in to stop the fight at 1:18 of the first round. Shamrock jumped up, furious at the quick stoppage, but even Shamrock wasn't as furious as the more than 11,000 fans in attendance. They had paid big money to see a blood feud come to an end, only to have the moment ruined by a premature stoppage.

"I was three elbows away from finishing him off. I dominated the fight. I think there's no question I won," Ortiz said. "Maybe next time, if you thought the fight was stopped short, next time you can bring a stretcher and a bunch of doctors and we can have the first death in the history of the UFC. Is that what you want?"

Officially, the UFC supported Dean's decision. "You have to remember, the referees have two people's lives in their hands every time they step into the Octagon," Dana White said. "Even if I don't necessarily agree with their calls, I respect their judgment."

The UFC's big show was once again marred by controversy. What should have been a night to celebrate ended up being the kind that could ruin a company's reputation. White and the UFC decided to offer a rematch for fans looking to see a decisive end to the feud. Instead of another pay-per-view fight, the UFC was going to treat its fans to the two biggest stars in history doing battle on free television. Shamrock–Ortiz 3 would be on Spike TV.

"I'm honest when I say this — this thing is giving back to the fans. I feel like so many times when I was growing up, me and my buddies couldn't wait for the big fight and ended up disappointed," White said. "I don't want people who waited 13 weeks [through the third season of *The Ultimate Fighter*] to see the end of this feel like that. The fight got stopped early. Whatever your opinion about whether that was right or wrong, it didn't matter. This is all about giving back to the fans . . . I would love to see a great rating. That means everyone would be tuning in to see the rematch. I have no expectations on the rating or the fight. I just hope it's a better fight than the second one. The first one was a great fight."[288]

Ortiz was reticent to fight Shamrock a third time. He felt that UFC 61 was a convincing win and an appropriate stoppage. Why fight Shamrock again, especially with a Chuck Liddell rematch in his immediate future? Still, Ortiz wound up doing what he thought was the right thing — beating up Ken Shamrock for a third time.

"The UFC called and said, 'Do you want to do this again? The fans are not happy about the last fight,'" Ortiz said. "The first question I asked was whether it was going to be on pay-per-view. When they told me it would be on TV, I told them to sign me up, and I was ready to do it. If people had to pay for another pay-per-view fight, I would not have done it. I wouldn't want to waste their time. Now it's free for them to see me beat in Shamrock's face."[289]

The fight, as expected, shattered all previous UFC ratings records. It drew an overall rating of 3.1 for the two-hour special and a 4.3 for the Shamrock–Ortiz fight. That equaled 5.7 million viewers for the main event. The previous record had been 3.4 million, although Zuffa had contrived a number of 10 million for the Griffin–Bonnar fight that had included everyone who watched the fight on subsequent replays. This number needed no spin. The fight even outperformed the baseball play-offs. "The fact that more young guys have chosen to watch this huge UFC fight over the baseball play-offs speaks volumes on the rising popularity of the UFC and mixed martial arts in America," Spike TV's Kevin Kay said.

The show was a huge ratings winner, but the actual fight was more of the same — almost a carbon copy of the previous encounter. Shamrock lasted two minutes instead of one, and took a few more blows to the head before the bout was stopped. It was his last fight in the UFC, and Ortiz sent him on his way with two middle fingers. Shamrock wasn't content to let it end that way.

"I have always been one of those people who you build up for something and the anger's there, and you step in there and you get it done," Shamrock said. "And win, lose, draw, or whatever it is, understand that at that point in time, you both went in there, you said the things you said, did the things you did, the fight happened, and boom, it's over. Move on."[290]

He tracked Ortiz down and tried to embrace him. "It was all business, man. You and me made a lot of money together. It was all business," Shamrock said. It was a pretty piece of business, indeed. But Ortiz had bigger fish to fry. He was looking to break his own pay-per-view record with another rematch, a battle with light heavyweight champion Chuck Liddell. The Iceman and the Bad Boy would face off in the final battle of a record-setting year.

22
ORTIZ VS. LIDDELL

The success of *The Ultimate Fighter* and the subsequent explosion of pay-per-view buy rates made 2006 a better and more profitable year for the UFC than the entire Zuffa era up to that point. The numbers were staggering. According to the *Wrestling Observer*, the UFC did about 5,225,000 pay-per-view buys, with a total gross revenue for pay-per-view events of an unprecedented $222,766,000. Even boxing's best year had seen pay-per-view incomes of just $200 million. The ten live UFC pay-per-view shows also earned more than $40 million at the gate.

"We exceeded a lot of the goals we set for ourselves," UFC president Dana White said. "It was an incredible year, but you ain't seen nothing yet. Wait 'til you see 2007. We're going to blow everybody's mind again."[291]

Just two years earlier, the Fertittas had been looking to sell. Now they were the proud owners of a company that was valued by some at over $1 billion.

"The Fertittas were smart enough to see what this was really worth. And Dana loves this as much as anyone. No one loves this more than Dana does," former SEG executive and creator of *The Iron Ring* Campbell McClaren said. "Joe Silva, he was fucking handing out quarters in a video arcade when I found him. But that guy would rather die than fuck with the integrity of the UFC."

The UFC's success brought plenty of media coverage, and plenty of comparisons to boxing, which was going through a rough time. Since the decline of Mike Tyson, no boxer had captured the attention of mainstream America. Oscar De La Hoya was a star, and boxing was still doing huge business in the Latino community, but for most sports fans it was a forgotten relic. The UFC brass, all former boxing guys, liked to call it "your grandfather's sport."

"We've already choked them out," Dana White said. "Boxing and the WWE, too. My opinion is, once Oscar is gone, boxing's in a lot of trouble unless another star breaks soon, which I don't see coming. We'll be the top dog once Oscar leaves."²⁹²

The UFC did have a knack for attracting a young audience. Younger fans were abandoning traditional sports in droves. The UFC was bucking the trend, attracting a bigger audience of young males than either football or baseball. People were taking note of the UFC's success, and even some boxing promoters were looking to emulate the most successful promotion in MMA.

"This era, this generation, grew up with much faster stuff. The Internet is faster; the video games are faster — it's a whole different thing," boxing promoter Gary Shaw said.

Shaw was branching out, moving in to the MMA game with his newly created Elite XC organization. "[In] boxing, you can have to sit there for a boring fight; you've got to sit there for twelve rounds, and they go back and forth and nothing happens. The fight can't stop; it's got to keep going. Here [in MMA], you can have someone submit and it adds another dimension."²⁹³

Not everyone in the boxing community was ready to embrace the new sport. HBO announcer Jim Lampley was a vocal critic, and so were some of the fighters.

"UFC ain't shit," Floyd Mayweather, Jr., said. "It ain't but a fad. Anyone can put a tattoo on their head and get in a street fight. These are guys who couldn't make it in boxing. So they do [MMA]. Boxing is the best sport in the world and it's here to stay. We should put Liddell against a good heavyweight, under Mayweather Promotions. If Chuck wins, then I'll give him a million dollars out of my own pocket."

Boxers were probably right to be a little touchy. They were being asked questions about the UFC in every press conference. Every newspaper and Web site was talking up the UFC and proclaiming boxing to be a dying sport. While the frustration was predictable, so was Dana White's response to Mayweather. White, who loved hamming it up for reporters, was quick to respond.

"You know, Floyd Mayweather just came out and said some stupid shit about Chuck Liddell. He'd pay a million dollars if Chuck could hang with a heavyweight boxer. How about if he pays a million dollars to see if a heavyweight boxer can fight MMA with Chuck Liddell? Or, even better, I'll put up a million dollars of my own money if Floyd Mayweather can sell more than ten tickets without Oscar De La Hoya," Dana White said. "Boxing and mixed martial arts are totally different. You distribute your weight differently because you have to worry about takedowns and leg kicks. It's completely different. Boxing and mixed martial arts are apples and oranges."

The truth is, MMA and boxing both did well in 2006. Both were filled with great athletes, and although reporters were drawing comparisons between the two, they actually weren't in close competition. They were attracting fans from two very different bases.

THE ZUFFA MYTH

The UFC was suddenly big news. It was featured in the *New York Times, USA Today*, and many of the nation's other leading newspapers; on television networks like CNBC and CBS, and even in *Sports Illustrated*. The rise of the UFC was a great rags-to-riches story. The Fertittas and Dana White had taken a struggling company and guided it to greatness.

The official story goes like this: Zuffa bought the UFC from SEG in 2001 and had a lot of work to do. SEG had run from sanctioning and didn't want to work with state regulators. Zuffa took the opposite approach and brought in many innovations. They added rules, created weight classes, added rounds, and allowed the referee to stop the fights. These innovative changes allowed the company to finally get sanctioned and get the sport back on pay-per-view.

This tale was repeated in a newspaper or magazine article practically every week in late 2006 and through 2007. The UFC was hot, and this was its spin. The problem? This tall tale is almost entirely untrue. The UFC had always had rules. The referee was able to stop the fight from UFC 3 onwards. The first weight classes were created at UFC 12. UFC 15 saw SEG ban head butts, kicks to a downed opponent, and strikes to the back of the head. Five-minute rounds, actually in effect at UFC 1 but never enforced because no fight lasted five minutes, were implemented again at UFC 21. By the time the UFC had its first show in New Jersey in November 2000, almost every one of the UFC's current rules was already in place. The sport Zuffa promotes is pretty much exactly the same sport SEG had been promoting for years. But that just makes the UFC story too complicated for a mainstream reporter looking for a quick and easy story about the next big thing.

SEG's David Isaacs said, "I think Dana has done a lot of really good things. I really, really do. But I also think he's kind of propagated this myth of the old UFC — that we had no rules, we were outlaws, not trying to get it regulated, and that they changed so many things. You know, I hired Joe Silva. What's he doing now? John McCarthy we hired through Rorion. Joe Rogan, Campbell found. Mike Goldberg? I found him. For Dana, it's probably good marketing. And maybe he believes it now? I bet he does. . . . It's funny, now, when I hear, 'We run to sanctioning and they ran from sanctioning.' Dana is telling a story that isn't entirely true, but I think it's a good story for the media. This is the new UFC. The mainstream press doesn't understand it, so they are looking for the headline. Human cockfighting was that headline. Today it's: fastest growing sport in the world. That's the story. They just don't have the time or the interest to really understand the details."

The press essentially reported the story Zuffa told them. There was no research or investigation. The reporters were no more than stenographers, and Dana White told a compelling story.

"Dana is what he is. He's a promoter," Dave Meltzer explains. "He says what he thinks is the right thing to say at that moment to make the company look good. Does he really believe it? Maybe he does. I don't know. Vince McMahon and Eric Bischoff were the same way. They became completely different people when they got on television, too. Obviously [Dana] likes being a TV character."

THE REMATCH

Even before the last show of 2006, it had been the UFC's breakout year. But the UFC saved the best for last. After his two wins over Ken Shamrock were the most watched UFC fights and the best-selling UFC pay-per-view bouts ever, Tito Ortiz was now going to step into the cage with Chuck Liddell once more.

Ortiz said, "I thought we were friends. When you share a household with someone, you feed them, they feed you, then I consider that a friend. But I guess money will change everyone's mind. Chuck sold out to the UFC, and more power to him. But I guess he is confused about what friendships are really about. It was a hard thing to overcome, but I did overcome it. Now it's strictly business . . . Chuck Liddell is always just going to be a fighter. That's why he'd better make all the money he can right now. Liddell will always just be a fighter. He'll be a karate instructor or an MMA instructor when he's 40 and 50. I own a clothing company."[294]

After enduring the bad rap that saw him portrayed as both greedy and a coward, Ortiz's star turn on TUF 3 helped change the way the public viewed him.

"I couldn't have asked for a better coach. Honestly, before I went on the show, I felt the same way everybody else felt about Tito," training partner and TUF 3 winner Kendall Grove said. "Oh, this guy's a cocky punk who cares about himself, you know what I mean? That's the image; he's a punk. But on the show, he kind of let down his guard and showed us the real Tito Ortiz . . . Working with him has changed my whole game."[295]

Ortiz was ready to try the Iceman on for size again, and was training harder than ever. He ensconced himself in his training camp in Big Bear, California, to work out with a team that included Grove, wrestler Jake O'Brien, and Saul Soliz. The training wasn't cheap, but a top camp was a necessity to beat a world champion like Liddell.

"Of course, it's a pretty expensive thing. I spend about $30,000 to $40,000 for a six-week camp. It gets pricey, but I get the most out of it," Ortiz said. "I get about $250,000 a fight, so it's worth the cost. Sponsors help a lot, as well. American Home Mortgage, for example, helped me out."[296]

Reports out of his training camp were positive. He was working to improve his standing skills, and was regularly dropping his sparring partners with crisp punches and kicks.

"He had a lot of good guys to push him. He's ready," training partner Jake O'Brien said. "We worked real hard, and he's going to be at his best. I heard from everybody how hard he works. . . . I found out it's true. There's no secret to why he's in such good shape for every fight. . . . I think he's going to win. I really like Tito a lot, and I think he's going to do it this time."[297]

In many ways, Ortiz had better technical striking than Liddell. He was a more traditional striker, and had better form after years of training with

Colin Oyama, Master Toddy of *Fight Girls* fame, and Saul Soliz. But there is a saying in boxing — you can't teach power. Liddell had punching power and Ortiz didn't. And in Liddell's mind, that would be the difference.

"I don't have to establish that I hit hard," Liddell said. "He already knows it." Liddell was as confident as he'd ever been in public before a fight. He never even considered the idea that he could lose.

"I'm going to come after him," Liddell said. "I don't think I've changed much of my game plan from the first time. I think I've improved. He's improved his game, but his style is still the same, so the fight doesn't change . . . I feel great, and this is the best shape I've been in. One of the things I've concentrated on is his trying to take the long way by hanging in there, trying to get me tired. I'll be ready to go for five straight rounds if I have to, but I don't think he'll survive that many."[298]

After more than three years without a loss, there were now people suggesting that Chuck Liddell might be the best fighter of all time. He had won six in a row, including avenging his first career loss to Jeremy Horn and beating Lion's Den standout Vernon White. At UFC 57, he had ended Randy Couture's legendary career by knocking him out in a rubber match.

"Chuck loves to fight, Chuck loves to compete, but I think more than anything, Chuck loves to win," Liddell's trainer John Hackleman said. "The reason he's so good, other than his God-given talent, is that he puts so much of himself into it. He studies. He listens. He doesn't settle for just all right. He wants to constantly push, to constantly improve. . . . He's the kind of guy you would want on your side in anything competitive, because he finds a way to win. I'm just kind of around here keeping an eye on things and trying to help him reach his goals."[299]

Couture was the only fighter to beat both Liddell and Ortiz. Since leaving the sport, he had gone to work for the UFC and was promoting his own clothing line and gym. He was also proving to be an astute analyst of fighters and fights. Couture thought Ortiz had the tools to beat Liddell, if he could get his head screwed on straight and overcome his fear.

Couture said, "I think it's going to be a good, competitive fight. Both guys are game fighters, and there's no love lost between them at this stage in their careers, so neither one wants to think about the possibility of losing to the other, which is pretty motivating. On the technical side, I think that if you look at the fights Chuck's lost in the last couple years, they've been against guys who have been able to take him down and make him work on the ground . . . Tito Ortiz has that kind of style. The problem Tito has is he doesn't favor the idea of engaging Chuck in a range of exchanges where he can hit, be hit, and be able to get his hands on him and take him down . . . I'm not sure if Tito can do that, but I think that's what he has to do to win. Whether or not he can get over his psychological issue with Chuck, and Chuck's power, and his [own] unwillingness to trade with anybody is going to be the huge issue."[300]

THE FIGHT

Ortiz had worked hard on his stand-up skills, and was winning some exchanges with Liddell. He'd done that in the first fight, as well. The difference was in power. When Liddell landed a hard left hook to the temple, Ortiz staggered back, and referee Mario Yamazaki almost stopped the fight. Even Ortiz's critics had to be impressed with his guts and will. After absorbing a storm of punches from Liddell, Ortiz rallied in the final seconds of the round and finished strong with a nice uppercut. The two smiled at each other as they went back to their corners.

The second round went better for the challenger, and he even managed to take Liddell down, if only for a moment. Ortiz had survived another hard blow from Liddell, this time an elbow that broke up a clinch. Going into the third round, cageside reporter Eddie Bravo's unofficial score card had the fight even.

In the third round, wrestling proved to be the difference. Ortiz tried to take Liddell down and just couldn't. After a furious exchange of wild haymakers, Ortiz was on his back, looking up as Liddell landed punch after punch. The referee stopped the fight with just more than a minute left in the round. Liddell had won again in dominating fashion. "I made a few mistakes," Ortiz said. "I tried to fight a smarter fight and not be as aggressive with Chuck. Chuck fought a great fight . . . I fought my ass off, man. I tried to stick to my game plan, throwing leg kicks, body kicks. People don't give enough credit to Liddell for being a great wrestler. He defended a lot of great shots that I had. Chuck Liddell fought the best Tito Ortiz . . . I have no excuses at all." Ortiz had given it his all, but it just wasn't enough. Without his trademark ground and pound, Ortiz was just a wrestler outgunned in a kickboxing bout.

"There is no doubt Chuck Liddell is the man," Dana White said. "The best 205 pounder in the world, and maybe ever, in mixed martial arts."

White had good reason to be excited. The event was the most successful in UFC history. Not only did they pack almost 14,000 people into the MGM Grand, Liddell and Ortiz had drawn more than a million buys on pay-per-view.

Little did the Fertittas know that they had peaked.

23
BOB SAPP

It was what Bob Sapp had always dreamed about. He was standing across from an all-pro defensive lineman (William "The Refrigerator" Perry), and beating the crap out of him, putting him on his ass. Too bad it wasn't on the football field. Too bad he was reduced to Celebrity Toughman contests on the FX Network. Too bad his life's dream was turning into a nightmare.

Sapp had been a great football player. He won the Morris Trophy in 1996 as the best lineman in the Pacific Ten Conference. He would live forever in University of Washington lore for his role in "The Whammy in Miami," the Huskies' upset win over the Miami Hurricanes, breaking the 'Canes 58-game home winning streak. The Chicago Bears drafted him in the third round, and his future seemed secure. Instead, he was bounced out of the league in four years after stints with four different teams, and was even suspended for a failed steroid test. "In the NFL, I was an ass-back," Sapp says. "The coaches were always saying, 'Sapp, get your ass back on the bench.'"

They say that when it rains, it pours, and Sapp was caught in a monsoon. His business advisor had stolen the money from his initial contract, and Sapp was forced to take the kind of work that men of his bulk are best at: picking up and moving large objects. Sapp felt he was destined for something more. Friends did, too. Maybe he didn't have the skills for football; he had always been more about raw ability than technique. But he did have the tools to be a success in another line of work.

"Mike Morris from the Minnesota Vikings said, 'You should

probably try some pro wrestling.' We did a video, and Jesse 'The Body' Ventura helped me out," Sapp said. The wrestling industry was in the middle of a ratings war between Ted Turner's wcw and Vince McMahon's wwe. Talented wrestlers with potential were being offered huge contracts, sometimes just to keep them away from the opposition. wcw had more than 150 wrestlers under contract at one point, and many of them never appeared on its popular *Nitro* or *Thunder* shows. Sapp became one of those guys and got paid six figures to learn the wrestling business. "I moved down to Atlanta, Georgia, and they were cool. wcw started me off with a rental car and 90 days in a hotel. Nice salary. Right before I got my television contract, they went bankrupt."

Things just seemed to fall into place for Bob Sapp. He was offered the fight with Refrigerator Perry as a representative of professional wrestling and asked fellow wcw wrestler Sam Greco to help him train. Greco was an Australian on the wrong side of 30, inexplicably under wcw contract despite having no wrestling experience or background. But he was a professional kickboxer who had been a journeyman with Japan's oldest and most successful martial arts promotion, K-1. When Greco saw Sapp fight, he saw dollar signs. Not only did Sapp fight with an uncontrolled fury, he also created a character for the show called The Beast that would be a certain hit in Japan.

"After my first fight, Sam Greco said, 'It looks like you have a pretty hard punch and could have a future in fighting. I'm going to give this video to my boss, Mr. Ishii.' So Sam showed my boxing and wrestling tapes to Mr. Ishii, and they came back and said that I had good conditioning, stamina, and endurance, but zero boxing skills," Sapp told InfinityFitness.com. "However, they had faith that I would improve with practice, and if not, due to my size, I could always get into Japanese pro wrestling."

K-1 had been struggling to find new stars. Its adopted son, "The Blue-Eyed Samurai," Andy Hug, had passed away in 2000 from leukemia. Its best fighters, men who had carried the promotion during the glory years in the mid-1990s, like Ernesto Hoost and Peter Aerts, were past their prime. Sapp would offer K-1 fans something different. Most of the kickboxers were big, but lean and lithe, built for speed and movement. Sapp was a 400-pound freight train. The contrast made for great television, and K-1 boss Kazuyoshi Ishii immediately made Sapp the focus of the entire promotion.

Sapp played a role as Mr. Ishii's bodyguard and looked for work with the major pro wrestling promotions. When no one bit, Ishii sent Sapp home to get ready for his fighting debut.

Sapp was fortunate that his home state was MMA's mecca. He started training with former kickboxing world champion Maurice Smith, spent time with Matt Hume and Josh Barnett at AMC Pankration, and worked out with Randy Couture at Team Quest. When the call came for Sapp to come to Japan and fight, he got a bit of a surprise — he wouldn't be debuting in a kickboxing match, he'd be fighting in the Pride ring instead. It was the calm before the storm in the vicious battle between Pride and K-1 for Japan's biggest fighting stars. For the moment, the two were working together, and that meant Bob was working for Pride, too. It didn't make much difference to Sapp; he was bringing physical tools into the ring that no one had seen before or since. He was 6'4" and 380 pounds; he bench-pressed almost 600 pounds. And he was so flexible that college football teammates called him "The Rubber Band Man" because he could stretch his legs all the way over his head. Yoshihisa Yamamoto didn't last long.

"I looked at Bob as a lump of clay when I got him. Now we're forging him into a fighter," trainer Maurice Smith said after the fight. "He's real young, he's real green, but he's learning and has a competitive spirit. He had no experience other than the toughman contest. What he has to his advantage is his size and his power and speed — his disadvantage is his inexperience." K-1 would do its best to make sure Sapp wasn't inexperienced long. The Beast was on the scene, and Japan would never be the same.

THE BEAST

His legend grew stronger with his next fight, just two months later. It was pure spectacle, Sapp against a skilled but undersized Japanese kickboxer, Tsuyoshi Nakasako. Sapp unleashed the Beast. In what would become a Sapp trademark, he bull-rushed his opponent into the corner and proceeded to go to work. Whether the blows were legal or not seemed incidental. Sapp knocked Nakasako down with an illegal elbow to the back of the head and hit his prone opponent with an illegal knee for good measure. After a red card and a point deduction, Sapp again threw his opponent to the ground and delivered punishment with a knee and a stomp to the head. The referee had seen enough. The fight was stopped, but the fighting in the ring didn't stop. Kazuyoshi Ishii himself had to come into the ring to restore order. The Beast was unrepentant, taking a page out of his friend Tank Abbott's playbook after the fight by telling the press it was clear who had really won. He made the tabloids the next day when the press caught him visiting a famous "massage parlor" after the fight. "The papers said I was on top of Nakasako by day, and on top of a woman at night," Sapp said.[301] He was already learning that what happened in the ring was just a small part of the show.

Sapp disposed of one of Japanese MMA's biggest stars just three weeks later, former UWF-I and RINGS standout Kiyoshi Tamura. It was a fight that saw Sapp benefit from a more than 200-pound weight advantage. Now it was time to get serious. K-1 and Pride were co-promoting a huge show at Tokyo National Stadium. Sapp would be in one of three main events in front of almost 100,000 fans. His opponent in his first heavyweight MMA fight was none other than Pride's heavyweight champion, Antonio Rodrigo Nogueira. The now-legendary fight almost didn't happen. Nogueira's original opponent was to be rotund K-1 star Mark Hunt, in a kickboxing match.

Nogueira said, "I asked for four months to prepare to fight under K-1 rules, so I could stop training ground fighting. Since I'm an NHB fighter, I train in several things, including Muay Thai around four to five times a week, but not with the level of intensity I needed to train if I was going to fight K-1. I'm a fighter with a name to take care of, so I always need to enter prepared when I'm going to fight. So I offered a fight against him under NHB rules now, with a rematch next year under K-1 rules, when I would be more trained for it, but Mark Hunt didn't accept. Since he didn't accept, Bob Sapp's name came up. I guess nobody wanted to fight Bob Sapp, and some other Pride fighters already had their fights matched. I accepted the fight, 'cause I'm not afraid of big guys. I think he is a very strong fighter, a dangerous fighter, but in terms of strategy he has some weak points in his game, and I'm going to exploit those points."[302]

Like any Sapp opponent, Nogueira had a hard time finding sparring partners who could mimic Sapp's combination of size and athleticism. When they got in the ring, he was quickly overwhelmed by Sapp's unorthodox approach and his mammoth size. Sapp said, "I didn't know anything about fighting. So I was confident I was going to win. The best way I could win was to do what I could do naturally. I just came from pro wrestling, so I only knew mainly pro wrestling moves. So, you can see during the fight, I used them." Sapp tossed Nogueira around like the proverbial rag doll, once even power-bombing him right on his head. It was a move right out of pro wrestling, one that Sapp had worked on with his training partner Josh Barnett.

"Josh was essential in helping me. Josh was like, 'Bob, you don't know anything about MMA, so just do it. Man, you can do that. You're strong enough to do it. Do it, and you'll hit every highlight reel, I'll tell you that much.' I said, 'I'll do it, whatever.' What happens with kickboxing, what happens with MMA, is that everyone follows a rule of thumb and gets used to doing the same stuff all the time," Sapp said. "And there's a million different moves in there that you can do. And nobody really wants to do them. But when you don't know anything, you can do everything and let your mind go crazy and utilize the essential parts of MMA. Use the basics, and the rest is up to the individual."

In just his third pro fight, Sapp was utterly destroying the world champion. But the fight isn't famous just for Sapp's impressive performance. In one of the most courageous comebacks in all of sports history, Nogueira managed to weather the Sapp storm and finally secure an arm bar to put a finish on the fight. It was one of the most exciting encounters in MMA history, and it taught Sapp an important lesson about fighting in Japan. Sometimes you can gain more in a great loss than you can with a dull win.

"Sometimes I win, sometimes I lose, but my popularity remains unchanged whether I'm winning or losing. That just says a lot about Japan and how I fight," Sapp said. "People love to come and see me fight. It's kind of like an amusement park ride. You come, you ride, you conquer it or it beats you, but either way you enjoy watching it."

THE LEGEND GROWS

He had already faced the world heavyweight MMA champion. Now he would test his skills against the best kickboxer in the world, Ernesto Hoost. Hoost was a three-time K-1 World Grand Prix champion. He had seen everything there is to see inside the ring — except for Bob Sapp. Sapp's inexperience worked to his advantage: his punches came from unorthodox angles, and his strength and size put Hoost on the defensive. Critics say Sapp had a little help in the form of a lenient official who allowed Sapp to manhandle Hoost, often holding him in the corner with one hand while clobbering him with the other, but Sapp bristles at this idea.

"Leeway as far as what? We're allowed to grab behind the head, we're allowed to do all of the things that were done in the fight, that's for sure," Sapp said. "Sometimes, when it comes down to it in K-1, many Americans don't get it."

In classic K-1 booking, Hoost got a return match, where it was expected that he would get his revenge on Sapp. K-1 was notorious for having its stars help with the process of getting new talent over. New fighters often looked dominant in the beginning of their K-1 tenure before falling back with losses in return matches.

"K-1 had its fixed fights, too. There were an awful lot of exchanged wins, and they would bring guys in strong. I was told that a lot of the spectacular 30-second knockouts when they brought a new guy in would be worked to get the new guy over," *Wrestling Observer* editor Dave Meltzer said. "Like when Fihlo first came in and he knocked out Andy Hug in seconds. I think Andy Hug was their house guy. I don't buy for a second that Patrick Smith could really beat Andy Hug. They just said, 'This guy is a UFC star, we need to get him over. You'll get your win back.' That's how they made people."

If that was what Hoost was expecting, that's not what he got. He found the Beast's weakness, dropping him with a body shot, but referee Nobuaki Kakuda was there to protect K-1's new star. Hoost was knocked down in the second round, but was controlling the fight, and Sapp was tiring. As the round ended, Sapp was getting desperate. He threw Hoost into the corner and threw a series of increasingly wild punches. Hoost was surviving, blocking the few that weren't outright missing, but Kakuda jumped in to call an end to the contest, keeping the Sapp train on track. All told, Sapp fought eight times in just eight months in his debut year, including a fight with Yoshihiro Takayama on New Year's Eve for Antonio Inoki that drew a 24.5 rating and made New Year's Eve MMA shows a fixture on Japanese television.

Buying (and Selling) the Beast

A strong first year made Sapp a legitimate celebrity in Japan. Things got weird quickly. Soon he couldn't even walk outside without an escort. "When I would walk down the street, everyone would start flipping over taxi cabs and going nuts," Sapp said. "The police would ask me not to walk outside. It was nuts." Japan had its share of gaijin stars in the pro wrestling and fighting industries, but none could compare to Sapp.

"He's been in more than 200 commercials, has his own rap song, Bob Sapp kendo boxes, he's on ice cream boxes. He's everywhere. He did really well for himself, the situation snowballed, and it helped him establish himself here as someone who's on his way to being larger than life," Strikeforce vice president Mike Afromowitz said. "It's his tremendous size and strength. In Japan, you don't see people who look like that. Even here his size is a rarity, there even more so. I think people were just incredibly intrigued by it. Then he made himself into a larger-than-life character and the people really took him in."

Sapp's life was so crazy, it's amazing that he had time to fight. He became a staple of the network Japanese morning and evening shows, and was on the air every day, sometimes on multiple channels.

"I would eat breakfast early, go to sleep, wake up again at eight a.m. From there, I'd go and do television shows from about eight to two o'clock. From two to four, I would eat lunch, from six to nine, I would have to do some more television shows and then some rest and go eat dinner. Then I'd have to do some commercials and television shows, some of the late-night television shows. The next day I'd get up and go anywhere from a pro wrestling match or pro wrestling practice, then kickboxing practice, followed by MMA practice," Sapp said. "A kickboxing or MMA match would be followed almost immediately by commercials or pro wrestling. Then the next day, I'd have a full onslaught of television. It was hard. And that's one of the reasons my records are going to stand. I don't think you'll find anyone who's going to be able to work and do that much stuff. I did comedy shows, and the only thing beating out my fights were my comedy shows. The entertainment I was providing was ridiculous. They had me doing absolutely everything and anything."

The schedule was deadly, and Sapp was spending more time becoming a television celebrity than he was becoming a world-class fighter. In many ways, his fighting career and abilities peaked in 2002 with the wins over Hoost. His celebrity, however, continued to grow.

Sapp's coach Matt Hume said, "Bob Sapp's meteoric rise to fame in Japan was an amazing thing to be part of. As a coach, it would have been very frustrating to try to get him ready for a fight with the crazy media schedule that he is on when he is in Japan. Fortunately, I have been involved in other areas of the business for many years and understand the situation well. He really didn't have much time to train, so we had to be creative and make the most of any time, but also know when to back off and let him rest. If he would have had time to dedicate to strict training, he would have been a better fighter, however K-1 and Bob's priority was media exposure, so we accepted it and worked with it."

THE RACE CARD

Bob Sapp was willing to do anything to make it big. He acted like a beast, literally. He crammed bananas into his mouth and mimicked a gorilla. It was pro wrestling at its finest, playing to people's fears and hidden prejudices.

"Kazuyoshi Ishii was brilliant at marketing Bob Sapp. He fit all the Japanese cultural stereotypes — a big, scary foreigner who also was black," FightOpinion.com founder Zach Arnold said. "There are still very negative or cartoonish stereotypes about black people in Japan. It's more a result of naivete than malice. So, Sapp fit in perfectly because he's this larger-than-life cartoon character who was willing to say or do anything to get over with audiences."

Sapp says the skits were all in fun. He was "The Beast," and simply playing a role. Still, the criticism obviously bothers him.

"I get asked about the banana thing and everything else. The bottom line is the Beast not only had bananas, I had raw meat and all kinds of crazy stuff going on. It wasn't anything that had to do with racism," Sapp said. "What happens, and this is very common, is that we in America assume that the rest of the world has all of our same views. I've been criticized for my Panasonic commercial. They say, 'You look like a pimp.' I start laughing and say, 'That's not the way the Japanese are going to look at it.' That's how Americans look at it. They don't have pimps over here, they have mama-sans. It's a female, the mama, who is in charge of the prostitutes. Not a male. Not a pimp. So they had no idea. But it's very common that it happens."

To Sapp, he and comedian Bobby Olugun are playing a major role in expanding Japanese horizons and helping the Japanese confront stereotypes. After all, you need your Mr. Bojangles before you can have your Sidney Poitier.

"If it's racism, why have there been no African-Americans, no Americans, who have come over to Japan and done what I've done? They aren't in the streets hollering Negro this, nigger that, they're out there saying, 'Bob Sapp, Bob Sapp,' and everyone is going nuts. Would you say it's because of racism that I've also got the number-one selling women's sex toy in Japan? The Bob Sapp Wild Sapp Dildo. The closest thing it compares to is a horse. I don't think it has anything to do with a gorilla. I think what's occurring is that things are going so well people say, 'Why don't we knock him down a peg?' In Japan, they're prejudiced against all foreigners. They call me Baka-Gaijin, super foreigner. The success I've had should show you something," Sapp said. "They've got an African comedian over there, Bobby Olugun, and he also does some things we couldn't do over here, but you can't find a single African upset with him in Tokyo. I read the stuff online, like Bob Sapp and Bobby Olugun, he's a sellout, he's perpetuating stereotypes of blacks. Every African loves him. You know why? They're happy just to see a black on TV in Japan. They know that with evolution, other things will come. They're excited about that, but everyone wants to get upset and push and shove, but one thing that's great about it: in Japan you can bitch and moan all you want to, brother, but I promise you it ain't going to change a damn thing. It's a different country, and you will never, never understand it."

In 2003, he had his first major setback. Sapp fought Mirko Cro Cop in K-1, and the Croatian frustrated him with a lot more movement than he'd seen from opponents like Hoost, who were happy to stand and trade blows with him. When Cro Cop cracked Sapp's arm and followed up with a big left hand to the eyeball, the big man went down, literally screaming in pain. He was coherent, but in excruciating pain, and took a ten-count and went to the back. He had suffered a broken orbital bone. In true Sapp fashion, he was able to turn this negative into a positive. The time off to recover just led to new business opportunities.

"You saw as soon as Mirko Cro Cop beat me he took off for Pride because he had beaten K-1's champion. I signed a deal for 400,000 slot machines in my image and Mirko became a politician in Croatia, so we both ended up doing pretty well," Sapp said. "It's just for me it ended up paying to be a loser a little more."

After taking five months to recover, Sapp made his North American debut for K-1, fighting UFC pioneer Kimo Leopaldo in Las Vegas. Kimo had been lit up in his prior K-1 fight, and seemed like a well-known but ultimately harmless opponent. Sapp had become a marketing force in Japan, and K-1 was banking on him being the fighter who could finally break kickboxing into the mainstream in America. Explaining Sapp to the American media wasn't always easy.

Afromowitz said, "We were in Vegas for the fight, and Maurice Smith was trying to explain the Sapp phenomenon in Japan. He said, 'You have to understand something, this guy is bigger than all of us combined.' Maurice has a big name, and the other guys he was referring to, like Ray Sefo, have big names, too. They have big endorsements. But Bob is bigger than all of them. A lot of Japanese people came to Vegas to watch him fight. He was a rock star."

K-1 was pulling out all the stops; Sapp went on *The Tonight Show with Jay Leno* to let Americans hear his maniacal chuckle, a laugh the Japanese just couldn't get enough of. They even planned a post-fight angle with Mike Tyson, the popular boxer K-1 had been flirting with for years. This was going to be K-1's biggest night. All Sapp had to do was knock Kimo out and the real show would begin. Someone forgot to tell Kimo.

He showed heart and skill, and knocked Sapp down with a left jab as the first round was coming to an end. Sapp's legs were wobbly, but K-1 house referee Kakuda allowed him to continue, and he was saved by the bell. Things got weird when Sapp couldn't answer the bell for the second round. As Kimo celebrated, Kakuda allowed Sapp two minutes of time by having the ringside physician check on Sapp and engaging in a long discussion with Sapp's cornerman, Maurice Smith. It was a true travesty, but K-1's shenanigans were far from over. Sapp was clearly outclassed in a conventional kickboxing match, so the bullying began. Sapp was allowed to push Kimo around, and finished the fight with a blatantly illegal punch to the back of the head.

As the crowd booed Sapp and chanted, "Kimo, Kimo," the real main event began. Tyson hit the ring and teased a brawl with Sapp, promising that if Sapp would sign for a boxing match, he would fight him then and there. "Sign the paper, big boy," Tyson said. Sapp promised to put him through the ground. It was a silly and staged spectacle, but it got K-1 on *Sports Center* and had the public primed for another Tyson spectacle. The fight never happened, and Sapp's 15 minutes of fame soon expired, at least in his home country. In Japan he was as popular as ever, and would prove it on New Year's Eve.

THE BATTLE OF THE GIANTS

New Year's Eve in Japan used to be all about music. The NHK network's New Year's Eve concert was the biggest television show in the country, not just for that night, but for the whole year. It was a tradition and a phenomenon untouched by competition for four decades.

"Unlike in the U.S., where people go out to celebrate New Year's, in Japan nearly everyone stays home for what is the most important television night of the year, and the concert is their version of the Super Bowl, the show that everyone watches," Dave Meltzer explains. "For years, the networks in Japan threw in the towel rather than compete with something so big."

But the competition had finally found its programming kryptonite. After Sapp's success in 2002, three different networks would air MMA shows against the New Year's concert. The most succesful would be a battle of the giants. For the first time, Sapp would be the smaller man in the ring. His opponent was the recently retired Yokozuna Akebono. In the 300 years of Sumo wrestling's history as a professional sport, there had only been 64 Yokozunas, or grand champions. Akebono was one of them, and the first foreigner to earn the distinction. This was a big deal. This was the new, flashy fighting icon against the traditional representative of Japanese culture and combat. The fight drew 54 million people. That's half the country. Keep that in mind when people go crazy when *The Ultimate Fighter* hits two million viewers, calling the sport mainstream in America. This was mainstream, and Sapp was atop the crest of MMA's cultural tidal wave.

He continued as a cultural icon into 2004, but it was becoming obvious that he would never live up to his potential as a fighter. It was the part of his act that he took the least joy in. His lack of time for proper training hurt quite a bit, as most fights ended when Sapp got so tired he could no longer compete. After the Kimo debacle, K-1 had to bring in a lower level of fighter to ensure a Sapp win, and even that almost failed in the case of Seth Petruzelli. Sapp was fed to Kazayuki Fujita, where he was absolutely brutalized by soccer kicks in a one-sided match and then knocked out by Ray Sefo a month later in K-1. It seemed like the Bob Sapp fad was finally coming to an end, yet his popularity lingered.

Sapp said, "What's most amazing about all this is that back in 2002 everyone told me, 'Bob, it's just a fad.' We're going on seven years later. I don't exactly know how long they want this fad to last. But let me tell you, brother, it's 2008, you know what I'm saying?"

After a brief resurgence in 2005, including winning the K-1 Japan tournament, Sapp and K-1 parted ways in 2006. He was scheduled to fight Ernesto Hoost in Hoost's retirement match in Amsterdam; Sapp was in the building, but chose not to fight due to a contract dispute.

Sapp said, "I had extreme popularity. Everything has blown up, MMA around the world is blowing up, and my popularity is blowing up. Again, Japan is a unique place, so you have to use Japanese logic. If you use American logic, we're just going to say, 'It's plain silly what they are doing.' I had a 20-fight contract that was supposed to last five years. Well, because of my popularity in Japan, they were fighting me once a month and sometimes twice a month. So that should tell you that 20 fights is going to go rather quickly, and they ain't going to last five years if you're blowing them out so fast. I did way more than that if we include pro wrestling. But we're talking about 20 fights, anyway, not including pro wrestling. I did 20 fights in just over two years. That left me with two and a half years left of no work. So, in my opinion, my contract is finished. Their opinion — no, it's not. They said, 'You still have to do five years worth of work.' I said, 'Okay, am I going to fight? How much?' They said, 'We don't know, we have to look at your contract. Contract says zero, so you have to fight for zero.' What? So it's kind of silly. I said, 'Okay, let's resign.' No problems. We go to Amsterdam, they were supposed to put almost a million bucks in, and they didn't. They said, 'Just trust us that you'll get it.' I said, 'Listen, I can't trust you. That's too much money to be trusting anyone with. So, I tell you what, I'll fight for free, and then you guys just have to leave me alone.' They chose not to do that . . . they chose to play games."

After Sapp no-showed at the event, he went into hiding. The rumor mill said he was hiding from K-1 yakuza who were looking from revenge. Sapp has a different story, insisting he was afraid of the reaction from the rowdy European fans. Either way, his storied K-1 career was at an end. It was time for the Beast to come to America.

Bob Sapp is a born entertainer. He's got an engaging personality and a great laugh. Combine that with his unusual physical size and you've got something, certainly enough for a career as a B-movie villain. Sapp was going to give Hollywood a try. While he was in Hollywood, Sapp was within a signature of a WWE deal. They planned to bring him in and use him both as a pro wrestler and as wrestling's representative in the world of MMA.

Sapp said, "K-1 was playing games, games that would consequently lead me to have one of the best years of my life and would save my career. Because I came over here, left K-1, and got ready to sign a huge contract with WWE, they threatened to sue WWE. WWE backed out, thank God, because my partner was going to be Chris Benoit." After a narrow escape from being partnered with a child murdering pro wrestler, Sapp's persistent good luck led him further and further up the Hollywood food chain.

"I was supposed to be on *The Anna Nicole* [Smith] *Show*, that's why I first went out to California. It didn't work out because she was sick and didn't show up for the scene the next day. However, I caught the attention of one of the producers from the movie *Elektra*. I did *Jay Leno* and *Jimmy Kimmel*. That caught the attention of the producers from *The Longest Yard*. I've done eight Hollywood movies so far, and I just did *Pros versus Joes*," Sapp said. "I'm 33 years old. Everything I've done, not only has it not required a job application, but every job I've touched has manged to make me well over six figures. Or in that six-figure range. My first pro wrestling contract was like $120,000, you've got the fighting, which is well over $1 million, you've got all the movie work, which is now adding up to be over $1 million. You've got the NFL in there, too, which is over $1 million. It's like, 'Bob, you've lived a huge and incredible life.' Everything I've done has been a kid's dream job."

Back in Japan, K-1 tried desperately to find the next Bob Sapp. Instead of looking for the most skilled and charismatic performers it could find, it instead tried to find another comical giant.

"It wasn't Sapp that was the problem. The problem was they tried to create a whole world of Sapps. It's like the next Hulk Hogan was Steve Austin, it wasn't Lex Luger. The next Bob Sapp wasn't going to be Choi Hung Man or Silva," Meltzer said. "It was probably going to be a great fighter. But instead they said, 'We got Bob Sapp over and he wasn't a great fighter. Now let's find another freak show.' I think people had seen their freak show and they needed a superstar fighter."

Sapp considers the legion of giants and showmen to be an acknowledgment of what he's brought to the sport. The "giant" is back, and it all started with Bob Sapp.

Sapp said, "K-1 does it, Pride's done it, and boxing's done it when they brought in their big Russian guy. That was their version of Bob Sapp. It's funny to me, because that's not what's making me popular. They've had big guys, bigger guys, stronger guys. It's just the sincerity. I don't have the ego that all the other fighters have. I'm not always, 24/7, talking about fighting. I'm not like that. A lot of these fighters are walking around tattooed up with a Mr. T starter kit, running around with two vicious dogs on chains. They want to scare the world. Team Killa! Team Criminal! Team Felony! It's just like everything they talk about is almost sheer evil. One of the main criticisms is that 'Bob's an entertainer, he's not a fighter.' Now when you talk about fighting you go, 'It's really not about the fight, it's about the entertainment.' Wait a minute. Y'all didn't start saying that until I came on the scene. Fighting's been here. I didn't create fighting. They're telling me, 'It's all about the entertainment.' Don't tell me! I'm mimicked throughout the fighting world. It's great. What's it led to? You've got Brock Lesnar in there, the big pro wrestler. Entertainment, entertainment. This is really a huge tribute to what I've been able to accomplish."

The break from K-1 also allowed Sapp to have his first cage fight in his home country. It was Strikeforce's first journey out of California, and it was taking no chances with its meal-ticket fighter. Sapp would face another K-1 giant, Jan Nortje, who had a losing MMA record. It's a fight Sapp should have won. Instead, it was an inglorious defeat.

What comes next is anybody's guess. On New Year's Eve 2007, Sapp showed he was still a big ratings draw, getting the highest rating of any MMA fight that night for his comedy match with Olugun. He's negotiating with K-1 for a full-time return to the Japanese scene, looking to do a reality show with Spike TV, continuing a regular television schedule in Japan, and wrestling for the HUSTLE promotion. After his early experiences and struggles, Sapp is taking no chances with keeping all his eggs in a single basket.

"I learned a lesson from being unemployed to always keep that Plan B, Plan C, it goes all the way down to Z, brother. If push comes to shove and all of this goes away, I'm fine, because I've got 95 percent of my money saved. I don't have to worry about nothing," Sapp said. "I live well beneath my means. I'm worth $7–$10 million, and I live off of around $50,000 a year. That's just the way I was taught and the way I was raised."

24

THE RETURN OF CAPTAIN AMERICA

It began, like many questionable decisions, with just a little too much to drink. Randy Couture was hanging out with friends at a sushi bar and had downed a few sakis. He'd been retired since the third Chuck Liddell fight, and retirement was turning out to be more work than fighting ever was. Between the announcing, acting, business ventures, and charitable work, Couture was run ragged. His friends that night were telling him: "You can beat the champ."

Fans worldwide despised Tim Sylvia, the new heavyweight champion, for his cautious and sometimes dull fights. Couture was in a playful mood and decided to show off just a bit. He whipped out his phone and left UFC president Dana White a text message challenging Sylvia. He thought White would get a kick out of it and get back to him later. Instead, the return call was almost instantaneous. It turned out the promotion was actively searching for someone with the skills and box office power to battle the giant champion. The comeback was on.

"It's hard to sit by the cage and watch these guys compete and not get excited about it. I find myself wrestling around in my seat while I'm watching. I kind of always said all along, 'You never say never.' And if the right opportunity came along, I'd definitely be interested in getting back in there," Couture explained. "It's the right opportunity. The people at 205 [pounds] right now are the same people I was fighting against when I retired. Chuck and Tito, they're just not terribly intriguing to me. I want to fight someone else. Basically, I fought Chuck three times, nobody really wants to see me fight Chuck again."[303]

Couture's comeback surprised no one in the industry. He had worked diligently to get in fighting shape for a grappling exhibition with Brazilian jiu-jitsu master Ronaldo "Jacare" Souza, and had been rumored as a possible opponent for Tito Ortiz if Ortiz had been able to upset Chuck Liddell. Not only that, but White had been asking Couture to return on the first day of the month, every month, since his retirement. "Bullshit," the UFC boss told him. "You're not retiring. When are you coming back?"

The timing was perfect. Sylvester Stallone's *Rocky Balboa* topped the box office, drawing $65 million with a story of a beloved former champion's return to face a younger, unpopular champion. Sound familiar? Couture was a real-life Rocky, and fans were thrilled with his return. Except for the ones who thought Sylvia was going to murder the old man.

Sylvia had been waiting some time for a challenger to appear. Andrei Arlovski and Brandon Vera had turned down the fight, but finally manager Monte Cox had good news. They had a lemming on the line. But the UFC wouldn't tell him who it was.

"He said they weren't telling him yet — that it was gonna be a big deal, so I just needed to wait and see," Sylvia said. "When I found out, I was like, 'Wow, Randy's coming out of retirement to fight me. That's crazy.' So obviously I called Randy up and asked him what the heck he was doing. Randy and I are good friends, so I wished him luck and told him I'd see him in the middle of the Octagon."[304]

Sylvia was saying the right things, but he was not happy with Couture's announcement. Not only was he sure he was more than a match for Couture, he was a little offended by the challenge. After all, Couture was coming off consecutive losses to 205-pound kingpin Chuck Liddell. The move to heavyweight was a tacit admission from Couture that Sylvia made easier prey than Chuck. Was the champ hot?

"Absolutely," Sylvia said. "He's 43 years old and has been retired for a year. I don't know what kind of competitive training he has been doing for the last year, but I fought four times in 2006. They were all very competitive fights, too. I think I still have my fighting edge. I don't know if he still has it."

Sylvia saw himself and Liddell as very similar fighters, and was sure Liddell had found the magic formula for beating the Hall of Famer. "If he tries to bum rush me, we are going to work angles the same way that Chuck

Randy Couture and Kevin Randleman

Minotauro and Heath Herring

Jens Pulver

Frank Mir (bottom) and Márcio "Pé de Pano" Cruz

Mark Coleman and Fedor Emelianenko

B.J. Penn and Renzo Gracie

Kevin Randleman

Matt Serra

Matt Hughes and Georges St. Pierre

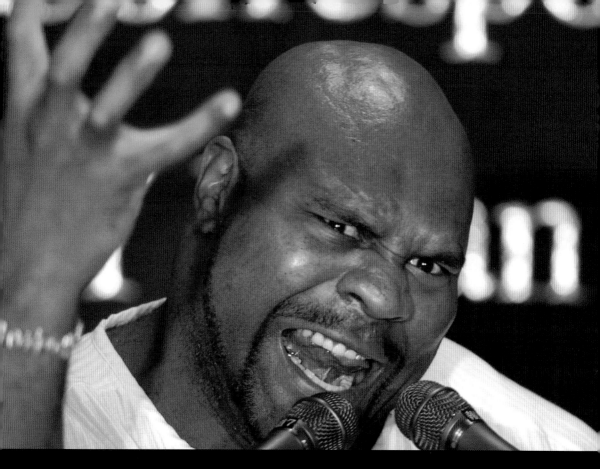

Bob Sapp

Tim Sylvia

Mirko Cro Cop

Chris Leben and Jason MacDonald

Roger Huerta and Kenny Florian

Stephan Bonnar

TUF winner Forrest Griffin and Quinton "Rampage" Jackson

**Tito Ortiz and
Rashad Evans**

**Jon Fitch and
Diego Sanchez**

Rich Franklin

Matt Hamill

Michael Bisping and
Rashad Evans

Kimbo Slice and
James Thompson

Brock Lesnar

Anderson Silva

did. Randy is a straight forward and straight backward fighter. He has a lot of trouble with angles," Sylvia said. "I really look at this as a way to propel my career to the next level. I'm very secure in my [financial] future. Now I'm focused on my fighting legacy, and Randy Couture is in my way."[305]

Couture the announcer had been very critical of Sylvia, saying the champion was too passive, was fighting to not lose. Since being submitted and almost knocked out by former heavyweight champion Andrei Arlovski, Sylvia had been tentative. He and the crowd suffered through some sluggish fights with Assuerio Silva, Jeff Monsen, and a rematch with Arlovski. His boring fights and cocky posturing had made him one of the UFC's least-popular stars. His new, cautious approach had also made him one of the most difficult fighters to game plan for. He was a 6'8" giant with power in his hands and feet and good takedown defense.

"I think Tim's stature, both in height and reach, and in weight, pose some interesting problems," said Couture. "For a guy who's 6'1" walking around at 225, that's part of the challenge when you face an athlete like Tim. He's a well-conditioned fighter who uses his range very, very well and puts great combinations together. The task at hand is to try and figure out a way to get past that."

Couture once again proved himself to be MMA's master tactician. Sylvia had been able to stay on his feet against other great grapplers because they respected his heavy hands too much. This led to shots on Sylvia's legs from way outside and takedown attempts that were easy for the giant to avoid and sprawl his way out of danger. Once again, like with dangerous strikers Vitor Belfort and Chuck Liddell, Couture's game plan was to strike with the striker. He would rely on his solid boxing technique to get in close enough to take the fight to the mat.

"Sylvia packs quite a punch. However, his punches are real straight and he doesn't throw a lot of combinations," Couture said. "With proper side-to-side head movement, along with some bobbing and weaving and a lot of movement of my feet, I felt I could avoid his punches, close the distance between us, and tie him up in the clinch. And once I tied him up in the clinch, I felt confident I could take him down and dominate from the top position."[306]

THE CHAMP

Tim Sylvia was one of the most hated men in MMA, but he could never understand why. Something about him just rubbed people the wrong way. Normally, UFC fans are especially jingoistic and borderline xenophobic. These are fans who chant "USA, USA" at Canadian fighters. But these same fans cheered a Belarussian with a thick accent over a homegrown American world champion on three different occasions. It was tough for the sensitive fighter from Ellsworth, Maine, who traveled 1,300 miles and 21 hours to train with Pat Miletich in Iowa.

"I have always had a self-esteem problem. I was physically and mentally abused as a child, growing up with my mother. So, I think it still sticks with me to this day that I have a problem with that," Sylvia said. "I just block it out [the boos from the crowd], man. That's gonna happen. A lot of the fans still aren't quite educated about all the stuff that's going on in a fight."[307]

Sylvia is a giant man and usually big guys are spared the Columbine-style abuse and psychological torture that can drive smaller men either to athletic success or into depression. But Sylvia was picked on, and still carries those scars with him.

"I didn't grow until my senior year of high school. I was bullied all through grammar and high school, getting picked on, beat on, you know — pushed up against lockers; people picked on me all the time," Sylvia said. "My senior year, I grew four inches over the summer and reached six foot four, and then grew a couple more inches throughout the school year. I started going out and looking for all these bullies, and they were very apologetic and very nice to me. . . ."[308]

Sylvia has come along way as a professional fighter. His size gives him a tremendous advantage, and his trainers give him the tools he needs to utilize his God-given gifts. And though it hasn't been easy, his teachers rave about him.

"Tim Sylvia has worked harder since he's been here than anybody I've ever seen. He had a lot of obstacles to overcome when he first came here, and he's climbed over all of them. He's a totally different fighter than when he first got here," Jeremy Horn said. The founder of Miletich Fighting Systems agrees. Sylvia, Miletich says, has gotten more from less than anyone else he's worked with in the gym. "Tim Sylvia has got an amazing work ethic. When he first got here he couldn't jump rope. Could hardly walk and chew gum at the same time, and he's worked so hard and been through such a roller-coaster. It shows what true hard work will do for somebody."[309]

He was making progress as a fighter, but still having problems fitting in. He tried too hard. When the guys went to Vegas for a fight, Sylvia tagged along, spending his own money to be part of the crew. The guys called him on it. You didn't buy your way into the MFS inner circle — you had to earn it. "No one wants you here," Jens Pulver told Sylvia. "You weren't invited." Sylvia left the group in tears. He eventually started to earn respect, but it wasn't easy.

Eventually his teammates' example took hold. Hard work took Sylvia to the top. Shortcuts sent him crashing back down to earth. After beating Ricco Rodriguez for the UFC heavyweight title, Sylvia was on top of the world. That feeling was short-lived because after his first defense, a knockout of fellow giant Gan McGee, a man who as a bouncer once beat up 12 Navy Seals without suffering a scratch, Sylvia tested positive for the steroid Winstrol. It was the second postive test for a UFC heavyweight titlist in a two-year period, a mini steroid scandal that was a precursor to today's steroid-obsessed sports world. The UFC's president, Dana White, had no choice but to act. "We are very disappointed that the lab tests came back and showed that he used steroids," White said. "We fully support Tim in his efforts to respond to these charges and to work with the Nevada State Athletic Commission to come to a fair and just resolution. We also fully support the NSAC in whatever its judgment might be."

Sylvia was suspended for six months and stripped of his heavyweight title. But, more importantly, he stripped his highly regarded fight camp and his friends of credibility and dignity. Although he never denied using steroids, Sylvia was defiant to the end that the drugs gave him no fighting edge. It was a marketing move, an attempt to give Sylvia the kind of lean musculature that MMA rewarded fighters for with endorsement deals and strong promotion.

Sylvia said, "What I took had nothing to do with my training at all, and I didn't it take long enough for it to have any effect on my fight anyway. Not that what I took had effect on my fighting, it was mainly for hardening and physique. What I used was just for my appearance. When I beat somebody, I knock them out. Steroids have nothing to do with my boxing skills."[310]

Upon his return, Sylvia would get an immediate shot at redemption. He and hot young heavyweight Frank Mir would fight for the vacant title. And while the athletic commission had put Sylvia on the shelf for six months, Mir would, too.

In one of the most sickening televised sports injuries since Lawrence Taylor snapped Joe Theismann's leg on *Monday Night Football*, Sylvia had his arm broken in half by a Mir arm lock. Mir had secured an arm bar, and Sylvia was trying desperately to escape. Without warning, referee Herb Dean jumped in and immediately stopped the fight. It wasn't evident right away what had happened, and Sylvia wanted to continue. As the crowd booed, the television replay clearly showed Sylvia's arm break. His radius bone had snapped three inches below his elbow joint. He was out of action for more than six months and had a titanium plate inserted into his arm.

When he returned, he wasn't the same fighter. The kill-or-be-killed attitude that had propelled him to the title was gone. In its place was a pure professional fighter. In his comeback fight against Andrei Arlovski for the vacant heavyweight title, there would be no valiant struggle; when Arlovski locked on an Achilles hold, Sylvia tapped almost immediately. Total ring time: 47 seconds. He would take his check and live to fight another day.

It took Sylvia a year to earn a rematch with Arlovski. It had been almost two years since he lost the title to Mir, and Sylvia was ready to get back on top of the food chain. The sport was exploding, and he wanted his piece of the pie.

"I just miss being recognized as the number-one man," Sylvia said. "I see more criticism now. When you're on top, everybody loves you, and just before you're there, when you're at the level I'm at right now, the people who are bandwagon jumpers aren't on the bandwagon. And the sport's gotten so much bigger now that when you're a champion you get rewarded more — by being a coach on *The Ultimate Fighter* and stuff like that, and getting bigger endorsement deals, which will set you up for the future. I'd love to be able to retire from the sport and stay retired in five years. If I'm heavyweight champion, there's more money, more endorsements, and that dream's possible."[311]

This fight was just as explosive as the first. It looked like another Arlovski win when a punch sent Sylvia plummeting to the mat. But Sylvia was able to recover, and soon put the glass-jawed Arlovski down. It was a situation Sylvia had spent a long time preparing for before the fight.

"Billy [Bill Rush, Sylvia's strength and conditioning coach] had me doing a bunch of agility stuff, as well, on the ground. You know, hopping back up real quick, moving my hips, and stuff like that," Sylvia said. "The main thing is to get into a scramble with him. Don't, you know, if you get on the ground immediately cause a scramble, and get the hell back up."[312]

Sylvia was once again the UFC heavyweight champion. And after a boring five-round decision win in an Arlovski rubber match and a boring five-round decision win against submission wrestling expert Jeff Monson, Sylvia was looking hard to beat. He was also hard to get an opponent for, especially with marketable heavyweights being few and far between.

Enter Randy Couture.

THE FIGHT

The pundits had it all figured out. Sylvia would use his size and reach to pound away at the old man's face with straight punches. It wasn't a question of who would win, only of which round Sylvia would knock Couture out in. If Couture had any shot, it would be to shoot and secure a takedown. The chances of him being able to do this ten times over the course of 25 minutes seemed unlikely, especially considering the takedown defense Sylvia had displayed against Monson, an excellent grappler. The odds were against Couture. Literally. He was anywhere between plus-200 to plus-300 at the online sports books. If you were willing to bet big on an old and retired fighter making a comeback against a dominant champion, you could win big. There were few takers.

"I guess that's what happens when you fight at 44. It does not bother me at all. I have come to expect it. I operate well when no one expects me to come through," Couture said. "He is younger, bigger, and stronger. This puts me in a spot I have been in several times, so I will have to go out and prove everyone wrong."

It started with a right hand. It was like Couture was determined to encourage the Rocky Balboa comparisons, because the punch was a ridiculous haymaker, the kind you only see in the movies. Except it landed. Within ten seconds, Sylvia was on the ground. No one in the crowd was more shocked than Randy Couture.

"Landing that first blow set the tone for the fight and gave me a boost of confidence," Couture said. "Over the next five rounds, I constantly moved my head and feet, making it difficult for Sylvia to pinpoint a target. Every time I took him down, he got more frustrated, and the more frustrated he got, the easier it was for me to enforce my game plan."[313]

The fans were watching the fight with bated breath. The old man was winning, even dominating the champion with his head movement on his feet and his strong takedowns. But the 19,000 fans who packed the Nationwide Arena in Columbus, Ohio, knew that Sylvia was only one strike away from victory at any time. The support for Couture was palpable. More than watching an exciting fight, you could feel the crowd wanting Couture to win, even if the fight was dull, which it sometimes was. Couture was workmanlike, using head movement to close the distance, winning the battle in the clinch, and methodically pounding Sylvia on the ground. It was an inspirational performance, one that moved UFC color man Joe Rogan to tears. He didn't know what to say. No one did. Forty-four-year-old Randy Couture was the heavyweight champion of the world.

CRO COP COMETH

Couture's first defense had already been set in stone. He would take on the dangerous Croatian striker Mirko "Cro Cop" Filopovic. Cro Cop had seen the writing on the wall and departed the floundering Pride promotion and made his way to the flourishing UFC. Cro Cop was Pride's Heavyweight Grand Prix winner and one of the most dangerous strikers around.

All he had to do was get by the relatively unknown Brazilian jiu-jitsu player Gabriel Gonzaga at UFC 70 in Manchester, England, and the dream match would be a reality. But sometimes dreams are meant to die. Oddly enough, Dana White was eerily prophetic.

"A lot of people think that the mystique over in Japan, they're bigger, better, making more money. All of it is bullshit. It's all a big myth, and now we're in a place where we can prove it."[314]

I don't think he intended for Gonzaga to prove it, however — that was supposed to be Couture's job, in a marquee main event. Before the fight, Couture, on commentary, predicted a Gonzaga upset and referee Herb Dean asked the fighters for a good, clean fight "with lots of action." Both would get their wish. Gonzaga was not to be denied. Cro Cop seemed shocked that Gonzaga was willing to stand and trade blows with him. Didn't Gonzaga know who he was? He wasn't just a pale white man in red and black checkerboard short shorts. He was one of the most feared strikers alive. Gonzaga caught a kick and took Cro Cop to the mat, but instead of looking for a submission he just pummelled him. Gonzaga was working hard and had bloodied Cro Cop when Dean ordered an early stand-up. It was shades of Bas Rutten's UFC tenure, when early stand-ups were de rigueur for the popular Dutchman.

Ironically, standing up cost Cro Cop dearly. The high kick came and sounded like a shotgun blast when it landed. But it wasn't Cro Cop's famous left foot. Gonzaga had scored the upset.

Gabriel Gonzaga had a great ground game, knockout power, and he looked like a Cro-Magnon. Randy Couture looked to be in real trouble. The match was made for August 25, 2007, at UFC 74. Once again, "The Natural" defied the odds. The ageless Couture looked ready to carry his title all the way to the retirement home.

25
RAMPAGE

Quinton "Rampage" Jackson says a lot of things most people couldn't get away with. He talks about sex: "I don't want people to know that I like fat Japanese chicks with stretch marks from ear to ear. I don't like people to know that I like the flabby labby. Yeah, that shit would get out, so don't you tell nobody I like the flabby labby."[315]

He talks about money, at a time when athletes everywhere insist they play for the love of the game: "If I forgot a sponsor, then you ain't paying me enough. . . . Yo, man, I need to get paid. I got a ton of kids. I have, like, a kid every 30 seconds. Wait, what time is it? Damn, there's another one. Told ya."

He talks about his opponents, and not just their game: "Man, that was like fighting a big-ass smelly skunk. Matt, you need to take a shower, man . . . I don't know if he didn't want the nuts in his face or the knees in the face. I don't know which one was worse for him. 'Cause I like to put my nuts in his face so he can smell my sweaty balls. That distracts him, then I come down with the knee. Hey, it works. See, look, look, here I go. Look at him; he turns his face, he tries to get out of that. There! Knee, boom, in the face. He's getting a face full of nuts right here, then I punch him."

And, more than anything, he talks about race.

Jackson is, as they say, black and proud. There's no reason for him to be anything other than what he is: a black kid from the ghetto who made it in a notoriously white sport. So white that when Jackson fought Kevin Randleman it was to maintain his spot "as the token black guy in Pride."

Jackson is so talkative that he was a guest commentator on some Pride pay-per-views, and that lead to this awkward exchange:

> **MAURO RANALLO:** "There's a left by Jackson . . . or make that Randleman, sorry."
> **JACKSON:** "That's all right, all black folks look alike."

Jackson can get away with it, however. He can touch on subjects no one else would dare go near, because he does it with a wink and a smile. And he's funny. No one is spared Jackson's wit. When an Israeli reporter asked him about the Middle East at a press conference, Jackson was quick to respond, "Are y'all the reason our gas prices are so high?"[316]

Every sport has a go-to quote. A guy that can't get enough of the media and will say whatever is on his mind, consequences be damned. In professional basketball, that was Charles Barkley, the "Round Mound of Rebound." Like Jackson, Barkley was a verbose kid from the South who wasn't afraid to let you know what he thought. Like Jackson, Barkley is very open about race. People love them, and they escape the media scrutiny somehow. Maybe it's because they can back their words up, on the field of play and in the streets.

Jackson grew up on the hard streets of south Memphis, Tennessee. When his grandmother told his mother she had a dream that all of her children would be successful, Mrs. Jackson asked, "Even Quinton?" His life could have gone down the wrong path, like so many young, poor black men.

"I grew up fighting. My mom says I've been fighting ever since I was in Pampers. I got a cousin who's six months younger than me, and we kind of grew up together and we always bumped heads, you know what I'm sayin'? My cousin, him and I have probably fought each other over 300 times. And that's probably a low number. There's 365 days in a year, and we grew up together for years and would fight most every day," Jackson said. His family started calling him "Rampage" because of the legendary tantrums he used to throw.

Family members weren't the only victims of those flying fists. "When I used to fight, crowds of people used to gather round and watch. I would fight a lot. I used to fight people from other neighborhoods, people who would pick on my friends and I had their back. People loved to watch me fight."[317]

He had started down an all-too-tragic path: prison, drugs, fights, death.

Wrestling saved him. Not professional wrestling, although he was a huge fan and has made a pretty penny stealing the Junkyard Dog's wrestling gimmick. It was amateur wrestling that turned his life around, gave him an outlet for his anger. It's not hyperbole to suggest that Peter Bolgeo saved Jackson's life. He was 17 when he heard Bolgeo talking about wrestling at a gas station. Jackson was interested, and had always loved wrestling on TV, so Bolgeo told him to come down to Raleigh-Egypt High School, where he was the wrestling coach. The problem? Jackson wasn't enrolled at Raleigh-Egypt High School. He was 17 and not enrolled in school anywhere. He was studying at the proverbial school of hard knocks, and hadn't been in a classroom since doing time at a juvenile detention center.

"One of my uncles once sat me down and told me that if I didn't change the way I was living and the way I was acting, I wasn't going to live long. I saw a lot of my friends disappearing, either going to prison or getting killed, and I didn't want that type of life," Jackson said. "Strangely, something changed when we moved out of the neighborhood and we moved to a place where they had better things. They had wrestling in school and a lot of other things. Normally, I was going to an all-black school, but there I went to a mixed school and was surrounded by a mixture of people. It was more positive for me, and I felt how good I could be."[318]

Jackson had developed a reputation around town as a street fighter, not only solving his own disputes, but also as a kind of a thug for hire. He was already wearing his trademark chain, already howling at the moon. None of that is a gimmick. It's Jackson personified. The school board didn't want Jackson, fearing it was too late to reach him. But Bolgeo took a chance on the young man and got him enrolled as a 17-year-old freshman.

Jackson said, "I left my reputation back in my old neighborhood. I came to this school and nobody knew who I was. I could turn over a new leaf. I was like an actor. Nobody knew I could fight. They could tell by the way I looked, so nobody really messed with me. I was always mean looking. I didn't have to beat nobody up. I quit smoking weed, quit smoking cigarettes, quit drinking. I quit doing all my stuff when I started wrestling. I fell in love with wrestling. My grades started improving. My family couldn't believe it. I went to summer school, skipped grades, and the next thing you know I went to junior college and started wrestling."[319]

Jackson was good. In his second year of high school Jackson finished fifth at the Tennessee State tournament at 189 pounds. By 19, he was already a senior thanks to summer school, but state rules made him ineligible to compete on the wrestling team. The lure of the streets was pulling him back into the gang life, but Bolgeo pulled harder. He helped get Jackson into junior college as a wrestler, but a racial slur led to a fistfight, and Jackson almost beat a teammate to death with his cell phone. Bolgeo helped raise his bail.

It seems like fighting is just a part of Jackson, something inside him that he just can't escape. His wrestling buddy Dave Roberts got him interested in MMA, and he had found his calling.

Jackson said, "The inner-city kids do the boxing, but there ain't too many martial arts gyms in the city, you feel me? So black folks who are good athletes, most of them are already doing stuff, trying to make millions, like in football or basketball. Mixed martial arts hasn't been described as a sport that is making millions yet, so black folks are trying to make their meal ticket, you feel me? They ain't trying to go out there and do mixed martial arts and not make the big money. Well, the weird thing about me is that I grew up fighting, and one of my friends introduced me to it and I was like, 'Whoa, you mean I can beat up white dudes and not go to jail?' I ain't racist or nothing, but it was just a bunch of white folks fighting, there weren't no black people fighting. I used to like to fight, and I'm from the South, you know what I'm saying, and it's like, 'Damn, beating up white folks and not going to jail?' That's, like, unheard of where I'm from. So when my family found out what I was doing, they didn't give me a problem. They were like, 'You mean they don't say nothing when you're out there beating up them white folks?' I said, 'Man, they don't say nothing, they're cheering me on.' I'm like, 'Damn,' it blew my mind. To be honest, though, the real reason was so I could keep up my wrestling, dog, just on the real. I don't want people to think that I'm racist or something, 'cause I really ain't. I just wanted to keep up with my wrestling."[320]

Soon Jackson was training MMA and fighting for west coast feeder shows like King of the Cage and Gladiator Challenge. He made an impact in his first fight for King of the Cage, back when that promotion still meant something as a stepping-stone to the UFC and Pride. He lost to Marvin Eastman, but put up a spirited fight that impressed the audience, both live and on television.

LAND OF THE RISING SUN

Jackson built a record of 11–1, and was finally given a shot at the big time. Pride needed a last-minute opponent for its superstar, Kazushi Sakuraba. Just getting to the fight would be the biggest challenge of Jackson's life. Police met him at the airport in Los Angeles with guns drawn. They were responding to an anonymous tip that an armed felon was trying to get on a flight to Japan. Jackson was not armed, but he was an ex-felon trying to get on a flight to Japan — an ex-felon who hadn't filled out the appropriate paperwork to leave the country. After eight hours in lockup, King of the Cage promoter Terry Trebilcock was able to sort out the situation and Jackson was on his way to Japan. Who phoned the tip in to the police was a mystery, but Jackson had some ideas. One of his training partners for the fight was Chris Brennan, from Next Generation jiu-jitsu, who expected to fight Sakuraba before the promoters decided that Jackson would be more marketable. Brennan took advantage of Jackson's difficulties and went on to Japan while Jackson sat in jail. Once there, he offered to take the fight in Jackson's stead.

Jackson said, "Well, it's kind of odd that when I got to the airport the police knew my business. They knew how many people I was with, they knew I was a pro fighter, and they said that I had beaten up police and stuff before, and they knew I was fleeing the country and I had a warrant out for my arrest. It was just kind of weird that they knew all of this and one of the police told me that somebody ratted me out. But I don't know who did. I don't have 100-percent proof, but I just know what somebody told me two days before I got arrested, that Chris Brennan was going to get me arrested because he trains undercover cops. He trains a whole police department out there. I've seen him do it. I've seen him train them. So, somebody told me, 'Chris Brennan is going to get you arrested,' but then other people told me that they don't think Chris Brennan did it because he was worried about me on the plane and wanted to bail me out real bad and stuff, no matter what my bail was."[321]

With the international intrigue finished, Jackson was out of jail and in his usual good spirits. "Yeah, I got bailed out. Terry Trebilcock — you know, he got trouble with his cock, but he bailed me right out," Jackson said. He was on his way, a day late, for the biggest fight of his life. Fighting Sakuraba was a tremendous opportunity for Jackson, a step up in class and a chance to make a name for himself on the big stage. If Jackson had any doubts that he was brought in to lose, those doubts were completely erased by Pride officials.

"I'm never the type of fighter who would lose for money. I don't do that. But they told me, 'If you win this fight, you get $10,000.' But they also told me — these are, like, the two people from Pride who got fired recently, I don't know if the president of Pride knew about it — but they told me themselves: 'If you lose by knockout or submission and you don't tap, you get $12,000.' I said, 'But what if I knock him out?' and they said, 'You get $10,000.' Then I understood what was going on," Jackson said. "This was my first time fighting in the big show in Japan, and I learned that sometimes they wanted the other guy to win. I knew it was going to be tough for me to win that fight, so I went out there and gave it my best to get my $10,000."[322]

In Pride, there were two kinds of fighters. There were guys they wanted to push to the top of the promotion and guys they wanted to lose. Jackson was a guy they wanted to lose. Although Pride officials denied there was a bribe, his contract did include a $2,500 bonus to lose the fight by submission or knockout. This wasn't an enticement to lose in their minds, just a way to encourage an exciting fight. Jackson didn't intend to lose, and he didn't intend to make a contracted weight of 194 pounds, either. Trebilcock had agreed to that weight without consulting Jackson, and he couldn't get there; he had arrived in Japan at 208.6 pounds. Instead, the Japanese agreed that Jackson would need to make 198.6 pounds, but it would need to be on the day of the fight. This was unheard of. It's routine for fighters to lose up to 15 pounds the day before a fight, but not the day of a fight. The day before allows them an extra day to rehydrate and recalibrate. Cutting that much weight on the day of the fight would be disastrous. What's odd was that Jackson was the only fighter on the card who had to make a specific weight.

King of the Cage representative Mark Davidson said, "My understanding is that Pride, historically, has not had weight classes. I believe that after the Silva fight there was a motivation to instill that weight class and not put Sakuraba against someone who was considerably heavier than him. That was the motivation. There was further discussion as to whether or not the weigh-in was to occur on Saturday or Sunday [fight day]. In multiple conversations with Terry, it was agreed with Pride that the weigh-in would be held on Saturday, allowing Jackson basically a day and a half to recuperate. Pride's interpretation of the agreement was that at fight time he was supposed to be 198.6 pounds. After many discussions and deliberations, most of which were very polite, but very tense, I would say, we agreed that he would weigh in on Saturday at 6:00 p.m. at 198.6 pounds."

Brennan had to help carry an exhausted Jackson to and from the weigh-in. The easy part was over. Now he just had to find a way to beat the best fighter in the world.

SAKURABA

Sakuraba was on top of the fight game. He had beaten four Gracies and established himself as the top drawing card in the MMA and wrestling world. The *Wrestling Observer* called him the best box office draw of 2001. Pride needed him to get back on track after a loss to Wanderlei Silva, and Jackson was thought to be easy prey. He was a relative novice, had never fought in front of such a large audience, and had never encountered an A-level fighter, either in training or in the gym. He would be nervous, they thought.

They didn't know Jackson. There were 35,000 people in the Saitama Super Arena, but that didn't faze him in the least.

Jackson said, "That stuff never even bothered me. I never even thought about all of that until after the fight. 'Cause you know, I'm an entertainer. A lot of people freeze up in front of a lot of people like that. I don't know what it was, but it's just crazy that it didn't bother me. The big crowd didn't bother me. I was more nervous for my first UFC fight than I was for all the Pride fights put together, and at the UFC it seemed like there was nobody there compared to the Pride shows I fought in. So no, it didn't bother me at all. I knew for a fact that I wasn't brought there to win, and when you fight in Japan against someone like Sakuraba, the whole country knows who you are. I was instantly famous as soon as I got off of the airplane. I had fans who had already made cards of me and photographs and stuff, so I was in the hotel going, 'This is nuts, everybody already knows who I am.' So it's kind of crazy. Also, you didn't know it then, but secretly you know most of the people want you to lose. Some people like you and don't care if you win or lose, but most people want you to lose, and that's kind of a weird feeling that goes through you like, 'Oh man, these people want me to get my ass kicked because I'm fighting their hero.'"[323]

Before the fight, Jackson introduced the audience to his winning personality. When announcer Stephen Quadros asked him where he saw himself in two years, he responded, "I'm 23 now, so in two years I see myself as 25." The room broke up. In the ring, he introduced the audience to another Jackson specialty: the big slam. After surviving an initial takedown, Jackson made his way to his feet and slammed Sakuraba down twice, hard. Sakuraba almost managed to secure a triangle choke, but again paid the price with three hard slams.

Suddenly the audience, and Sakuraba himself, knew that this "opponent" was here to fight. "It doesn't feel good to get slammed on the back like that," Quadros said. That is expert analysis. When Sakuraba transitioned to a beautiful arm bar, Jackson picked him all the way up and tried to toss him out of the ring. Color commentator Bas Rutten was getting pumped up: "What an exciting fight!" Sakuraba eventually secured a rear naked choke and the win. But Jackson had made an impact. "My God, man, what a talent," Rutten enthused.

Pride management agreed. They were going to make Jackson a star, feeding him a succession of Japanese pro wrestlers like Yuki Ishikawa from Battlearts and Masaaki Satake from RINGS. Jackson established himself as more than a personality. He put himself on the map as a genuine contender by beating former heavyweight star Igor Vovchanchyn with a trademark Jackson slam, and outwrestling and knocking out former UFC heavyweight champion Kevin Randleman. Going into the Pride Middleweight Grand Prix in 2003, Jackson was among the favorites. He beat the UFC middleweight champion, Murillo Bustamante, by a controversial decision to move on to the semifinals: Pride Final Conflict 2003. His opponent was the handpicked UFC entrant, "The Iceman" Chuck Liddell. Liddell had won ten in a row before losing to Randy Couture in June 2003. He was still widely regarded as one of the top five fighters in the world at 205 pounds, and was expected to knock Jackson out on his way to the finals, where he and Wanderlei Silva would settle the debate over which company had the top fighters in the weight class. "The UFC is here to make a point," Rutten said. "Chuck is here to make a point." After years of waiting, fans were finally going to see Pride versus the UFC. Dana White was just as pumped as the fans.

"Really, this whole thing started between me and Mr. Sakakibara, the president of Pride. He started trash-talking the UFC a little bit, and then I said, 'Let's talk about some real issues like Chuck Liddell knocking out Wanderlei Silva.' That's a fight I've wanted to do for a long time, but Pride would never do it," White said. "They ended up coming back saying, 'If he wants to fight Silva so bad, why don't you put him in our eight-man tournament?' If there's any guy I would put in an eight-man tournament, it's Chuck Liddell. Because I'm kind of an old-school kind of guy and I like real fighters. Chuck Liddell is a real fighter. There's no BS with him. He likes to fight. He'll fight anybody, anywhere, anytime. He's definitely one of the best."[324]

CHUCK AND THE UFC INVASION

"All the fighters in Pride know I'm coming," Liddell said. "They'd better be ready. When I come to Pride, I will be ready." Liddell was eager to redeem himself after losing to Randy Couture earlier in the year. He had been the uncrowned champion of the UFC for years, waiting for his shot as Tito Ortiz refused to face him. When he finally got his chance to become the champion, he lost. This was a second chance, an opportunity to reclaim his place at the top of the world rankings, to prove to fans and to himself that it hadn't just been hype.

Liddell worked as hard as he ever had to get ready for the fights in Pride. Dana White was confident that his former client would establish the UFC as the top company in the world. White was so confident he bet $250,000 that Liddell would take the tournament. He did his part by making sure Chuck had an all-star lineup of trainers to get him ready. Liddell worked with his regular trainer, John Hackleman, but White also brought in John Lewis to work on jiu-jitsu, Matt Hughes and newcomer Jay Hieron to work with Chuck on his wrestling, and Phil Baroni and Ganyao Fairtex to work on his striking. White was thrilled with his training camp, comparing it to Rocky's workouts in Russia prior to dismantling Ivan Drago. This was similar: a tough-as-nails American traveling to a foreign land to beat the odds. But longtime trainer John Hackleman wasn't sure about deviating from Chuck's regular routine. After all, it had served them well to this point.

Hackleman said, "Well, that was Dana White's idea. He had an idea and we were willing to go with it, and it didn't seem to work out that well. We were kind of breaking up the training. And when two guys are trying to work on the same thing, but they're not on the same page, you know, over-training some things, undertraining others. It just wasn't the whole Pit feel. Chuck likes the Pit feel, he likes the old-school pit. He's been here since '91, you know, we kind of have a rapport with all of our team. I think he's more comfortable training the way he's always trained."[325]

There was trouble in paradise. White was sweating bullets. Every time he was on camera in Japan, he looked like he had just finished a strenuous workout. Maybe that was why he thought he was a part of the training and part of the fight. "We trained hard for this," White said. "I keep saying 'we.' I've invested a lot emotionally, mentally, and financially."

Jackson delved deep prior to the fight, offering some stunning analysis into his own skills as a fighter. "My biggest strength is my strength, because I'm strong. That's my biggest strength." Jackson said. He was a strong man and also a broke man: "I need that money!" Jackson was more famous for his powerful slams than his powerful punching, so White was surprised when Jackson decided to stay on his feet and slug it out with Liddell. If there was any doubt that Jackson could take a punch, Bas Rutten put it to rest: "One time he was at my party, Quinton, and I was drunk and I showed him a combination I had won with. And I hit him by accident with a left hook, full. I thought I broke his jaw and he didn't flinch at all. So I think he can take a shot."

Jackson took all of Liddell's shots and delivered plenty of his own. He was better than Liddell in every way that mattered, beating him to the punch, taking him down, and stopping the fight with a sustained ground-and-pound beating. Jackson, and not Liddell, advanced into the finals to face Wanderlei Silva. The Liddell versus Silva dream match would remain a dream, and Silva knocked Jackson out to cement his place on top of the 205-pound weight class.

LIDDELL 2

The 2003 fight was a turning point for both men. Liddell went four years without a loss, while Jackson fell to .500 over the next six fights. Liddell went back to training at the Pit, and established himself as the most feared fighter in the UFC, if not the entire world. For Jackson, the question wasn't whether he was the best in the world, but whether he was washed up. He had seemingly lost his edge after being knocked out three times by (the

Brazilian fight team) Chute Boxe's Silva and "Shogun" Rua. It was a constant question, and he heard it before every fight, from every reporter.

"It's not a stupid question, because fighting is very mental," Jackson said. "I think it's mostly mental. Think about it, you gotta have the right mentality to get up every day and train. To not be such a party guy and want to go to the clubs and clubbing every night, and then you've got to get mentally strong and eat the right food and go on a strict diet. You gotta be very mentally strong to lock yourself in this cage with this guy who's trying to knock you the hell out."[326]

Many people thought Jackson was done as an elite fighter. He had lost to the top fighters in Pride, and had struggled even with average fighters like Marvin Eastman. Jackson had lost his fire, but Liddell's camp knew he was still dangerous.

"Quinton is a very tough guy," Liddell training partner and UFC veteran John Lewis said. "He is definitely a worthy opponent for Chuck right now, and he's certainly not shot like some people believe. He's a very strong individual. His hands and his striking have really come a long way, and I consider him a real striker now, and he's won his last few fights. He's also hard to take down. He's very athletic and agile, so I think he's definitely a tough match, in general, for anybody, including Chuck."[327]

The fight was one of the most heavily publicized in UFC history, and it enjoyed huge coverage on the ESPN networks. ESPN was treating the UFC title fight like it was a big boxing match, covering the weigh-ins, interviewing the fighters, and talking about the fight on its signature show *Sports Center*. It just so happened that ESPN was negotiating for the UFC television rights that were owned by Spike TV. ESPN was just showing what it could bring to the table. All the extra attention brought extra distractions, and distractions are a trainer's worst nightmare.

"I don't really like it, but it comes with the territory and the UFC likes it," John Hackleman said. "You know, as a trainer, I don't like it, but the promotions always like it. It's coming from a lot of different places. It's good overall, but if you remember *Rocky III*, I'm the Mickey. I'm more like Mickey: 'Ah just get in there and fucking train.' They want him to do all of the press stuff, but hey, it comes with the territory. He handled it well. I didn't like it, but it didn't make a big difference in the fight."[328]

Liddell was focused like a laser beam on avenging his loss. He had made a point of beating everyone who had conquered him. Jeremy Horn, who had submitted Liddell at UFC 19, was brought back specifically for Liddell to beat. He was committed to erasing the black mark Jackson had put on his record, as well.

"When Chuck trains for revenge fights, he's extremely focused," long-time training partner Scott Lighty said. "He's always focused with other fights, but there's always just a little more with these types of fights because he just can't stand to lose. He trains with just a little bit more of an edge, and you can see him working every possible move that Quinton can do against him."[329]

The Jackson who had struggled in the recent past was gone. He had left Team Oyama, where he received less than world-class training, and connected with boxing trainer Juanito Ibarra.

"I'm going to have reputable sparring partners and I'm going to do my thang like I always do. Win, lose, or draw the fans will be happy. Chuck Liddell is going to be happy because he made his money. I'm going to be happy because I made my money," Jackson said. "Dana White should be happy, the UFC going to be happy, reporters going to be happy, the president going to be happy, the governator going to be happy, everybody going to be happy. My momma going to be happy, my daddy going to be happy, my cousin going to be happy, my brother going to be happy, my homeboy going to be happy, my homegirl going to be happy, my ex going to be happy, her ex going to be happy, my ex-ex going to be happy and you going to be happy. Everybody is going to be straight because it's going to be a nice and exciting fight."[330]

The feeling in Jackson's camp was that he had Liddell's number. He was simply well-suited to fight Liddell. His boxing was improving by leaps and bounds, and he had the quickness to make Liddell pay for his looping shots with quick, straight punches. Ibarra thought Liddell wasn't his usual self against Jackson.

"He was totally intimidated. I saw it, absolutely," Ibarra said. "Chuck's the kind of guy who will shoot laser beams through you with his stare. He has those piercing eyes. Like Tito. Tito gets intimidated by that stare. When Tito tries that, it doesn't work. Chuck is a true warrior, but I'll tell you I saw it in Dana's eyes. I saw it in Dana when he was looking at Chuck's eyes, and then he looked back at Rampage and then looked at Chuck again, and really stared at Chuck's eyes. I saw it and I told Rampage after. I said, 'You got in his head right now, son.' I see it in his eyes. Absolutely, I saw it. Rampage was definitely in his mind."[331]

Liddell had been a two-to-one favorite, but the betting lines started to shift in the week leading up to the fight. Liddell had been seen out partying late into the night every evening. Coupled with a disastrous appearance on *Good Morning Texas* where Liddell slurred his words and mentioned that his next opponent would be boxer Tommy Morrison, there was some concern that Liddell was more focused on living the good life than he was on training. The interview had been bad enough that host Gary Cogill seemed legitimately concerned for Liddell, saying, "Uh, you hang in there today, take care of yourself." The Liddell camp blamed the stammering and slurred words on a late night and too much Nyquil. Dana White was concerned enough to pull Liddell off the road. There were rumors that Liddell was in rehab. The Nevada State Athletic Commission was concerned enough to bring Liddell in for a drug test, which he passed. Whether he was having drug problems or not, something was definitely up with Liddell.

The fight started slowly, with both men circling each other. Jackson taunted Liddell to bring it on. He was mad that Liddell had predicted a first-round knockout. The rabidly pro-Liddell crowd was restless.

"The crowd seemed to want them to mix it up a little faster, but you can't buy into that. You've got to stick to your plan," Ibarra said. "The only thing I asked for was for Rampage to double jab a little bit more, and that's what I was yelling. But I know how Chuck opens up, and we worked on that right. It's a timing punch, and he steps in, boom. He stepped right, he threw right, and Chuck was done. I knew once Chuck fell, just by looking at his legs, he wasn't getting up. I was already jumping up. I already knew it."[332]

Liddell had reached down to try to throw a lead right to the body. Jackson countered perfectly with a right hook. It was sloppy and lazy, and Jackson had made Liddell pay.

Hackleman said, "He got caught. He could've done things different, but it happened. He saw an opening and he took it and Chuck got caught. It happens to everyone. If no one ever capitalized on mistakes, no one would ever lose. He got caught. He made a mistake, and that was it."[333]

RAMPAGE ARISEN

Just like that, there was a new light heavyweight champion. Liddell had been the face of the UFC. He was the one UFC fighter with his own DVD, his own book, a featured role on HBO's *Entourage*, and the first MMA fighter featured on the cover of *ESPN: The Magazine*. Jackson, after winning the title, got none of that special attention. He was a forgotten man.

"Why should I look like every other fighter, walk down, be quiet, and not show who I am? Hide my personality. Why should I do that? You can't please everybody," Jackson said. "You can knock somebody out quick. You can whoop their ass, and people will still boo, so why worry about it? . . . I know it's a white sport. To be honest, I'm all for white people having a fighting sport. I think white people need something besides boxing. I think that's good. It's an extreme sport, and white people are good at extreme sports. I just so happen to be a black guy who's good at this sport. They say wrestling's a white man's sport, too, and I wrestled. I was okay at it; there's some good black wrestlers. I just think the world needs to quit stereotyping and seeing race. It's 2007, for God's sake; we're all human."[334]

Jackson finally got his due in 2008, when he was tapped to coach the seventh season of *The Ultimate Fighter*. But the pressures of life on top got to him. After a slow climb to the pinnacle of the sport, the ensuing fall would be fast and hard.

26
UFC BUYS PRIDE

In 2006, Zuffa and the UFC exploded into the mainstream consciousness, firmly establishing themselves as the top promotion and the most recognizable brand name in the sport of MMA. In 2007, Zuffa intended to consolidate that power.

"Football is the NFL," said Paul McGuire, vice president, integrated media at R&R. Zuffa had hired the marketing company to help it put the UFC on the corporate map. "The ultimate goal is you don't say MMA, you say UFC. UFC represents mixed martial arts. It's kind of like Coke and Kleenex. You don't say, 'I want a soda,' you say, 'I want a Coke.' You don't say, 'I want a tissue,' you say you want a Kleenex. . . . We're looking to maintain and increase our dominant role in the sport of MMA."[335]

The goal for years was to get sanctioned, get on pay-per-view, get on television, and turn a profit. They had done all of that. Each UFC event was now grossing tens of millions of dollars. The new goal was to maintain market dominance. New competitors were eyeing the fight game, and Zuffa didn't want anyone getting a foot in the door. They needed to make sure they had all the fighters they needed to put on the best shows and to keep competitors like the IFL and Elite XC from doing the same. If they had to buy those fighters, they now had the resources to get that done. They purchased two companies, the WFA and the WEC, at the end of 2006.

"Zuffa is committed to giving our fans the best fights between the best fighters in the world. This acquisition helps us continue fulfilling that goal," White said in the press release announcing the WFA deal. The WEC would be run as a separate promotion. The television contract they secured with Versus for the WEC was a deal that wouldn't go to a competitor. The WFA would cease to exist as a separate entity. That deal would prevent WFA fighters from signing with the newly created Elite XC, which had a deal in place with Showtime.

"The main score in that deal was Quinton 'Rampage' Jackson," White said. "We got some good guys out of this. . . . We bought the WFA for the contracts. We bought the WEC, and we're going to take that to a whole other level. Put it on television and blow it up. Pretty soon the WEC will be number two. . . . Showtime's got nothing. I don't see the Showtime thing lasting for long," White said. "They don't know what they're doing. And there's no hard feelings [with Showtime]. They can do a deal with the WEC when their other thing doesn't work."[336]

Elite XC's parent company, Pro Elite, quickly purchased a hodgepodge of MMA companies from around the world, including England's Cage Rage, Hawaii's Rumble on the Rock, and Korea's Spirit MC. The buys didn't make much sense for the fledgling company, which might have been better off concentrating on running its first few shows rather than creating a massive conglomerate. But there was a legitimate fear that if the company didn't act, the UFC would simply end the potential promotional war by buying all the available marketable talent. By securing these established MMA companies, Pro Elite was able to assure that it would have at least a few established fighters at its beck and call for its major shows.

BUYING PRIDE

The UFC purchases were merely an appetizer compared to what was still to come. The most significant purchase of all was Zuffa's acquisition of Pride. For years, the UFC and Pride had been bitter rivals. Zuffa had initially intended to work closely with Pride. Dana White and the Fertittas were fans first, and wanted to see the UFC's best take on the top fighters from Japan. There had been very little intermingling of fighters between the promotions, and hard-core fans were intrigued by the idea of seeing Wanderlei Silva fight Chuck Liddell or Fedor Emelianenko fight Randy Couture.

Unfortunately, Zuffa's burgeoning relationship with Pride was strictly a one-way affair. They sent Liddell and Ricco Rodriguez to Pride to fight. They were promised fights with Silva and Kazushi Sakuraba in exchange — fights that never took place. Pride was such a great success that it didn't need to work with the UFC. It would gladly use the UFC's talent on its shows, but it had no intention of sending its top stars to the United States. It needed top fighters, like Sakuraba and Silva, to sell its own shows.

While the UFC was still struggling in the pre–*Ultimate Fighter* years, Pride had thrived. It routinely attracted huge crowds to its stadium shows and drew huge ratings on Fuji television. Almost since its inception, the company had been the biggest and best MMA promotion in the world. The UFC had lagged a step behind: in fighter salaries, in television production values, and in revenue. In 2006, that paradigm shifted. The UFC was suddenly in the driver's seat. The success of *The Ultimate Fighter* had led to pay-per-views that routinely grossed tens of millions of dollars. At the same time, Pride was knocking on death's door, but not because its show was no longer popular. Pride was dying because of scandal. There had been whispers about yakuza connections for years. Pride president Naoto Morishita had committed suicide in 2003, supposedly over a failed affair. No one was sure whether to believe it. There was speculation that he had been killed in a yakuza hit. The yakuza had always played a major role behind the scenes in Japanese business. But with Pride, they had moved to the forefront.

Japanese MMA expert Zach Arnold, from Fightopinion.com, said, "When the wrestling business started to falter in the late 1990s, the yakuza became more prevalent in terms of actually financially propping up promoters. The yakuza went from being on the periphery to becoming the primary backers. This increased the level of volatility in the business, and what you ended up with were organizations that were 'fronts.' In the past, you always knew who the owners of a company were. However, the legacy of Pride's death was that Pride [and perhaps other groups] was nothing more than a 'front' for the gangs. Instead of a company with real owners and tangible assets, you have front companies that were very high profile and didn't maintain a lot of hard assets."

Pride yakuza had threatened Inoki Bom-Ba-Ye promoter Seia Kawamata when he signed Pride champion Fedor Emelianenko to fight wrestler Yuji Nagata on his December 31, 2003, show. Kawamata had Emelianenko fight anyway. The show ended up being a complete disaster, finishing third of the three MMA programs that aired that night. Kawamata went into hiding, fearing for his life after crossing the yakuza. In 2006, he emerged to give an interview to Japanese magazine *Shukan Gendai*.

Kawamata told his story and implicated Pride head Nobu Sakakibara, who he said was present when yakuza threatened his life. Fuji Television, which was still getting monster ratings for its Pride television specials, was forced to remove the show from the air. Yakuza ties were a barely hidden truth in the Japanese entertainment industry, but Fuji TV wasn't comfortable with the yakuza connection being so public.

"In many ways, the death of Pride was great symbolism for how volatile business in Japan is with the rise of aggression by the top yakuza gangs. Gangs like Yamaguchi-gumi and Sumiyoshi-kai were tolerable when they could be dealt with outside of company infrastructure, but once those gangs actually started owning companies and providing the cash to run activities, the whole ballgame changed," Arnold said. "In 2004–2005, the company generated between $50–$60 million. Which is why it's fascinating that they had 'money problems' only a couple of years later after losing their Fuji TV deal. Where did all the money go? We all have our suspicions. . . ."

Overnight, Pride went from the biggest and best MMA company in the world to one struggling to stay afloat. The company should have had plenty of money from its boom period to sustain it during the hard times. That was how SEG's UFC had survived. Pride, on the other hand, was seemingly without assets. Although Sakakibara claimed that television made up just 10 percent of Pride's income, and it continued to run big shows as a symbolic gesture of good health, the company was losing money quickly — money it didn't have.

"I don't think it was run like a business. And losing TV was a killer. But they were going down, too, even before all that happened. Their popularity was based on Sakuraba and then Yoshida. They didn't really have a Japanese star to follow up on," Dave Meltzer of the *Wrestling Observer* explained. "It's that Japanese thing where it's really big for three years and then it isn't. That's Japanese culture with rock stars and everything. It's a fad culture. And Pride was a fad. They'd have survived if they'd kept television, but they were on their way down. The fad period was over."

Pride's last-ditch move was to market the company's shows to the growing U.S. market. It badly needed a new source of income. The UFC had shown how profitable Las Vegas could be, and Sakakibara decided to follow in its footsteps. He brought in entrepreneur Ed Fishman to help get him into Las Vegas.

Fishman said, "I immediately got them probably the best name in the world as far as casinos, Caesar's Palace, known for boxing and special events, to be the main sponsor, along with a dozen other casinos who never really participated in buying tickets for a fight event other than the UFC. And they were responsible for buying over a million dollars worth of tickets right off the bat. That was the main thing DSE [Pride owners] wanted me to do. Get them into Las Vegas, get them the sponsor. The problem really was, as we all discussed, they would not make money for the first several fights. I explained to them the difference between the 15,000 to 20,000 names they had in their database of people who, for the past six or seven years, had bought $39.95 pay-per-views. That person, who has been buying pay-per-views, doesn't necessarily spend several hundred dollars to fly to Las Vegas and buy tickets that could be anywhere from $50 to $700."[337]

Both of Pride's Las Vegas events had memorable moments. At Pride 32, Fedor Emelianenko defeated Mark Coleman in a rematch of their 2004 bout. Pride 33 saw Wanderlei Silva's long reign as middleweight champion finally come to an end. His 205 pounds of fury ended up staring at the ceiling, looking up at the new Pride middleweight champion, Dan Henderson. A left hook put him there, a big right made sure he stayed down.

"It was the highlight of my career because I dominated the whole fight and knocked him out," Henderson said. "And no one expected that. And to do it to a fighter of his stature . . . definitely the highlight."

Henderson was a two-time Olympian in Greco-Roman wrestling, but had won the biggest match of his career by standing and punching with the feared Silva. Knocking people out comes easily for Henderson. Despite his Olympic wrestling background, he relies more on a heavy right hand than any wrestling throws or submission locks.

"I've just got a natural ability to hit hard," Henderson said. "And I've worked on my total game because the sport has changed. Wrestling just isn't enough."

Pride 32 and Pride 33 were both big successes at the live gate, drawing more than $2 million apiece. They were less successful as pay-per-views, bringing in less than 50,000 buys. Without a strong television deal, Pride just couldn't survive as a pay-per-view entity. And getting television took time. Pride needed money now, and didn't have the five years it had taken the UFC to turn a profit. Sakakibara started looking to sell the company.

ENTER ZUFFA

Lorenzo Fertitta said, "Initially, we had a dinner about ten months ago [May 2006] to talk about the business and the future of MMA. We talked about the fact that the fans weren't getting to see essentially what they wanted. We wanted to put together a plan to figure out how we could deliver the best product to the fans. We actually had dinner at the Italian restaurant at our casino, the Red Rock Casino. We talked for a couple of hours, and that was the beginning of our discussion. It really took a lot from both sides to give and not be selfish and really make this happen. It really took both parties staying focused on what the goal was, and that was making history. This is a history-making event. These two organizations coming together, and we are going to be putting on events that are going to blow people's minds."

Lorenzo Fertitta was excited to have the chance to buy Pride. Not everyone inside Zuffa felt that way. White and others had been against the move. Why purchase the company, they asked, when you could just pick up the pieces when it inevitably went out of business?

"They were going to be the biggest company in the world, and promote all over the world," Dave Meltzer said. "They were going to have the UFC, they were going to have Pride, they were going to do the Super Bowl. When they bought it, I was just like, 'What are you doing?' All the fighters you want you could just get. They're going out of business either way. Why would you spend that much money on the tape library?"

What the UFC envisioned was a thriving company in Japan with Pride, a thriving company in the United States with the UFC, and regular super-fights between the two promotions' top champions.

"This is really going to change the face of MMA," Fertitta said. "Literally creating a sport that could be as big around the world as soccer. I liken it somewhat to when the NFC and AFC came together to create the NFL. . . . Bottom line, I'm a huge fan of MMA. This is not about business. This is not about making money. This is about putting together the dream fights that me and you, as fans, have always wanted to see. The UFC is, like, my baby, and now I have another and I love both just the same."

Sakakibara had chosen to sell the company to Fertitta despite offers from other companies. Pride was like his child, he said. It was leaving his home, but he wanted it to find a safe place to reside. "I really feel refreshed.

To see Pride, which I gave birth to, grow up," Sakakibara said. "Pride has left my nest, graduated from DSE, and to have a situation arranged where it can flap its wings and face the world, I feel like my duties are completed. Pride has become that big under a private owner, but I couldn't carry on by myself. Personally, I feel lonely, but when I look at Pride's future I am full of refreshing and joyous feelings." The Fertittas seemed like the best choice to keep Pride running. In Japan, the sale of Pride was met with mixed reaction.

"I had predicted that this type of evolution could happen," SEG head and K-1 front man Sadaharu Tanikawa said. "But I wonder, why did the UFC buy Pride? It's a freedom for a buyer to do anything he wants, but this business won't exist without the fans. Regardless of the circumstances, the fact that Pride was destroyed, that is big. It's definitely a minus for this industry."[338]

Others wanted to do nothing more than gloat. Pride had been ruthless in taking top talent from smaller Japanese rivals. It took many of its biggest foreign stars from RINGS and stocked its lightweight Bushido show with SHOOTO stars like Takanori Gomi and Hayato Sakurai.

"Look at yourself! It's a divine justice," former RINGS promoter Akira Maeda said. "They enticed Gilbert Yvel away from RINGS, headhunting with large amounts of money is something they used to do, so if the UFC is doing the same, they have no right to complain. . . . [It's] a divine punishment to someone who has done a bad thing. When TV stations pulled out of broadcasting Pride, the other MMA promotions were perceived in the same manner, and it was an inconvenience to everyone."[339]

The UFC went into the Pride purchase with good intentions. It really did intend to keep the promotion alive. It wanted to run cross-promotional shows. "It's one of those things, in my opinion, why this thing is so great, when fighters fight, obviously, the money is great and the fame and everything that goes along with it, but at the end of the day it's about their legacy," Dana White said. "Pride and the UFC have the best fighters in the world in all weight classes. Finally, we are going to find out who is the best fighter in the world. Whoever wins that fight will be looked at as the best heavyweight, the best light heavyweight, the best middleweight in the world, and possibly one of the best, pound-for-pound, of all-time. I think that is really what is going to come out of this. The fans win. Both of the organizations win. The fighters win."

They couldn't make it work with the Japanese television industry. And without TV, Pride was as much of a money-losing proposition for Zuffa as it had been for Sakakibara. "I've pulled everything out of the trick box that I can, and I can't get a TV deal over there with Pride. I don't think they want us there," said White. "I don't think they want me there. Pride is a very powerful brand, and we want to keep it alive, but I'll tell you what, the brand is very tainted, not only over there but over here. . . . The problem is, Pride was never a big company in the United States, and I'm not going to drop another $44 million to try and straighten it out."

Japanese television stations make programming decisions in April and October. April was too early to expect a new Pride deal. The arrangement between Pride and the UFC hadn't even been finalized yet. But when October's announcements for new television shows didn't include Pride, Zuffa pulled the plug. Pride president Jaime Pollack fired all of the Pride employees during a conference call. After ten years, Pride was dead. Instead of running cross-promotional matches, the UFC changed tactics. It would still pit its best fighters against the best from Pride. But instead of inter-promotional dream matches, they would be simply UFC fights on UFC cards.

"We're going to have them all," White said. "At the end of the day, if you want to fight the best fighters in the world, if you want to cement your place in history . . . and at the end of the day, the money is great, all that stuff is good, but I'm one of those types of people . . . it's all about cementing your place in history. Who is the greatest fighter in every weight division? It's here. It's in the UFC. They're all going to be here."

FEDOR FALLOUT

The one that got away in the Pride buy was Pride heavyweight champion Fedor Emelianenko, who had a non-exclusive contract with Pride. He was available for Pride fights, but was also free to fight for anyone else of his choosing. This wasn't acceptable to the UFC — all of its fighters had exclusive contracts. Try as they might, Dana White and Zuffa could not get Emelianenko to sign with the UFC.

It wasn't that he was opposed to fighting in the UFC. Emelianenko had great respect for UFC champion Randy Couture and wanted a unification match. It was the UFC contract that Emelianenko didn't like.

"The contract the UFC presented us with was simply impossible, couldn't be signed — I couldn't leave. If I won, I had to fight eight times in two years. If I lost one fight, then the UFC had the right to rip up the contract," Emelianenko said. "At the conclusion of the contract, if I am undefeated, then it automatically extends for an as-yet-unspecified period of time, though for the same compensation. Basically, I can't leave undefeated. I can't give interviews, appear in films, or do advertising. I don't have the right to do anything without the UFC's agreement. I could do nothing without the okay from the UFC. I didn't have the right to compete in combat sambo competition. It's my national sport. It's the Russian sport, which in his time our president competed in, and I no longer have the right to do so. There were many such clauses; the contract was 18 pages in length. It was written in such a way that I had absolutely no rights, while the UFC could, at any moment, if something didn't suit them, tear up the agreement. We worked with lawyers, who told us that it was patently impossible to sign such a document."[340]

As the Emelianenko negotiations continued with no signs of success, White's notorious temper was getting hotter and hotter. "All this stuff they're talking is bullshit," White said. "The problem with those guys — the deal was never, ever, about Fedor. It was all about his management. It was what his managers were going to get. Not once during the negotiations for Fedor did they give a shit about what Fedor was going to get. That's why the deal fell apart. . . . His manager, I'll tell you right now, is a fucking liar. . . . Good luck to them, wherever they go, because I don't want him fighting in the UFC."

White and Emelianenko hadn't just failed to come to terms. White had insulted the Russians, calling them crazy and calling Emelianenko a pawn. "Numerous times have I read Mr. White's statements on the Internet concerning me. In my opinion, allowing yourself to say those things is not a sign of a gentleman or a grown man at all," Emelianenko said. "If he candidly wants to prove himself right, then let my fight with Randy happen. . . . In the future, I wouldn't want to hear those statements in my address ever again, and I won't tolerate that."[341]

The two sides were drifting further and further apart. Soon, White was saying Emelianenko wasn't that good after all. He was barely even a top-five fighter. Fans and fighters were incredulous. "The best fighter ever to climb into any arena is Fedor Emelianenko," Kevin Randleman said.

"There's nobody better. He's the best fighter I've ever seen, fought, or trained with. He's been through some hardship, too, and that's what you need in this. Some people come to this and learn how to be tough. And then there are people who are just tough, and they're trying to learn how to be better fighters. Fedor is just tough. And he's a great fighter. He's in his own league."[342]

The Emelianenko situation bothered Randy Couture. The champion was 44 years old. He had a very limited number of fights left, and he wanted to fight Emelianenko. It was a fight to cement his legacy as perhaps the all-time best MMA fighter. Couture had beaten everyone the UFC had to offer. Now he wanted to fight Pride's best. When White couldn't make that happen, Couture shocked everyone by announcing his resignation. He was done with the UFC.

27
THE COUTURE CONTROVERSY

Randy Couture was nicknamed Captain America, and like the Marvel superhero, he was a beloved institution. He inspired everyone in MMA when he returned to the Octagon at the age of 43 to regain the heavyweight title. In a sport filled with a thousand bad tattoos and plenty of people you'd never want to meet in a dark alley, Couture was a breath of traditional fresh air. He was college educated, a military veteran, a health nut, and an all-around good guy. When he spoke, people listened. And in October 2007, fans around the world heard Couture's words.

"I appreciate the opportunity the sport of MMA and the UFC have given me," the UFC Hall of Famer said. "However, I'm tired of swimming upstream at this stage with the management of the UFC. It only makes sense at this point in my career to fight Fedor Emelianenko, and since he's now signed with another organization, I feel like it's time to resign and focus on my other endeavors."

Couture had faxed in his resignation while filming the movie *The Scorpion King 2: Rise of a Warrior.* That fact alone showed just how far the sport had come. The problem was that fighters' salaries weren't matching up with their newfound status as celebrities. Couture had gotten rich with the UFC. He was in a perfect position to challenge anything he found unfair and make a stand for all of the UFC fighters who would follow in his footsteps.

"Randy's contract was on a fight-by-fight basis, and that's the way he said he was always going to take it — fight by fight," said Matt Walker, Couture's agent at The Gersh Agency. "His acting career is accelerating at an astronomical rate, and without the support he felt some of his peers were receiving in the fight business, this was the logical choice."[343]

Couture wasn't willing to take just any fight. He had beaten the champion, Tim Sylvia, and defended his title against top young star Gabriel Gonzaga. Now he wanted to fight the best. The problem was Dana White.

White had failed to sign Fedor Emelianenko, and the Russian star had joined the fledgling M-1 Global group. M-1 CEO Monte Cox was willing to talk to the UFC about an Emelianenko-Couture fight. "We really want to work with all the other organizations," Cox said. "For example, if Randy Couture was still with the UFC, we'd make an offer for Fedor to go to the UFC and fight Randy Couture." This kind of cross-promotion was common in boxing. Zuffa wanted no part of it. As the country's only established MMA company, it didn't make sense for it to share the stage with another player. Emelianenko versus Couture was off.

"The motivation for the decision is twofold," Couture said. "I know Fedor just signed with another organization, and that's the only real fight that makes sense for me at 44 years old and the heavyweight champion of the UFC. That's the fight I wanted, and if that can't happen it doesn't make sense for me to compete with all these other guys. And then, obviously, that's not going to happen now. And, two, I'm tired of being taken advantage of, played as the nice guy and basically swimming against the current with the management of the UFC. I have a lot of other things going on in my life that I'm doing just fine with. I don't need the problems. I don't feel like I get the respect I deserve from the organization, and that's motivation number two for the letter of resignation that was sent today."[344]

Respect was athlete code for money. Couture was upset about not fighting Emelianenko, but he was more upset that he wouldn't be paid nearly as much as the Russian if they did battle.

"I think the final straw for me was meeting with Dana and Lorenzo [Fertitta], where they claimed I was the second-highest paid athlete in the organization, which I know is a bold-faced lie," Couture said. Couture had said his dispute with the UFC wasn't about money, but it now seemed like it was. The multimillionaire felt underpaid. The UFC was making a fortune, and he wanted his share. Or at least as much as the other top guys were getting. "All of us athletes are pretty tightly intertwined. You hear what other guys were paid as signing bonuses, and what other guys were paid, on the record and off the record, with bonuses. I've heard Chuck's numbers. Tito's numbers. Hughes's numbers. Quinton's numbers. Cro Cop, Wanderlei. I heard what they were offering Fedor, and it's insulting."[345]

It was a shock to most MMA fans, but not to insiders. "I'm not surprised at all by Randy's decision," UFC president Dana White said in a statement published on UFC.com. "I talked to Randy several weeks ago and he said that if he couldn't fight Fedor, then he has nothing left to prove in the sport of mixed martial arts."

Through his proxy in the media, Yahoo's Kevin Iole, White said he knew that Couture had been upset about his contract, and that he and Lorenzo Fertitta had sat down with their champion before he left to film the movie. White just didn't realize how truly angry Couture was.

White told Iole, "He felt he was not getting paid as much as Mirko Cro Cop, as much as this guy and as much as that guy," White said. "We told him he was our second-highest paid fighter, but he didn't believe us. Chuck [Liddell] is the only guy who makes more, but he kept hearing all these rumors and he wouldn't believe us. This business is like a beauty salon. These guys are all the toughest guys in the world, but they're like bitches in a beauty salon. They pass along rumors and gossip that have no basis in reality and they believe all the [rumors] they hear. The Internet is very powerful, and one of the best promotional tools we have, but it's a crazy place."[346]

The UFC put the focus squarely on the money. Through Iole, it released a statement that said Couture could be leaving behind up to $15 million if he walked out on his contract.

"This was never a money issue," Couture said. "It's been a prevailing feeling of respect that wasn't being given." The dispute was getting personal. The two sides held competing press conferences, and Couture's family and friends chimed in.

"Dana and the Fertittas, in particular, have never been anything but nice and genuine to me. It's not a personal issue with them, but my experience with the organization," Couture's wife, Kim Couture, said. "When anyone from our staff has called to ask for anything, be it tickets to a fight, rooms, or something that was very important to me and Randy, like the Xtreme Couture GI Foundation charity fundraiser, the answer was always no or no response at all. . . . Every time we asked them for anything they acted like we were bothering them, unless they needed something from Randy; then their attitude was different . . . the UFC saying this is about the money is a joke; they know better. Our other businesses, Xtreme Couture Clothing, Couture Nutrition, and the gyms, have paid Randy more money in the last year than he has ever been paid in a fight. Over and over again, he has stated it isn't about the money. . . . If it were about compensation, he'd have gone elsewhere a long time ago. The offers have been out there before, and are out there now, and he hasn't considered any of them."[347]

Fighters rallied around Couture. "It didn't surprise me because of what they did to me," Ken Shamrock said. "I basically sold my body to them. I mean, I fought hurt all the time — and I got paid, of course . . . [UFC management] seems to think that the UFC is everything and that it doesn't have to respect anybody. The guys who built this sport are thrown outside — the guys who were there before Dana White. Dana's not a fighter, and he's not a tough guy, and he walks around talking to people, treating people with disrespect, talks about people's managers because he doesn't like them. Randy Couture was an absolute gentleman in the sport. Me, Royce Gracie, and other people who developed the sport before Dana White ever got in there, he treats us like dog crap. . . . The fans need to understand that the money they're putting into the UFC is going into Dana White's pocket and the Fertittas' pocket. They made billions of dollars on this company, and they're selling souls."[348]

Tito Ortiz had been through it all before. Zuffa had put him through the PR wringer, characterizing him as money hungry and greedy, just like it was doing with Couture. He could also understand Couture's frustration that the company hadn't taken enough steps to promote individual fighters.

Ortiz said, "I've been living with this for the last four years, you know. Randy Couture's going through exactly the same thing that I went through. For me, getting on *Celebrity Apprentice* was my own doing. It had nothing to do with Zuffa or Dana or anything like that. Donald Trump came to me and he noticed my skills and he wanted to see how I could show them on the *Apprentice* and I came in and I did it. Dana is really out for himself and his company. He doesn't give a shit about the fighters. Couture was their number-one guy, he was doing all the commentating, doing everything, doing this and doing that, then all of sudden when Randy stepped down [and said], 'I'm starting to see the big picture now, and you guys are making all the money and I'm making nothing.' People say, 'Well, you guys make a million a fight.' Well, yeah, we make a million a fight . . . and the company's making $45 million. What's wrong with that picture right there? And Randy Couture sees that. . . . 'I'm going to make you a superstar. . . .' How many times has Dana White said that? . . . I don't want to be a superstar, I want to be a multimillionaire when I put my life on the line."

Couture said the UFC was overstating his income. He claimed to have only been paid an average of $500,000 a fight for UFC shows that grossed almost $50 million. Couture had credibility with the fans and media. This prompted the UFC to settle the dispute by doing something it had never done before: it opened its books to the world to show exactly what Couture had been paid.

"I sat back and watched his press conference last week on TV, on Thursday, and I have to be honest with you," Fertitta said. "I felt that the statements he made had so grossly misrepresented the facts that we needed to protect ourselves, because I felt that the statements were made in a way meant to hurt us. The fact is you can only sit back and be silent for so long. The facts are the facts. We have the facts."

The facts met somewhere in the middle. Couture had made $1,186,000 for UFC 68, a show that had sold 534,000 pay-per-view buys. For his fight with Gonzaga at UFC 74, he had made $1,072,000. That show had sold 485,000 pay-per-views. Including an annual salary for helping promote UFC events and for his commentating duties, Couture looked to make almost $6 million over the course of his contract.

"At some point, the best fighters have to be allowed to fight each other regardless of promotion or production," Couture said. "Otherwise, we're going to lose the trust of the fans we worked so hard to gain over the years."[349]

Couture and the UFC sat down around Thanksgiving 2007 to try to find an equitable resolution. There was still some hope that the situation could work out for both parties.

"We've cleared the air, and hopefully we'll move forward with some sort of relationship," Couture said. "I've got a lot of fighters and a lot of things that hinge around mixed martial arts and the UFC as well. I want to continue to work with them, and I think they want to continue to work with me, so we'll figure out how that happens. . . . This whole resigning thing took on a life of its own. There were 72 media outlets trying to get a hold

of me. [I was] on the cover of *Yahoo*, it was just insane to me. I figured I'd
go away quietly, maybe MMAWeekly.com would cover it, *Full Contact
Fighter* or something like that would do a blurb on it, but it would be
confined to the small niche . . . of mixed martial arts. The reaction to me
stepping down is truly a testament to how big the sport has gotten."[350]

The reconciliation was short-lived. Couture reaffirmed his intention to
wait out his contract and fight Fedor Emelianenko for another company.
The UFC struck back by taking him to court and banning his clothing line
from its shows.

"What's really tough for me, to be honest, is we have been friends for a
very long time," White said. "The hard part is that he is not living up to his
obligations. Captain America is not keeping his word. . . . I expect Randy to
honor the obligations in his contract, which he signed [a year ago]. I tried
to resolve it by talking to this guy, whom I've had a relationship with for
eight years, and was unsuccessful. Now this thing's in the hands of the
justice system."[351]

It appeared the UFC and Captain America had parted ways for good.
Zuffa moved forward with an exciting crop of new heavyweights and a title
fight between two grizzled warriors. Since it couldn't get Emelianenko and
Couture, it settled for the men Emelianenko and Couture beat for the UFC
and Pride titles. Antonio Rodrigo Nogueira would face Tim Sylvia for the
interim heavyweight title. More importantly, however, Zuffa introduced the
UFC's next big thing.

HERE COMES THE PAIN

Brock Lesnar and Tim Sylvia both entered the Octagon at UFC 81, Lesnar for
the first time. They both had something to prove, to themselves and to the
fans. Sylvia should by rights be a legend. He's a two-time heavyweight
champion at the peak of his powers. He's decisively beaten some of the best
heavyweights in the world, a who's who of heavyweight MMA: Arlovski,
Rodriguez, Monson, Vera. Despite this, he is despised by the fans, or worse,
ignored. When he fought Antonio Rodrigo Nogueira for the UFC's heavyweight title, it was in the very long shadow of Brock Lesnar. And Tim Sylvia
was not happy.

Sylvia said, "Brock's done a lot in WWE. He has a big name. Is the
wrestler going to beat the fighter? They're trying to hype it that way. I

understand the philosophy of him getting all the exposure. I think they're bringing him in to get him beat. That's why he's getting all the exposure he's getting. Your average bozos who don't know anything see Brock coming in, or these superstars like Kimbo Slice who haven't really done anything, and they think they're studs."

To say Sylvia was bitter is an understatement. He was furious. This was a man who was desperate for attention, desperate to establish a legacy. Most fighters are happy to oblige fans when they see them on the strip in Vegas. Sylvia courts fans, walking around with his title belt on and introducing himself to total strangers. He wants to be loved. Yet at the weigh-ins he barely got more reaction than the preliminary guys. And all the marketing and publicity for the show was focused on Lesnar. After six years with Zuffa, Sylvia was fighting for the title on the undercard in all but name, beneath a debuting fighter.

"Brock Lesnar hasn't done anything in this sport to even stand next to me, let alone having UFC All-Access [the UFC Spike TV preview show], let alone being on the fight poster," Sylvia told UFC.com. "He's a great athlete, don't get me wrong, and I was a fan of his when he was in WWE, and I trained with him, but he's just getting a little too big for his britches when he starts talking about me, talking about the heavyweight division. He hasn't even fought in the UFC yet; where does he get off talking like that?"

For Sylvia, this was old hat; he'd been here before. He was the secondary attraction under the Tito Ortiz–Ken Shamrock 2 fight and the George St. Pierre–Matt Hughes fights, too. In his title challenge to Arlovski, he was given a very strong Tito Ortiz–Forrest Griffin fight as the co-main event. In boxing, heavyweights have always been the biggest draws, yet Zuffa has felt the need to give Sylvia's title fights plenty of support. Sylvia is one of the strongest fighters of his era, but he seemingly doesn't draw fans, which is why the UFC was so happy to gamble on Lesnar.

Lesnar said, "Dana's no dummy. He sees some credibility in Brock Lesnar as an amateur wrestler, and I've got a lot of notoriety. This is a business, and I'm very fortunate to be involved in it. I think there's a lot of interest. There's a lot of interest in the MMA world, there's a lot of interest in the sports entertainment world. There's a huge following from all of the pro athletes. Everybody's talking about it. Everybody's talking about the UFC."

Lesnar is everything Tim Sylvia is not. He looks like a fighter, like he would be happy hurting people. He has a chance to be MMA's first real heavyweight star in America. "I've never taken any of the WWE guys seriously, but I take this guy for real," White said. "He's a big, strong guy, he's a great wrestler, and I actually think this guy can adapt to MMA and do well."

The big money in the UFC has always been at light heavyweight. This was the guy who could change all that — if he could fight. Reporters at a pre-fight conference call were focused on his transition from the WWE to MMA, to the point that Lesnar felt the need to let the cat out of the bag all over again.

"Let's get one thing straight here. Pro wrestling is purely entertainment. We go out there and know the outcomes of the bouts and obviously this is real. It's the real deal, so I've taken my training back to exactly how I was training as an amateur wrestler. It's apples and oranges. You can't even compare the two," Lesnar said. Lesnar did pro wrestling for a short time, but it was never in his blood. WWE was all about making the most of his limited opportunities. "When I got out of college, after I won my NCAA title, I didn't have a lot of options. There aren't a lot of options for an amateur wrestler. You can go to the Olympics or you can become a coach. The bottom line was Vince [McMahon] had $250,000 waiting for me and a contract on the table and I was 21 years old and didn't have a pot to piss in. Come on. You make the decision."

Lesnar was making huge money, and was the youngest WWE world champion in history. Yet the urge to compete never left him. On tour, he would take down the 500-pound Big Show for fun and challenge Olympic gold medalist Kurt Angle to impromptu amateur wrestling contests. It wasn't enough. He left to try his hand at pro football. "He is a good athlete. He has a history of achievement. And you know he has a work ethic," Scott Studwell, the Minnesota Vikings director of college scouting said at the time. Ultimately, he was too old and too raw to make it to the NFL. But those same physical skills make him a threat to break into the upper echelon of MMA fighters because they will be applied in a more familiar setting. Lesnar compiled a 106–5 record in four years of college wrestling. In his two years at the Division I level, he won the NCAA championship for the University of Minnesota in 2000, after finishing second to New England Patriots star Stephen Neal the year before.

"Competition is in my blood, and I've done it for a number of years, whether it's on a wrestling mat, in the ring, or in an octagon. It's gonna be no different when they close the door on the Octagon. It's me and one other man out there. I've been in those positions before. I'm going to be very comfortable," Lesnar said. "Obviously, I'm going to have a lot to prove. There's going to be a lot of people gunning for me. I'm going to have to come out and prove myself, even to Tim [Sylvia], even to the other fighters. There's going to be some people who disapprove of where I am on the card because of who I am. There's going to be a lot of animosity toward me because of the visibility I have."

Both men faced significant challenges. Both opponents would be looking to score submission victories. Lesnar's huge salary meant he wouldn't have the luxury of developing slowly, as a fighter ideally should. Former heavyweight champion Frank Mir would test him right away — and Mir wasn't taking this fight lightly. People always say that, of course, but Mir watched all the Lesnar amateur wrestling DVDs he could find. He knew his opponent had physical tools that most in MMA can only dream about.

"Obviously, Brock Lesnar is stronger than I am. It doesn't take a genius to figure that out. He's stronger than most anybody he'll ever compete against. So if I just lay there, I'm going to get crushed," Mir said. "But if I can use constant motion and speed . . . like when a little guy fights a big guy in the gym, he has to use motion, movement, keep moving all the time. Because if you stand still, all that weight is going to bear down on you."

Lesnar had been working on his boxing and Muay Thai skills, but it would be a mistake to test Mir too much on his feet. Gold medalist Karam Ibrahim fell in love with his rudimentary boxing skills and got put to sleep by Kazayuki Fujita, who, like Mir, is a competent but unspectacular striker. Lesnar planned to focus on his strength, wrestling, and hoped Mir would be just the first pit stop on the road to the championship.

"I'm tabbed as a professional wrestler. People tend to forget that I was an amateur for 18 years at a high level," Lesnar said. "I've got a lot to lose in this. This is my road to hopefully becoming the UFC heavyweight champion."

Sylvia's opponent was Pride legend Antonio Rodrigo Nogueira. His new teammate, Anderson Silva, had helped Nogueira make the journey to UFC. "Anderson Silva got me in contact with Dana White about four months ago. But the proposal was made when I went to UFC *Fight Night* to help Roan Carneiro," Nogueira said in the Brazilian publication *Tatame*. "I have to thank Anderson Silva, it was his idea, and his manager Eddie also helped a lot. I'm 30 years old and able to negotiate my own stuff. I know what is good to me, [Brazilian Top Team] is an excellent place for me to train, but I got this contract through Anderson Silva and his manager."

Nogueira's debut was a rematch with his old nemesis Heath Herring. Herring had knocked Nogueira out cold, but somehow the fight was allowed to continue. Nogueira made another of his legendary comebacks and won a decision. Now he was fighting Sylvia for the interim title.

It was an incredible fight. Sylvia started strong, knocking Nogueira down and almost finishing him off in the first round. Nogueira, like he always seemed to do, survived. "He takes a beating and keeps on ticking . . . he's got one of the biggest hearts in the game," Sylvia said. "I rocked him and hurt him, but I couldn't finish him. So I jumped back up, scored another knockdown, and scored the rest of the round. . . . I didn't make the mistake Heath Herring did. I had him hurt, and I tried to capitalize on it."

Nogueira looked fresh in the second round, but Sylvia was still controlling the action. He was keeping the former Pride champion at bay with a crisp jab. "At the beginning of the fight, it was very hard for me," Nogueira said. "He has a very good right hand, which came over my jab." Nogueira, despite his skilled boxing, wasn't going to be able to beat Sylvia standing. He needed a takedown, and when he couldn't get it in the third round, he simply pulled Sylvia on top of him.

Once the fight hit the ground, it was all Nogueira. "He hooked the inside of my glove and got the sweep," Sylvia said. "I went for the escape out the back door, he went for the guillotine like we knew he was going to do. I was just about two seconds too late from spinning."

Sylvia had shown solid submission defense in an earlier fight with grappler Jeff Monsen. Nogueira was simply on another level. The Brazilian set Sylvia up for an arm bar, expecting him to counter it. Like a chess master, a good Brazilian jiu-jitsu player is always thinking several moves ahead. Nogueira had expected Sylvia to counter the arm bar. That put him in the perfect position for a guillotine choke. "I played his game for almost three rounds," Nogueira said. "He played my game for two minutes and I won the fight."

In just his second fight with the UFC, Nogueira had established his legacy as one of the all-time greats in the sport. He had beaten the UFC's best heavyweight of the decade and was the new champion. "I hate jiu-jitsu," Sylvia joked.

He wasn't the only one. Even though Nogueira had put on a display of heart for the ages, the night belonged to Brock Lesnar, even in defeat. Lesnar lasted just 1:30 with Mir, but in that minute clearly established himself as a future star. He moved in for the takedown with a speed and ferocity unmatched by any other MMA heavyweight, even Fedor Emelianenko. "I didn't expect his shot to be as fast as it was," Mir said. "When he changed levels and exploded on me, I thought I could kick him and get my foot down fast. That was hopeless."

Once he got Mir down, he was relentless, attacking him with wild ground and pound. He hit Mir on the back of the head and referee Steve Mazzagatti took away a point and stood the two fighters up. "Brock was excited," Mazzagatti said. "It was a big, big opportunity for him, and — in my opinion — he looked down and saw the head there, and he took three shots at him and caught him. I jumped in and said, 'Don't hit at the back of the head.' A few more seconds went by, Mir tucked up under there again, and Brock came down with the second couple of hits to the back of the head. That's when I jumped in and had to do my job. That's what I saw."[352]

The deduction was controversial. It came quickly, and many fans actually thought Mazzagatti was stopping the fight to award it to Lesnar. On their feet, Lesnar dropped Mir with a punch and was right back on top, pounding away with strong punches. "Constant motion was the key to not getting the fight stopped. I was not winning that fight in the first minute and twenty seconds," Mir joked. Eventually, Mir went for an arm bar. When Lesnar stood up to escape, Mir hooked onto his leg like an anaconda, securing the knee bar that would finish the fight.

"I must have worked on getting out of that leg lock a thousand times," Lesnar said. "That's the beauty of this sport. I got a little overzealous. I thought I was going to get out, but he held on for dear life."

Mir was back in the mix at heavyweight, but it was Lesnar who had impressed the fans with his abilities and the UFC brass with his drawing power. UFC 81 drew 650,000 pay-per-view buys, just 25,000 short of the biggest pay-per-view of 2007, the UFC 71 showdown between Chuck Liddell and Quinton Jackson. It was a good sign for a company that had struggled to find a pay-per-view attraction to replace the aging Iceman and the absent Captain America.

"Hopefully they can see through my defeat a little bit," Lesnar said. "And see in that minute and half that maybe there's some credibility there. I hope so. There's no shame in losing. When I was a young kid, my very first wrestling match I lost . . . my coach told me, 'You have to learn to lose before you can learn to win.' I don't like to lose, and I took that with me all these years."

THE CRAZY HORSE AND THE NEXT BIG THING

Lesnar was going to be one of the faces of the new UFC. His next match would follow the standard UFC template of matching the rising star with the past-his-prime legend. Lesnar would fight "The Texas Crazy Horse" Heath Herring. Herring was primarily a stand-up fighter who had trained for years in Holland with some of the world's best kickboxers. After fighting for most of his career in Japan, he was best known in America for a popular YouTube clip that saw him knock out Yoshihiro Nakao before the fight ever started after Nakao kissed him on the lips.

His UFC run had been less memorable. Herring had been taken down and controlled on the mat, not just by wrestler Jake O'Brien, but by kickboxer Cheick Kongo, too. He was an experienced veteran, but his main weakness was Lesnar's greatest strength. The UFC was setting Lesnar up for success. Lesnar was proclaiming himself to be a much better fighter. He had learned plenty from the Mir fight, and was excited to test his new skills in the Octagon.

"I've got 15 minutes to try to win a bout. I really rushed that fight, and I made a foolish mistake," Lesnar explained. "I had Frank in a dominant position, and I stood up and fed him a foolish amateur mistake, and it was something we worked on a million times. Just to be a more controlled fighter and a little more relaxed in there. We've been working on that. It has to do with just putting time in the gym, and that's exactly what I've been doing. Just trying to polish every aspect of the fight game and trying to better myself every day."

At UFC 87, on August 9, 2008, in his adopted home state of Minnesota, fans saw a much more cautious and controlled Lesnar. As expected, Lesnar outwrestled Herring easily, and even knocked him down with a fast right hand on his way to an easy three-round decision. "I came with the right hand and I put it where I needed to put it," Lesnar said. "It's one of those things. I was stunned for a second."

It was a dominant performance, but there was some concern in Lesnar's camp about his failure to stop Herring. Lesnar was unable to take advantage of all the great positions he secured, and it was immediately clear that he didn't have any finishing techniques at his disposal. More than anything, Lesnar resembled a 275-pound version of Dan Severn. He could win matches like this, could probably even dominate most competition in the UFC's weak heavyweight division. What he wouldn't do with that style is win any new fans or wow the audience.

"I think a victory is sweet anyway," Lesnar said. "I've got to keep evolving. This fight is in the record books already. I'm turning the page and going back at the gym."

Lesnar tried to insert some of the spark the fight lacked into the post-fight celebration, where he awkwardly pretended to lasso "The Texas Crazy Horse." Those kinds of shennanigans, so effective for Tito Ortiz, don't really work when you've spent the last 15 minutes warily riding your opponent's back with no attempt to finish the fight.

"I got really excited after I won and I've got every right to be," Lesnar said. "I was coming off a loss and it was tough."

Lesnar's cautious performance may have been the result of pre-fight rumors that a loss would end his run with the UFC. His huge money guarantee made it untenable to use Lesnar as anything but a main eventer. And after two losses in a row, it might have been hard to convince fans that he merited that position. But after dispatching Herring, the future for Lesnar and the UFC heavyweight division looks bright.

"Let me tell you, Brock Lesnar is a mixed martial artist," White said. "Heath Herring was 29–13 and he's fought all over the world: Holland, Pride. He's been here for two years and he's fought the best fighters in the world. He got dominated tonight. Dominated by Brock Lesnar. Brock Lesnar is a mixed martial artist, no doubt about it." Randy Couture was the old version of the world-class wrestler turned fighter. Zuffa hopes Brock Lesnar can carry that role well into the next decade.

Inside the cage, 2007 was the year of the upsets. Tim Sylvia fell to Randy Couture, Takanori Gomi lost to Nick Diaz, Gabriel Gonzaga knocked out Mirko Cro Cop, and both Quinton Jackson and Keith Jardine stopped the seemingly invincible Chuck Liddell. But the biggest upset of all was career 155-pounder Matt Serra knocking out welterweight champion Georges St. Pierre. St. Pierre was the prohibitive favorite. The betting oddsmaker had the champion as high as minus-1,000 to win. That meant you'd need to wager $1,000 to get a $100 payoff. That's as big a favorite as they come.

GSP

Georges St. Pierre was seen as the heir of both Frank Shamrock and Randy Couture. He was the most well-rounded fighter in the sport, like Shamrock had been in the late '90s. And, like Couture, St. Pierre was seen as a true gentleman, a classy, soft-spoken warrior.

"Guys like Georges are extremely important in this sport because they remove this idea of the brutish or dumb fighter," Canadian promotion TKO's announcer Jay Mozen said. "Georges comes off as very, very polite, as a gentleman — he has time for you, he has time for his fans, you know, he's gracious in victory, gracious in defeat. When you look at him or David Loiseau fight, these are not just two guys who went into the ring to try to beat each other up. For that, they're really good ambassadors, because they bring a class to it, they eliminate the brutish mentality, and they also show the athleticism involved."[353]

Despite St. Pierre's reputation as a great guy, he might not be a St.

Pierre fan. "The funny thing is, most of my favorite fighters are trash talkers," St. Pierre said. "They are my favorite fighters to watch. I like Tito Ortiz, Phil Baroni. They make the fight exciting. It's not my style, but we need both types of guys. We need gentlemen and guys who are more like characters in the sport. It's like Muhammad Ali used to say, 'Love me, hate me, but don't ignore me.' And I think that's what the sport needs. We don't play hopscotch, you know, it's fighting, so it makes the fight more exciting."[354]

St. Pierre was a product of the old UFC system. He hadn't gotten to the top by winning a reality show. He had worked his way up the card the old-fashioned way — by winning fights. He started by beating other top prospects, like Jay Hieron and Karo Parisyan, before being thrust into a fight with longtime UFC welterweight champion Matt Hughes. St. Pierre was just 23.

"When I fought Hughes, I had no choice. Because the UFC offered me that fight, and I took it. But I didn't want to fight Matt Hughes," St. Pierre said. "I thought I was not ready. But my manager thought it was a good opportunity, and it was, so I took it. I took it with fear. When I was going to that fight, I was going to survive. I was thinking, 'I'm going to lose, but I'll do my best.' Usually when I fight, it is impossible, in my mind, to lose. When you go fight you have to think you are going to win and nothing else. You see yourself as a winner. But when I fought Hughes, it was not like that."[355]

Hughes was actually on the losing end of much of the fight's only round. But he was ahead when it counted, at the finish. Hughes showed his complete game, reversing a St. Pierre Kimura attempt into a beautiful arm bar. As the final seconds of the first round ticked away, St. Pierre tapped the mat.

"Matt Hughes beat me fairly, squarely, but I think I lost that fight more because I gave him too much respect. I was so afraid," St. Pierre said. "I watched this guy fight since I started my career, and then he was in front of me. He is one of my idols in MMA. Now I'm two times better than I was when I fought Matt Hughes. I'm not impressed or intimidated by nobody right now. I lost that fight, but it's the fight that made me grow up the most. After that fight I realized, 'I can beat this guy.' I realized I'm on the top of the food chain. After, when I saw the fight, I said, 'Goddammit, I did well.'"[356]

THE COMEBACK TRAIL

They say a champion shows his true mettle by how he responds to adversity, and St. Pierre responded very well. After the loss to Hughes, he went on a tear through the UFC's welterweight division. It wasn't just wins over top names that impressed, it was the manner of those victories. Frank Trigg had almost beaten Hughes twice. St. Pierre treated him like a child. Not only did St. Pierre submit him in the first round, but he outwrestled the wrestler. St. Pierre said, "My strategy was to put Frank on his back, because he's an elite wrestler, and usually when he's fighting he likes the top position. So my plan was to put him on his back, because he's never been there before except against Matt Hughes, and Matt beat him like that. When Frank's on the bottom, he doesn't defend himself very well. So that was my strategy. I exchanged with him a little bit first. He tried to shoot me, but I swept him and put him on his back. Then I submitted him with a rear-naked choke."[357]

Sean Sherk had pushed the champion to five rounds. St. Pierre finished him in the second, the first fighter to ever beat Sherk decisively. St. Pierre re-established himself as the top contender with a three-round decision over B.J. Penn. He would get another shot at the champion.

HUGHES 2

When St. Pierre suffered an injury, Zuffa went with B.J. Penn as a replacement. Penn had upset Hughes years earlier, at UFC 46, and a rematch was long overdue. Penn took Hughes three tough rounds before referee John McCarthy stopped the fight. After the fight, St. Pierre jumped into the ring. Everyone knew that St. Pierre would be the next challenger, and he was expected to congratulate Hughes and wish him well in their matchup. Instead, the gentleman of MMA lashed out. "I'm not impressed by your performance," he told Hughes in his heavily accented English. Tension had been building since Hughes had come to the set of *The Ultimate Fighter* 4, where St. Pierre was serving as lead trainer. Hughes had been cocky and arrogant, trying to get in the shy St. Pierre's head like he had with another MMA star, Hayato Sakurai. When St. Pierre finally lashed back, live on pay-per-view, Hughes was shocked.

"Whenever they've asked me to go into the Octagon, I've always said no," Hughes said. "I never wanted to steal someone else's glory." Hughes waited for St. Pierre to finish and let him know how he felt. "You just showed me who you really are," Hughes told the affable young Canadian. Backstage, Hughes was legitimately angry, and St. Pierre was upset. He had been pushed into hyping the fight this way, and, in retrospect, he didn't think it was the right move.

"He had an altercation with Matt Hughes in the ring about something Georges thought Matt had said, so Georges kind of lashed back at him," future St. Pierre trainer Greg Jackson said. "I was there for that fight, one of my other guys had fought and won. Georges went and apologized to Matt Hughes afterwards, and I said, 'Well, Georges, why did you do that?' And he said, 'I'm not that kind of person. I'm not the kind of person who's going to be a negative guy or a jerk.' And I was just so impressed by that. Not only is he a great fighter, but that's the kind of guy who can hang out at the dojo any time."

To prepare him for the Hughes fight, Jackson sent several of his students to work with St. Pierre in Montreal. Jackson is picky about his students, because his dojo is like his home. It's important for everyone to get along. St. Pierre fit right in.

"There are several things that really impressed me about Georges. First of all, even before I trained him, I was impressed with the intelligent way he fought, with his athleticism, with his technique," Jackson said. "I was always impressed with him. Rashad Evans actually worked out with him and asked me, because we're a close-knit bunch, 'Would you mind me working out with Georges?' I said, 'Sure. Have fun. He's a 170-pounder, so I'm sure you'll take him down and maul him.' And he came back and said, 'Holy God, you have no idea how good that guy is.' Really? Wow. He's that good?"

St. Pierre was that good, and proved it in the cage against Hughes. This time, St. Pierre met Hughes's eyes in the pre-fight stare-down. The fight began with no touch of gloves. The two had made amends publicly, but make no mistake, this was a grudge match between the two best 170-pound fighters in the world.

Hughes decided to keep the fight standing early. He was at his best in the ground and pound, but St. Pierre had dangerous submissions. Besides, Hughes always wanted to test his stand-up skills.

"I just enjoy hitting," Hughes said. "With throwing punches, you get to do it all the time. Hitting. The one thing that came hard to me was the footwork, because it's just so backwards from wrestling. I've got to try to throw wrestling out the window when I'm working my stand-up, but in MMA you have to put them both together. It's just hard. You see a lot of wrestlers who don't do well in fights because they can't combine MMA and wrestling. And you have to do that. If you can't, you're limiting yourself out there."

St. Pierre was getting the better of the exchanges, thanks to his length. This let him get to Hughes without Hughes being able to counter. Two kicks caught Hughes low, and after a break in the action Matt decided to take the fight to the mat. But St. Pierre didn't want to go. This was new ground for the champion. Hughes had always been able to take the fight down anytime he wanted. St. Pierre just muscled him away. Like he had against decorated wrestler Frank Trigg, St. Pierre was winning the wrestling war. He nailed Hughes with a flying "Superman" punch, and followed up with a left hook that sent the champion to the mat. The bell saved him, but it couldn't help Hughes in the second round.

St. Pierre came out throwing low kicks, and as Hughes concentrated on blocking low, St. Pierre went high. He knocked Hughes silly with a left high kick and finished him off with elbows to the head.

"Everybody has good days and bad, Georges is a heck of a fighter, there's no doubt about it," Hughes said. "Tonight he was better than I was. Now does that mean tomorrow he will be? No it doesn't. . . . Everybody's got their day. . . . He's the future of the sport, there's no doubt about it."

St. Pierre wasn't just the future. He was the present, the world champion. A rubber match with Hughes was at the top of the UFC's to-do list. It would be a tremendous fight between the top fighters in the game. But first there would be a perfunctory title fight with TUF 4 winner Matt Serra. They had promised it on television, and it shouldn't be much of a challenge. Serra was just another stepping-stone for St. Pierre, a small obstacle on the path to a blockbuster rematch.

What could go wrong?

THE UNDERDOG

Matt Serra was simply not supposed to win.

He was the feel-good victor of TUF 4, a collection of fighters who were washed up or treading water and needed a second chance. Serra had been a career underachiever. He was Renzo Gracie's first American black belt, a ground wizard who could hang with anyone on the mat. He just wasn't able to show it. Six of his eight fights had gone to a decision, and he had lost half of them. Serra, as it stood, would be remembered for his spectacular loss in his UFC debut when Shonie Carter knocked him unconscious with a highlight-worthy spinning backfist. Serra had been on the road to nowhere when opportunity knocked in the form of reality TV.

Serra was made for a show like *The Ultimate Fighter*. He was a prototypical brash New Yorker, and he quickly became the dominant personality on the show. Not only was he never afraid to open his mouth, he also showed he was a savvy coach and mentor to the other fighters he helped corner. Statements like, "It's okay, you've been here before," and "Hammerfists are fine" became the show's mantras. Not only did Serra display a dominant personality, he was also a much-improved fighter. He won a rematch with Shonie Carter and beat Chris Lytle to become the TUF 4 winner.

Serra got just as much attention for what he said on the show as for what he did in the cage. When Matt Hughes visited the training center to torment St. Pierre and instigate a fight between Serra and trainer Marc Laimon, Serra told the cameras exactly how he felt. Matt Hughes was a bully and a dick.

"I would never disrespect the guy as a fighter because he's a powerhouse. He's done a lot in our division. But as a person he's so arrogant. Being a great fighter doesn't give you an excuse to be an asshole," Serra said. "I mean, I used to hang out with guys like Tim Sylvia and Matt Hughes. We used to be cool, but I don't know, you win a few fights and get yourself some airtime and all of the sudden you're walkin' around like your shit don't stink. My attitude is you meet the same guys on the way down that you met on the way up."[358]

His higher profile didn't make Serra any less of an underdog against St. Pierre, who was considered the top young fighter in the sport. Serra was just a blown-up 155-pounder who had beaten some other washed-up never-weres. St. Pierre was suffering though a difficult time in his personal life. He would later say that if the fight had been against Matt Hughes, he would have postponed it. But even St. Pierre didn't take the Serra challenge that seriously.

"I was there for the [first] Matt Serra fight and I could see that he wasn't there mentally. He had partied too much and he wasn't focused," Jackson said. "There's a certain confidence that Georges has when he's ready, and he didn't have it that night. He was nervous. But it wasn't my place to say anything. I wasn't the lead guy in the corner where the metal meets the meat. After that fight he wanted me to be the lead guy."

In a year full of upsets, Serra's was the biggest. Matt Hughes was scheduled to face the winner of the fight in a title match. When it was Serra instead of St. Pierre, Hughes looked like he had won the lottery. Even in victory, Serra wasn't getting any respect.

"People love GSP, but you can't deny what I have done," Serra said. "You have Matt Hughes saying it was a lucky punch, but he's a retard. Georges was supposed to be the new MMA god; the guy on the Wheaties box. As far as everyone was concerned, I was just a little Italian guy who got lucky. It wasn't one punch. I got the better of every exchange. I had a game plan, and it was my night."[359]

Serra was known as a Brazilian jiu-jitsu expert, a ground fighter. That didn't stop him from knocking St. Pierre out. St. Pierre had a good chin, but the fight clearly proved that, on any given day, anyone is vulnerable in MMA.

"The shot that really hurt hit him on the back of the head," Greg Jackson said. "It never hit him on the chin. He spars at the Grant Brothers gym in Montreal with these world champion boxers, and they nail him. They nail him. He has a really good chin. He just got caught. Keith Jardine has a really good chin, too. But he can get caught as well. Anybody can get caught if they're hit in the right spot."

The myth of the MMA superman has been exposed many times. At the dawn of the decade, both Pride and the UFC had fighters who were deemed too hard-headed to be KO'ed. But Kazayuki Fujita was stopped by Wanderlei Silva. And Wesley "Cabbage" Correira has been stopped a number of times, most notably by Tank Abbott. The tiny four-ounce gloves make it impossible for anyone to be an unstoppable Tyson-esque killing machine. They magnify the puncher's chances significantly.

"What Georges did in that fight was, he bent down at the waist and got hit right behind the ear," Jackson said. "And it knocked his equilibrium off, and he never really recovered from it. Georges has a great chin, and I'm sure Matt Serra's going to hit him at some point [in the rematch], and everybody will be able to see it."

The announcers and the crowd were in a state of shock. But the likeable Serra was never at a loss for words: "Joe [Rogan], I'm really hungry, man. I was wondering if you and Dana had some humble pie in the back?"

JACKSON'S

After the fight, Georges St. Pierre had to re-evaluate the way he prepared for the Octagon. He was still working primarily with Canadian training partners and old friends. But St. Pierre was a world-class athlete; he needed more, including people who would push him. He decided to turn to Greg Jackson. The training at Jackson's was a perfect fit for St. Pierre. "It's absolutely great, and I think I am blessed because I am able to train with such a great group of guys under Greg Jackson, who is the best MMA coach, in my book," St. Pierre said. "People say you're only as good as your training partners, and I believe that is the truth."[360]

Jackson would push St. Pierre, physically and mentally. Now, when he arrives in New Mexico, St. Pierre comes with a notebook full of philosophical and mathematical questions to discuss. He's ready to work.

"That's where their teammates come in. Because they're really competitive guys. Their teammates will really push them," Jackson said. "Instead of sitting back on their laurels, a guy like Georges St. Pierre comes down and they train, and their teammates can really push them. Hold them down, tap them out, rock them with punches, or whatever it takes. The team is a real key element at that point, because you're able to say, 'You're this great guy, but so-and-so just whacked you in the head. You can't have that happening, and it's because you're doing this or that.' I just try to keep them improving, keep them focused on constantly getting better, constantly looking for a new challenge, even if it's outside the cage. Trying to keep them interested — that's my job."

Greg Jackson is good at his job. Growing up as the only white kid in a primarily Hispanic neighborhood, he'd learned how to fight and ended up making it his life. When he saw Royce Gracie, he had the same reaction many in the traditional martial arts had — I have a lot to learn. The dearth of Brazilian jiu-jitsu black belts in Alberquerque, New Mexico, meant Jackson had to teach himself jiu-jitsu from instructional manuals and videos. Soon he was teaching others. His fighters' local wins turned into regional wins and then King of the Cage wins. And then *The Ultimate Fighter* came along.

No trainer in America has benefited from the reality show more than Jackson. His first great fighter, Diego Sanchez, was a first-season winner. Rashad Evans won season two, and Keith Jardine was a memorable contender. The show changed the sport for everyone involved, but for nobody more than the fighters at Jackson's gym.

"It's a great vehicle, that thing. Dana White is a genius," Jackson said. "That show really changed everything. I hate reality TV. I can't stand it. I don't watch much TV, anyway, but reality TV is the worst. When Diego came to me and said, 'They want me on this reality show,' I was like, 'Oh, God, don't do that, Diego. Give me a break!' He's like, 'Please coach, I really want to.' I said, 'All right, when you're done with it come back and we'll get back to fighting.' I had no idea. We've trained two of the winners, and I've never actually seen a complete episode. That being said, despite my own personal bias, it's the best thing that's ever happened to mixed martial arts. That vehicle is why people are asking me questions, it's why I had to get a bigger gym, it's why the guys are making a living."

The guys who train with Jackson are more than a team, they're family. Jackson makes sure it stays that way. While fighting is a business for many, it's not for Greg Jackson. He won't manage his fighters, and doesn't take an interest in any of the backroom shenanigans that make up so much of a fighter's life. He won't even take a percentage of his fighters' pay, as is customarily due the trainer, although he admits the guys do usually give it to his wife.

"I'm here to be an artist. I put friendship before everything else. People say, 'I didn't get into this business to make friends.' Well, I kind of did. I really like my art, and I really like my friends. Money doesn't mean that much to me. I've got enough to feed my kids and I run a successful business and that's great. I don't need more. The money is never the prime motivator for me. And if I made it the prime motivator, my personality would change. I'm very cautious about that. I don't manage fighters, either. I just do the game plan stuff, because I don't want to get into arguments with anybody about money. I just want to do my art and be the best martial arts trainer I can be. You bring money into it and people change, stuff gets weird. I want it to be about the art and the friendship."

There's a purity to the training. More than anything, Jackson just wants his guys to be better fighters.

"He's a unique person because he doesn't want anything from you," Rashad Evans said. "He has the ability to gain your trust right away. He does it on a personal and a professional level. His reputation is very big in this sport. He could charge a lot of money and guys would still want to work with him because of who he is, but he's very sincere and he doesn't want anything from you. When you work with him, you see how well he knows his stuff. He gets his point across to you so easily, and it's easy to learn from him. He's my idea of what a coach should be."[361]

The Jackson camp is about loyalty and friendship above all else. They will absolutely not fight other guys from the camp. When Dana White suggested that Evans and Jardine would fight if he demanded it, the two emphatically denied that was the case. And it's not just because of the friendships involved. A potential fight in the future between the guys in the gym would hurt the training.

"People think, 'It's just business.' That's bullshit. That's just fucking bullshit to me," Jackson said. "If you are friends, then you are not going to fight each other. Then you give to each other. If you're going to fight each other in the future, you're always going to hold something back. You're always going to be studying the other guy. It has to be a competitive and co-operative balance. And that just tilts the balance to competitiveness more, without enough co-operative. We keep that whole vibe out of our gym. It is a business, but being a fighter is something special. It's not like going to be an accountant. It means something to me."

This credo allows Jardine and Evans to give each other more than a normal training partner might. It's a close bond that has helped both men develop as fighters and friends. It is a relationship that Jackson hoped might develop between Georges St. Pierre and his longtime student Diego Sanchez, who also fights at 170 pounds, when he brought St. Pierre in.

"I brought in Georges St. Pierre because I wanted those two to work together the way Keith and Rashad work together," Jackson said. "I still believe that if Diego wanted to come back, we could do that. He never told me Georges St. Pierre was why he was leaving. What he said was he was engaged to a girl, he had a son in California, and he wanted to get his family together and do right by his son. I said, 'More power to you.' I love Diego to death, we still have a good relationship. He just wanted to go find his family and find himself. He's been in New Mexico his whole life, and I've trained him since he was 17. I think he should go see what else is out there. It's not like it's some cult here, where I'm like, 'Oh, you've got to stay.'"

Sanchez was hurt by the St. Pierre move, and thought he was being pushed out the door. He thought that he and St. Pierre were the best welterweights in the world. If Jackson was bringing in St. Pierre, what did that say for Sanchez's future prospects as a champion?

"I have so much respect for the Jackson camp. Keith Jardine, Nate Marquardt, all those guys, they're still my boys," Sanchez said. "My loyalty was very strong. But St. Pierre could have gone to any camp he wanted. He knew that place was my home, my dream. That took a little something out of my heart. He's training in the cage that I bled in, that I sweated and cried in. . . . Put yourself there for a minute. You're an undefeated fighter coming off two of the biggest wins of your career. Now they're bringing in the champion of your weight class to train with your guys? For three months, I was telling Greg that my heart wasn't feeling it. Greg kept telling me, 'Trust me, trust me, you guys are going to make each other the best,' but I kept feeling like their true intentions were to make me go down to 155 pounds. I mean, most of the Jackson fighters cut a lot of weight, and that's not me. I wasn't going to do it. I wasn't bowing down to Georges St. Pierre. I ain't riding nobody's coattails."[362]

The fighters and Jackson pushed on without Sanchez. Their first fight as St. Pierre's primary training partners was against wrestler Josh Koscheck.

"I think Georges St. Pierre is a well-rounded fighter, a good fighter, but I think he has one area he's very weak in and that's his mind. I think he's not mentally as strong as his skills are. That's the area I'm gonna work on, and hopefully exploit, in this fight, and hopefully I'll come out with a victory," Koscheck said. "If you look at the past history of Georges St. Pierre, he said the reason he lost against Matt Hughes was because he was fighting his idol. You don't come out and say that. And after his loss to Matt Serra, he came out and said he didn't train, and then came back and said he did train hard and he made a mistake, that type of thing. From the outside looking in, you would obviously think something's wrong with this kid if he's making up those kinds of stories. But now I'm glad it's out because it's just an advantage for me, because I'm mentally tough. I come from a wrestling background, so the mental toughness aspect is there, so it's just a matter of getting my skills to the level that I need to compete with those guys."[363]

Koscheck was one of the most decorated wrestlers in the UFC. But when St. Pierre told Jackson he wanted to take Koscheck down, no one blinked. St. Pierre was that special of a fighter. They needed all the fighters at the camp to keep St. Pierre busy and challenge him like he needed to be challenged.

"There are things that a lightweight can bring to the table that a heavyweight cannot. So if I'm working speed, I'm going to need to use a lighter guy," Jackson said. "Whether Georges can beat that guy or not is not really relevant, as much as him dealing with the factor I want him dealing with. If I need somebody who can hold Georges down and make sure he can work up off his back or do submission holds, then I'll bring in a heavier guy. It's not like this guy can beat that guy, so he can't work with him. Everyone has certain elements they can work on. The thing is, in terms of personal growth plans, you have to think in smaller areas. For instance, I need Georges to handle a fast left hook. The heavyweights aren't going to be able to throw that fast left hook like I need it thrown so Georges can defend it. There's a time and a place for lightweights, a time and a place for heavyweights, and a time and a place to just go. It's segmented, but you also have to put everything together. A lot of times they have their individual coaches for boxing and wrestling, and it's my job as a mixed martial artist to put them all together."

Under Jackson, St. Pierre was ready. He would fight the winner of a Matt Hughes and Matt Serra fight that had building for a full season of TUF. St. Pierre was biding his time. Until an unexpected phone call came; Serra was out with an injured back. St. Pierre was in on short notice. He was fighting Hughes for the third time, for the interim title.

HUGHES 3

"I view this a couple different ways," Matt Hughes said about the last-minute change in opponents. "Number one, it's bad in the fact that I'm fighting a lot tougher opponent than Matt Serra. Another thing I dislike about the situation is that I feel Matt Serra is getting the easy way out. If he would have beaten me, then he would have fought Georges again, he would have possibly fought both of us. Now he's getting the easy way out by fighting just one of us."

Hughes and Serra had worked each other up to the boiling point.

Fighting St. Pierre was a tougher fight, and a bit of a let down. Hughes was emotionally ready to deal with Matt Serra, not someone he respected.

Hughes said, "As you can tell, I'm not a big Matt Serra fan right now, with what he's said about me. The good thing about the fight is that I'm not fighting this guy who's been bad-mouthing me, but I'm fighting somebody who I really respect, so it will be a pleasure to face Georges St. Pierre, a stand-up character like he is, as opposed to somebody like Matt Serra, who's just running his mouth. I was really looking forward to fighting Matt, with what he's said and done against me, and so now I just don't have that hunger I had before."

If he was expecting an out-of-shape St. Pierre, he was out of luck. St. Pierre had been spending his downtime preparing to try out for the Canadian Olympic wrestling team. He was in great shape, and his wrestling was better than ever.

"I'm at the top of my game right now. I'm in great shape. I've been training with Rashad Evans to get him ready for his fight," St. Pierre said. "The loss to Matt Serra was probably the best thing to ever happen to me in my career. I don't want to make any excuses. In any sport, like if you take baseball, for example, it's not always the best team that wins. It's the team that is the best prepared and plays the best that wins the game. The same thing is true in fighting. It's not always the best fighter who wins the fight. It's the fighter who comes the most prepared and fights the best."

In the fight itself, St. Pierre made it clear to the world that he was prepared. Hughes was the past. He was the present. It wasn't even a contest. Everything Hughes could do, St. Pierre could do better. Hughes was outwrestled, outstruck, and submitted at the end of the second round.

"No excuses," Hughes said after the fight. "I came in 120 percent and really trained hard for this fight and had a great game plan. Georges is the better fighter."

St. Pierre was glad to have conquered Hughes again. But winning the interim title wasn't what he wanted. "It's a good honor, but Matt Serra is the target," said St. Pierre of his interim title win. "Until I get my belt back, I'm not gonna consider myself a real champion."

Serra versus St. Pierre seemed likely to be what wrestling fans would call a babyface match. Two good fighters would do battle to see who the better man was. Since the fight would be held in St. Pierre's hometown of

Montreal, Serra decided to go in the opposite direction.

"Georges St. Pierre is a pathetic liar," Serra said. "He stood up after the fight, like a man, and admitted he got beat. Now this bullshit? How do you do a total 180? It's so disheartening. I earned this. I worked my friggin' ass off for this fight. All I did was give him respect, and now he wants to save face by shitting on me? All I heard before the fight was how he was going to train like he never trained before, and that he had to be absolutely perfect, and now he says he didn't train. So which is it? Are you a liar now or a liar then?"[364]

Serra's confidence was at an all-time high. His boxing coach, Ray Longo, had kind of expanded his horizons with an offhand comment. "[Longo said] 'You're trying to get to your world when your world is everywhere. Why don't you believe in it?' And I did, and it paid dividends," Serra said. "I'll be clocking in over 80 rounds for this fight. I'm sparring hard. I'm sparring with guys — every two and a half minutes a new guy. Tough guys, big guys. We don't pitter-patter. We whack. I'm used to the shock treatment. I'm used to getting whacked, and I hit right back. So I'm not going to be gun shy. A lot of guys say, 'Tone it down, tone it down.' No. We fight, you know? That's how I train. And that's what gave me the confidence. I know if I can do it in sparring, or I can do it in rolling, I can do it in the fight."[365]

St. Pierre and his team had studied the first fight carefully. Serra still had that puncher's chance, but the old St. Pierre was back. He wasn't planning to lose in his hometown, in the first UFC event ever held in Canada.

"I am going to come with a specific strategy, and it's going to be a different story. They're going to see my eyes when I step into the Octagon. I'm going to have a different look. I'm going to look like a totally different guy, and people will understand when they see that fight," St. Pierre said. St. Pierre always had the best physical tools in the fight game. Now he was developing his mind, as well, first with the philosophical Greg Jackson and later with a sports psychologist. "I used to think that people who needed to see a psychologist were crazy or weak. But at a certain level you need it. Visualization and positive imagery are very important. People underestimate the power of the mental aspect; it helped me a lot."[366]

While St. Pierre was trying to get his head straight, Serra was doing everything he could to get throw St. Pierre off. He was even willing to reignite that classic feud: Canada versus the United States. He called St.

Pierre "Frenchy" and insulted Canada. "Drink your red wine, go to your hockey game, and shut up," Serra said on *MMA Weekly Radio.*

St. Pierre was trying his best to stay above it, just delighted to be competing in his home country. The show was a huge success, and the crowd was amazingly hot. The largest crowd in UFC history, 21,000, packed the Bell Centre for a gate of more than $5 million. "I'm thrilled to be in Montreal, and I am so excited to fight in front of all my Canadian fans," St. Pierre said. "It's amazing. The sport is starting to take off, and I'm so happy we can finally bring live events to Montreal, and Canada. I'm shocked and so privileged to be part of it."[367]

St. Pierre gave the crowd a performance that sent them home happy. Serra, who entered the ring with a T-shirt representing his sponsor, GunsAmerica.com, was badly outgunned. St. Pierre looked like the young champion he had always been advertised as. The crowd was worked into a fever pitch, and the Canadian dominated Serra by taking him to the mat and pounding him out. Serra was taking such a beating, he turtled into a ball and was defenseless as St. Pierre landed knee after knee. St. Pierre had regained the world welterweight title. He was 26 years old and looked like he would be champion forever.

"It's the most beautiful day of my life. A dream come true. And I couldn't wish for a better scenario, honestly," St. Pierre said. "It's like a dream, it's amazing."

29
THE BATTLE FOR BRITAIN

In Britain, MMA was slow to develop. England was the spiritual home of boxing, and the sweet science still held the hearts of the British people. And just as it is in the United States, boxing as an institution was rabidly anti-MMA.

"I bet certain members of the public would buy a ticket for a public hanging. Extreme fighters wouldn't last five minutes with a proper, schooled boxer," UK promoter Frank Warren said. "Boxing is an art, a way of life. That ultimate fighting stuff is for guys who chuck steroids down their neck, pump weights in the gym, and run out of breath after a couple of minutes. I hope it doesn't catch on."[368]

Still, though progress can be slowed, it can't be stopped. As people across the Atlantic watched MMA matches on third-generation videotapes, a small-but-passionate fan base developed. The early British fighters came from a street fighting or stand-up boxing and kickboxing background — Britain didn't have a strong amateur wrestling program. If Brits were going to compete at the sport's top level, they were going to have to go elsewhere to learn how to wrestle.

"Most of our guys come to it through boxing, but the wrestling side of the sport is actually getting bigger over here now," British MMA legend Ian Freeman explained. "I think we're just a few years behind. The top guys, like me and Michael Bisping, who have traveled abroad and trained and fought in other places, we've progressed a little quicker. . . . A guy like Mike Bisping, though, he's gone around and trained with other people, and he's far ahead of everyone else here."[369]

Early British MMA pioneers were often introduced to the sport outside the country and brought it back to Britain when their travels were done.

"One of the main pioneers of MMA in the UK was Mr. Lee Hasdell, a professional fighter in Japan for several years. During the late 1990s, he promoted several large MMA shows that changed the face of martial arts in the UK forever," BAMMA (British Association of Mixed Martial Arts) general manager Mark Woodard said. "UK fighters have been steadily improving with the development of the sport, and we have already produced some truly homegrown talent."

Hasdell had been fighting for K-1. Dutch fighter Bob Schrieber had told him about the shoot-fighting scene in Japan. Hasdell's kickboxing career was stagnating, and, on Schrieber's recommendation, he gave RINGS a try. He had learned judo and some ground fighting in an information exchange with some of his Japanese kickboxing students. This seemed like the perfect sport for Hasdell.

He promoted some of the early MMA shows in England, often gym shows that didn't attract a huge audience but attracted plenty of negative attention from the media. "It was quite difficult at the time, because I didn't have much backup because the sport was very, very small and there were only a handful of people who were involved in it," Hasdell said. "I had almost no way of justifying it — as opposed to now, where a lot of events have taken place and people haven't died or been carried away on stretchers . . . which is what they were prophesizing would happen."[370] Just like in the United States, the British struggled with the idea of MMA. Sportsmanship was ingrained in athletic tradition: the idea of hitting a man when he was down seemed barbaric to the uninitiated. But the sport continued to grow.

In 2000, MMA in Britain got a huge boost as Ian Freeman became the first British fighter to ever compete in the UFC. He was a last-minute replacement for Travis Fulton in a fight with leg lock specialist Scott Adams at UFC 24, in Lake Charles, Lousiana. Freeman's experience was an eye-opener. He still had much to learn about fighting, especially on the ground.

"I'd like to think I would have put up a better performance. I'm not taking anything away from Scott . . . he's good at legs, really good," Freeman said. "I was talking to Tito Ortiz and he said Scott gets him in a leg lock every time. John Lober said, 'Be careful of his leg locks, he came down to train with me and he got me with a leg lock.' So the guy is really good at them. Where I went wrong was, I got out of the first one, got out of the second one, got out of the third one, then I thought, fuck it, instead of just getting out of it I'm gonna try to make one. So I exchanged leg locks when I should have just got out of there and stood up. Trying to exchange leg locks with a leg lock merchant."[371]

Freeman would be back in the UFC, and two wins over Nate Schroeder and Tedd Williams made him a rising star. He was fighting for the UFC and Pancrase in Japan, and finally making some money, but his lack of polish soon caught up to him. He lost four in a row, and his career as a major international star seemed finished. Then the new Zuffa-led UFC decided to make its first foray into Europe.

"I never thought the UFC would get here so quickly. I thought, when I started fighting two years ago in the UFC, that it would open doors for more English fighters to come fight in the States, but that never happened," Freeman said. "So, the show actually coming to England was something I never thought would happen — not in my lifetime, anyhow. Obviously, I'm overwhelmed. To be back for my fourth time, I want to show the English fans that I can do it just as well here as I can abroad."[372]

The Royal Albert Hall in Westminster had hosted all kinds of events since it was built in 1871. Classical music concerts were the typical fare, but the hall had seen boxing matches and even the first Sumo contests held in the UK. This was, however, surely the first cage fight in one of London's most historic buildings. And since UFC 38 was the company's first-ever UK show, it wisely decided to bring in some of the best homegrown talent. Leigh Remedios, James Zikic, and Mark Weir were all on the undercard, and Freeman was selected to give an easy win to the UFC's rising heavyweight star, Frank Mir.

Then Freeman overwhelmed Mir, known for his technical jiu-jitsu, with hard punches and a street fighter's mentality.

Mir said, "I kind of feel like I was a victim of my own success. I felt very comfortable that I could take people out extremely quickly. But I didn't have a backup plan. So when Plan A failed, I didn't have a Plan B. That's what you saw against Ian. When I didn't get him to submit, I had no backup plan. His tenacity was very much an eye-opener. It has definitely changed my style as far as fighting goes. You have to be ready to go, every second, in this game."[373]

The Freeman win and 26 weeks of the UFC on television was the start of a UK MMA renaissance. The UFC wouldn't return for five years, but it left a growing local market. In the interim, the dominant players on the British scene were Cage Rage and Cage Warriors — the two outfits had dramatically different approaches.

"We've followed the Pride influence more than, shall we say, the UFC influence," former Cage Rage co-owner Andy Geer said. "We've had a few open-weight fights, we do rely heavily on entertaining the crowds, and we make some great TV."[374]

While Cage Warriors focused on homegrown British talent, Cage Rage aimed higher. It brought in top foreign talent and got a show on Sky TV. The show was intended to be a one-off fundraiser, but was soon the biggest thing going.

"We actually sat down — after putting our guys into different tournaments and realizing how badly they were run. . . . We said it would be nice to put them in a tournament that we would run, and show how to do it properly. Basically, we were just going to do one tournament, and after the first one we said never again. But so many people wanted more, more, more," former Cage Rage owner Dave O'Donnell said. "Then, for our second one, we were lucky because I'd just trained with Royce Gracie and received my blue belt with him, and we asked him to be our special guest at Cage Rage number two. He actually refereed some of the fights for us. That was after having Frank Shamrock as our special guest at number one. Both were sellouts, and both had documentaries made about them, so we've done really well."[375]

While Cage Rage brought in Gracie and Shamrock, and had top fighters like Anderson Silva and Matt Lindland on their cards, Cage Warriors set about developing the best fighters in the UK.

"Cage Warriors has always been about the development of the UK scene, maybe even to its own detriment. It is content to continue to run smaller venues than Cage Rage, but run on a tenth of the payroll," British MMA expert Iain Liddle, of Total-MMA.com, said. "If you look at the fighters who have made a name for themselves, the vast majority have been through Cage Warriors as a testing ground. Denis Siver, Gerard Mousasi, David Baron, Paul Daley, Michael Bisping, Dan Hardy, and Paul Taylor all started out with Cage Warriors before Cage Rage or people overseas blinded them with dollar signs."

Daley and Hardy are developing stars. But the biggest and most important fighter to come out of Cage Warriors is Michael Bisping. Bisping was an undefeated prospect when he and fellow Briton Ross Pointon were chosen to join the cast of *The Ultimate Fighter.*

THE COUNT COMES INTO HIS OWN

Bisping was already a rising star when he traveled to America for reality television fame and fortune. Like many of Cage Warrior's stars, Bisping was taken into the Cage Rage family for a time. Cage Rage had a distinct sink-or-swim philosophy. With just a few fights under his belt, Bisping was going to be fed to international star Renato "Babalu" Sobral. When Sobral was injured prior to his trip to the UK, Bisping fought UK star Mark Epstein instead. This was the win that got people talking.

"My proudest moment, I'd have to say, is when I beat [Mark] Epstein for the second time, because I was quite new to the sport," Bisping said. "It was my fifth pro fight, but I beat Epstein at Cage Rage 7 and a lot of people said it was a fluke because he took the fight on short notice. So then to beat him again, and beat him in style . . . that was a proud moment."[376]

Bisping was the pride of Team Ortiz at TUF 3. Or at least felt he should have been. One of the show's most memorable side plots was Bisping's war of words with Ortiz's favorite pupil, wrestler Matt Hamill. But Bisping doesn't bear his flashy coach any ill will.

"I can't bad-mouth his coaching abilities on the show. He did a good job. You can't deny it. He brought in Saul Soliz [kickboxing coach] and Dean Lister [Brazilian jiu-jitsu coach], who are both world-class in their own rights. Saul's a fantastic coach, Tito showed us wrestling things and takedown defense, and Dean Lister showed us some great stuff on the floor. So as a team, it was very, very good," Bisping said. "A lot of the guys came back from the show and said they hated it and would never do anything like that again. I loved it. It was one of the best experiences of my life. It changed my life. Usually, the guys who don't like it are the ones who don't make it very far. The guys who are there to the end usually love it."[377]

When Hamill left the house with an injury, Bisping cruised to the finals to fight for the six-figure TUF contract. He was fighting scrappy and undersized Team Quest fighter Josh Haynes for a shot at being a UFC regular. For a family man like Bisping, that meant everything.

"When I got to *The Ultimate Fighter* finale, I thought, 'Well, I've got to win this fight for my family because I need that contract,' so I'd better win this fight," Bisping said. "So I think about my family and the reason why I am doing this. I look at my opponent and think he is trying to take away from my family, and you know, it sounds corny and a bit cheesy, but that's just the way it works. I think, well I need to beat this guy, you know, and my family is going to have a better life and this guy is trying to take it away, so I just go at the guy."[378]

The win gave Bisping a UFC contract and the UFC a star to promote in the UK. It was determined to capture the European MMA market, and Bisping had become the name Britons associated with the sport. The UFC was thriving in the United States, and making a profit would take some time in Europe. The short-term strategy would be to drain the well dry in the U.S. before looking to expand, but the UFC's owners were looking further into the future.

"We invest in the sport to try to grow it by doing things like going to Europe. We took major losses in Europe [in 2007]. We didn't make money on any of those European shows," UFC owner Lorenzo Fertitta said. "But looking forward five years, we realize that Europe is going to be bigger than the U.S., and a lot of those fighters are going to benefit from the way we've cultivated the European market. The boxing way is to take a short-term approach, but we're focused on the long term, both for the brand and for the sport."[379]

At UFC 70, the UFC returned to Britain for the first time since UFC 38 in 2002. The crowd in Manchester was absolutely electric. The card featured international star Mirko Cro Cop and rising talent Forrest Griffin. But the man fans wanted to see was Bisping. His TUF win didn't just attract a fan base in the United States. For the first time, the Brits were watching closely, as well.

"The first two series of TUF didn't penetrate at all over here to people that weren't on the Internet. The third series saw Bravo [which isn't a huge channel, but is well-known by cable standards] start promoting it because of the two Brits on the show," Iain Liddle said. "It definitely helped in that respect, and it was also the first show where we didn't have to wait three months or something to see the episodes, so people could watch it unfold in real time. The emergence of Bisping was the first time I have heard my casual UFC-following friends talk enthusiastically about the sport. It's the British mentality. We don't get excited about something until we think we have someone who can take on the world in it. I didn't realize how popular he was until UFC 70, when I saw the reception he received."

Bisping was a rock star that night to his UK fans. It was just his second fight in the UFC, and he was facing the tough Australian journeyman Elvis Sinosic. Sinosic was on the losing end of many of his fights, but that was because he had fought the very best, including Frank Shamrock and Jeremy Horn. He was not going to let the young British star walk through him. The crowd was wild for Bisping, but Sinosic almost put a damper on the fun with an arm lock that nearly ended the fight.

"Unbelievable, to say the least," Bisping said. "I was expecting a good reception from the crowd, but nothing like that. Never in my wildest dreams. It absolutely blew me away. It kind of took over me a little bit. Once the fight starts, you've got a job on your hands and you kind of blank it out a little. Although [the crowd] did help during that submission. At one point I thought . . . I wish I could tap here, but I found the extra strength and got out."

THE REAL TUF 3 FINAL

"I want to fight Bisping to see who should have been the TUF 3 champion," Matt Hamill said. The UFC had spent hours of television time building for a fight between Bisping and Hamill that had never taken place. That wasn't going to be squandered, so after both men won their early UFC fights, the match was booked for UFC 75 in London.

"Look, I can understand why the UFC wanted this fight. A lot of people watch the show and want to see us fight," Bisping said. "It's the fight the fans want, so that's good enough for me. Yeah, I didn't want it at first. I wanted to put the whole 'Ultimate Fighter' thing behind me and move on with my career in the UFC. But the fight's booked. I look forward to going out there and shutting him up and putting on a good show. . . . They portrayed him as this big, gullible, bloody puppy-eyed deaf kid, but that wasn't the case at all. The guy's an asshole, for lack of a better word. He came on the show for the wrong reasons. He's a bit of a bully. He didn't respect anyone. When it's universal that every guy who met him thought he was an asshole, well, he's got to be an asshole. You'd think someone —

at least one person — would like you, but no one in the house, except for his buddy Danny [Abbadi], did."[380]

Quinton Jackson beat Dan Henderson to unify the Pride and UFC titles at 205 pounds, and the event was a tremendous success on Spike TV. The fight card drew 4.7 million viewers — the most watched UFC event ever in North America and the most viewed show ever on Spike TV not produced by the WWE. The fight that everyone was talking about after the show wasn't the great main event, which saw two evenly matched warriors trading punches and slams for five rounds. It was the semi-main event between Bisping and Hamill. Hamill had shocked fans by coming out swinging. Conventional wisdom said that Hamill was just a wrestler and didn't have anything to offer standing on his feet. He put that idea to rest early by showing just how far his game had progressed since TUF.

"I came right out and started throwing heavy punches," said Hamill. "I was actually surprised at how easy it was for me to connect. I knew he was going to run, so I walked him down. I felt like I hurt him right off the bat. I saw a different look in his eyes. I landed a flying knee that surprised him. It made me hungry for more. I felt like I completely dominated him in the first round. I landed numerous shots, most of them power shots, and completely outboxed him. I felt in complete control of the fight, and easily won round one."[381]

Bisping came back strong, and it was a close fight for the final two rounds. When the scorecards came back, it was a split decision for the home-country fighter. Hamill was incredulous, and fans on the Internet exploded in righteous anger. Even some of his countrymen in the O2 Arena booed the decision that night. "I've seen a lot of bad decisions," White said. "This is why I tell these guys to never leave it in the hands of the judges, because everybody sees a fight differently. The bottom line is, both Michael Bisping and Matt Hamill fought their hearts out Saturday night, and I hope this scoring issue doesn't put a damper on what was a great fight between two fighters who have bright futures in this organization, and this is a no-brainer for a rematch."[382]

Backstage, Bisping was not happy, especially when reporters asked if he thought he had really earned the win. "Of course. Don't insult me like that," Bisping snapped. The fight had soiled Bisping's reputation with many fans, and Internet message boards were particularly brutal. One close decision had turned a rising star into a sham, a company-made artificial fighter who needed the help of corrupt hometown officials to win.

"Of course I care what people think, especially because I'm not that kind of a guy," Bisping said. "If you read the Internet message boards after that fight, I think I was more hated than Saddam Hussein. If I had a time machine, I'd go back in time and handle myself a lot differently. Of course I felt I won the fight, but I had no business reacting to the journalists the way I did."[383]

THE REMATCH THAT WASN'T

"Wow! Let me just say . . . I am in shock," Hamill said. "First, I get hosed by two judges in London and now the much-anticipated rematch has evaporated in front of my eyes."[384] Hamill would have to miss a few months after minor surgery. Instead of holding off on the rematch and moving it from UFC 78 to UFC 79, the UFC had gotten Bisping a new opponent — TUF 2 winner Rashad Evans.

Originally, the show was going to be headlined by a rematch between Evans and Tito Ortiz. Their first fight was a draw, and fans were ready to see a rematch. Ortiz was more interested in filming Donald Trump's *Celebrity Apprentice*. He told the UFC he had an injury. They found out about his network television star turn when the rest of the country did. The UFC was short one main event for its return to the New York metropolitan area. When the fight was cancelled, the UFC needed another star capable of headlining a pay-per-view event. Dan Henderson was considered, but the UFC ultimately decided that Bisping was ready for the role.

It was the right move. Bisping and Evans provided the UFC with its most cost-effective main event ever. Although New York fans, and the media, weren't happy with what they felt was a subpar main event, MMA fans didn't seem to mind. The fighters drew an average number on pay-per-view, and did it while still under their TUF contracts. The main eventers for a pay-per-view show that would gross tens of millions of dollars were paid a combined total of less than $50,000.

The fight also paid off in the ring. Evans was the overwhelming favorite because of his strong wrestling base, but Bisping was aggressive early. Eventually, Rashad's strength and size advantage wore on Bisping, who seemed tentative when he had opportunities while standing.

"Early Bisping fighting Rashad would have gone for it more in the third round," Liddle said. Bisping feared the takedown. It is a hurdle that all fighters from a striking base have to overcome in order to become world-championship caliber fighters. Despite Bisping's loss, and the loss of his undefeated record, there were positive signs. He had taken one of the best fighters at 205 pounds to the limit.

"If Rashad was fighting his best, it proves that Mike really belongs in there with anybody," Freeman said. "He had kind of a bad fight with Matt Hamill, and a lot of people thought he lost that fight, but whether he did or didn't, I think he proved his worth against Rashad. I believe he did lose the fight, but it was very, very close. I was proud of how he fought."[385]

Bisping was proud of his performance, but had a decision to make. For years, people in the sport had been suggesting that he move down a weight class, to 185 pounds.

MIDDLEWEIGHT MICHAEL

"Even as far back as the TUF 3 tryouts in London [in December 2005], Dana White looked at me and asked me if I was sure I wanted to try out for the light heavies rather than the middleweights," Bisping said. "Then I was asked the same question again when I was invited to Las Vegas to do the interview to get on the show. I've been asked about middleweight loads of times, not just by writers, but also other fighters, so I started thinking about it more seriously this year . . . Dana thought it was a great idea, he said I'd be 'a monster' down at middleweight. In fact, all sorts of people, like Rampage [UFC light heavyweight star Quinton Jackson], were telling me this was the best thing for my career. Really, I knew middleweight was the place to be. When I went to train with Rampage in America over the summer, when we'd go eat, he'd have half a lettuce leaf; I'd have a pizza or a couple of foot-long Subways and a couple of sneaky cookies."[386]

Bisping's regular weight was around 210 pounds. He barely had to cut weight at all, and was giving up a significant size advantage in every fight. He knew middleweight was his division. Still, he had a stubborn streak, like Dan Henderson, who actually won titles at 205 pounds despite weighing in under 200.

"I was going to try my normal weight. People said I should drop to middleweight now, because a lot of [light] heavyweights are huge, you know, which they are, to be honest," Bisping said. "But, you know, I won my first fight. Then I won my second time and third time, and I thought, 'Well, I'll keep going until I lose one' and then I'll drop down, because I had to finally drop down at some point, and I thought it wasn't fair while I was still winning the fights. . . . He got the win, so I decided to move down. To be honest, it's the best thing I have ever done. My performance is so much better. I'm eating a better diet, my body is performing better. I'm gaining less weight, so I am faster, and I just happen to be more disciplined, you know, and perhaps I reap the benefits."[387]

His first fight at middleweight was against TUF 4 veteran Charles McCarthy. McCarthy let Bisping have it verbally before the fight, and fans on the Internet chimed in, as well. Bisping was only successful, the argument went, because he was carefully protected.

McCarthy hadn't gotten the memo that he was just a tune up fight for the young star. He was confident that Bisping was the decided underdog.

"Bisping's never fought anybody as good as me on the ground. He's fought some decent guys, but what I bring on the ground is just a different level," McCarthy said. "When I get it to the ground, you can start your stopwatch, it'll be about a minute and I'll have that fight over with."[388]

"His skill level is not real impressive to me," McCarthy said. "I know he doesn't want to go to the ground with me. . . . You won't see him have any strengths in this fight . . . I fully expect to go in and finish this fight quickly and move on to better things."[389]

Bisping didn't take kindly to what he considered a series of insults. He had earned more respect than he was being shown. He was a TUF winner, and had done well with some of the top fighters at 205 pounds. This tune up was now personal.

"I know some people think I've taken my eye off the ball by getting into a bit of a war of words with my opponent, but, believe me, I am going to fight my fight and do what I was always going to do," Bisping said. "Don't blink. I'm not going out there like a maniac, but I will be starting very fast, pushing the pace and showing what I can do now that I am at my proper weight class."[390]

Once the bell rang, Bisping attacked his opponent aggressively, but McCarthy was almost as good as his word. He trapped him in a tight arm bar and looked to be on his way to a first-round submission win. When

Bisping escaped, he was out for revenge and quickly finished McCarthy with a series of punches and knees. McCarthy, who was so confident that Bisping would be easy prey, retired after the fight. The UFC breathed a sigh of relief. A potential Bisping versus Anderson Silva title match at middleweight was still on the table. The UFC intended to continue its push into the European market, and the fight would be the perfect main event for a UK show.

THE FUTURE OF EUROPEAN MMA

"I don't think there's anything profitable about the European market right now. We're getting our ass kicked over there. But the bottom line is to grow this sport. I'm always, you know, yapping about the boxing promoters and how they don't spend the money to build their sport and secure the future of the sport," UFC president Dana White said. "For this sport to grow, we need to move into Europe. As far as the sport goes, I think that this sport is the most exciting. . . . Once people are introduced to it, they love it . . . look at the NFL. Right? There's nothing bigger in this country than the NFL. I don't care if you didn't watch one football game all season. Everybody watches the Super Bowl. Okay? They've been spending billions of dollars to try to break into Europe, and they can't do it. You know why? Because nobody gives a shit about football in Europe. They didn't grow up playing football, they don't know about it. I take two guys, put them in the Octagon, and they can use any martial art they want. It transcends all different cultural barriers, language barriers. People love fighting. It's inside of us as human beings. We're born with it. People love fighting. And I think that this thing can be global, I think this can be the biggest sport in the world. I already know it's the most exciting sport in the world. And, you know, we'll see in the next five or six years if I'm right or wrong. If I am wrong, we spent a shitload of money, you know, in places we'll never go again."

Bisping would be called on to rescue a UK card just a month after his middleweight debut. Chuck Liddell had gone down with an injury, and the UFC would again need a main event star to carry the show. Bisping stepped up, as he did at UFC 78, to help make the night a success. The UFC would continue to lead the way in the development of MMA in Europe, and Bisping would be its first poster boy.

"Brits are definitely excited about him, and he remains the most popular UK name by some distance," Liddle said. "Unless he loses a couple of fights in a row, he'll remain a draw over here. He's the only fighter to have infiltrated the public consciousness in any way. He had a column on *The Sun* Web site [the biggest newspaper in the country], and radio appearances on a number of national stations. He's the unofficial spokesperson for the sport in this country, and if he suddenly excels, then the sport will proportionally increase its awareness and attendances, I am sure."

In the long term, the UFC and MMA look like they will be huge successes in Europe. The initial invasion took place in England, but there is a strong interest in MMA in eastern Europe, Germany, and Holland. It's a market the Fertittas are keen to tap. The WWE has shown that a strong European fan base can help prop up a struggling company when domestic revenues are down. The UFC would like that kind of recession-proof fallback as well.

One of the biggest challenges will be shifting the model the UFC has always used in America, where for years the show was relegated to pay-per-view, because that was the only place it could be broadcast. In the UK and elsewhere, there is actually a demand for the UFC on regular television. It's a huge paradigm shift, one Zuffa will eventually maximize to its best advantage. The thousands of screaming fans are the proof.

"There's no arguing with selling out events, breaking merchandise records, having good ratings on television, doing good numbers on pay-per-view, having enough success that just about every significant network in the UK wanted to license our rights," The head of the UFC's UK division, Marshall Zelaznik said. "So while the overall profits may not have met the desired goals, I think the amount of revenue we created in this office is about where we thought it would be — it's just that we spent more money. And we did that because we could see the upside of the market pretty early, based on how UFC 70 tickets were going, so we started spending to make sure we hit it out of the park.

"That was an investment that will come back in the next few years, but overall there are no targeted goals here — it's kind of 'you'll know it when you see it.' I'm so optimistic for this year in terms of the measurable things, like ticket sales, merchandise sales, total revenue, and profits, for this office. So, for me, we're ahead of targets, when you look at the five-year plan."[391]

It didn't take long for that initial investment to pay off. By mid-2008, the

UFC's UK ventures were turning a profit. All the hard work promoting Michael Bisping as a main event star was also paying dividends. His fight with journeyman Chris Leben was moving tickets for UFC 89, in Birmingham, England, without any established names in a supporting role. Zuffa also signed Dan Hardy, perhaps Britain's best fighter, to bolster its lineup of native stars.

Having conquered the United Kingdom, the UFC turned its attention to mainland Europe and even dared to look further abroad — to India, Mexico, and South America.

30
LOOKING FORWARD

The success of the UFC has spawned many competitors. Some, like BoDog Fight, a creation of gambling impresario Calvin Ayre, quickly flamed out. Others, like the IFL and Elite XC, have lasted longer, but only because investors were willing to lose millions of dollars against the promise of future returns. Others, like Scott Coker's Strikeforce, have had limited success promoting shows on a smaller scale. Strikeforce has drawn several million-dollar gates on the strength of local stars Frank Shamrock and Cung Le. But, as yet, no one has emerged as a true challenger for Zuffa.

UFC owner Lorenzo Fertitta said, "A lot of people talk about the growth of MMA. I don't believe in that. I don't know where anybody can show me there is this great success in MMA outside of the UFC. There has been explosive growth for the UFC, but in MMA in general, nobody is making a breakthrough. The biggest non-UFC pay-per-view, you might know better than me, is something like 25,000, maybe 30,000 buys. There is a bit of a misnomer there. It's not the growth of MMA. It's the growth of the UFC. Based on our success, as with any business, you're going to get guys who are going to try to be the 'me, too' person, and want to try to hang on and build on the success that we've had. I don't necessarily think that that's a bad thing. There are always going to be others in the business, and I respect what they're doing. I understand that. It's our job to stay ahead and continue to be the leader. At the end of the day, a lot of people are going to try to take shots at us. But what I like to say is, 'You can only tackle the guy with the ball,' and we have the ball."[392]

That may change. For years, the UFC aggressively pursued a network television deal. But when the deal was announced, it wasn't Dana White standing on stage beaming.

CBS

The biggest MMA card in televised history happened with no UFC involvement. For the first time, MMA, a sport once banned throughout much of the nation and not even suitable for an audience that paid for the privilege of watching, was going to air on network television. Over the years, the audience for network television, at one time the only television channels there were, has eroded. Yes, there are 500 channels to choose from, but the big three networks (CBS, NBC, and ABC) still pack the biggest punch, draw the most viewers, and carry the most prestige. An MMA company had finally broken the network barrier, and to everyone's surprise it wasn't the UFC.

"They have their eye in the right place, in the cage of Elite XC. It's big for Elite XC, it's big for CBS, but it's biggest for the sport of mixed martial arts," Gary Shaw said. Shaw is the driving force behind Elite XC, a former New Jersey State Athletic Control Board member, and a longtime boxing promoter. "It's the final validation that it is a real sport. That it has real athletes who have real disciplines and are highly trained. . . . I think we're drafting right behind the UFC. I don't think we're there, but we're close."[393]

Some media critics were amazed that CBS would stoop to this level of programming, especially ESPN's *Pardon the Interruption* duo of Tony Kornheiser and Michael Wilbon. Although the UFC had received laudatory coverage in plenty of national media outlets, CBS was different. Network television was supposed to be too classy for cage fighting.

"Sure, the 'Tiffany network' did bring us *All in the Family* and Edward R. Murrow, and these fights may not be what the network's older audience is used to," said Robert Thompson, director of Syracuse University's Bleier Center for Television and Popular Culture. "But have you watched *Big Brother* this season? CBS and all the networks are desperate to find the next big idea, and it's not completely wrong to think this is it."[394]

White wanted everyone to know that he could have signed the deal. There were lots of offers he turned down flat because they involved giving up control, or even selling part of the company Zuffa had built into a money machine from bankruptcy. It wasn't that Elite XC had swooped in to take a CBS deal from the UFC. It had simply been willing to take an offer the UFC wouldn't.

"It's a lot trickier than people realize," White said. "The reality is that Elite XC didn't sign a deal with CBS, that's not what happened. CBS bought Elite XC — big difference. I don't think it's a great deal at all. I've talked to every network, including CBS. The thing is with me — I say it all the time — I'm not going to cut a stupid deal."395

Still, the UFC had been angling for a network television deal for some time and could never quite get it done. It had also lost a high-profile deal with the top pay cable network, HBO. Many speculated that the UFC was leaving offers on the table because it insisted on a level of control these traditional media outlets wouldn't allow. HBO would want to be free to have its own announcers, and to criticize UFC decisions they didn't agree with on the air. A professional announcing team would mention the fact that the UFC had lost its heavyweight champion, Randy Couture, to a contract dispute, or that its lightweight champion, Sean Sherk, had been busted in California for using steroids. The current UFC production swept these issues under the table. Instead, it simply stopped mentioning Randy Couture on its programs, as if he never existed. This couldn't happen when legitimate journalists started covering the sport on television, and it was a significant issue for Zuffa. Gary Shaw thought that Zuffa's single-minded focus on protecting the UFC name would allow other promoters to get their foot in the door, not only to sign deals like the CBS coup, but to sign the bigger-name fighters when their contracts expired, as well.

Shaw said, "If you fight for the UFC, you can't be bigger than Dana White and the UFC. If you fight for Elite XC, as a fighter, you're bigger than Gary Shaw. It's about the fighter. It's not about me. Whether it's Kimbo [Slice], who was signed to us, or any other fighter, I believe we represent some of the greatest fighters in the world. I believe that Antonio 'Big Foot' Silva could knock out any heavyweight in the UFC. Now, I'm not disparaging the UFC. They have some great fighters and great fights. They have a good brand. They do a good job marketing their brand, but they don't own MMA. They don't own the space. They have a brand. You know what, if you hold up the belt there, all you are is the club champion. Until Dana White is willing to fight his fighters against other brands, they are only club champions."

White had seen competitors come and go. Since *The Ultimate Fighter*, plenty of promoters had thrown their hats into the ring. None were significant threats in the minds of Zuffa brass because they didn't understand the MMA business.

White said, "The next company that was going to take me out has been coming for the last eight years. Every time somebody puts something new together, it's been, 'Oh, these guys are gonna kick Dana's ass and put his ego in check.' There ain't anybody kicking our ass. It isn't going to happen this year with CBS and Elite XC or any year. We'll see who's around in five years, me or Gary Shaw. There's some ego for you. The reality is I know what the fuck I'm doing and Gary Shaw doesn't. If you go and search Gary Shaw and mixed martial arts [on the Internet], this guy was saying five years ago that mixed martial arts was a joke . . . it's not a real sport, these guys are barroom brawlers. Now that fat, bloated fuck is running around acting like he loves mixed martial arts."

Shaw was building a mini-empire for Elite XC's parent company, Pro Elite, but was doing it at a significant cost. Pro Elite lost more than $31 million since its inception, $27 million in 2007 alone. The company made frivolous choices, like spending millions of dollars on a Web site, proelite.com, that is essentially unnavigable and has no chance of earning back that kind of money. In its annual 10-K report, the promotion indicated "our auditors have expressed substantial doubt about our ability to continue as a going concern." Pro Elite would not survive long at its current rate of growth and its ever-increasing rate of expenditure. Company spokesmen remained confident that the CBS deal would be the first step toward solvency.

"I know we'll be profitable because my mother and father are backing me," Shaw joked. "But on a serious note, Elite XC is all about the fighter. It's a fighter-friendly company. We care about the safety and welfare of every fighter we represent. We have, probably, the biggest mixed martial arts library in the world today. We have several brands around the country. We have a huge Internet play, which works for the fighters and works for the fans, that is an important part of the company. We have a contract with Showtime where we'll have roughly 14 fights on Showtime and millions of eyes this year. . . . We have a lot of opportunities. We're growing every day. We're really excited. We think we bring the best fights. I believe we put on exciting events for the fans. We're event-friendly in the arena. We're on TV and get the eyeballs that watch our fights. A lot of people said a lot of nasty things last year about us, and never thought we were going to really get off the ground. But this rocket ship launched."

Despite the huge money losses and the UFC's established place on the top of the pecking order, fighters and a series of promoters were confident that success was just a good idea away. The UFC's idea to put its fighters in the classic reality television structure had opened the door to success, but it was a great fight between Stephan Bonnar and Forrest Griffin that had made UFC must-see programming. Any company that got the right platform to show its fighters to an audience, and then delivered a compelling show, had the potential to thrive.

"Anybody who does good business and has a good business model can compete," Frank Shamrock said. "The UFC is just a bunch of guys with a bunch of money who learned through trial and error and bought a brand that was already established. They didn't do anything spectacular. I'm sure if I bought Kleenex I could make Kleenex a stronger brand. You know what I mean? It's not rocket science. I don't think they have a competitive edge or anything. Their advantage is that they have made the first move. Elite XC can definitely compete, and I'm really pleased to see them bringing in as many people as possible. Having a monopoly doesn't help everyone, it just helps one person, and there is enough talent, enough fighting, and enough marketing. Everyone should be sharing the marketing dollar and developing new stars instead of their own stars. So I think they have a tremendous opportunity, and I'll help them anyway I can."[396]

KIMBO SLICE: INTERNET WARRIOR

Elite XC was betting everything on the idea that mainstream America would be as interested in Kevin Ferguson as the Internet had been. As Kimbo Slice, Ferguson drew thousands of eyeballs to YouTube for televised street fights. Slice would bring a camera crew with him to film him beating the crap out of a collection of out-of-shape fat guys, bouncers, and other sundry non-athletes. He was bringing this Internet fame into the world of MMA.

"I'll take anybody on. Everybody says I'm the new kid on the block or whatever. But it's the era. Being street certified mixed with MMA, tae kwon do, jiu-jitsu, kickboxing, and wrestling. You combine that, and you're going to have a type of fighter like me," the Internet legend explained.

Kimbo Slice had charisma and looked the part of the tough street warrior, the kind of bar brawler that, for years, critics had insisted all MMA fighters were. But actual MMA-style fighting was new to Slice. He had always insisted his street fights be nothing but bare-knuckle boxing. When off-duty police officer Sean Gannon tried to utilize kicking techniques, knees, and throws in their Internet fight, Slice's people were vehemently opposed. The new style would be a challenge.

"It's really hard. It's more skilled fighters and better fighters. I'm proving myself now, because people feel like the guys I fought were pretty much nobodies. But you never know what another guy has," Slice said. "I'm dying to get the opportunity to show off a little stuff. I've got a lot of tools in my arsenal now. I'm not afraid to use them. I'm getting to the point where it's second nature. I'm just excited to be where I am . . . and make a good future and a good name for myself."

Elite XC was where he was, not the UFC. The UFC was very careful about the fighters it promoted. It made a point of telling people that these athletes were just like them. They went to college and loved their kids. The racial subtext was startling. The UFC had safe, white, middle-class athletes. Elite XC was going to give America something different. The company was confident that Slice exuded the kind of masculinity and dangerousness that had made Mike Tyson such a popular boxer.

"He is a superstar in the making. He can punch maybe bigger than any heavyweight, both in boxing and in mixed martial arts," Elite XC's Gary Shaw said. "He's being trained by Bas Rutten. I think, in a short time, he will be in the top ten. I think Kimbo's story is still yet untold. I would just wait and let Kimbo see where Kimbo goes. There are fighters who were supposed to be great but never matured into greatness. For me, you've got to give Kimbo time to ferment."[397]

Slice's main supporter at Elite XC was a former Pride executive. Pride had always placed a premium on star potential and the spectacular, sometimes at the expense of legitimate athletic prowess.

"Several years back I spoke to Kimbo's manager, Icey Mike, and I thought the same thing," Elite XC vice president and former Pride executive Turi Altavilla said. "I definitely thought he could be a star in Japan. You could just see it from watching the YouTube fights. It's partially his ability to fight, but also his look, his charisma, everything. In Pride, a lot of emphasis was put on the total package; you had to be a great fighter, but you had to be marketable, too, and he was definitely that. Unfortunately at the time, my access to [Pride president Nobuyuki] Sakakibara was not direct, and I had to go through several channels to bring fighters into him. The two at the Dream Stage [Entertainment] L.A. office didn't think Kimbo was for real. I think they've been proven wrong."[398]

To help Slice develop his fight game, Elite xc turned to Bas Rutten. Rutten had been one of the sport's top fighters, and was well-regarded for his ability to teach strikers how to survive on the ground.

"He's doing really good. The instructions you give him, he takes to heart," trainer Bas Rutten said. "And he actually does it. He doesn't complain. He trains hard. He's always there, he shows up. I'm very impressed with Kimbo."

Fans seemed impressed with Slice, too. Or, if not impressed, at least interested enough to watch. Elite xc had drawn good ratings on Showtime for matches headlined by Frank Shamrock, but Kimbo Slice and Tank Abbott had outperformed even Shamrock's best match, drawing 522,000 viewers to the premium network. Abbott had been the perfect opponent for Slice. Before the fight, he provided plenty of fireworks.

"I'll tell you what's up. Kimbo's going to be on his back," Tank Abbott said. "This fight is going to last about as long as his opening interview did. 'What's up' is about how long it's going to take for him to end up on his back, knocked out . . . I will give him his props. Kimbo goes out there, he's tough, he's got balls and he's got heart. Those are things you can't teach. But I've been swinging around wrestling rooms for over 30 years, and I've been in boxing gyms for over 20, and I've been in the street a lot longer than that. You can never tell. All you can say is that Kimbo is a tough man as far as his heart and his balls and his mind, but I don't know how polished he is."

During the fight, Abbott was just a slow and old version of Slice. Both were cut from the same cloth, but Slice was still in his athletic prime. He beat Abbott to the punch, and Abbott fell to the mat the first time it was convenient. Slice had passed his first test, but not everyone was impressed.

"If he [Kimbo] fought anybody who mattered, I would book that tomorrow," UFC president Dana White said. "Tank Abbott? I mean, come on. That guy was a bad UFC fighter. A friend of mine said he was out at a bar the week before that fight and he saw Tank there drinking beers. He went up to him and was like, 'Aren't you supposed to be fighting Kimbo soon?' . . . The fact is, Kimbo's not there yet. He would get destroyed. I heard he just got knocked out by Forrest Griffin last week in a sparring match after a kick to the head."[399]

It was true that Kimbo wasn't there — yet. He was a developing fighter with only two professional bouts. The perception and the reality were very different. Because of Elite xc's marketing, Kimbo was a main-event star, even as his skills dictated he should be fighting other developing fighters, not main event–worthy opponents. Fighters who trained with him thought he was learning quickly. He had a lifetime of fighting experience; it was just a matter of learning some specific MMA techniques and defenses.

Former UFC champion Kevin Randleman said, "I've trained with him out in Vegas, and he is a very good athlete and he wants to be the best. He's a street fighter, so throwing punches is nothing to him. He's game for that, but can you imagine what kind of beast Kimbo will be when he learns how to triangle choke a man? He isn't going to move around on the ground like the Nogueiras, but once he has knowledge he is going to be a beast. He's already a bad man, but can you imagine what he'll be like once he learns all that shit? Be ready for it, 'cause he's learning it. Learning MMA is like learning sex, and I'm learning new techniques every time I do it."[400]

Not everyone was so generous with praise. The truth was, Slice had garnered more money and notoriety than most veteran fighters had ever received. There was a feeling among many fighters that he hadn't earned it.

UFC legend Chuck Liddell said, "Kimbo's one of those guys who doesn't have any ground game. He's training and he's learning, but he's been built up as such a big star, and that's the thing that bothers me. People talk about him like he's the next great thing, when he really hasn't done anything. He's been built up because of the Internet and him beating a bunch of guys on the street. I could make some impressive knockout videos, too, if you let me walk outside and just punch people and knock them out — 'Hey you, come fight!' Fuck, we can make a highlight reel tomorrow and go around beating people up and talking about it — we could just go up to people and start dropping them — wow!"[401]

ELITE XC ON CBS

Elite xc was ecstatic to get the first major broadcast deal on network television. And the company brass knew, immediately, who they wanted to headline their first show. Kimbo Slice was going to be a network star. This flew in the face of years of hard-won MMA wisdom. For years, the UFC had taken pains to convince fans and decision makers that the UFC was more than a collection of thugs and street fighters. And now Kimbo Slice, famous for illegal underground brawls, was going to be Elite's poster boy. "In terms of recognition and perception, I believe May 31 is the biggest and single most important MMA fight card ever. It will forever change the landscape of the sport and how it is perceived," Gary Shaw, Elite xc live events president said. He had the opportunity to change the way the sport was perceived, and he was wasting that opportunity on an inexperienced fighter who was best known for beating up fat guys on the street.

"You've got to be kidding? The face of MMA? If so, then something is really wrong out there," UFC ring announcer Bruce Buffer said. "No disrespect for Kimbo, but he has a long way to go to prove to me he is the face of MMA. What you have is a marketable fighter who will be brought up carefully against distinctly selected opponents and showcased as a main event in the process. I wish him all the success, but he would be beaten by many UFC light-heavyweight and heavyweight fighters."[402]

Regardless of whether the move was wise, soon Kimbo Slice would be the most watched MMA fighter on the planet. The question would be, for how long? The UFC had drawn respectable audiences for some of its programming on Spike TV, but if Elite xc only drew UFC-level numbers on CBS, it would be considered a big disappointment. If the show thrived, the UFC would have its first real opposition. If the CBS show was a failure, the company would drown in its millions of dollars of debt. There were no other options. For Elite xc, it was sink or swim. That was a lot of pressure to put on Slice's broad shoulders.

His handpicked opponent was Englishman James Thompson. Thompson was a Pride veteran who didn't seem to be a threat to take Slice to the mat. Thompson would stand and trade blows with Kimbo, but his brittle jaw likely wouldn't stand up to the pressure of Slice's powerful punching.

Thompson gave Elite xc promoters a real scare by doing what they were sure he wouldn't — taking Kimbo to the mat. He got Slice down and landed more than 20 unanswered elbows and punches on the street fighter. Slice was lucky the referee didn't stop the fight, and luckier still when, minutes later, Thompson's grotesque cauliflower ear exploded, drenching the fighters with pus and blood. Slice pounced, rocking Thompson with punches and forcing a stoppage. The decision was controversial, with announcer Gus Johnson loudly complaining that the fight was called too soon, but Thompson was clearly out on his feet. Slice had survived, and, more importantly, had defeated an established pro in his prime for the first time.

The show was a hit. Even though it drew a relatively low 4.85 million viewers (more than 6.5 million saw Slice fight in the main event), it drew huge numbers in the all-important young male audience. Unfortunately for Elite xc, those fans were tuning in to see Kimbo Slice specifically, not MMA generally. The follow-up show, featuring a return match for the middleweight title between Robbie Lawler and Scott Smith, fell 43 percent in the ratings, attracting less than three million viewers. If Elite xc was going to survive as a television product, it would need Slice on every show.

A strong television platform was just the first piece in the puzzle. Any success in the ratings could only help so much. The company was still losing millions of dollars a quarter. Real progress would be made only if it could make the successful jump to pay-per-view, a move the company was exploring for 2009.

PUTTING THE I IN TEAM

The UFC's other major domestic competition was the International Fight League. The founders were an unlikely duo who had a new way of doing business.

Men with big muscles punching each other in the face always appealed to Gareb Shamus. He had made them his life's work, building an empire in the comic book industry and selling violence to young men. *Wizard* magazine, devoted to chronicling and commercializing the comic book business, was an incredible success. Shamus sold almost 200,000 copies of the magazine every single month, a magazine he had created as a 21-year-old kid still living at home with his parents. Now he was a media mogul with five magazines, one comic book line, and a successful pop culture convention circuit that drew hundreds of thousands of fans every year. *Wizard* had started out as a magazine about comic books, but had morphed into a lifestyle magazine for the trendy nerd. Its pages were filled with comics, video games, movies, and television shows, and whatever the hottest trend was going to be. *Wizard* didn't just predict the next big thing, it helped create it. Shamus was always looking for the next big idea, like Pokémon, that he would use to expand his empire. When his architect, of all people, lifelong martial artist Kurt Otto, came to him with an idea for an MMA magazine, Shamus was intrigued. After a little research, he saw the market was ripe, not just for a magazine, but for a new product. Shamus thought he and Otto should think bigger than a new MMA mag. It was time to promote real-life musclemen.

"Well, my whole life I've been dealing with superheroes; characters with exceptional abilities above and beyond the usual. When Kurt introduced me to the world of MMA, I immediately recognized that these guys have extraordinary skills and abilities that go beyond those of a typical human. As we went along, I understood exactly who these guys are and why fans admire what they are capable of, which is the ability to do what most people can't. These fighters are essentially real-life superheroes, and I get why they appeal to others," Shamus said.

When he went with Otto to see MMA live, he saw an audience that looked very familiar. This was his market, men 18-34, and he was confident in his ability to manipulate them out of their money. Shamus's readers were consumers first. They were more likely than others their age to buy the latest DVD or gadget. If anyone had an iPhone, it would be a *Wizard* reader. "When a new movie comes out, they are first in line," said Shamus. "Then they tell all their friends and go online and talk about it. They're a very influential group."[403]

He had sold them so many things, MMA would be easy. Shamus was all business, but the man who nurtured the idea of bringing the legitimacy of team sports to the world of MMA was Kurt Otto. "Kurt and I really are that chocolate and peanut butter situation. I have the business perspective. I run a nice company. Kurt is really, really smart about how to work with fighters, what he wants to see in the ring, and how that's going to operate," Shamus said. "From that perspective, we really have a great chemistry between us. He deals with his side of the business and I deal with my side of the business."[404]

Otto had been selling the idea for some time, ever since watching Mark Kerr self-destruct in the outstanding documentary *The Smashing Machine*. Otto's ideas went beyond the usual filching of the UFC game plan. He had a different plan: the biggest sports in America weren't individual contests, like tennis and golf, he reasoned. The team competition in football, basketball, and baseball really captured the interest of Americans. The benefit to the owners was twofold. Not only did the team focus take some bargaining power away from the fighter, but it also provided an easy way to infiltrate a market. Promoting an individual fight was hard, especially a fight between relative unknowns. But it was easy to sell Portland versus Seattle or Iowa versus Toronto. Otto also saw a sport in desperate need of reform. *The Smashing Machine* clearly showed how easy it could be for a fighter to fall victim to the lure of drugs, and how fragile the human body really was.

"There's no support system, no organization in place to take care of the fighters similar to what you see in other professional sports. Collegiate wrestlers, like Kerr, for example, really have nowhere to go afterward because the sport pretty much ends there," Otto said. "Some will be Olympic hopefuls, and might be able to continue in the sport for a few more years, and others may transition into coaching positions, but an overwhelming majority of these guys hit a dead end because there are no stepping-stones in place to advance their careers."[405]

Soon, Otto had some of the sport's true legends on board to serve as recognizable coaches and occasional superfight participants. Convincing them was easy, because they had an interest in staying involved with the sport they helped build, but had no real vehicle to do that. Zuffa had left a bad taste in their mouths. There was a time when you'd see every former heavyweight boxing champion at a big fight at Madison Square Garden or in Las Vegas. Zuffa didn't have time for its old champions, wouldn't even leave them a ticket at the box office for a show.

Former UFC champion Maurice Smith said, "Listen, before all of this came about I had made my mind up that I was out of this industry. I was disgusted with it. People would ask me if I saw that fight or knew this person and I didn't care or didn't want to know. These fighters who are up-and-comers now? I don't know any of them." Smith would be one of the IFL's original coaches for one of its teams, the Tigersharks. "I was involved with SEG and K-1. I fucking hate Zuffa and I fucking hate K-1. I never considered myself a Zuffa champion. I was an SEG champion. Zuffa never gave any of us that respect. I shouldn't have to call and ask for tickets to an event. I shouldn't have to negotiate the best deal for a trip. I'll bet Michael Jordan doesn't, or John Elway. That's what I mean; I am a former UFC heavyweight champion and a former K-1 champion. Do I get treated like one? Fuck no. These guys fighting in those organizations now have to sell their souls. One paycheck to the next. They don't care about these guys. All they care about is how much money they can make off of these athletes' blood and injuries. I'm not saying I want Zuffa to fail, because they have done a lot for the sport, but without these athletes they wouldn't be making all that money. They are not letting most of the fighters see any of it."[406]

Otto was committed to taking better care of fighters than promoters traditionally did. He offered health insurance and a solid income for guys who might otherwise have been working intermittently on one of the UFC's onerous "3/3" contracts. That's $3,000 to fight, $3,000 to win. The average IFL fighter made about $60,000 for five fights, fights that would take place in a ring. Shamus had decided that Americans were more comfortable with fights in a ring, it was what they had been conditioned to see by years of boxing and professional wrestling matches. This comfort zone would help attract sponsors to a sport they had typically viewed as too risky. Besides, the ring offered better sight lines for spectators and more and better shots for video production. The IFL would also offer a more sporting approach, eliminating elbow strikes in order to keep the action as blood-free and advertiser-friendly as possible.

"We make it a sport. We don't make it a spectacle. We take the elbows out," Bas Rutten said. "It's kind of cheating. How many people do you know who've gotten knocked out by an elbow? Not a lot. I really don't exaggerate when I say I know five. Ninety-nine percent of the cases [of fights ending with elbows] it's because they got cut."

While the pundits viewed organizing fighters into teams as revolutionary, it was only revolutionary to those who never wrestled in high school or college. What the IFL proposed were events where four teams would compete in two separate heads-up battles on the same day. The idea was comfortable to many MMA competitors who had grown up wrestling and were used to working with a team of guys in different weight classes. The IFL was clearly taking a different approach than the UFC, which was promoting individuals. But in reality, it was using the same concept: putting the brand ahead of the fighter. The UFC promoted the UFC much more heavily than it promoted any one fighter, to the point that "UFC" is synonymous with MMA for many fans. The IFL, hiding behind its fighter-friendly guise, was trying to do something similar by promoting the teams more heavily than the fighters. Instead of the IFL name, it was going to have 12 brands to promote: each of the 12 teams.

Otto said, "We believe, because of the individualism of the sport, if that man or woman gets hurt and blows their knee or shoulder out and they are done, if a popular individual is hurt, then that individual franchise is done. A team situation, though, with the five weight classes: lightweight, welterweight, middleweight, light heavy, and heavyweight . . . those five weights will always be on that team. If we took a legend in the business and made him the coach, you would have five individual fighters competing under that legend's system. There are all kinds of great camps that have their own specific style. Some have the ground jiu-jitsu style as their base, while others preach other styles. So we thought it would be exciting to bring these camps together in a league and find out which style has the better style and who is more dominant."[407]

Although he put on a grin in public, the UFC's Dana White was furious. He was indignant that the IFL had the gall to hire away two of his top talents. These weren't fighters — the IFL raid went deeper. They hired his vice president, Keith Evans, and top television producer Steven Tornabene. Not only that, but the IFL was getting some big-name fighters involved. MMA legends Bas Rutten, Pat Miletich, Renzo Gracie, and Maurice Smith coached the four original teams — the Anacondas, Silverbacks, Pitbulls, and Tigersharks.

The IFL still had eight coaching slots to fill, and White was going to make sure none of his guys got involved. These guys looked like serious competition, and White was going to try to eliminate them before they got too strong. Calls were made, and threats were issued. If you coached in the IFL, you were done with the UFC. "We are going to fucking crush these guys," White told UFC legend Pat Miletich. The Fertitta brothers had given him permission to go after the IFL with both barrels. "When the dust settles, anyone associated with the IFL would not be associated with the UFC."[408] Threats went far and wide: to Randy Couture, Ken Shamrock, and

Matt Hughes. If you had a fight camp, and you wanted guys in the UFC, you'd better not be working with the IFL.

"He had a vendetta with the International Fight League because he felt they had stolen concepts, or fights, or personnel, or paperwork, or something," Ken Shamrock said. "He tried to sue them. He lost in court, and that pissed him off. So then I was going to put an IFL team together [in 2006] where I was going to be a coach, which was not against my [UFC] contract. There were no rules that I couldn't corner my fighters in the IFL. I was going to go in the IFL and bring a team so some of my fighters could get some fights under their belt, get some exposure on TV, because they weren't going to get it with the UFC. They just weren't there yet. So Dana White tells me that if I go with the IFL, he will not use me. I was like, 'But I have a contract,' and he said, 'I'll rip it up.' I mean, I'm like, 'What are you talking about?' I thought, well, okay, I'm going to respect his wishes right now because I don't want to ruffle the feathers and maybe he'll get over this or whatever, so I did my thing later on and promoted my own shows, and then I put the team together. I get my fighters out there, they're getting TV exposure, and Dana White cuts my contract. He cuts my contract and doesn't give me a reason. Obviously, we know why. That's personal. It's nothing to do with business. . . . He was pissed off because he had some employees who went to work for the IFL. And he said this to other people about the IFL, that they're scumbags, that they're no good, and that they're thieves and he's going to crush them and that if anybody works for them, they won't fight in the UFC."[409]

Just as the IFL secured Fox Sports to air its inaugural show, the UFC sued the IFL, looking for an injunction to stop the show from taking place.

Miletich said, "They thought we were trying to steal trade secrets, but it's just fight promoting. I was forced to give a written statement stating the facts of a phone conversation I had with Mr. White. They're not very happy with each other. I'm stuck in the middle and I don't like it. If I'm watching a boxing match, I don't care if it's Bob Arum or Don King promoting it. Dana wants a bigger piece of the pie and our mentality is that we want a bigger pie. This league is just going to make a bigger fan base for the sport as a whole."[410]

Eventually the dust cleared from the IFL–UFC scuffle, and the company went about the business of putting on fight shows, securing broadcast deals with Fox Sports and MyNetwork television. The MyNetwork deal could have been huge. It was a large station with a broad reach, actually available in more homes than the UFC's home network, Spike TV.

You only get one chance to make a good first impression. And the IFL's first impression on MyNetwork TV was not good. It was a flashback to the greatest hits of SEG's Campbell McClaren, highlighting the "bone-crushing"action, insinuating that the losers would be leaving on a stretcher, and even playing a soundover of a heartbeat flatlining on top of video footage of a rear-naked choke. The show was promoting extreme violence and mayhem, exactly the opposite of the pure sport approach the IFL had championed. Not only did the show do a bad job of showing the skill level of the athletes and the multiple techniques that make MMA so great, it didn't even do a good job of showing the fights. The four-minute rounds were edited down, often in half, and they tried to jam too many fights into one program. The show had a solid debut, drawing 1.12 million viewers and doing well with the coveted 18-34 demographic, but fans were upset, and many indicated they would not give the show another chance. Instead of digging in their heels, the IFL did something unusual. It apologized.

"I would like to apologize on behalf of the IFL and MyNetwork if we upset or disappointed anybody in the MMA world. We're all about MMA being seen in a positive light," Otto said on MMA *Weekly Radio*. "In this instance we dropped the ball, and we promise to make everybody proud. We realize, as a group, that we made a mistake with some parts of the show, but we will learn from this and grow. We want to make this the best possible platform for the sport. The IFL would also like to apologize to our athletes and our coaches. We promise that it will be corrected, and we as a group will learn from this . . . I look at an organization like the UFC, and they have really accomplished some unbelievable things, and I don't want this to be viewed as something that sets the sport back five or ten years."

If ratings held steady, things would have likely been fine for the growing company as it looked for a more lucrative television deal. Instead, they plummeted. There were too many fights on the show, and the team concept was never developed in a way that made sense to the viewer: soon the audience was down to 730,000.

The league was struggling to make ends meet. It had gone public with a stock offering that brought in $24 million, but even this windfall wasn't enough to cover the losses. The IFL needed to make some changes, and brought in Showtime boxing guru Jay Larkin to right the ship. Larkin immediately set to work.

"We're making some major changes in the IFL, and we're making them in a very short amount of time. I've been on board now for a little less than two months, and one of the very first things I did when I came on was examine the original team concept," Larkin said. "As an observer, before I joined this organization, I felt that those teams were contrived. I learned that a large majority of the MMA public agreed. We had teams with contrived names fighting out of cities they had no connection to, in cities that neither team was from. That did not make a strong basis for fan support. The first major change I made was to address that, eliminate that. Those teams are now gone. We have changed that to camp-based competition. Now we have a Gracie team fighting a team fielded by Miletich Fighting Systems."

This was a change in name more than in spirit. Instead of connecting each team to a city, a city where they would likely never hold a live show, the teams were connected to one of the coaches or an already established camp. The team concept was safe.

"People said the team format doesn't work. Fighting is not a team sport. They don't realize that fighting is a team sport," Bas Rutten said. "Of course it's one-on-one once you step into the ring. But teams train together, and together everyone achieves more. [With the IFL] You're never short on sparring partners. There's structure. You need that, because every fighter lives on Brazilian time, they always show up late. On a team, one guy specializes in wrestling, another in striking. Normally those guys don't give their secrets away to training partners because they want to keep on using those techniques in order to beat them in training. Since this is a team, and they want their team to win, they now pass on those strengths. I truly believe this is the main reason you see the fighters of the IFL making so much improvement in such a short time."

The IFL shows were often delivering spectacular fights. They were establishing several homegrown stars, most notably Chris Hordecki. But the IFL was also spending way too much money.

"We have changed the pay structure because it's wonderful to be altruistic and good-hearted and support the fighters above all else," Larkin said. "But at the end of the day it's a business. We're a public corporation with a responsibility to the shareholders to make money. At some point we need to look at a way to become cash positive. It's no secret that we are not a cash positive company. . . . We're not talking about degrees of profit. We're not talking about shaving dollars off to make more money. That doesn't trouble me very much because we're just a year and a half old. If you compare where we are now to where the UFC was a year and a half into its existence, we look like Microsoft."

The cost of each card averaged $1.2 million, a cost that was prohibitive for a company with no significant revenue streams. The television deal with MyNetwork only paid the company $50,000 per show. The IFL would be forced to cut costs. Founding fathers Shamus and Otto were out, although Otto would stay on as a consultant.

"There were some missteps in the beginning," Larkin said. "One thing we don't want to do, that I don't want to do, is to perpetuate a mistake. Regardless of how honestly that mistake was made and the good intentions. We're looking at a lot of the things done out of necessity as a start-up organization that may not apply right now in this ever-changing MMA environment. We have to adapt and change with that."

Larkin and Otto knew that the fights needed to be live to make an impact. The shows on Fox Sports and MyNetwork were tape delayed. The hard-core MMA fan base that made up the bulk of the IFL's audience demanded live fights.

"You never want to watch a fight when you know the results already," Bas Rutten said. "For them to do every show live, I think, is going to be a real success."

The IFL was able to put its theory to the test. The 2007 IFL World Grand Prix aired as a one-hour special on MyNetwork TV. The rating was a colossal disappointment. The live show only attracted 450,000 viewers, and was eventually cancelled. Although the IFL was able to get its events on HDNet, that channel only reached a very small audience.

"I think if these guys don't start to figure out how to make money fairly soon, I don't care who you are, you're going to be in trouble," Dave Meltzer said. "The IFL, they're in a lot of trouble. I don't see how they can make it work at this point. When they didn't draw ratings on MyNetwork, that was the kiss of death. They needed to draw ratings there and they didn't. They had a good time slot on a good station."

Today, it looks like the IFL is dead. The company lost $21 million in 2007, and with CBS going with Elite XC and NBC signing a deal with Strikeforce, a white knight in the form of a television network never rode in to save the promotion. Dana White left the IFL a fitting obituary: "The IFL was gonna take us out last year, and they were offering stock options and other stuff to all of the fighters," White said. "Some guys we had long-term relationships with left and went there. A year later it's gone. . . . It's been like this for eight years. For eight years there's been a new three letters popping up and they buy a cage and they're in the business. We love this shit. This is what we do for a living. We love it. We do it 24/7 and nobody is going to beat us at it."

Venturing into the unknown, the UFC is well-positioned to continue its incredible success. Much of the credit for turning the promotion around has to go to President Dana White. White is bombastic and aggressive, and becoming a character on *The Ultimate Fighter* hasn't helped that. He's very passionate about his business, and is known to hold a grudge. This is a double-edged sword. His passion drives him to be a workaholic, constantly looking to make the UFC better and more successful. But it may also drive him to make rash statements and decisions. The UFC saw the ill effects of a White tirade when it lost Fedor Emelianenko. That could just be the beginning.

Whether he wants to or not, White may become the foul-mouthed fight promoter he plays on TV rather than a savvy operator heading a billion-dollar company. He was the perfect fit for a struggling company trying to make it. For the company trying to negotiate big deals with corporate and network partners, however, he may be the wrong man for the job. White is street educated, a former doorman, boxercise instructor, and fight manager. But to his boss, it's this experience with the hustle that makes him a great fit for this unique sport.

"Bottom line, and I've said this before, I don't think anybody could have accomplished what Dana has," Lorenzo Fertitta said. "It took somebody like Dana, who's got street smarts, who doesn't pull punches, who speaks his mind, who never bullshits, to do this. At the end of the day, if we had taken a Harvard MBA and hired him in 2001 to run this company, we'd probably be bankrupt right now . . .

I truly believe that Dana was put on the earth to run the UFC."[411]

The UFC has continued to grow. Although the company failed to score the long-promised HBO or network-TV deal, it has partnered with some impressive mainstream corporate entities. The Bud Light and Harley Davidson logos now adorn the Octagon, a far cry from Mickey's Malt Liquor or the Fertittas' own Gordon Biersch Brewing Company.

"The UFC has developed a huge following in recent years, and is wildly popular with the 21-34-year-old fans we want to reach," said Tony Ponturo, vice president, global media and sports marketing of Anheuser-Busch, Inc. "The number of people attending live events, buying the pay-per-views, and talking about the UFC around the water cooler continues to grow. It's just a great place for us to be."

The athletes are finding some success in the corporate world, as well. For a basketball star, a signature sneaker is a rite of passage into stardom. For an MMA fighter, it is unheard of. Rampage Jackson not only has his own shoe, from Osiris, he starred in a Nike commercial with Lebron James and others. The sport is going mainstream and corporate at a dizzying pace.

'ROID RAGE

Despite its tremendous growth and seemingly limitless potential, the UFC still faces some substantial obstacles. Like every other sport in America, the scourge of steroids lurks around the corner. The UFC is particularly vulnerable because its fighters are so out in the open. NFL football players are covered by uniforms, padding, and a helmet. Fighters stand exposed, in little more than their underwear. If someone has an unusual or suspicious physique, everyone knows. If someone has telltale signs, like acne or gynecomastia (unusually large male breast tissue — a common side effect of anabolic steroid use), it can't be hidden from the world. And MMA now has a history of significant steroid and illegal drug use. In California in 2007 there were 15 positive steroid tests in the 54 shows run there, including MMA legend Royce Gracie. Compare that to boxing, which saw just two positive tests in the course of 85 cards held during the same time frame.

"I'm very concerned. If I told you anything different, it would essentially be a lie. I am very concerned. When you look at the high number of positives it's really scary," California State Athletic Commission executive director Armando Garcia said on MMA *Weekly Radio*. "You know what, people are using drugs. People, unfortunately, are uneducated that drugs will kill you and will greatly damage your quality of life as you get older. And it's cheating. I don't care how much you candy coat it, it's cheating. Performance enhancing or not, an athlete who is looked up to by kids should not be using drugs. They need to grow up a little, you know?"

MMA clearly has a problem, and it exploded into the mainstream when UFC lightweight champion Sean Sherk tested positive for the anabolic steroid nandrolone after his first title defense against Hermes Franca. Franca, incredibly, was also dirty for the fight.

Sherk's case was particularly egregious because the UFC had just devoted a one-hour special to his training regimen. Sherk went on and on about his work ethic and his drive, the whole time knowing his nickname, "The Muscle Shark," and his conditioning program were fraudulent. They were seemingly the product of illegal drugs. Worse, he tried to deny any use after his positive test.

"This is not even about getting a suspension lifted or whatever, but I want to get this thing overturned," Sherk said. "I didn't take nandralone, and I don't want this crap on my record for the rest of my career. I've already lost everything . . . I'm just fighting for my dignity. . . . People look at me and the first thing they think is steroids. People don't realize how much training and how much effort and dedication goes into what I do. I train 12 weeks for a fight. I start dieting 12 weeks before my fights . . . the people who want to make these accusations are the lazy people who sit around eating Doritos and they figure the only way you could get in shape is if you do steroids."[412]

It was an award-worthy performance, with the fighter blaming the regulators, the media, and the fans. Everybody, apparently, was at fault — except for Sherk himself. Later, his story shifted. Sherk still wasn't to blame. He had taken a bad supplement; a tainted supplement had ruined his reputation; or maybe the lab was at fault. Fans turned on Sherk, and fighters did, too.

"That's one thing no one can ever say about me, you know? That I was a coward and took sports enhancement drugs, because I was afraid I was going to get my ass kicked in front of millions of people," B.J. Penn said. "To me, in this sport, it's fighting, it's mixed martial arts, and I feel there's too many athletes and not enough fighters. I think these people going in taking these sports enhancement drugs, they're not real fighters, they're athletes . . . I'm not going to say, 'Oh, Sean Sherk is doing something illegal!' I could care less about that. The guy was cheating, trying to steal somebody else's dream."[413]

The UFC's official response was to take a hard stand against steroids. "Our policy on fighters using steroids, illegal drugs, or any banned substance remains the same," Dana White said. "You cannot use them. It's not only unhealthy and unsafe, it is against the law. The UFC fully supports the commission's efforts, and we will continue to take measures that keep this sport clean and keep the athletes safe."

In reality, very little real harm was ever done to steroid users in the UFC. Recent test failures like Nate Marquardt were right back in the promotion when their state-enforced suspensions were served. And Sherk was not only welcomed back with open arms, he was actually given an immediate main event title shot against the new champion, B.J. Penn.

"Dana basically said that he wants to stay consistent with what he has done in the past. In the past, if you did it or not, you got the belt stripped," Sherk said. Sherk wasn't the first UFC champion to test positive for steroids. Tim Sylvia and Josh Barnett both lost the heavyweight title after positive tests. "He believes that I didn't do it, and I know that I didn't do it, but the belt gets stripped. That's just the way it is. . . . To be honest with you, I still feel like I am the champion. . . . To be the champion, you have to beat him, and no one has beaten me yet. I still feel like the champion because no one has beaten me."[414]

Nevada Changes the Game

Since the promotions can't be trusted to enforce a strict anti-drug policy, the State of Nevada found it necessary to step in. The tests the State had been running on the day of the fight were ultimately ineffective. A fighter could carefully time his steroid cycle in order to take advantage of the drug and be clean when the test was administered. And fighters, of course, are free to use drugs as often as they like when they aren't scheduled for a fight. The only way to really stop steroids was to test randomly, so a fighter never knew when the test was coming. This is exactly what Nevada regulators had in mind.

Athletic Commission chairman John Bailey, in a memo to all state licensees, explained Nevada's new policy: "In addition to the steroid and drug tests performed on contestants on fight night, the Commission will be requiring fighters licensed by the Commission, and applicants for such licensure, to submit to these tests when ordered by the Commission at other times during the year. (The costs of these tests will be paid by the Commission.) The process for selecting which fighters are required to submit to these tests will be based on: (1) a random selection; (2) some indication that a particular fighter may be using a prohibited substance; or (3) the fact that a fighter has previously tested positive for using a prohibited substance."

Nevada was getting serious about steroids. Marc Ratner's replacement as director of the Nevada State Athletic Commission, Keith Kizer, was committed to cleaning up the sport.

"If you want to come [to Nevada] to fight, you are subject to testing. No one is forced to come here and fight. It's a privileged license. It's no different from other medical tests, requiring guys to get MRIs, to get tested for HIV, or hepatitis B and C," Kizer said. "First you have a duty to your opponent and the sport to compete fairly. In addition to that, unlike Olympic sprinters such as Tim Montgomery or Marion Jones . . . you're hitting your opponent in the head in your competition. So, therefore, I think [combat-sports participants] should be held to an even higher standard than athletes like Olympic sprinters. It should be a really high standard."[415]

The new testing regime could change the face and physique of the sport if the commission is serious about enforcing it. Dave Meltzer said, "If they test and they test off season, most of the guys will clean up. It may take one or two guys getting caught for everyone to get the message. And there will always be some guys who figure out a way through it. But it will tone down usage a lot. Most of the guys are going to do what they need to do to compete. Most guys who fight in California are not on steroids. They may do growth [hormone], but if tests come for growth, then they won't do growth. These guys don't want to be suspended, because suspensions are harsh. It's not like professional wrestling or bodybuilding, where the guys are psychologically addicted. The guys in MMA who do steroids do it because they figure the other guy is. It's not like the steroids are part of their lives."

BUILDING STARS

The UFC's other big challenge is building new stars. The current crop of headliners is aging, and legitimate sports are not friendly to older athletes, with Randy Couture as the exception that proves the rule.

"Zuffa doesn't create stars," former UFC owner Bob Meyrowitz said. "Almost all of the big names that we have in the world of mixed martial arts today are people who fought for me. Randy Couture, who is an incredible athlete, happens to also be 44 or 45 years old. Tito, Liddell, all the names are all older fighters. One problem is, with very few exceptions, they haven't created a newer younger generation of stars."[416]

The UFC has found two superlative fighters in Georges St. Pierre and middleweight champion Anderson Silva. Neither, as yet, is a huge box office star. *The Ultimate Fighter* has been an effective tool for making stars, but the show's ratings are in a steady decline, and many of the star-making coaching slots were used on older fighters like Liddell and Couture, or on already established stars like Ken Shamrock. One of the few big stars the show has created is Dana White, and White loves his on-screen role.

"Vince McMahon and [former wrestling promoter] Eric Bischoff were the same way. They became completely different people when they got on television, too. Obviously [White] likes being a TV character. I see a lot of similarities between him and Vince McMahon and Eric Bischoff," Meltzer said. "And it scares me. Because I don't want to see him end up being like Eric Bischoff. Because then there will be no UFC in two years. And it can happen. I saw it with WCW. Staying on top can be pretty damn hard. They need to create that second generation of drawing cards. This year [2008] will be the big test. If people just want to see Chuck Liddell and Randy Couture, they're in a lot of trouble."

Finding a star America can get behind is more art than science, and the seventh season of *The Ultimate Fighter* was a critical time for the UFC. The light heavyweight champion, Quinton Jackson, had star potential, but fans didn't seem to have forgiven him for beating fan-favorite Chuck Liddell. Forrest Griffin had already charmed fans on the first season of the show. Now he needed them to take him seriously as a challenger for the title.

"The thing with Forrest is, he's real, real popular but at some point people are going to realize that Forrest is never going to be a world champion," Meltzer said prior to the show. "If Forrest goes and beats Quinton

Jackson, then Forrest will be a drawing card. The thing with Forrest is that he doesn't have to win every fight to be a star. As long as Forrest fights tough, and has a good fight, to him that's as big as a win. Because people don't really expect him to be a world champion. They just expect him to be a fun fighter to watch."

The show continued its downward spiral, falling in the ratings for the fourth season in a row. While Jackson and Griffin both seemed to be likeable, they did little to build interest in their fight at UFC 86 on July 5, 2008. The company tried its best to build tension between the two, but both were laid-back professionals. It was thought that Griffin and Jackson would captivate audiences with their infectious personalities, but it just didn't seem to work. The two men seemed to like each other, perhaps a little too much, and the spark just wasn't there for a compelling grudge match. To Griffin, that was missing the point. "Whether you like the guy or hate him, it doesn't matter," Griffin said. "You're still going to hit him as hard as you can. It doesn't really matter how you feel about him."

Even without histrionics or hatred, this was a big fight. And in big fights, Forrest Griffin delivered. When the UFC needed a great fight, when *The Ultimate Fighter* concept was still hanging by a thread with Spike TV executives, Griffin delivered.

And it wasn't just Griffin's crowd-pleasing style that made him a big star. He and the UFC also carefully manufactured an everyman persona. The television Griffin is always cracking jokes and is the model of the self-deprecating good guy. Sometimes that shell cracks a little, like when he couldn't hide his dismay about being back on *The Ultimate Fighter*. Despite being a product of the reality television show, Griffin hated it.

"It was annoying. I didn't really like cameras or having to be certain places," Griffin said. "It felt like you always had to be somewhere doing something stupid you didn't want to be doing."

That's the real Forrest Griffin — the guy who is notoriously difficult with reporters and single-mindedly ambitious. But that's just real life. The TV character Forrest Griffin was more important here, and he was finally getting a title shot.

"It's the biggest fight of my life," Griffin said. "I realize that. And I've done everything right for it. So I've got no doubts and no worries. Quinton makes fun of me because I don't hit that hard, but he doesn't realize I was a black belt in tae kwon do, and if you hit too hard you get penalized for it. So I'm working on the hitting harder thing."

He might have joked about it, but Griffin's first title shot was a big deal. He was Zuffa's first homegrown star, and fans watched him grow from an unrefined brawler taken to the brink by Stephan Bonnar into a slick professional capable of beating the world's best in his weight class. Griffin's growth as a fighter was astronomical. In 2005, he and Bonnar were as evenly matched as two fighters could be, mirror images with roughly the same skill sets. By the time they had their rematch in 2006, Griffin had moved light years beyond Bonnar. By the time he was in the cage with Mauricio "Shogun" Rua, Griffin was hardly even recognizable as the guy who went to war on the TUF finale. He was a different fighter: his footwork was great and his striking had developed to the point that he could hit without being whacked back.

Even though he beat the world's best in Rua, Griffin realized that Jackson would be his biggest challenge.

"Without a doubt," Griffin said. "He has power. You know he hits hard. I don't have the best chin in the world." Jackson hits harder, has better wrestling, and even showed improved cardio, an area where Griffin had hoped to have an advantage. "The one thing that I thought maybe I could exploit in Jackson was his conditioning, but he went five rounds with a guy who wears you down [Dan Henderson]."

For his part, Griffin was ready for five rounds of action. He was well-known as the hardest working man in the business, and adapted his routine to prepare for the two extra rounds. His training camp went exceptionally well (except for being knocked out by Wanderlei Silva in a sparring session), and Griffin was prepared. Things didn't go as smoothly for Jackson.

"Everybody knows the truth. They watch *The Ultimate Fighter,*" Jackson said. "I got fat as hell, I took nine months off, not just from fighting. I took nine months off from training. I went to camp and started training nine weeks out, which is perfect. But training so hard, with so much weight to lose, I got injured very badly in camp."

The training camp seemed cursed. First, Jackson's Muay Thai instructor was injured. Then Jackson broke trainer Juanito Ibarra's ribs with body shots and had no one to hold the pads for him. And then the injuries came:

elbow, hamstring, and ankle. Although he was ready by fight night, most of his camp was spent getting into fighting shape. Little, if any, time was spent specifically preparing for Griffin. Jackson was dismissive of Griffin, and indicated that he didn't think his fellow coach was a worthy challenger. It was an assumption he would pay for in the cage.

The fight itself was exceptionally close. Griffin won a decision after five rounds of pitched battle. Jackson landed the consistently harder shots, but Griffin was more active, especially with debilitating leg kicks.

"I'm not the super submission guy. Unfortunately, I don't hit [hard]. I'm not a super knockout guy," Griffin said. "I could have tried to hit Quinton a little more, but the thing is, he's just got so much power. I tried to tink-tink-tink him away. I had to move instead of standing in front of him and taking that big shot. I'm not a feared guy, but I'm going to fight you for 25 minutes. Whoever you are, anybody at 205. I'm not going to break, I'm not going to quit. It's the same shit, I always say . . . the one thing I've got is that I'm going to fight you until the end like a dog."

Jackson was gracious in the ring after the fight, but he and his corner were furious, going so far as to challenge the decision with the Nevada State Athletic Commission.

"It was a close fight, but I thought I won," Jackson said. "I thought I did enough to win. I felt like I won the first round. I feel like I won the third round, and I felt like I won the fourth round. I felt like he won the . . . second and fifth. That's how I feel, but I'm not a judge."

The result was everything the UFC could have possibly wanted. Griffin and Zuffa had grown together. Now he was the champion, a huge potential star, and the company was thriving. Not only that, but the fight had been so close, and so fun to watch, that a ready-made rematch was just waiting in the wings to draw even bigger money. But the shock of losing after three undefeated years pushed Jackson over the edge.

RAMPAGE ON A RAMPAGE

An MMA star in trouble with the law was hardly shocking news. As might be expected, men who sought violence in the cage also had plenty of drama in their real lives, and MMA fighters were being arrested on a fairly regular basis as the sport grew and the fighter base increased in number. But Quinton "Rampage" Jackson? Fans had invited Jackson into their homes via *The Ultimate Fighter*. He seemed so laid-back and chill. How could this happen?

"For one week, I couldn't sleep because of this fight . . . I couldn't eat. I was getting kind of depressed," Jackson told Throwdown TV. Lack of sleep and driving don't mix, and when a tired and delusional Jackson got behind the wheel of his monster truck ten days after losing his title, he allegedly went on an automotive rampage, terrorizing fellow drivers and pedestrians.

According to the Costa Mesa, California, police report: "An officer saw Jackson weaving in and out of traffic with a flat front left tire, speaking on his cell phone. The officer activated his lights and siren and initiated a traffic stop. Jackson ignored the officer and continued southbound on 17th [Street] weaving in and out of traffic to avoid being stopped. Jackson drove over the raised center portion of the roadway at Cabrillo Avenue. He lost control and drove up onto the sidewalk, causing pedestrians to flee for their lives. Jackson regained control and continued southbound in the north-bound lanes of Newport Boulevard. As he crossed through the intersection with 17th Street, he collided with a vehicle that was legally in the intersection. Jackson continued southbound on Newport Boulevard, running several red lights. The rubber from his left tire began to disintegrate at the PCH [Pacific Coast Highway] overpass. Jackson continued southbound onto the Balboa Peninsula, running several more red lights and causing pedestrians to flee in terror. Jackson's vehicle finally came to a stop at 18th Street and Newport Boulevard, in the city of Newport Beach. Costa Mesa police officers took him into custody without incident.

"Jackson was transported to the Costa Mesa City Jail and booked for felony evading, reckless driving, and hit-and-run. He was transported to the Orange County Jail and is being held in lieu of a $25,000.00 bail."

When his former champion was arrested at gunpoint, Dana White flew in from Las Vegas to arrange bail. The next day, friends were concerned about Jackson's continued erratic behavior, and police were called to take Jackson in for a mental evaluation.

"Mentally he wasn't there," a confidential source told SI.com's Josh Gross. "It was almost as if he was possessed. He heard voices. He thought he was a God."

Three days later, Jackson was released and the healing could begin. The emotional breakdown, it turned out, was as much physical as it was mental.

"He was hanging out by the pool and he was fasting. He wasn't drinking, he wasn't eating, but he was drinking energy drinks," Dana White said. "You saw what happened on TV, the problems that he had. They took him in for psychiatric evaluation for over 72 hours and what they came back with was that there was nothing wrong with him mentally. It was physically — he was exhausted, he had severe dehydration, and that caused something called delirium."

A split with longtime trainer Juanito Ibarra after the fight may have led to Jackson's loss of control. Ibarra was a father figure to Jackson, but after the fight Jackson railed to friends about a "wolf in sheep's clothing" inside his camp. "I'm devastated by what he's been through, and some of the things I've heard," said Ibarra. "I've not sat down with Quinton to this day to discuss things. I pray for his well-being, and if I helped Quinton out a little bit with his growth in the sport, then I've been very blessed and honored to do that. I love this kid with all my heart, and I wish him nothing but the best. . . . This is a kid I've been with for almost four years. I have nothing but love and support for him. All I want for Quinton right now is what's best for him. Whatever he needs from me, in any way, I'm here for him and always have been."

Just as the saga seemed to be reaching an end, it took a dramatic turn for the worse. One of the alleged hit-and-run victims was an expectant mother. She lost her baby after the crash, and held Jackson responsible. What seemed to be a traffic incident was now a tragedy. Jackson and the UFC seemed to take it all in stride. Jackson made a public appearance at UFC 87 and laughed and joked with the media and fans.

"That was the worst mistake I ever made," Jackson said. "Now Dana is all over my back all the time. 'Did you eat? Did you sleep? You drinking water?' Acting like I'm two years old."

Jackson didn't address the woman whose life he had allegedly shattered. Dana White did, and didn't make even a perfunctory attempt at expressing sorrow for a family's loss. Like the worst fans on MMA message boards, White was sure this was just a naked grab for money.

"That one is out there like, 'He hit her and she lost her baby,'" White said. "It was a week later. He knocked her mirror off her car. Rampage said, and he'll tell you when you talk to him, 'I care about everybody. I care about all life. I would never hurt anybody.' That's the way he is. Now he's in a situation where somebody's trying to sue him and make some money . . . this is not a criminal thing. No way. I'm no lawyer and I'm no judge. This stuff will be worked out in court."

CHALLENGERS TO THE THRONE

Jackson and a lack of new stars weren't the only issues plaguing the UFC. Beyond making stars, the UFC will need to keep the stars it already has to remain the industry leader. Andrei Arlovski and Tito Ortiz both left the company, embracing the clothing company Affliction's new promotion, which also featured former heavyweight champions Fedor Emelianenko and Tim Sylvia. The UFC had never faced a serious domestic competitor, but that could happen if Elite XC takes off on CBS, Affliction finds a home on television, or if HDNet is able to expand its presence on cable systems nationwide. Dallas Mavericks owner Mark Cuban also runs HDNet, which has used MMA to attract a growing list of subscribers to his fledgling network.

"Now the big, scary guy is Mark Cuban. Mark Cuban is coming in. Mark Cuban doesn't give a shit about mixed martial arts. Mark Cuban has dumped millions of dollars into HDNet and he wants subscribers," White said. "He's a businessman. He'll build up the subscribers and sell it to Comcast and get out. I think he's passionate about basketball, [but] I don't think he's interested in mixed martial arts, and he'll be on to the next business venture."

White contends that Cuban doesn't know much about the fight game. That's true, but he's hired longtime fighter Guy Mezger to help show him the ropes.

"A lot of the fighters think Mark is going to come in and start spending a billion dollars on these shows. Mark became a billionaire because he's a freaking genius, not because he's going to throw good money after bad," Mezger said. "Our intention is to start slow, have good cards, consistent cards, and grow. Every show will be a little better, a little better, a little better, until we become a real contender. Too many guys come in and are a flash in the pan. They talk a good shop and then they are out. Our intention is to come in, start slow, and build up an audience. We have a little jump-start with the UFC's success. We'd like to grow and then eventually build our own stars and create a desirable pay-per-view."

It's a sensible plan. If it works, the UFC could be in for a true test. The

UFC currently only employs three of sherdog.com's top ten heavyweight fighters. There is plenty of talent up for grabs, and more on the way every day. Some of the sport's top stars will be willing to test the market, and major names like Tito Ortiz may soon be fighting somewhere other than the Octagon. A new competitor emerged on July 19, 2008, when the clothing company Affliction made a huge splash on the North American scene. The company spent wildly, and its first show was a star-studded affair headlined by Fedor Emelianenko taking on recently deposed UFC heavyweight champion Tim Sylvia. The card featured top talent from top to bottom, including Vitor Belfort, Matt Lindland, Josh Barnett, Andrei Arlovski, and Ben Rothwell.

The UFC was concerned enough by this new competition that it arranged a last-minute *Ultimate Fight Night* special to air in competition on Spike TV. It even decided to give away a fight with its top pound-for-pound fighter, middleweight champion Anderson Silva.

"It's just an example of how they want to control everything, but at the same time it's flattering, as well," Affliction vice president Tom Atencio said. "I guess they do view us as a threat . . . absolutely."

Despite the UFC's best efforts, Affliction drew more than 100,000 pay-per-view buys. It wasn't enough to make the show profitable, but it was a surprising figure for a show that didn't receive any television hype. The company also produced a great show, filled with compelling matchups and competitive fights. If HBO, long in the market for an MMA show of its own, needed proof that a group was capable of putting on a major-league show opposite the UFC, this was it. Russian Fedor Emelianenko dispatched Tim Sylvia in just 37 seconds and immediately became a marketable star.

"I was amazed at how good he is," Sylvia said. "The guy's a stud. I don't think he's human. He's incredible. I don't think anybody's going to beat him for a while."

The next logical matchup for Emelianenko was the long awaited battle with Randy Couture, but that fight became more unlikely than ever when Couture returned to the UFC's open arms. After an 11-month legal dispute, Couture was running short on money and time: after all, he was 45 years old. He agreed to fight Brock Lesnar at UFC 91 (November 15, 2008), for the heavyweight championship at the MGM Grand in Las Vegas.

"It feels pretty damn good. I feel like I've been walking under a black cloud for a year. So to have the cloud dissipate and walk in some sunshine feels pretty nice," Couture said. "There were some compromises made on both sides. I think, overall, we're both happy and we both want to move forward in a positive way."

Couture recognized that the UFC was more than willing to battle him in court — until he was either broke or too old to fight. Despite all the harsh words they'd exchanged, Dana White was thrilled to have "the Natural" back.

"I like Randy, I always have. This whole thing never made sense to me," White said. "We've never had that kind of relationship where I was like 'There's that fucker. I don't want to talk to him . . .' I never felt that way about him ever."

Couture, of course, was still interested in taking on Emelianenko — but he was no longer afraid that *not* fighting the Russian star would change the way fans thought about his career.

"I don't think anything's missing from my legacy. I could retire today and be perfectly fine," Couture said. "I'm fighting because I love to fight. Do I want to fight Fedor? Absolutely. Most people consider him the number one heavyweight. I want to take that away from him."

White indicated a willingness to sign the fight to appease his sensitive champion, but he clearly wasn't willing to violate another company's contract to make it happen: "[Couture's] made it very clear how bad he wants to fight Fedor. We're going to do everything in our power to make a Fedor fight happen, but we're not going to mess with anybody's contracts. He's under contract right now to another promotion. Obviously everyone knows how crazy we are about protecting our contracts and we would never do that to anybody else."

The most obvious return bout for Couture was with UFC interim heavyweight champion Antonio Nogueira, to reunify the title. Nogueira, unfortunately, was tied up with the next season of *The Ultimate Fighter,* and already scheduled to fight fellow coach Frank Mir in December 2008. Rising to the challenge, White faced down critics by matching his champion with Brock Lesnar.

With just three pro fights under his belt, Lesnar leap-frogged established pros like Fabricio Werdum for his shot at the title; and some reporters criticized the move, saying he was too inexperienced to have earned the privilege. Ironically, Couture himself had received *his* first title shot after just three fights. But the bottom line was simple: White knew that what Lesnar lacked in experience, he more than made up for in potential and star power.

"At the end of the day, the great thing about the UFC is that we aren't caught up in all the boxing political bullshit," White said. "So we can basically put on fights the fans want to see. I can tell you right now, and mark my words, Couture and Lesnar will be the biggest fight in UFC history."

While talk focused on Couture's potential fight with Emelianenko, Lesnar thought it made more sense to focus attention on the match at hand. The Russian star was mostly unknown to UFC fans, while he was now one of the promotion's top drawing cards.

"I'm hearing all this talk about Fedor Emelianenko. Who gives a shit about Fedor? I'm fighting Randy Couture. That's what this press conference is about," Lesnar roared. "I don't give a damn about Fedor. I'm tired of hearing about fucking Fedor. Randy Couture is fighting Brock Lesnar on November 15th. His number one concern should be Brock Lesnar. You want that fight, I don't give a damn. But I'm sick and tired of sitting on the phone and listening about Fedor. He's not with the company and he might not ever be with the company. So who fucking gives a shit?"

Affliction, however, was still gambling that people did care about Emelianenko. . . . They postponed their second show until early 2009, waiting for the Russian to be available. Clearly, his popularity would help decide whether the company lived, or died.

It's a wide-open playing field, but one thing cannot be denied. It's a game worth playing because of Zuffa and the UFC's dedication to the sport and the fans. With a long-term contract with Spike TV, experienced promoters and matchmakers like Dana White and Joe Silva, and an enterprising and aggressive ownership group in the Fertitta brothers, the UFC seems likely to continue its growth. SEG and Rorion Gracie planted the seed, and Zuffa provided plenty of fertilizer. Now MMA is primed to spread and grow all around the world.

ENDNOTES

1. *Full Contact Fighter*, 07/02
2. Graciemag.com, 07/11/07
3. *Kodokan Judo*, Jigoro Kano, Kodansha International
4. The History of Kodokan Judo, http://www.judoinfo.com/jhist.htm
5. *The Gracie Way*, Kid Peligro, Invisible City Press
6. *Full Contact Fighter*, 01/03
7. *Playboy* (Brazilian Edition), 02/01
8. *Mastering JuJitsu*, Renzo Gracie and John Danaher, Human Kinetics Publishers, 2003
9. *Grappling Masters*, Jose M. Fraguas, Unique Publications
10. *Judoka*, National Film Board of Canada, 1965
11. *Kakuto Striking Spirit*, 05/01/02
12. *Global Training Report*, 12/01
13. *Tatame Magazine*, 1997
14. *Full Contact Fighter*, 01/03
15. Graciemag.com, 04/20/06
16. *Grappling Masters*, Jose M. Fraguas, Unique Publications
17. *Gracie Magazine* no. 109, 03/16/06
18. *Brawl*, Erich Krauss, ECW Press, 2002
19. *Full Contact Fighter*, 05/2002
20. http://www.gladiatorchallenge.com/news.asp?ID=13
21. *Pro Wrestling Torch* no. 334, 3/13/95
22. *Brawl*, Erich Krauss, ECW Press, 2002
23. *Grappling Masters*, Jose M. Fraguas, Unique Publications, 2003
24. *Pro Wrestling Torch* no. 335, 3/20/95
25. *Full Contact Fighter*, 03/2000
26. Ken Shamrock Shoot Interview, RF Video
27. UFC Classics Volume I, Hall of Fame Interview, Lions Gate, 2006
28. *FIGHT Magazine*, October/November 2007
29. UFC Classics Volume I, Hall of Fame Interview

30. Ken Shamrock Shoot Interview
31. *No Holds Barred*, 02/04/2008
32. Ken Shamrock Shoot Interview
33. *Inside the Lion's Den*, Ken Shamrock, Tuttle Publishing, 1997
34. UFC Classics Volume I, Hall of Fame Interview
35. *Full Contact Fighter*, 05/2002
36. *Brawl*, Erich Krauss, ECW Press, 2002
37. *Beyond the Lion's Den*, Ken Shamrock and Erich Krauss, Tuttle Publishing, 2005
38. Ifl.tv, 12/22/06
39. *Inside the Lion's Den: The Life and Submission Fighting System of Ken Shamrock*, Ken Shamrock and Richard Hanner, Tuttle Publishing, 1998
40. *Full Contact Fighter*, 03/2002
41. *Beyond the Lion's Den*, Ken Shamrock and Erich Krauss, Tuttle Publishing, 2005
42. *Full Contact Fighter*, 11/2000
43. Ifl.tv, 12/22/06
44. *No Holds Barred*, Clyde Gentry, Milo Books Ltd., 2002
45. *Full Contact Fighter*, 03/03
46. http://www.ultimate-fighter.ca/Forum/viewtopic.php?id=3202
47. *Pro Wrestling Torch*, 01/02/95
48. UFC *Ultimate Warriors: The Top 10*, Jeremy Wall, ECW Press, 2005
49. *Pro Wrestling Torch*, 12/24/94
50. http://www.sportsline.com/print/mmaboxing/story/10722212
51. UFC *Classics: UFC V*, Lions Gate, 2006
52. UFC *Classics: UFC V*
53. *No Holds Barred* podcast, 02/04/08
54. UFC *Ultimate Warriors: The Top 10*, Jeremy Wall, ECW Press, 2005
55. http://www.martialtalk.com/forum/showthread.php?t=11784
56. http://www.aikidojournal.com/article.php?articleID=90
57. *Full Contact Fighter*, 05/02
58. *From Sport to Spectacle*, CNBC
59. *Off The Record*, February 2008
60. UFC *Ultimate Warriors*, Jeremy Wall, ECW Press, 2005
61. http://www.onzuka.com/news_2001July2.html
62. *No Holds Barred*, Clyde Gentry, Milo Books Ltd., 2002
63. *No Holds Barred* podcast, 02/04/08
64. *PWTorch Newsletter* no. 334, 05/13/95
65. *Brawl*, Erich Krauss, ECW Press, 2002
66. *PWTorch Newsletter* no. 334, 05/13/95
67. *No Holds Barred* podcast, 02/04/08
68. Ken Shamrock Shoot Interview
69. *Beyond the Lion's Den*, Ken Shamrock, Tuttle Publishing, 2005
70. *New York Times*, "Outcast Gladiators Find a Home: New York," 01/15/97

71. *New York Times*, "Giuliani to try to prevent "'Extreme Fighting' Match," 01/01/97

72. *No Holds Barred* podcast, 07/19/06

73. http://www.geocities.com/capitolhill/lobby/8271/PMC/bjm.html

74. *Daily News*, "The Media: ABC Leads a Charmed Life," 06/06/97

75. *Iceman: My Fighting Life*, Chuck Liddell, Dutton, 2008

76. http://www.thesweetscience.com/boxing-article/1716/joke-almost-ended-ali-career/

77. http://ejmas.com/jcs/jcsdraeger_alivsinoki.htm

78. http://www.scientificwrestling.com/public/320.cfm?sd=2

79. http://www.thesweetscience.com/boxing-article/4326/talking-boxing-angelo-dundee/

80. http://www.thesweetscience.com/boxing-article/1716/joke-almost-ended-ali-career/

81. http://www.puroresu.com/wrestlers/gotch_karl/article.html

82. http://www.sportsline.com/mmaboxing/story/10443463/1

83. http://www.charleston.net/news/2007/aug/05/god_professional_wrestling_gotch_dead_at12244/

84. *The Authoritative Encyclopedia of Scientific Wrestling: Volume III*, Jake Shannon, Lulu.com, 2004

85. Ken Shamrock Shoot Interview

86. http://www.Pridefc.com/Pride2005/index.php?mainpage=news&news_id=145

87. http://www.onthemat.com/articles/Rickson_Gracie_Interview_3_10_13_2005.html

88. *The Gracie Way*, Kid Peligro, Invisible Cities Press, 2003

89. http://www.boutreviewusa.com/Columns/02maeda03.html

90. http://www.japaninc.com/article.php?articleID=1026

91. http://nation.bodoglife.com/fight-files/ground-and-pound-mark-coleman-interview-part-i-80862.html

92. *Brawl*, Erich Krauss, ECW Press, 2002

93. http://www.fcfighter.com/don-frye-0305.htm

94. *No Holds Barred: Evolution*, Clyde Gentry, Archon, 2001

95. Sherdog.com, 11/18/2000

96. *UFC's Ultimate Warriors*, Jeremy Wall, ECW Press, 2005

97. *No Holds Barred: Evolution*, Clyde Gentry, Archon, 2001

98. *No Holds Barred: Evolution*, Clyde Gentry, Archon, 2001

99. http://www.ifl.tv/News-07Apr27-Smith-Ready-For-Comeback.html

100. *Brawl*, Erich Krauss, ECW Press, 2002

101. *UFC Ultimate Behind the Scenes Volume 1*, Van Gold Productions, 1997

102. *UFC's Ultimate Warriors*, Jeremy Wall, ECW Press, 2005

103. *UFC Ultimate Behind the Scenes Volume 1*, Van Gold Productions, 1997

104. *UFC's Ultimate Warriors*, Jeremy Wall, ECW Press, 2005

105. *Full Contact Fighter*, 11/2000
106. *No Holds Barred: Evolution*, Clyde Gentry, Archon, 2001
107. *Beyond the Lion's Den*, Ken Shamrock, Tuttle Publishing, 2005
108. *Winners Dead or Alive* vol. 1, 2000
109. *Winners Dead or Alive* vol. 1, 2000
110. *Gong Kakutougi* no. 91, 11/99, (translated by Kondo Yoko)
111. *Pride: Decade*, 2007
112. *The Gracie Way*, Kid Peligro, Invisible Cities Press, 2003
113. ibid.
114. *Full Contact Fighter*, 04/2000
115. *Full Contact Fighter*, 06/2000
116. *Full Contact Fighter*, 04/2000
117. *Winners Dead or Alive*, vol. 1, 11/2000
118. *The Gracie Way*, Kid Peligro, Invisible Cities Press, 2003
119. *Winners Dead or Alive*, vol. 1, 11/2000
120. *Gong Kakutogi Plus*, vol. 9, 11/2000
121. *Kakutogi Tsushin* no. 254, 06/11/2000
122. ibid.
123. *Kakutogi Tsushin* no. 254, 06/11/2000
124. *SRSDX*, no. 27, 08/10/2000
125. *Pride: Decade*, 2007
126. *60 Minutes*
127. *Playboy* (Brazilian Edition), 02/01
128. *SRSDX*, no. 38, 01/25/01
129. *SRSDX*, no. 38, 01/25/01
130. No Holds Barred with Eddie Goldman, podcast, 07/19/06
131. *Full Contact Fighter*, 02/01
132. No Holds Barred with Eddie Goldman, podcast, 07/19/06
133. *Hartford Courant*, 01/11/02
134. *Full Contact Fighter*, 11/2000
135. *Full Contact Fighter*, 12/2000
136. http://forum.kungfumagazine.com/forum/archive/index.php/t-2394.html
137. *Full Contact Fighter*, 12/2000
138. *Full Contact Fighter*, 01/02
139. *Full Contact Fighter*, 07/01
140. *Iceman: My Fighting Life*, Chuck Liddell, Dutton, 2008
141. http://www.evancarmichael.com/Famous-Entrepreneurs/1166/The-Ultimate-Fighting-Champion-Dana-White-is-Born.html
142. *Business Nation*, CNBC
143. *Full Contact Fighter*, 07/02
144. *Time Magazine*, "Gambling in Texas," Monday, Jan. 12, 1953
145. *Time Magazine*, "Texas Pleasure Dome," Monday, Jul. 09, 1951

146. http://www.happyhareonline.com/happyhare-88.htm

147. *Galveston: A History of the Island*, Gary Cartwright, 1998, TCU Press

148. http://abclocal.go.com/ktrk/story?section=local&id=5390951

149. *Galveston: A History of the Island*

150. *Full Contact Fighter*, 04/01

151. *Wrestling For Fighting: The Natural Way*, Randy Couture, Victory Belt Publishing, 2007

152. *1 on 1 With Randy Couture*, The Fight Network

153. *Brawl*, Erich Krauss, ECW Press, 2002

154. *No Holds Barred*, Clyde Gentry, Milo Books, 2002

155. *1 on 1 with Randy Couture*, The Fight Network

156. *Full Contact Fighter*, 05/01

157. http://sfuk.tripod.com/interviews_04/randy_couture.html

158. *Full Contact Fighter*, 07/02

159. http://www.mmaringreport.com/text-interviews/ufc-president-dana-white-7.html

160. http://primetimefighters.net/interview2.htm

161. *Brawl*, Erich Krauss, ECW Press, 2002

162. http://www.entrepreneur.com/ufc/index.html

163. *Brawl*, Erich Krauss, ECW Press, 2002

164. *Brawl*, Erich Krauss, ECW Press, 2002

165. Shoot Interview with Ken Shamrock

166. 411mania.com, 7/17/07

167. Thesportscritics.com, 8/14/05

168. *Brawl*, Erich Krauss, ECW Press, 2002

169. *Full Contact Fighter*, 06/2000

170. *Ultimate Miletich*, UFC pay-per-view

171. *Irish Whip Fighting*, 10/31/07

172. thaformula.com, 05/07

173. *Full Contact Fighter*, 01/02

174. *Fight Magazine*, October/November 2007

175. *Mixed Martial Arts: The Book of Knowledge*, B.J. Penn, Victory Belt Publishing, 2007

176. *Full Contact Fighter*, 09/2000

177. *Brawl*, Erich Krauss, ECW Press, 2002

178. *Mixed Martial Arts: The Book of Knowledge*, B.J. Penn, Victory Belt Publishing, 2007

179. *Full Contact Fighter*, 04/03

180. *Full Contact Fighter*, 01/02

181. thaFormula.com, 05/07

182. *Full Contact Fighter*, 02/02

183. thaFormula.com, 05/07

184. *Full Contact Fighter*, 10/02
185. *Beyond the Lion's Den*, Ken Shamrock, Tuttle Publishing, 2005
186. http://www.kenshamrock.com/news.php?id=116/articles/news
187. *1 on 1 With Tito Ortiz*, The Fight Network
188. Relentless: "Tito Ortiz -vs- Ken Shamrock: The Untold Truth Behind UFC's Legendary Feud," Progressive Arts Media Distribution, 2006
189. http://www.baltimoresun.com/sports/bal-ortizqa1218,0,3366285.story?coll=bal-sports-headlines
190. *1 on 1 With Tito Ortiz*, The Fight Network
191. *The Ultimate Fighter*, Season 3, Episode 1
192. *Fight World* Video Magazine
193. Wrestlingobserver.com, Alex Marvez interviews Dana White, 4/27/03
194. *Full Contact Fighter*, 11/02
195. http://www.boxinginsider.com/mma/stories/61387905.php
196. MMA *Weekly Radio*, 06/05
197. *Iceman: My Fighting Life*, Chuck Liddell, Dutton, 2008
198. MMA *Weekly Radio*, 06/05
199. *Full Contact Fighter*, 04/03
200. *Full Contact Fighter*, 04/03
201. *Full Contact Fighter*, 05/03
202. http://sfuk.tripod.com/interviews_04/randy_couture.html
203. *Ultimate Iceman*
204. http://thenatural.tv/content/view/42/1/
205. *Iceman: My Fighting Life*, Chuck Liddell, Dutton, 2008
206. *Full Contact Fighter*, 06/03
207. *Full Contact Fighter*, 10/03
208. *Full Contact Fighter*, 10/03
209. http://www.boxinginsider.net/mma/stories/80336746.php
210. http://www.onzuka.com/news_2004Mar3.html
211. UFC 47 DVD special features
212. http://www.icemanmma.com/content/view/112/51/
213. *Gong Kakutougi Plus*, 10/2000
214. *SRSDX*, no. 47, 3/8/01
215. *Gong Kakutougi*, no.108, 04/01
216. *Gong Kakutougi*, no.108, 04/01
217. *SRSDX*, no. 44, 4/26/01
218. *Gong Kautougi Plus*, vol. 16, 11/21/01
219. *Gong Kautougi Plus*, vol. 16 11/21/01
220. *Gong Kakutogi*, no.113, 09/01
221. *Gong Kakutogi*, no.113, 09/01
222. *Gong Kakutogi*, no.113, 09/01
223. http://www.bodybuilding.com/fun/mahler31.htm

224. Sherdog.com 7/21/2007

225. http://www.m1mixfight.com/info/publications/2007/12/26/finding-fedor-part-
    II/

226. *St. Petersburg Times*

227. http://fedor.bel.ru/index_eng.shtml?id=138

228. http://www.sherdog.com/news/interviews.asp?n_id=8356

229. *Kami no Puroresu Radical*, no. 60, 2003

230. *Gong Kakutougi*, no. 134, 06/03

231. Portal do Valetudo

232. Pride FC

233. *Gong Kakutogi*, no.144, 04/04

234. *Minneapolis Star Tribune*, 06/06/07

235. *Men's Fitness*, 09/05

236. Sherdog.com, 04/07/05

237. Sherdog.com, 04/07/05

238. MMAfighting.com, 04/08/05

239. http://www.kosmma.com, 09/23/05

240. *MMA Evolution Radio*

241. *MMA Weekly Radio*, 03/05

242. *Quad City Times*, 13/17/05

243. *OC Register*, 10/5/06

244. *Boston Globe*, 4/11/05

245. Boxinginsider.com

246. *Tapout Magazine*, issue 21

247. *Gainesville Sun*, 07/07/07

248. *USA Today*, 04/10/05

249. http://mmaringreport.com/fighter/index.php?option=com_content
    &task=view&id=274&Itemid=42

250. http://www.ufc.com/index.cfm?fa=news.detail&gid=2634

251. MMAfighting.com

252. http://www.mmaringreport.com/text-interviews/royler-gracie-talks-about-
    royce-gracie-in-the-ufc-again.html

253. http://www.newsday.com/sports/ny-ufc-royce,0,3892826.story?coll=ny-sports-
    mezz&gid=2637

254. http://www.ufc.com/index.cfm?fa=news.detail&gid=2634

255. http://www.boutreviewusa.com/Interviews/05yoshida.html

256. http://www.judoinfo.com/temp/Pride/yoshida.htm

257. *SRSDX*, 10/10/

258. http://www.Pridefc.com/Pride2005/index.php?mainpage=news&news_id=338

259. http://www.boxingscene.com/forums/archive/index.php/t-8214.html

260. *Pride Decade*

261. http://www.Pridefc.com/Pride2005/index.php?mainpage=news&news_id=320

262. http://www.Pridefc.com/Pride2005/index.php?mainpage=news&news_id=338

263. http://www.Pridefc.com/Pride2005/index.php?mainpage=news&news_id=320

264. http://www.Pridefc.com/Pride2005/index.php?mainpage=interview&interview_id=16&itemID=167

265. *A Fighter's Heart*, Sam Sheridan, Atlantic Monthly Press, 2007

266. http://www.Pridefc.com/Pride2005/index.php?mainpage=interview&interview_id=10&itemID=110

267. http://www.Pridefc.com/interviews/fedor_04

268. http://www.graciemag.com/?c=147&a=3190

269. *A Fighter's Heart*, Sam Sheridan, Atlantic Monthly Press, 2007

270. http://www.graciemag.com/?c=147&a=3190

271. http://www.graciemag.com/?c=147&a=3190

272. http://fedor.bel.ru/index_eng.shtml?id=138

273. http://www.graciemag.com/?c=147&a=3190

274. http://www.boutreviewusa.com/SpecialFeatures/280gawayoshida.html

275. http://www.Pridefc.com/Pride2005/index.php?mainpage=interview&interview_id=35&itemID=270

276. http://www.boutreviewusa.com/RingSide/91Prideotoko.html

277. http://www.Pridefc.com/Pride2005/index.php?mainpage=interview&interview_id=35&itemID=270

278. http://www.ufc.com/index.cfm?fa=news.detail&gid=2892

279. *MMA Evolution Radio*, 01/10/05

280. http://www.reviewjournal.com/lvrj_home/2006/Aug-20-Sun-2006/news/9032763.html

281. www.mmaringreport.com/text-interviews/tito-ortiz-interview.htm

282. http://www.kenshamrock.com/news.php?id=133/articles/news

283. wrestlingobserver.com, 09/07/06

284. http://www.ironlife.com/forum/showthread.php?t=76539

285. http://www.kenshamrock.com/news.php?id=138/articles/news

286. http://www.newsday.com/sports/ny-ufc-tito,0,6353246.story

287. *Gross Point Blank*, 01/20/08

288. Wrestlingobserver.com, 10/5/06

289. Wrestlingobserver.com, 09/07/06

290. http://www.ufc.com/index.cfm?fa=news.detail&gid=2892

291. http://www.baltimoresun.com/sports/custom/mma/bal-whiteqa122,0,7658660.story

292. http://www.thesweetscience.com/boxing-article/4815/year-ufc-choked-out-boxing/

293. http://www.extremeprosports.com/MMA/mixed_martial_arts_boxing.html

294. http://www.insidefighting.com/betweenRoundsDisp.aspx?uid=3332

295. http://www.buddytv.com/articles/ufc/more/exclusive-interview-kendall-gr-2766.aspx

296. http://www.insidefighting.com/betweenRoundsDisp.aspx?uid=3332
297. http://www.mmaweekly.com/absolutenm/templates/dailynews.asp?arti-cleid=3179&zoneid=13
298. http://www.rockymountainnews.com/drmn/other_spotlight/article/0,2777,DRMN_23960_5242406,00.html
299. http://www.reviewjournal.com/lvrj_home/2006/Dec-28-Thu-2006/sports/11662008.html
300. http://www.washingtonpost.com/wp-dyn/content/article/2006/12/29/AR2006122901556.html
301. ESPN The Magazine
302. Fullcontactfighter.com, 8/26/02
303. The Canadian Press, 01/15/07
304. Media conference call, 02/26/07
305. UFC.com, 02/22/07
306. *Wrestling for Fighting: The Natural Way*, Randy Couture
307. Baltimoresun.com, Pramit Mohapatra, 03/16/07
308. MMAfightline.com, Jason Perkins, 10/18/07
309. *Ultimate Miletich*, UFC pay-per-view
310. ironlife.com, 2003
311. *MAT Magazine*, 12/08/05
312. MMA *Weekly Radio*, 09/02/05
313. *Wrestling for Fighting: The Natural Way*, Randy Couture
314. nbcsports.com, 02/27/07
315. boxingtalk.com, 03/27/07
316. http://www.fox5vegas.com, 05/29/07
317. MMA *Today*, 06/12/07
318. ufc.com, 05/21/07
319. *The Orange County Register*, 07/13/06
320. thaformula.com, 03/07
321. fullcontactfighter.com, 07/28/01
322. MMA *Today*, 06/12/07
323. thaformula.com, 03/07
324. directtv.com, 11/07
325. http://www.boxingscene.com, 04/09/04
326. http://www.freerepublic.com/focus/f-chat/1840238/posts
327. http://sports.espn.go.com/extra/mma/news/story?id=2880225
328. http://www.icemanmma.com/content/view/160/1/
329. http://sports.espn.go.com/extra/mma/news/story?id=2880225
330. www.boxingtalk.com/pag/article11726.htm
331. http://www.thaformula.com/rampage_trainer_juanito_ibarra_thaformula.com_sports.html
332. http://www.thaformula.com/rampage_trainer_juanito_ibarra_thafor

mula.com_sports.html

333. http://www.icemanmma.com/content/view/160/1/

334. http://www.ocweekly.com/features/features/get-in-the-cage/27701/?page=2

335. http://publications.mediapost.com/index.cfm?fuseaction=Articles.show
ArticleHomePage&art_aid=67875

336. http://www.ocregister.com/ocregister/sports/other/boxingmma/article
_1381274.php

337. http://www.boutreviewusa.com/Interviews/040407FISH1.html

338. boutreviewusa.com

339. boutreviewusa.com

340. http://www.m1mixfight.com/info/publications/2007/12/26/finding-fedor-part-
III/

341. http://www.m1mixfight.com/news/2008/2/9/Fedors-official-open-letter-to-the-
UFC-president-Dana-White/

342. *Pride: Decade*

343. http://www.thefightnetwork.com/news_detail.php?nid=5085

344. http://www.sherdog.com/news/news.asp?n_id=9455

345. http://www.sherdog.com/news/news.asp?n_id=9455

346. http://sports.yahoo.com/box/news?slug=ki-
white101107&prov=yhoo&type=lgns

347. http://www.xtremecouture.tv

348. http://mmajunkie.com/news/3041/an-interview-with-ken-shamrock-thoughts-
on-randy-couture-dana-white-and-upcoming-tryouts.mma

349. *Inside MMA*, 02/08

350. http://www.mmaweekly.com/absolutenm/templates/dailynews.asp?arti-
cleid=5189&zoneid=2

351. http://www.lvrj.com/sports/13794082.html

352. http://mmajunkie.com/news/3684/referee-steve-mazzagatti-discusses-lesnar-
mir-fight-an-mmajunkiecom-interview.mma

353. http://www.hour.ca/news/news.aspx?iIDArticle=8504

354. http://www.subfighter.com/article-3280.html

355. *MMA Evolution Radio*, 07/20/05

356. *MMA Evolution Radio*, 07/20/05

357. http://www.knucklepit.com/mixed-martial-arts-georges_st._pierre_page2.htm

358. http://mmamania.com/2007/03/10/reign-of-terror-exclusive-interview-with-
matt-serra/

359. http://mmamadness.com/insight.html?newsitem_id=274

360. http://www.mmaontap.com/mma/entry/afternoon-news-and-notes1/

361. http://sports.yahoo.com/box/news?slug=ki-greg-
jackson050707&prov=yhoo&type=lgns

362. http://mmamania.com/2008/02/08/their-worst-nightmare-mmamaniacom-
exclusive-interview-with-ufc-welterweight-diego-sanchez/

363.   http://www.ufc.com/index.cfm?fa=news.detail&gid=7300

364.   http://mmamania.com/2007/05/16/exclusive-serra-on-gsp-hit-the-road-frenchy/

365.   No Holds Barred with Eddie Goldman, podcast, 03/30/08

366.   http://www.sherdog.com/news/articles.asp?n_id=10826

367.   http://www.mmacanada.net/home/view/173

368.   *Front Magazine*, 06/02

369.   http://www.ifl.tv/News-07Nov21-Ian-Freeman-interview.html

370.   *Full Contact Fighter*, 11/02

371.   http://sfuk.tripod.com/interviews/freemanufc.html

372.   http://www.fcfighter.com/news0207.htm

373.   http://www.boxingscene.com/forums/showthread.php?t=8494

374.   http://www.mmaworld.org/showthread.php?t=2851

375.   http://www.knucklepit.com/mixed-martial-arts-cage_rage.htm

376.   http://www.ironlife.com/forum/showthread.php?t=65432

377.   http://mmajunkie.com/news/2800/michael-bisping-discusses-ufc-75-a-ufcjunkiecom-interview.mma

378.   http://www.chokehimout.com/index.cfm/Get/vart/ID/934

379.   http://sports.yahoo.com/mma/news;_ylt=Ak4ccV9FmtohWREW4.3e3Kg5nYcB?slug=ki-fertittainterview010308&prov=yhoo&type=lgns

380.   http://mmajunkie.com/news/2800/michael-bisping-discusses-ufc-75-a-ufcjunkiecom-interview.mma

381.   http://www.ufc.com/index.cfm?fa=news.detail&gid=7746

382.   http://www.ufc.com/index.cfm?fa=news.detail&gid=7746

383.   http://sports.yahoo.com/mma/news?slug=ki-111007&prov=yhoo&type=lgns

384.   http://www.mmatko.com/matt-hamill-in-shock-over-michael-bisping-vs-rashad-evans-at-ufc-78/

385.   http://www.ifl.tv/News-07Nov21-Ian-Freeman-interview.html

386.   http://bisping.tv/2007-12-20/bisping-the-middleweight/

387.   http://www.chokehimout.com/index.cfm/Get/vart/ID/934

388.   http://www.mmauniverse.com/news/SS2807

389.   http://www.jarrypark.com/2008/03/06/the-chainsaw-is-about-to-rev-up-again/

390.   http://www.ufc.com/index.cfm?fa=news.detail&gid=11404

391.   http://www.mmapayout.com/2008/04/marshalls-law-extended-version.html

392.   http://sports.yahoo.com/mma/news;_ylt=Ak4ccV9FmtohWREW4.3e3Kg5nYcB?slug=ki-fertittainterview010308&prov=yhoo&type=lgns

393.   No Holds Barred with Eddie Goldman, podcast, 02/29/08

394.   http://www.latimes.com/sports/la-sp-mma29feb29,1,1189820.story?ctrack=1&cset=true

395.   http://www.bostonherald.com/sports/other_sports/ultimate_fighting/view.bg?articleid=1078976

396.   MMANews.com, 05/10/07

397. No Holds Barred with Eddie Goldman, podcast, 02/29/08

398. http://cbs.sportsline.com/mmaboxing/story/10500706/1

399. http://deadspin.com/378886/dana-white-says-kimboliddell-fight-not-out-of-
the-realm-of-possibility

400. http://www.MMAnews.com/other/MMANews.com-Exclusive:-Interview-with-
Kevin-Randleman.html

401. http://www.thesun.co.uk/sol/homepage/sport/ufc/article986050.ece

402. http://www.MMAmemories.com/interviews/talklin-mma-with-bruce-buffer/

403. inc.com, 04/06

404. Sherdog.com

405. MMAfighting.com, 02/09/06

406. *MMA Ring Report*

407. MMAweekly.com, 02/16/06

408. Pat Miletich deposition

409. http://mmajunkie.com/news/3041/an-interview-with-ken-shamrock-thoughts-
on-randy-couture-dana-white-and-upcoming-tryouts.mma

410. http://www.qctimes.com/articles/2006/04/17/sports/doc44432455586
38969787406.txt

411. http://sports.yahoo.com/mma/news?slug=ki fertittainter-
view010308&prov=yhoo&type=lgns

412. http://www.fighthype.com/pages/content1505.html

413. http://www.mmaweekly.com/absolutenm/templates/dailynews.asp?article
id=5689&zoneid=13

414. http://www.mmamadness.com/insight.html?newsitem_id=193

415. http://mmajunkie.com/news/3640/nsac-executive-director-keith-kizer-dis-
cusses-year-round-drug-testing-an-mmajunkiecom-interview.mma

416. *Gross Point Blank*, 01/20/08

PHOTO CREDITS